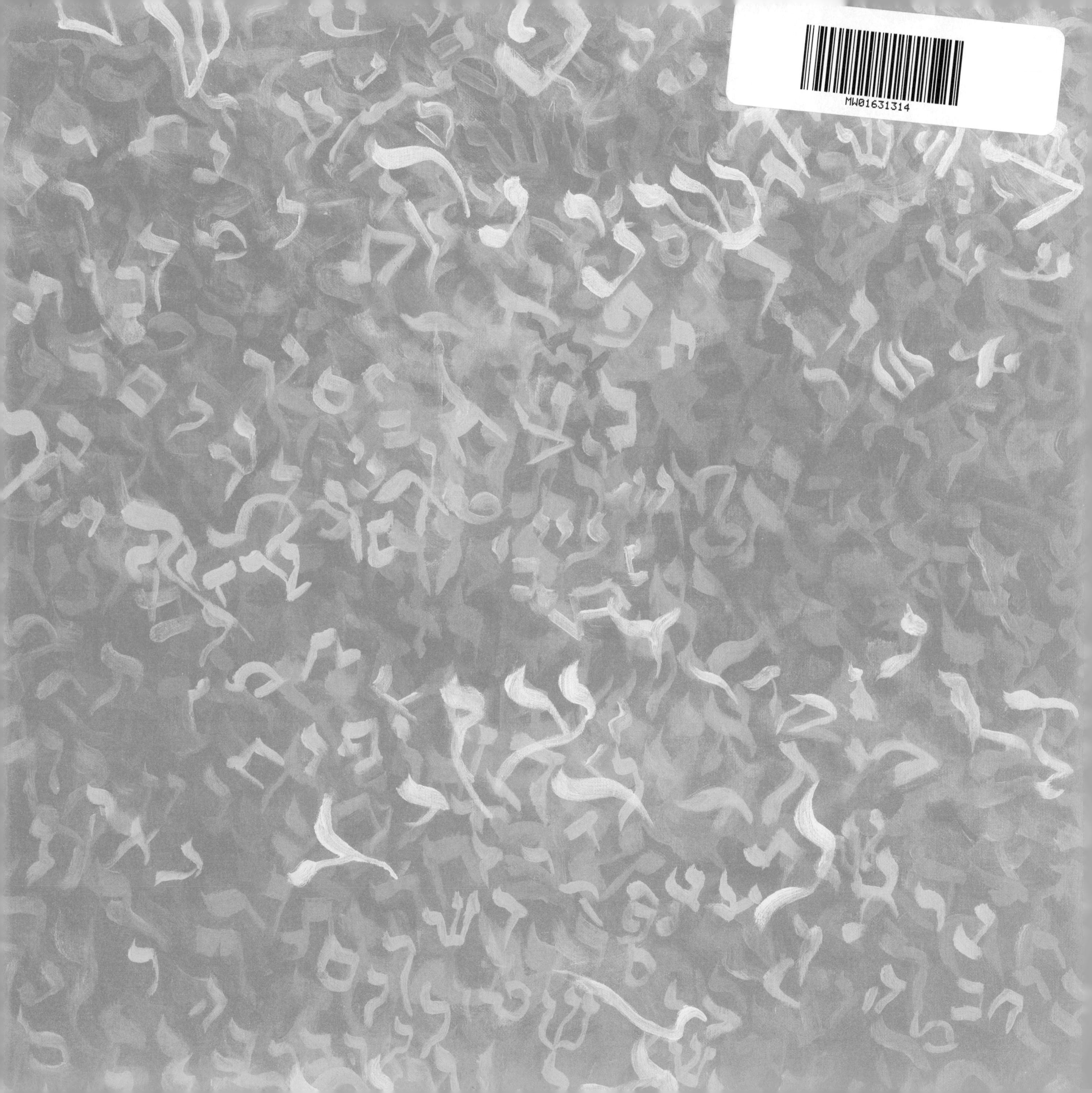
MW01631314

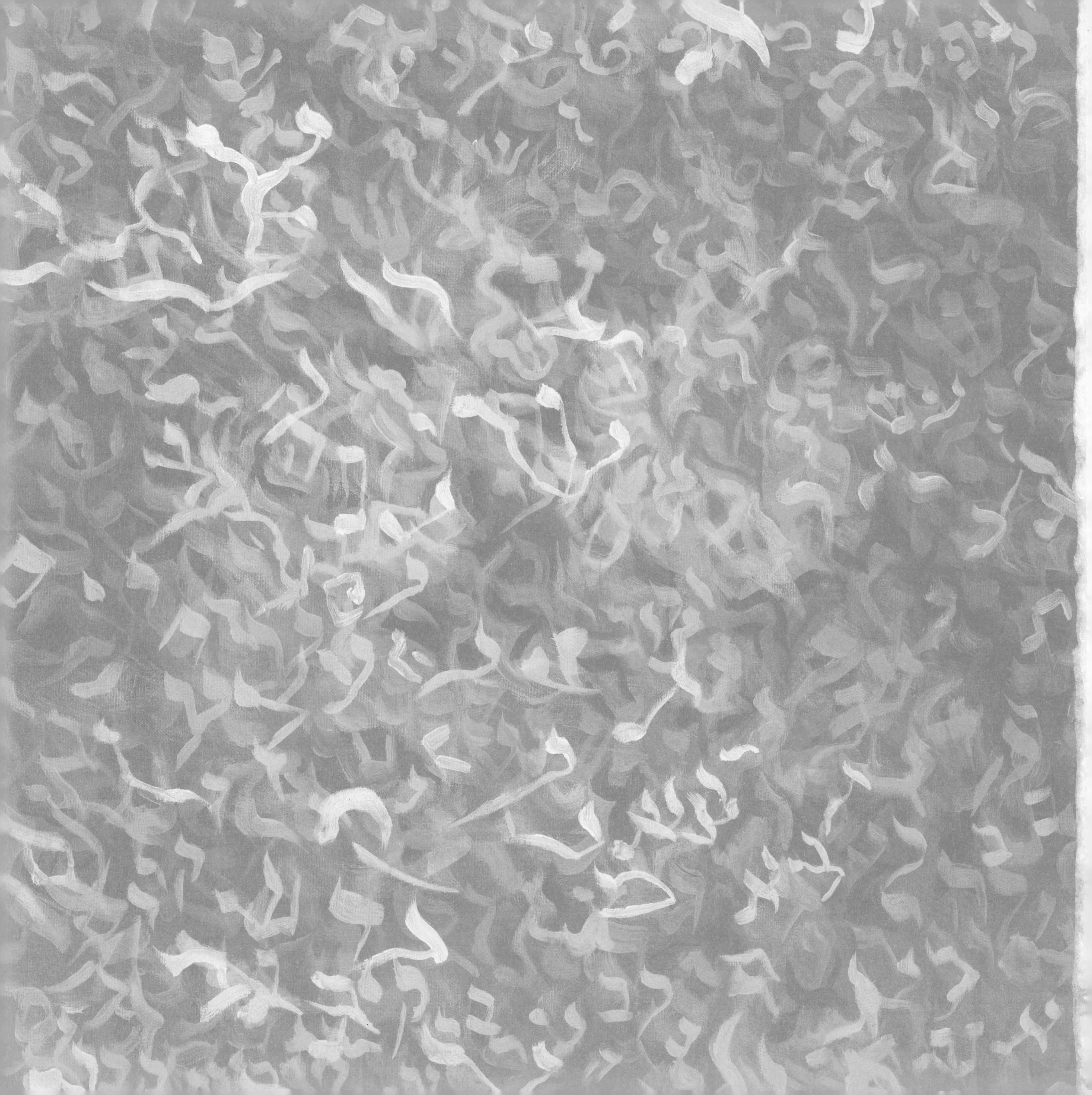

THE BEAUTY OF THE HEBREW LETTER

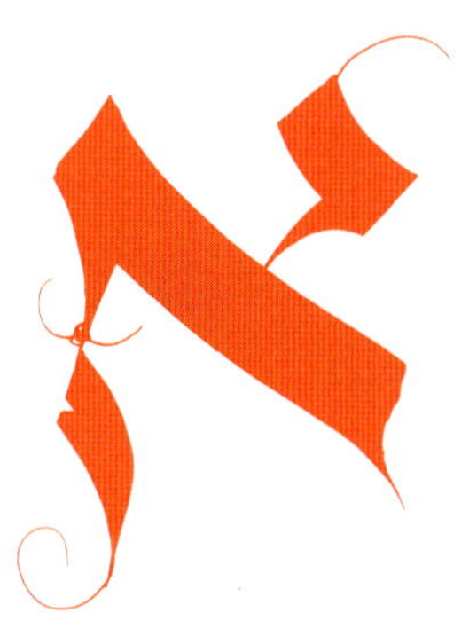

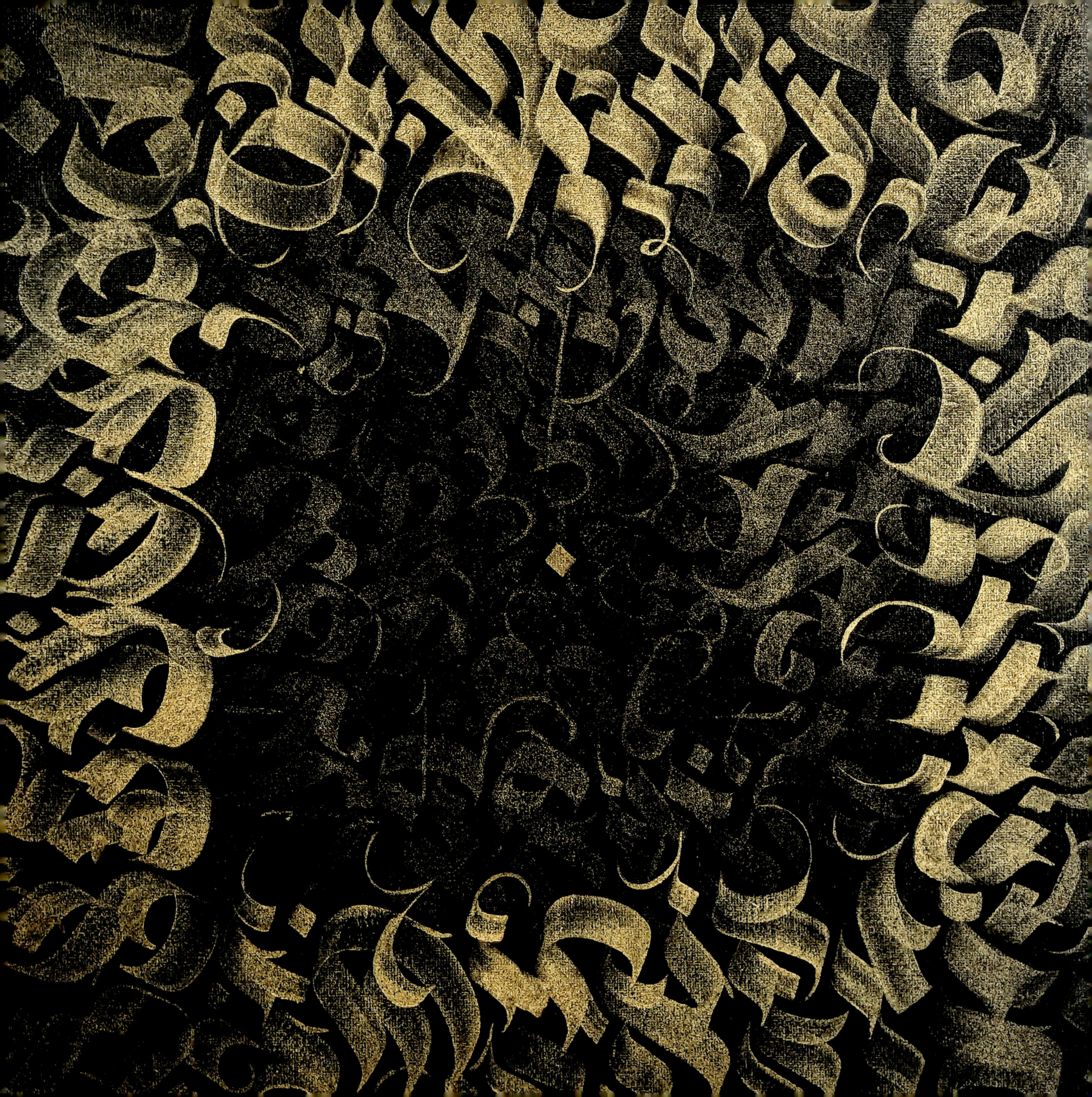

IZZY PLUDWINSKI

The Beauty of the Hebrew Letter

From Sacred Scrolls to Graffiti

Brandeis University Press
WALTHAM, MASSACHUSETTS

Brandeis University Press

Manufactured in China
Designed by Misha Beletsky
Typeset in TEFF Trinité

BINDING: Josh Baum, *Aleph-Bet*. See p. 123
ENDPAPERS: David Rakia, *Letters in Grey*, detail. See pp. 192–93

Library of Congress Cataloging-in-Publication Data

Names: Pludvinski, Yitshak, author.
Title: The beauty of the Hebrew letter : from sacred scrolls to graffiti / Izzy Pludwinski.
Description: Waltham, Massachusetts : Brandeis University Press, 2023. | Includes index. | Summary: "This book celebrates the beauty of the Hebrew aleph-bet by visually chronicling its earliest appearance in ancient inscriptions and its subsequent reception and representation by scribes and artists over the last three millennia"— Provided by publisher.
Identifiers: LCCN 2022050264 | ISBN 9781684581467 (cloth)
Subjects: LCSH: Calligraphy, Hebrew. | Alphabet in art. | Hebrew language—Alphabet. | Inscriptions, Hebrew.
Classification: LCC NK3636.A2 P575 2023 | DDC 744.4/29924—dc23/eng/20221109
LC record available at https://lccn.loc.gov/2022050264

5 4 3 2 1

This publication was made possible through the generous support of the Martin J. Gross Family Foundation

אלפיים שנה מטרם שנברא העולם, היה הקב"ה מסתכל
ומשתעשע באותיות—הקדמה לזוהר

Two thousand years prior to the creation of the world, the Creator was observing and playing with the letters

—from *Introduction to the Zohar*

Contents

Preface

WHY BEAUTY?

THERE WAS AN UNUSUAL TRADITION IN ONE OF the yeshivot I attended as a young adult in the early 1980s. Once or twice a year, we were all sent to a graphologist/psychologist/rabbi for a consultation. This was not intended to test our mental health but rather, through the graphologist's analysis, to allow us to become more aware where our unique talents lie, and to receive advice on how to use those talents in our individual spiritual paths. After the analysis of my handwriting and drawing of a tree, one of the things I was told was that I have a unique talent/desire for surface beauty. (At first I was a bit insulted by this; after a further talk we clarified things, but that is neither here nor there). Regardless, there was definitely a certain truth to this—I *am* attracted to surface beauty. However, for me, that beauty cannot just remain on the surface. Beauty is not just a static presentation of form. A truly beautiful letter, word, or composition, besides being the carrier of content, will possess a dynamism, an internal lifeforce. Calligraphy is like dance—the strokes that form the letters are the embodied gestures of the moving hand and body. One senses the vitality in the movements that underlie these forms. They make the letters come alive, and it is this lifeforce that resonates with the viewer and ultimately what distinguishes strong calligraphy from weak.

A story: I first visited Japan in 2005, during which time I attended a Zen calligraphy workshop given by Sensei Tanchu Terayama. It was my first day on my own in Tokyo, and I went to visit the National Museum. There, in one of the exhibition rooms, I came across a very large screen/panel of calligraphy that simply took my breath away, and I sat down on a bench facing the work, just taking it all in. I was all alone in the room. After a couple of minutes, an elderly Japanese man came in and stood in front of the panels, admiring them. He then raised his hand and began to make gestures, obviously following the rhythm of the writing. He had a smile on his face and was humming a tune as he was writing in the air, rewriting the piece, moving along the panel, making the strokes, reliving the piece. I sat hypnotized watching this. What was clear to me was that the vitality that the calligrapher, perhaps hundreds of years before, had put into the characters was now being embodied by this man and in a subtler way being passed on to me as my eyes followed his movements. It was a powerful experience that filled me with joy and enthusiasm.

This reaction to the experience of beauty is described nicely by the author André Aciman: "Suddenly, we are marveled and uplifted, pulled out of our small, ordinary lives and taken to a realm far richer and more eloquent than anything we know. Call it enchantment, the difference between the time-bound and the timeless, between us and the otherworldly. All beauty and art evoke harmonies that transport us to a place where, for only seconds, time stops and we are one with the world." It sounds quite mystical. Indeed, in Midrashic lore, it is said that the Hebrew letters existed before the creation of the world; they are beyond time and contain within them the potential energies of creation. It is that energy within the Hebrew letter, in all its many forms, that I seek in works—energies that have the power not only to delight, but to transform. As overreaching as it may sound, I believe an exposure to sensitivity, beauty, lifeforce can bring the viewer to a deeper place. How might it have this effect? As Aciman says, continuing: "because they promise to realign us with our better selves, with the people we've always known we were but neglected to become, the people we crave to be before our time runs out." In other words beauty both takes us beyond ourselves and brings us closer to our truer selves.

Beauty also has the potential for goodness. In a certain sense, beauty means the work has quality; caring went into it. As Robert

Pirsig wrote, "Care and Quality are internal and external aspects of the same thing. A person who sees Quality and feels it as he works is a person who cares."

And if quality is so closely related to caring, it is reasonable, or at the very least hopeful, that this caring of the artist will come across and affect the viewer in a positive way. And so my reason for this book is to showcase the beauty of the Hebrew letter and through its beauty to delight, uplift, and transport the soul, both outwards and inwards.

WHY HEBREW?

MY FIRST FASCINATION WITH THE HEBREW LETTER came as a result of seeing a poster pinned to a board at the back of the synagogue where I prayed. It showed an enlarged picture of the Hebrew letter *yud*, and it said that if an entire Torah scroll, which consists of over three hundred thousand letters, was written correctly but one *yud* was missing that little thorn-like protrusion at the bottom left of the head of the letter (called an *oketz*; see figure below), the entire Torah scroll would be invalid for ritual use.

"Wow," I said to myself. What mystical secrets must lie in that *oketz*? I was drawn to these sacred letters, and I decided to study to be a Sofer STaM, a religious scribe, and immerse myself in learning this sacred aleph-bet and in writing the ritual objects for which this script was intended.

A few years later, I was exposed to other expressions of the Hebrew letter in the art form known as calligraphy. Being subjected to less rigid rules, these newer forms, rooted in the same skeletal shapes as the Torah script, held a different fascination for me, and I found beauty in these letters too—not only for their form, but for their being the carriers of Jewish content. Texts have an emotional as well as a literal content. Calligraphy seemed to be the ideal way to holistically express both of these aspects.

It is difficult to explain the Jewish person's connection to the Hebrew letter. From an early age, Jewish children learn the Hebrew letters. The love for the letters is demonstrated by an old custom of covering the letters in honey and encouraging the child to dip his or her fingers in the honey and "taste" the sweetness of each letter. Jewish thought, starting from the Torah, is conveyed in Hebrew. Even in places where Jews did not write in the Hebrew language, they still chose Hebrew letters as the vehicle to convey their ideas—whether that language was Aramaic, Arabic, or Yiddish, to mention a few.

But the connection goes deeper; it is even otherworldly. In Midrashic tradition, the Hebrew letter is not simply an arbitrary symbol meant to express a certain sound. There is meaning in the shapes themselves. The letters are the potential energies through which the universe was created. They are beings. They have personalities. They talk. They are spoken to. One develops a relationship with each of the letters. When one writes them, one respects their individuality, on the one hand, and their sense of community, on the other. They belong together. One way to show this respect is to write them as beautifully as possible, to enliven them, to make them shine.

There are many words in Hebrew that can refer to beauty, such as *hadar* and *tiferet*. Interestingly, these words have wider connotations, such as glory, splendor, and majesty. The common word for beautiful in Hebrew is *yafeh*, a word which comes from a root that means "expansion." A beautiful Hebrew letter, as I understand it, needs to have not only surface beauty but also an expansive quality, whether that expansion is a physical manifestation, a spiritual one, or an expansion of consciousness. To play on the words of Ben Shahn, the form of the Hebrew letter is the very shape of its content.

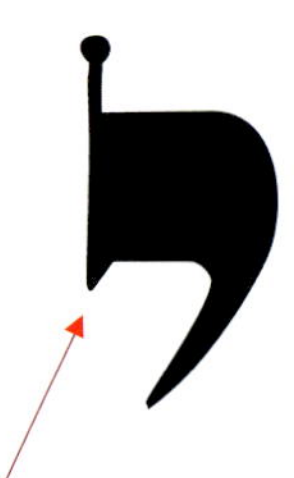

The letter *yud* with its *oketz*.

A Few Words about Image Selection

IN CHOOSING TO CALL THIS BOOK *The Beauty of the Hebrew Letter,* I am quite aware that, of necessity, the artworks presented in this book are based purely on my subjective taste. The process of choosing was not simple, and I struggled in many of my decisions. I had several criteria. The first was that the major part of the work had to feature the Hebrew letter. This eliminated many beautiful and worthy works whose compositions and artwork were of high quality but did not feature the Hebrew letter as the main element. For works that did feature the Hebrew letter, my next concern was their beauty. My standards for beauty were first shaped by my studies as a Sofer STaM (religious scribe). Here the laws (halachah) define the ideal skeletal shapes of each of the letters. In other words, what makes an *aleph* an *aleph,* what makes a *beit* a *beit,* etc. The same applied to halachic rules of spacing. Rhythm lies at the root of good calligraphy, with music, and perhaps dance, being the art that calligraphy most resembles. A calligraphic work that has beautiful letters can be ruined by poor rhythm. Conversely, a work that has a clear and flowing texture, even though its letterforms might be less than ideal, can still be attractive. The ideal strives for both.

The works in the book are loosely organized into different sections. There is nothing intrinsically exclusive about these categories, and several works could have comfortably been placed in a different section. I begin chronologically, first offering historical examples, which are sometimes interlaced with modern interpretations of said scripts. From historical I move to traditional works, then works made mostly, but not exclusively, in the mid-twentieth century, often for utilitarian purposes. I added marginal comments to many of the works in these first two sections to give some context and aid the reader when looking at these works.

Next is a chapter presenting complete aleph-bet compositions as well as individual letters. These provide a constant source for calligraphers, typographers, and lettering artists to play and experiment with, often producing improvisational works.

The section "Stretching the Boundaries" showcases more experimental works, where legibility is allowed to take a back seat and the works show more of an expressive interpretation by the lettering artist.

I had to make a difficult choice regarding Hebrew typography. There is much creativity and beauty in works done by today's Hebrew graphic artists. To be fair to the subject, there deserves to be an entire book dedicated to contemporary Hebrew typography, but that was beyond the scope of this book. However, I didn't feel I could ignore the field completely, so I included a very small taste of some typographic works.

Next follows a section presenting both street art and graffiti, on the one hand, and what I call fine art, on the other. In this latter category, I put works that are either more painterly or are conceptual in nature.

There exists, of course, a completely different scribal tradition of Hebrew lettering—the art of the Sofer STaM, the Jewish religious scribe. This art or craft or profession is dear to my heart as the letters of the Torah, Mezuzot, and Tefillin are what first enticed me to begin my calligraphic career—first as a Sofer STaM and later as a calligrapher. The mystic power in the letters as well as their beauty presented a fascination that held and still holds a spell over me. And so for this book I sought out what I hope to be among the finest examples of these holy articles.

I sincerely hope the reader enjoys and is enthused by the wide variety of forms Hebrew has taken and will continue to take. As a living force and a visual medium for a living language and a living people, its expression will undoubtedly take on new forms, inevitably test limits, and yet remain rooted in its noble tradition.

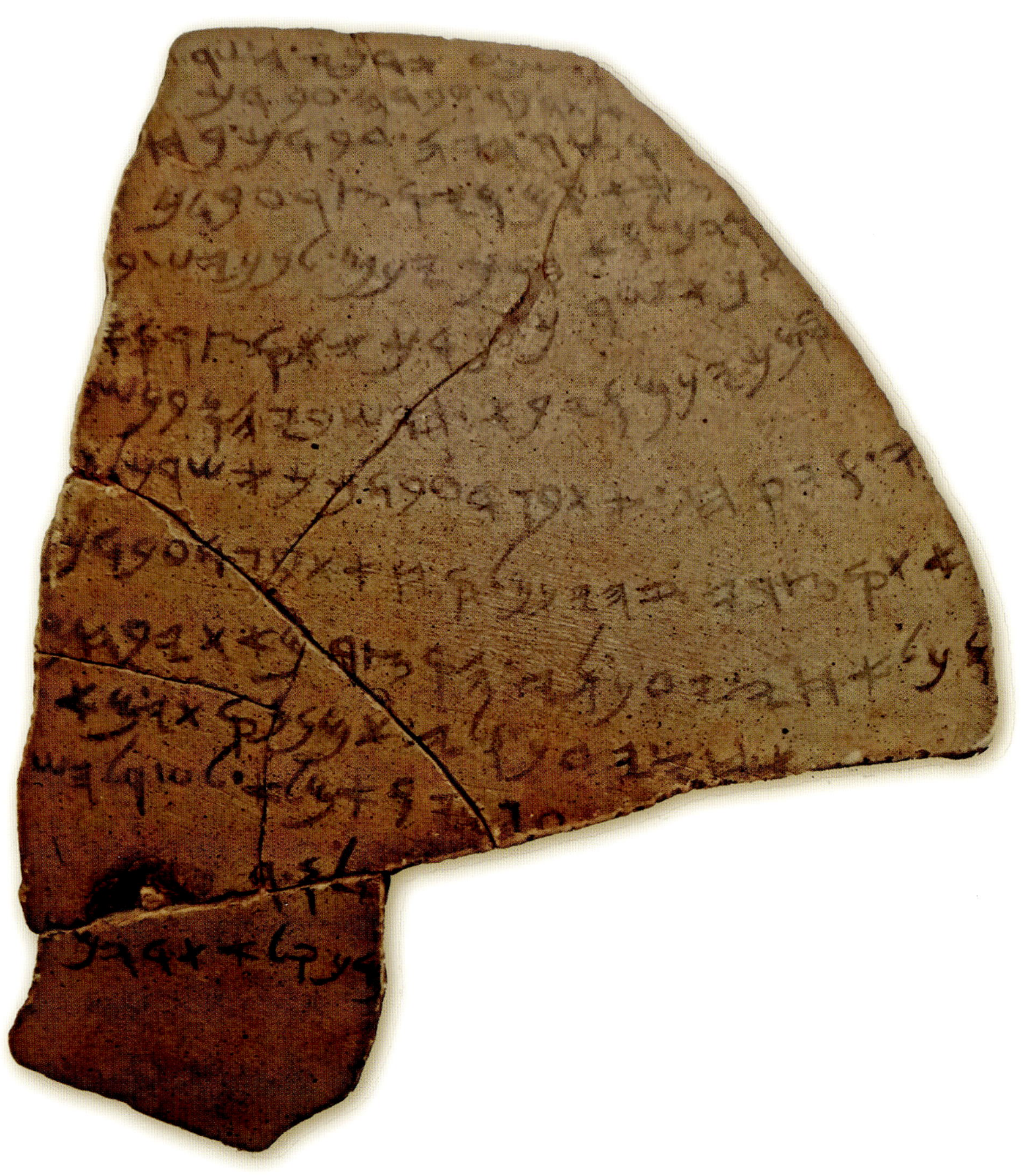

Mesad Hashavyahu Ostracon Replica, seventh century BCE
Archaeological Museum Beit Miriam, Kibbutz Palmachim.
Photo by Hanay

I

Historical Manuscripts and Their Influence

There are two very broad categories of Hebrew scripts: The Paleo-Hebrew script, and the present-day Square Hebrew script (with all its variations). Although the great majority of artists and letterers use the latter, some opt to refer back to the ancient Paleo-Hebrew script, as, by being almost indecipherable, it lends a mysterious air to their creative work.

This is how it all started: sometime about 1000 BCE—the first Hebrew aleph-bet. These twenty-two forms (with slight variations), called Paleo-Hebrew, which look strange and unfamiliar to the modern eye, were the letters used by Israelites throughout the First Temple period.

The Meshe Stele, dated to about 840 BCE, is one of the earliest examples of Hebrew writing. The artist here forms a dialogue between past and present in this work, which began as a rubbing of the Meshe Stele; she then added her own brushstrokes of paint.

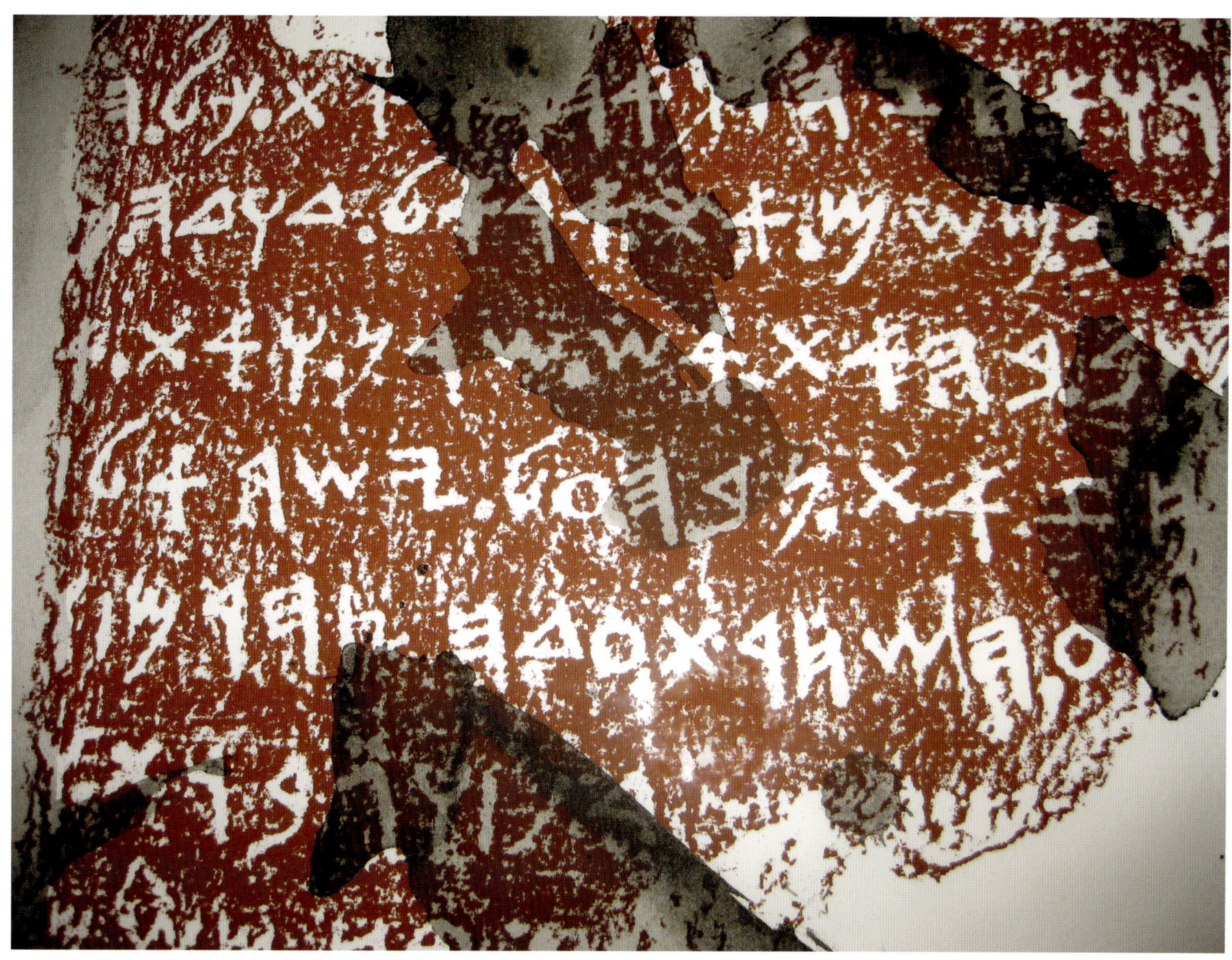

Edna Miron Wapner
Silkscreen print from a rubbing of the Meshe Stele, 1998–1999

Before evolving into more abstract symbols, the shapes of the letters in the ancient Hebrew script were more pictorial. In this, they have an affinity with East Asian characters.

One can see the influence of Japanese calligraphy in these two contemporary Hebrew works, both in the use of the brush, which is not a traditional tool for Hebrew writing, and the addition of an element in red.

*The work on this page consists of three letters in the ancient Hebrew script—*chet, samech, dalet*—spelling* chesed: *"loving kindness."*

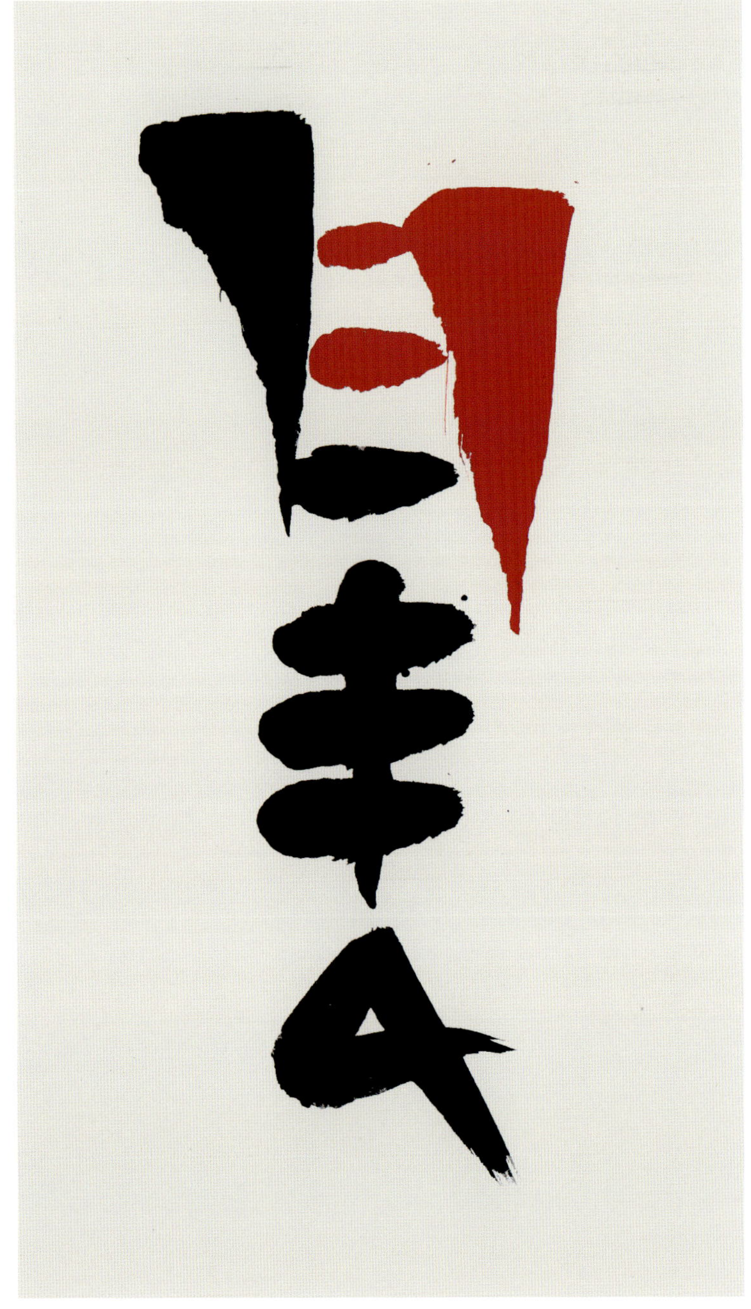

Izzy Pludwinski
Chesed, Paleo-Hebrew script, 2017

The ligature most often found in Hebrew is the aleph-lamed, *which represents God's name. Interestingly, the artist here uses a creative ligature of* yud *and* heh *for another one of God's names*—Yah.

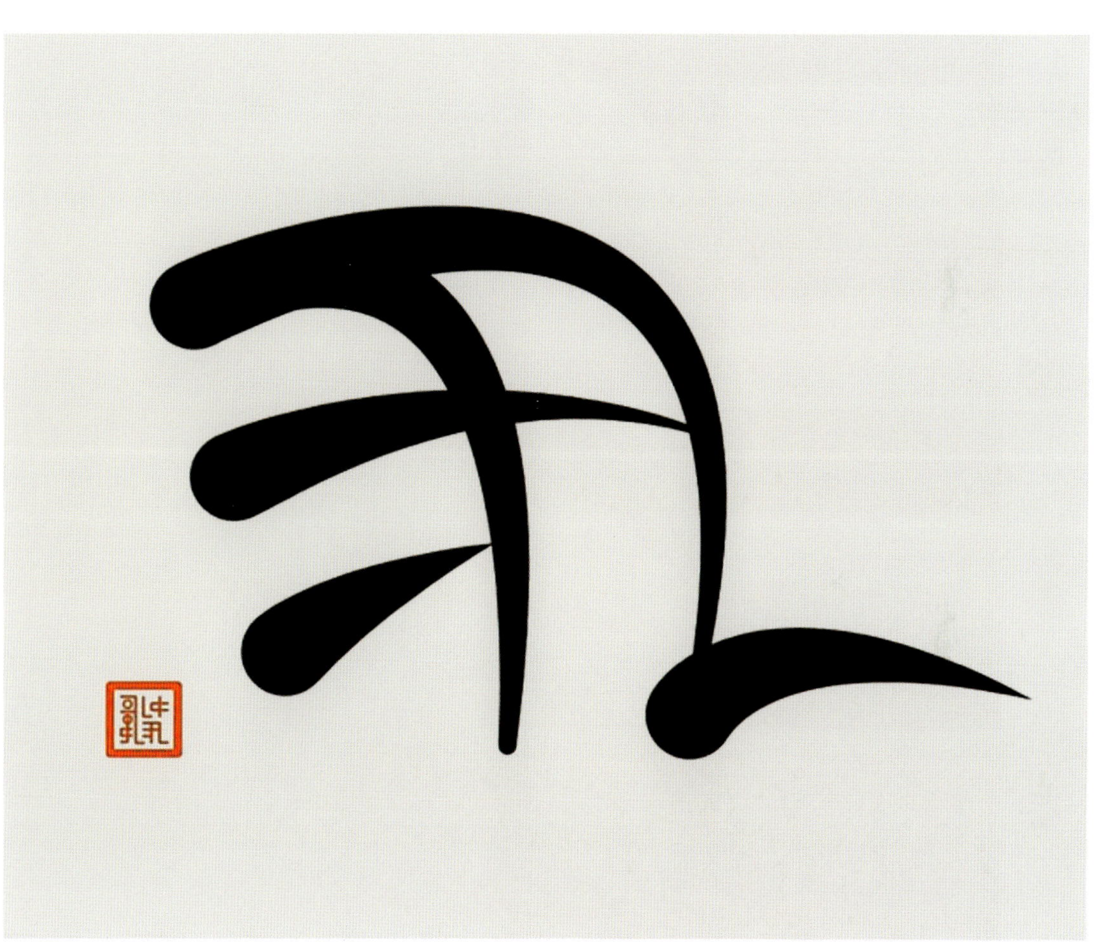

Ilya Yakubovich
Yah (*Yud-Heh* ligature), Paleo-Hebrew script, 2019

According to opinions expressed in the Talmud, it was Ezra the Scribe, during the early part of the Second Temple period, who changed the script from Paleo-Hebrew to the square script that we are familiar with today. In the Qumran manuscript shown here, the Commentary on Habbakuk*, one sees a clear example of this script. What is especially interesting in this manuscript is that one also sees the ancient Hebrew script (see the seventh line and the last full line), which was used for writing God's name.*

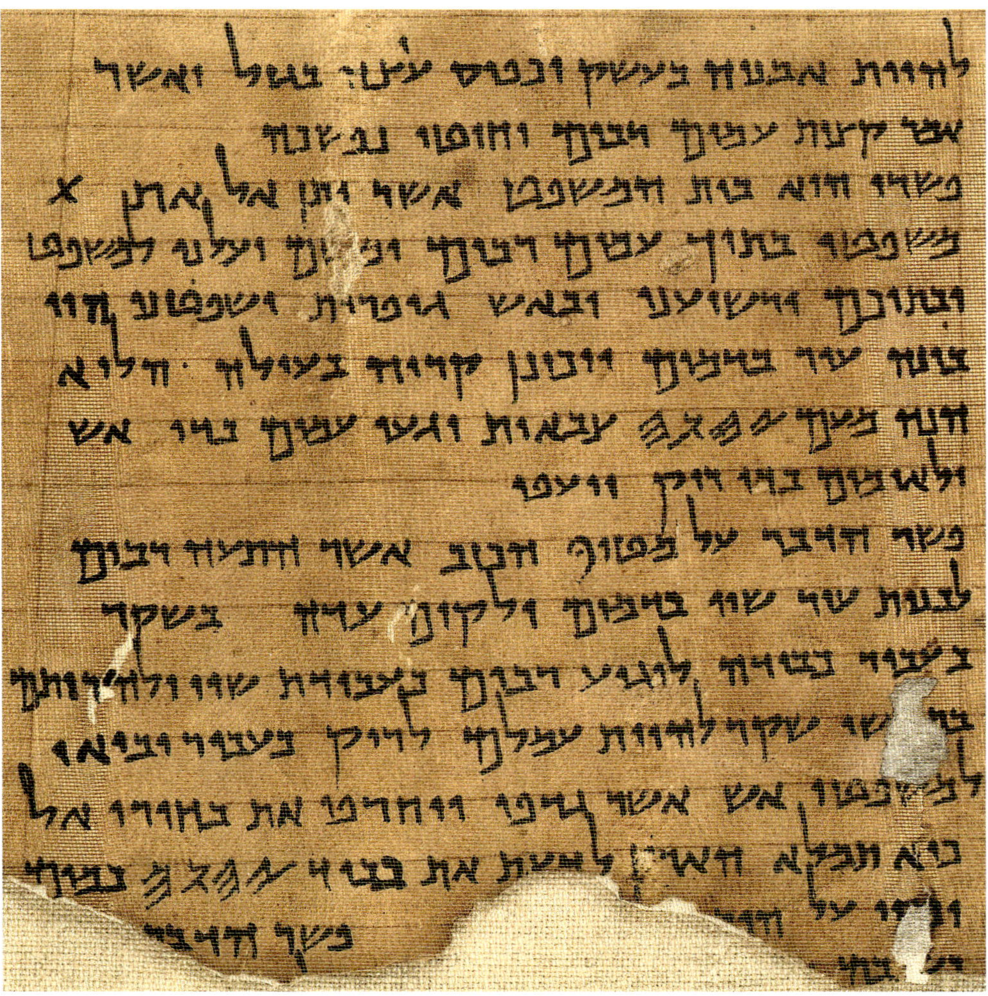

Commentary on Habakkuk
Qumran, first century BCE
Shrine of the Book, The Israel Museum, Jerusalem

In the mid-twentieth century, Yerachmiel Shechter taught calligraphy at the New Bezalel School in Jerusalem. It is clear from many of the students' works, as in the one shown here, that they worked on a script influenced by that of the Qumran scrolls.

גאל־לך אתה את־גאלתי כי לא־אוכל לגאול: וזאת לפנים ב
בישראל על־הגאלה ועל־התמורה לקים כל־דבר שלף איש נעלו ונתן
לרעהו וזאת התעודה בישראל: ויאמר הגאל לבעז קנה־לך וישלף נעלו:
ויאמר בעז לזקנים וכל־העם עדים אתם היום כי קניתי את־כל־אשר ל
אלימלך ואת כל־אשר לכליון ומחלון מיד נעמי: וגם את־רות המואב
המואביה אשת מחלון קניתי לי לאשה להקים שם־המת על־נחלתו ולא
יכרת שם־המת מעם אחיו ומשער מקומו עדים אתם היום: ויאמרו כל־
העם אשר־בשער והזקנים עדים יתן יהוה את־האשה הבאה אל־ביתך
כרחל וכלאה אשר בנו שתיהם את־בית ישראל ועשה־חיל באפרתה וקרא־

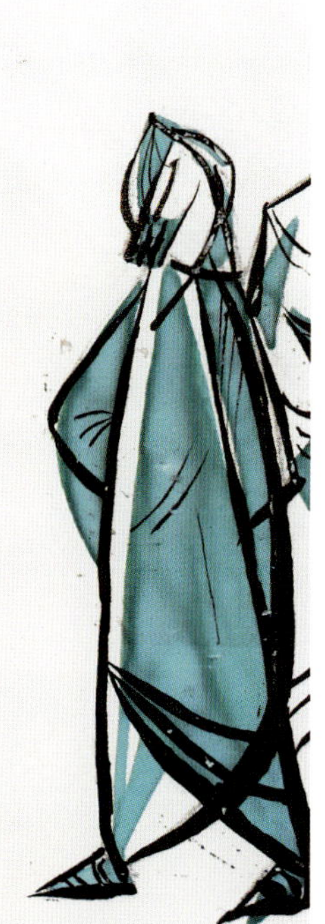

Felix Greenberg, *Book of Ruth*, 1959
Emunah Academic College of Arts and Design

From the first century onward, the square forms developed and became more formal and stylized. There is clearer contrast between thicker horizontal strokes and thinner vertical strokes.

Shown here is a good example of the oriental, or Mizrachi, square script. Notice that, as opposed to our modern letter, the left "leg" of the letter heh *is attached to the roof of the letter (as well as that of* kuf*, which is not shown in this example). Notice too, the very long necks of the* lamed*, a characteristic found also in the Qumran scrolls.*

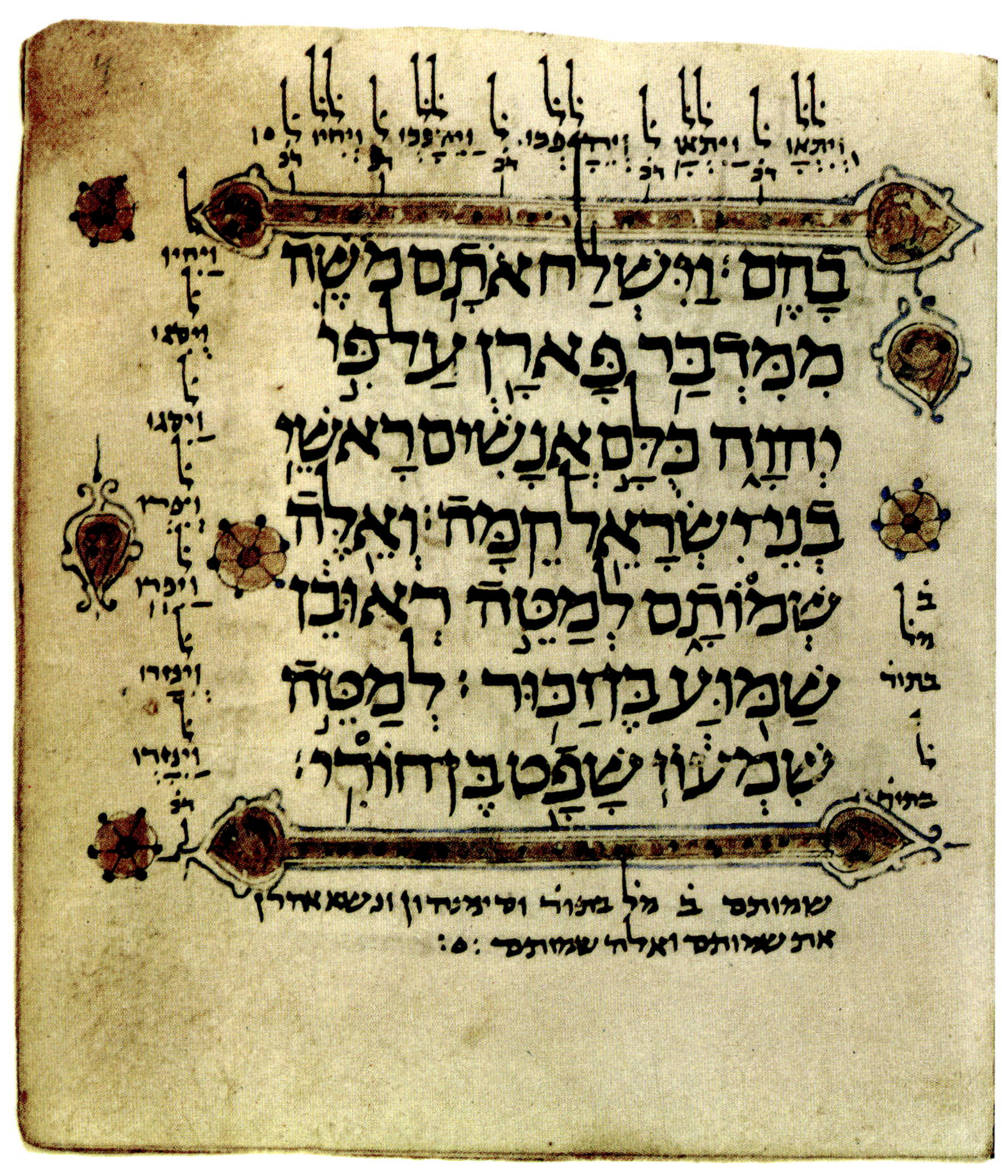
בהם וישלח אתם משה
ממדבר פארן על פי
יהוה כלם אנשים ראשי
בני ישראל המה ואלה
שמותם למטה ראובן
שמוע בן זכור למטה
שמעון שפט בן חורי

Shelach Lecha, portion of the Torah
Egypt (?), Persia (?), 1106–1107 CE
Jerusalem, Jewish National and University Library

הַחוֹחִים כֵּן רַעְיָתִי בֵּין הַבָּנוֹת׃
כְּתַפּוּחַ בַּעֲצֵי הַיַּעַר כֵּן דּוֹדִי בֵּין
הַבָּנִים בְּצִלּוֹ חִמַּדְתִּי וְיָשַׁבְתִּי
וּפִרְיוֹ מָתוֹק לְחִכִּי׃ הֱבִיאַנִי
אֶל־בֵּית הַיָּיִן וְדִגְלוֹ עָלַי אַהֲבָה׃
סַמְּכוּנִי בָּאֲשִׁישׁוֹת רַפְּדוּנִי
בַּתַּפּוּחִים כִּי־חוֹלַת אַהֲבָה אָנִי׃
שְׂמֹאלוֹ תַּחַת לְרֹאשִׁי וִימִינוֹ

Zvi Narkiss was commissioned by the publisher Nachum Ben Zvi to design a font inspired by the script of the tenth-century Keter Aram Tzova *(the Aleppo Codex), which is similar in style to the writing on the manuscript on the facing page. The publishers produced the* Keter Yerushalayim *Bible with this font, a detail of which is shown here.*

Details from the *Keter Yerushalayim*
N. Ben Zvi Printing Enterprises, 2002
Zvi Narkiss, font designer

An example of Yemenite script. These letters are quite bold. Like the Ashkenazic script, they demonstrate thick horizontal strokes and, in this manuscript, show very thin vertical strokes. Note how the head of the aleph *and the middle head of the* shin *are attached directly to the adjacent stroke rather than being connected with a thin line.*

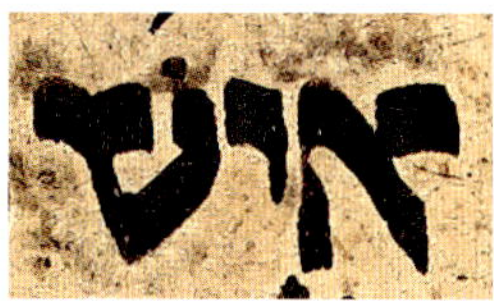

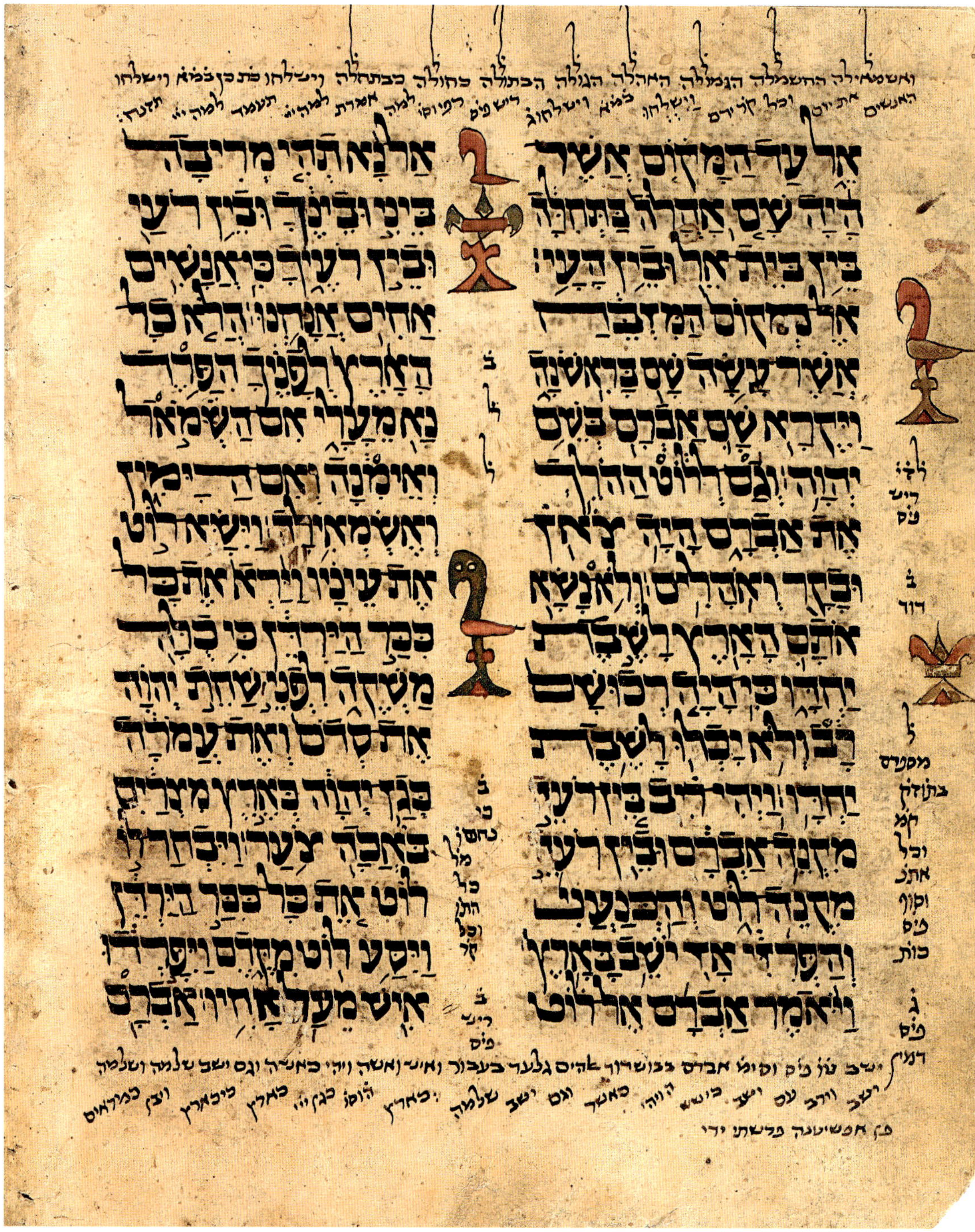

Mahberet Hatigan Bible, Pentateuch
Yemen, 1400 CE
The Library of the Jewish Theological Seminary

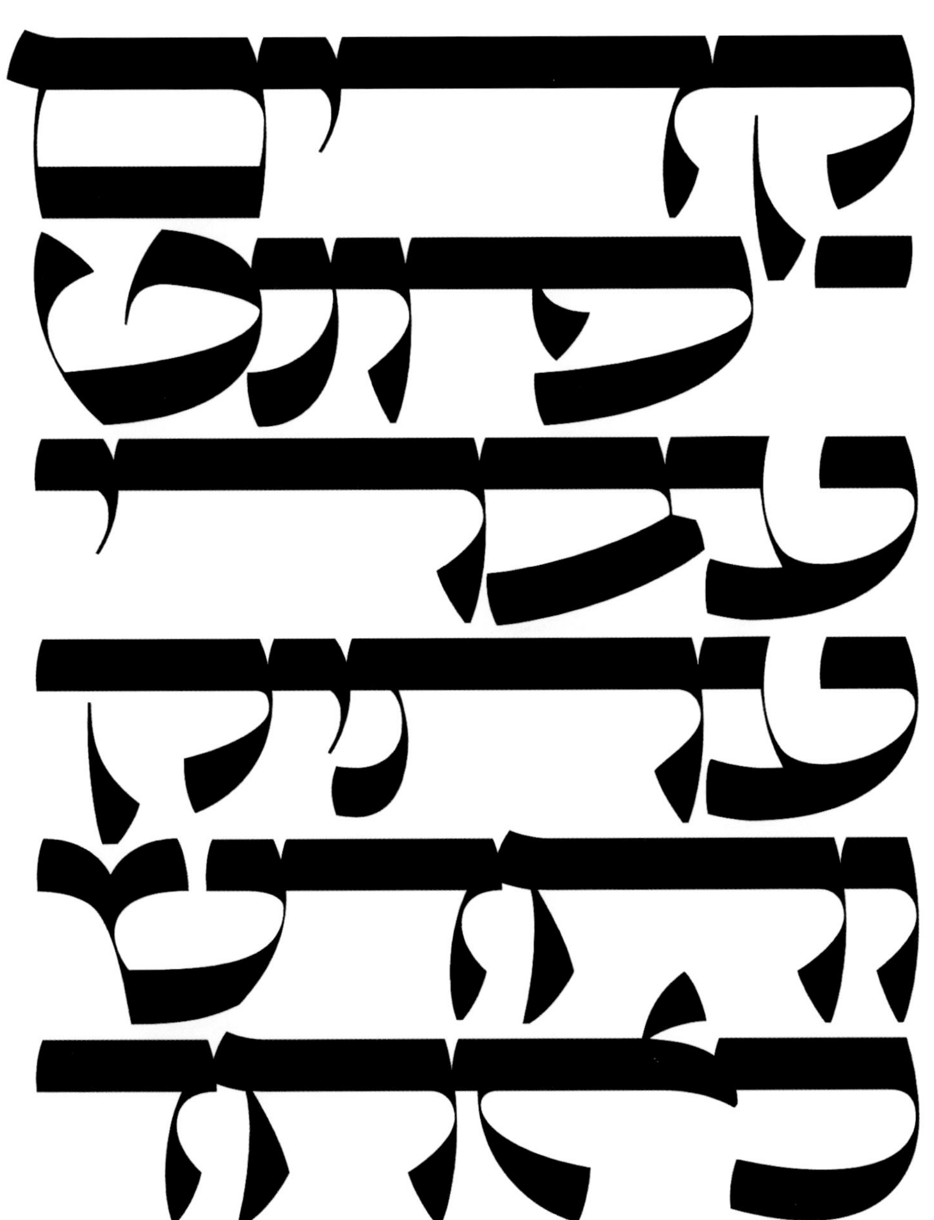

Type designer Oded Ezer studied the Yemenite script and shows how a modern font can be developed from a traditional historical style in his Kadim *font.*

Oded Ezer
Kadim font, 2020

The two broad classifications of Hebrew square script are Sephardic and Ashkenazic. Ashkenazic scripts (facing page) were written with a quill and are characterized by extreme contrast between the thick horizontal strokes and thin vertical strokes. Sephardic scripts were written with reeds and have less pronounced contrasts. Here are classic examples of medieval Sephardic and Ashkenazic square scripts.

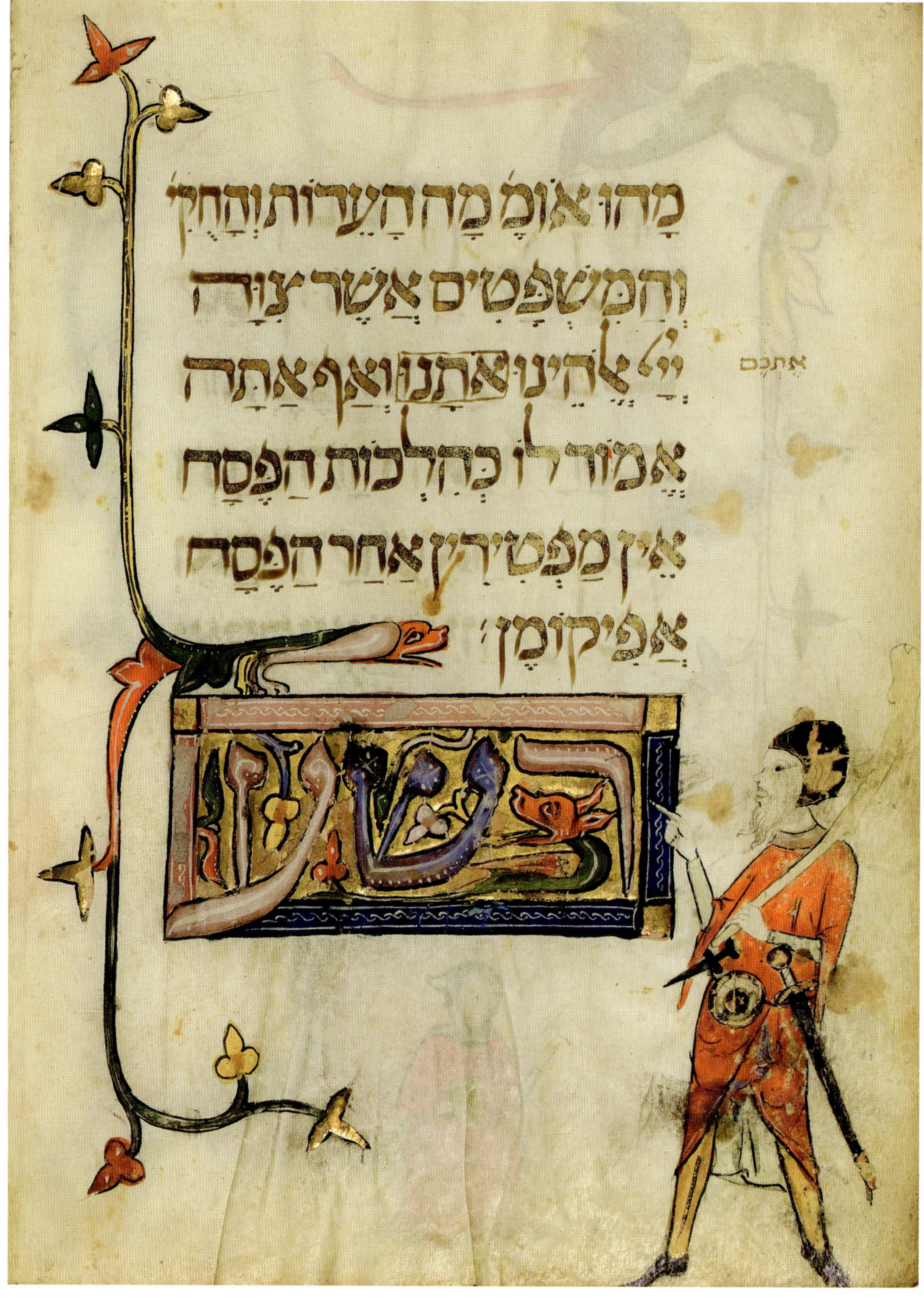

Prato Haggadah
Spain, 1300 CE
Library of the Jewish Theological Seminary

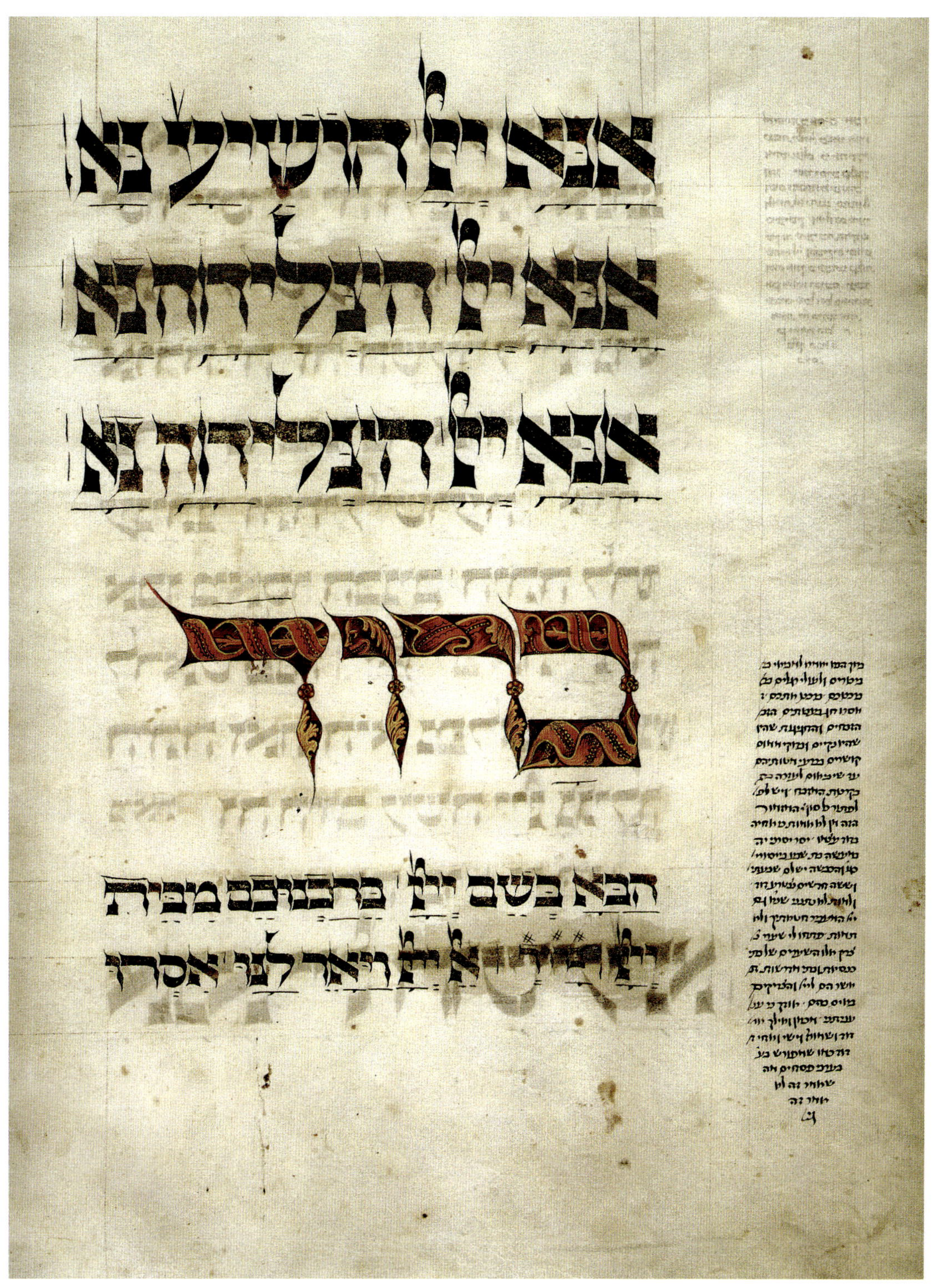

אנא יי הושיעה נא
אנא יי הצליחה נא
אנא יי הצליחה נא
ברוך
הבא בשם יי ברכנוכם מבית
יי אל יי ויאר לנו אסרו

Ashkenazi Haggadah
Germany, fifteenth century CE
British Library

The **Shiviti** plays a strong role in Judaic art. Expressing the phrase from Psalms "I will always set God before me," these works are usually hung in synagogues but are also found in homes and in prayer books.

Highlighting the Tetragrammaton, Shivitis also incorporate various verses and kabbalistic meditations, some written to the shape of the seven-branched menorah, and are thus also used as a visual meditation. Most often they are written in Sephardic script.

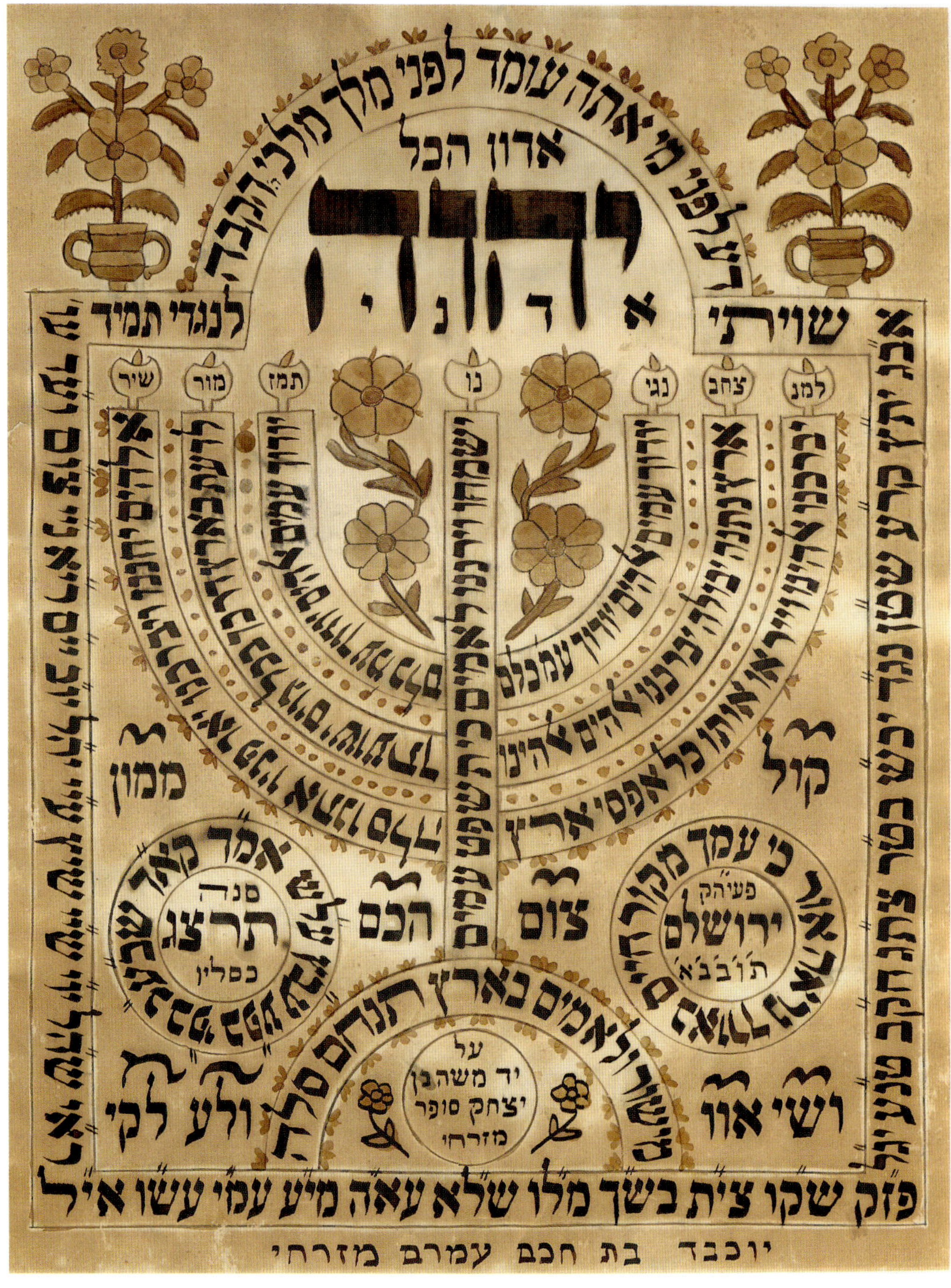

Shiviti
Jerusalem, 1932
Beinecke Rare Book & Manuscript Library, Yale University

This is a twenty-first-century Shiviti*-inspired work written in the Sephardic-style script that is also used for writing Torah scrolls. This script differs somewhat from the classic Sephardic script. See for example the letter* chet*, which is split and connected with a "spiked" roof, as well as having crowns, called* tagim*, on some of the letters.*

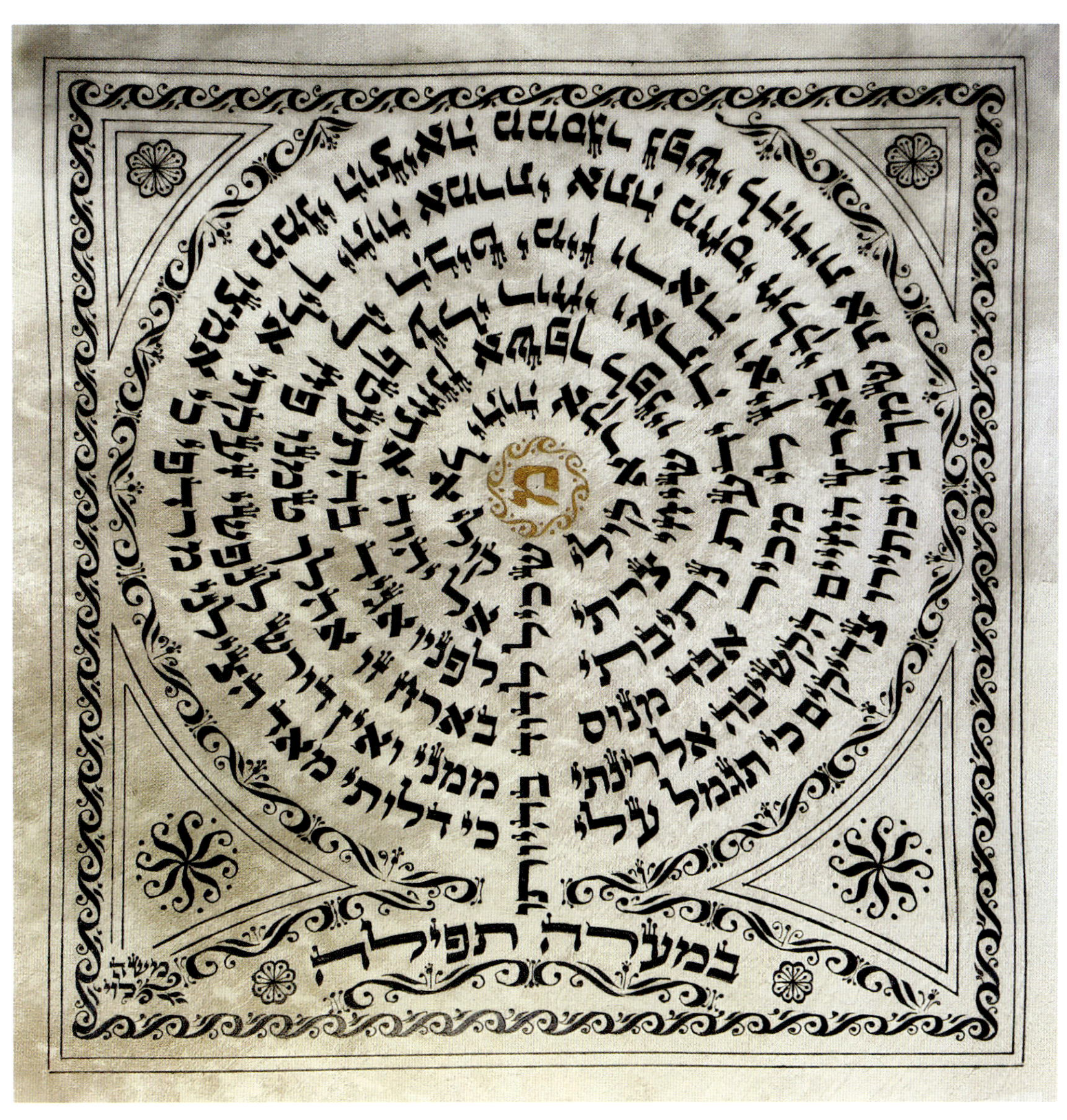

Moshe Levi
Psalm 142, 2021

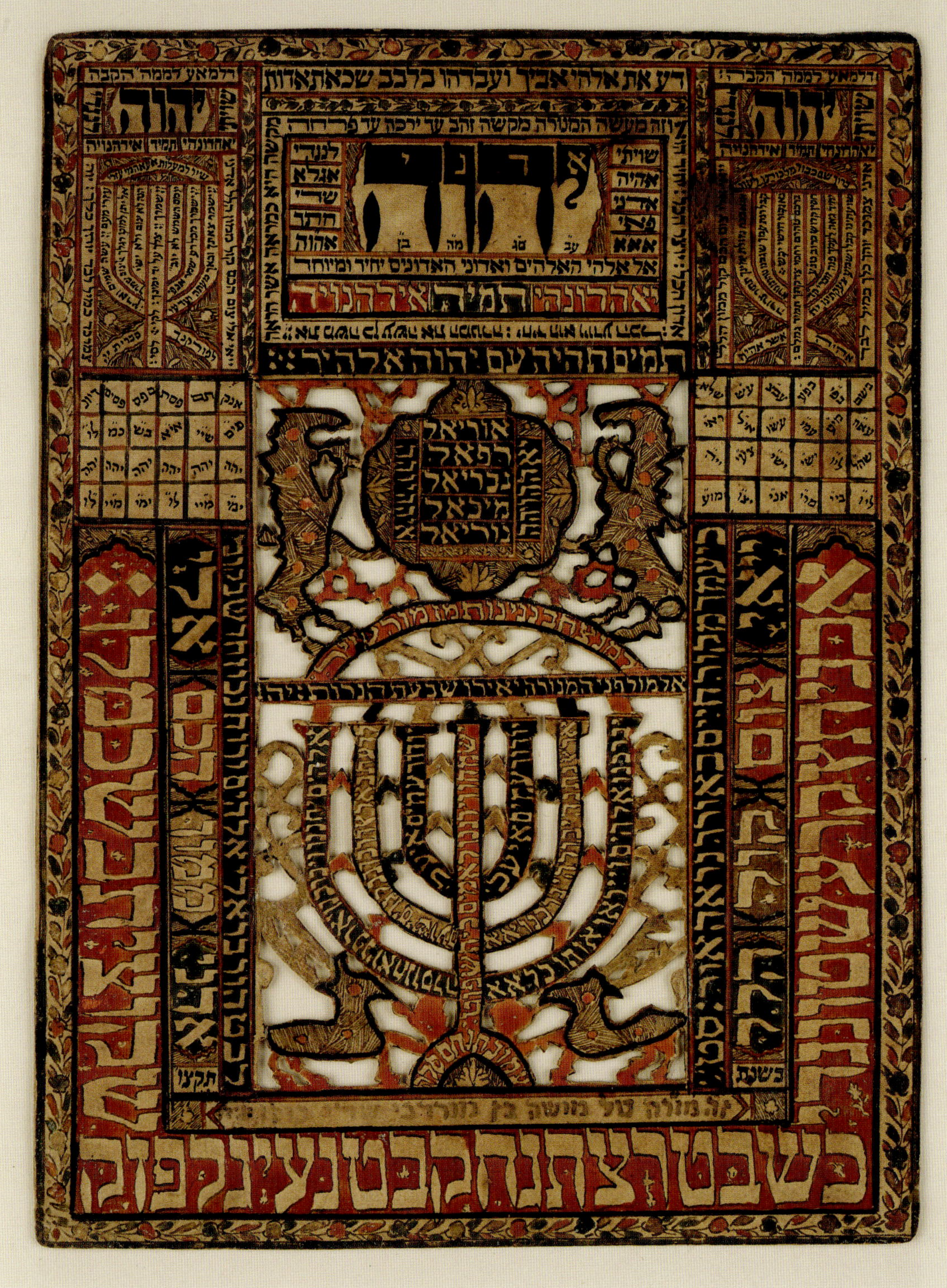

This elaborately decorated paper-cut Shiviti is part of a prayer book.

Moshe ben Mordechai
Shiviti
Iraq, 1875
Gross Family Collection, Tel Aviv

The Hebrew text in this work is also translated into Judeo-Arabic and written in an Iraqi Hebrew script.

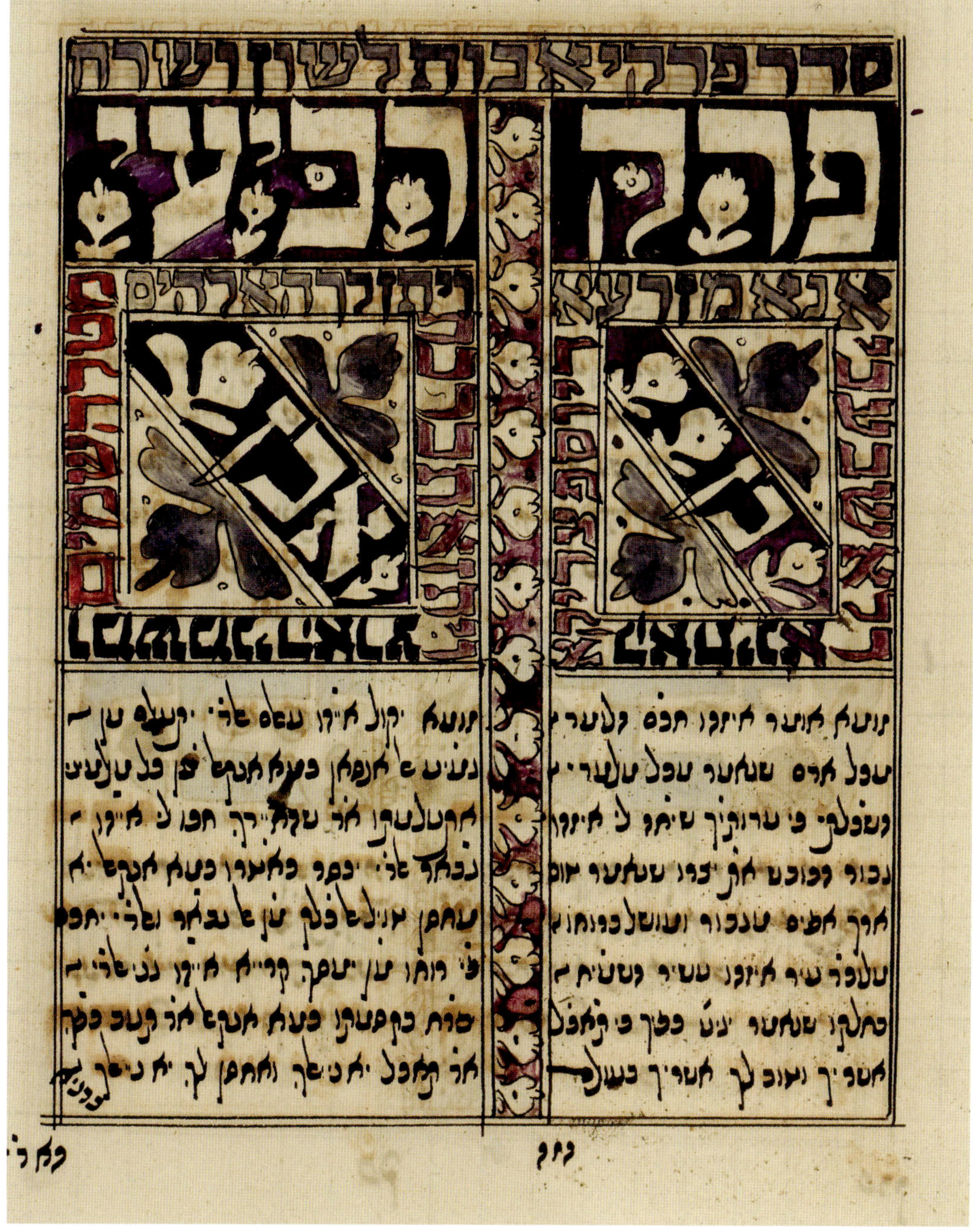

Moshe Yosef Avraham
From an illuminated compendium of texts for Passover
Iraq, 1883
Gross Family Collection, Tel Aviv

Jewish amulets, often containing kabbalistic texts or prayers, were meant to offer protection or good fortune to those who carried or wore them.

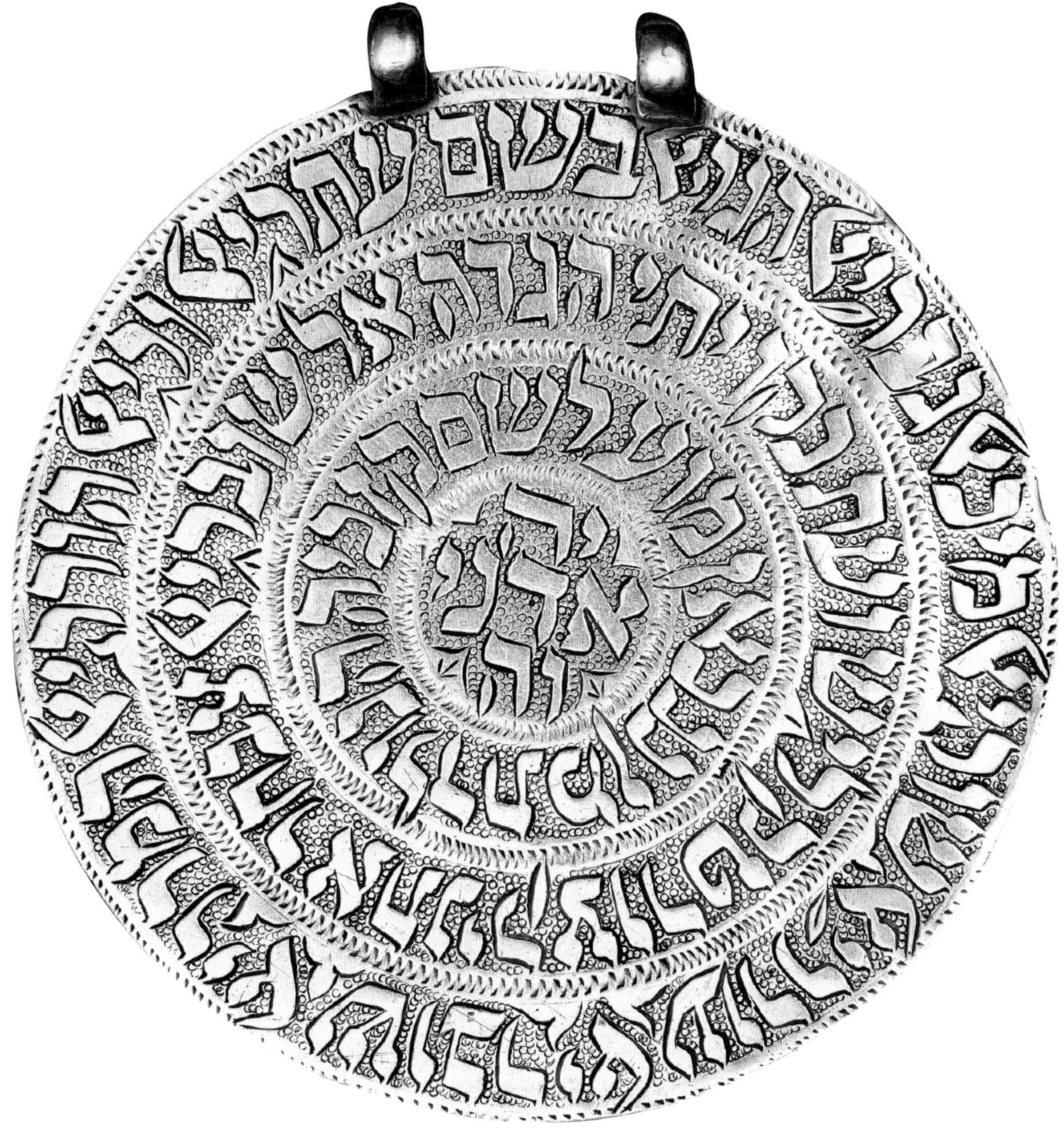

Amulet
Iran, c. 1900
Gross Family Collection, Tel Aviv

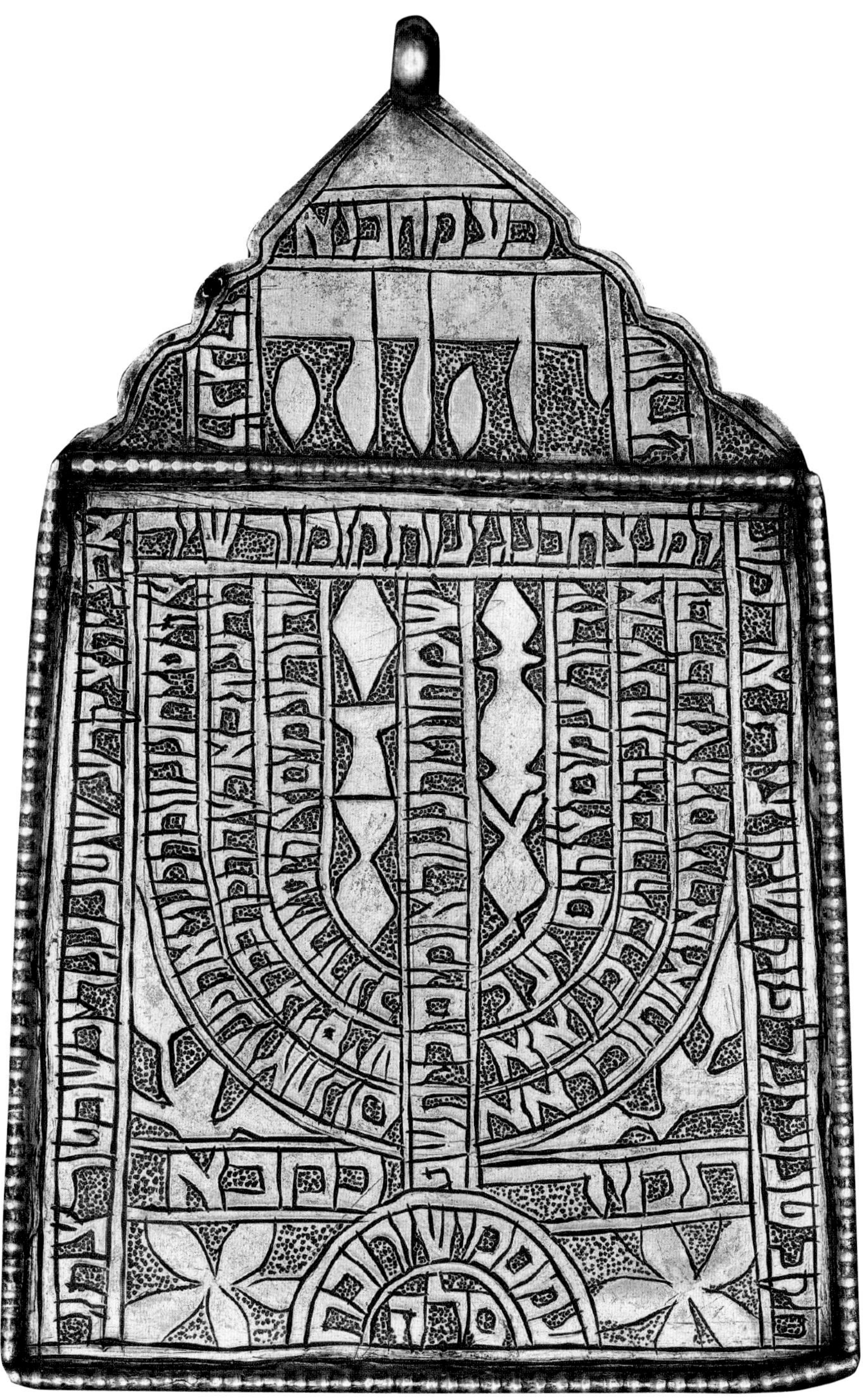

The lettering on this amulet, although not as refined as the one on the previous page, has a folksy charm of its own.

Amulet
Iran, c. 1930
Gross Family Collection, Tel Aviv

Here is a very lively and skillfully written French Ashkenazic script, a bit less formal than the German Ashkenazi Haggadah. *Notice the slight forward leaning of the letters, which gives an almost cursive feel to the writing.*

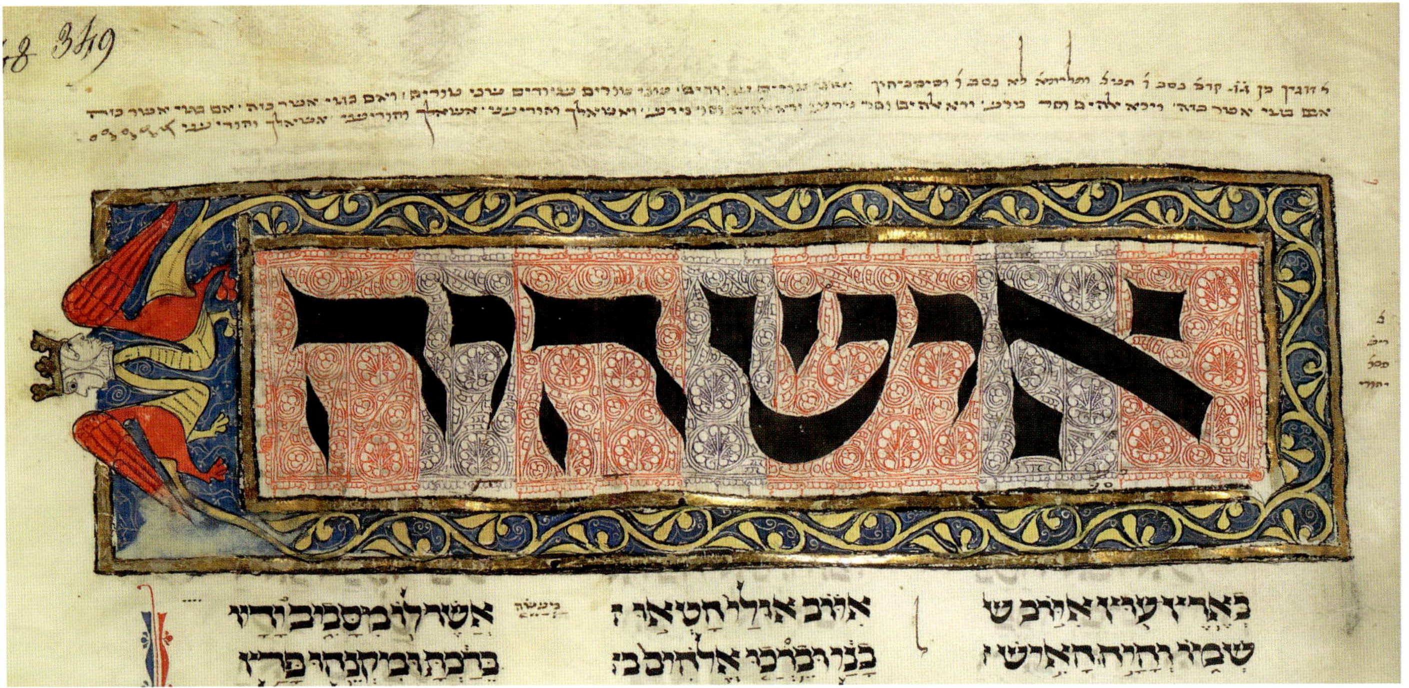

An illuminated heading from the same Bible.

Details from *Bible*
Poligny, France, 1300
Bibliothèque Nationale de France

לחה׃ ומשה בר מאה ועשרים שנין כד מי

לא שנא זיו יקרא דאפוהי׃ ויבכו בני ישר

ערבת מואב שלשים יום ויתמו ימי בכי א

ית משה במישרא דמואב תלתין

בכיתא דאיבלא דמשה׃ ויהושע בן נון מ

כי סמך משה את ידיו עליו וישמעו אל

שו כאשר צוה יהוה את משה׃ ויהושע בר

חכמתא ארי סמך משה ית ידוהי עלוהי ו

ראל ועבדו כמא דפקיד יי ית משה׃ ולא

ראל כמשה אשר ידעו יהוה פנים אל פנ

יא עוד בישראל כמשה דאתגלי ליה יי

לכל האתת והמופתים אשר שלחו יהוה

Pages from two Renaissance script-specimen books, "in which writing in any kind of letter, of any nation, ancient and modern, with its own rules and measures, and examples, is taught."

For the most part, these books showcased Latin letters in various styles, but a page of Hebrew was included, too. Here you see two samples of Ashkenazic scripts. On this page, one sees highly stylized letters (some quirky, such as the tzadi, called here Zzadi). On the following page, the letters appear to be broken up into their individual strokes, perhaps to give the reader an idea of how to form them.

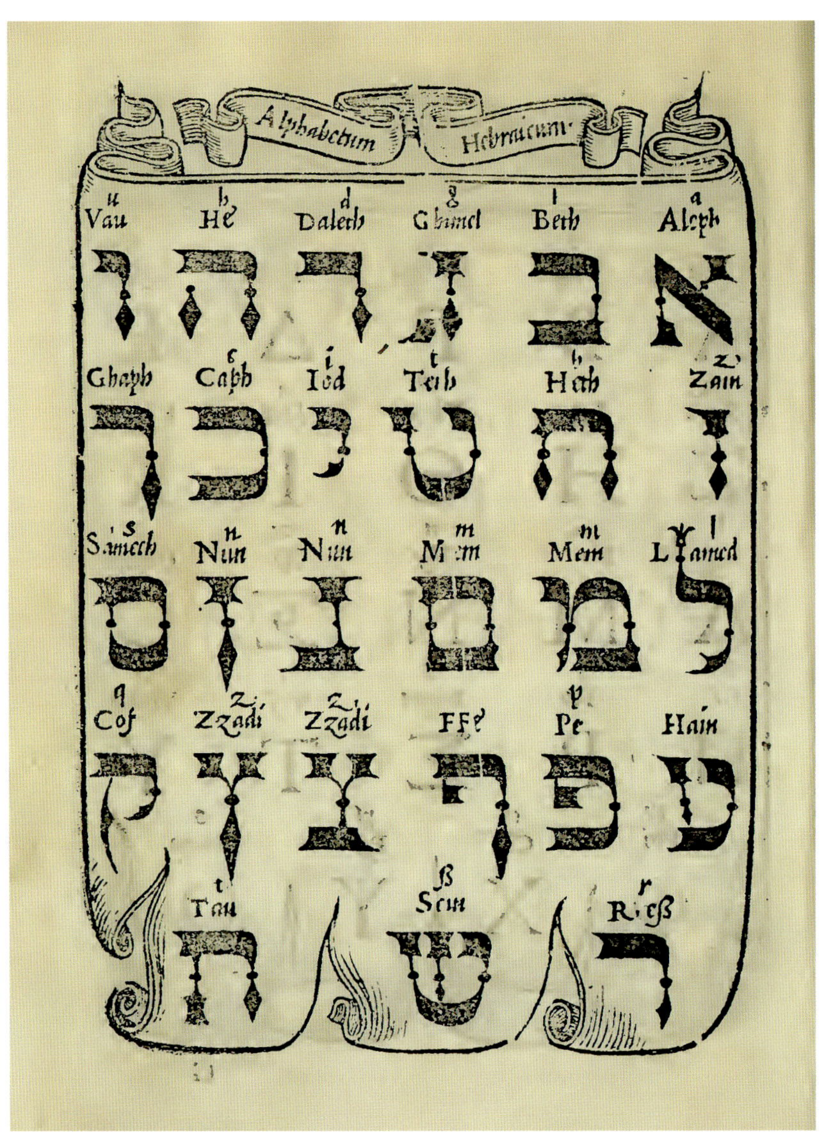

M. Giovanbattista Palatino
From *Tools of Handwriting*, 1540–1545

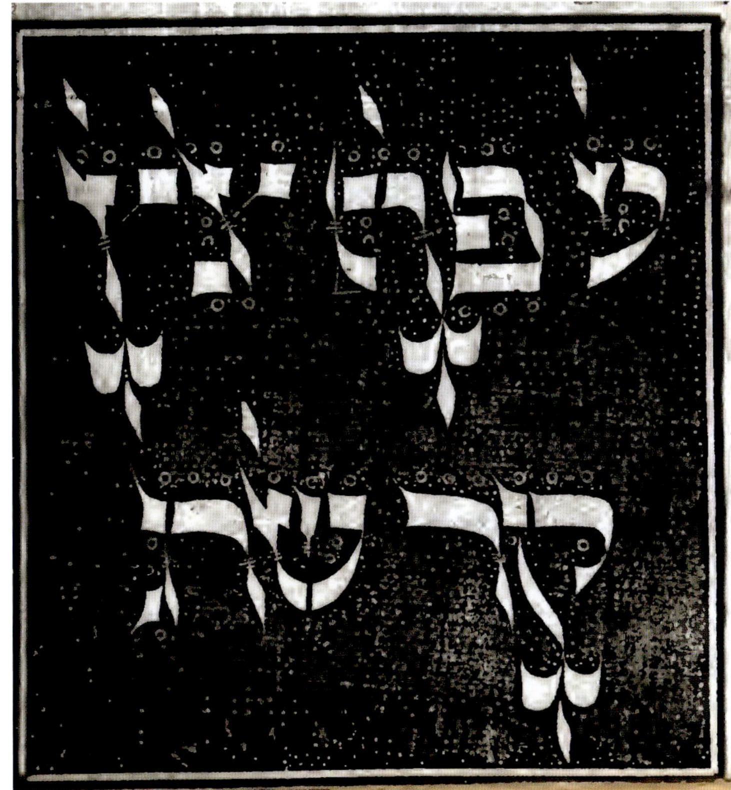

Il ſopraſcritto alphabetto e hebraicho for
mato ⁊ li hebrei dice che la ſua raggione e
che la lettera o die eſſere vno quadrato di
penna e la lettera mezza o de eſſere mezzo
quadrato adoncha la lóghezza e la larghe-
za vol eſſere longhe e larghe táti quadrati
di penna come tu uedi in queſta monſtra.

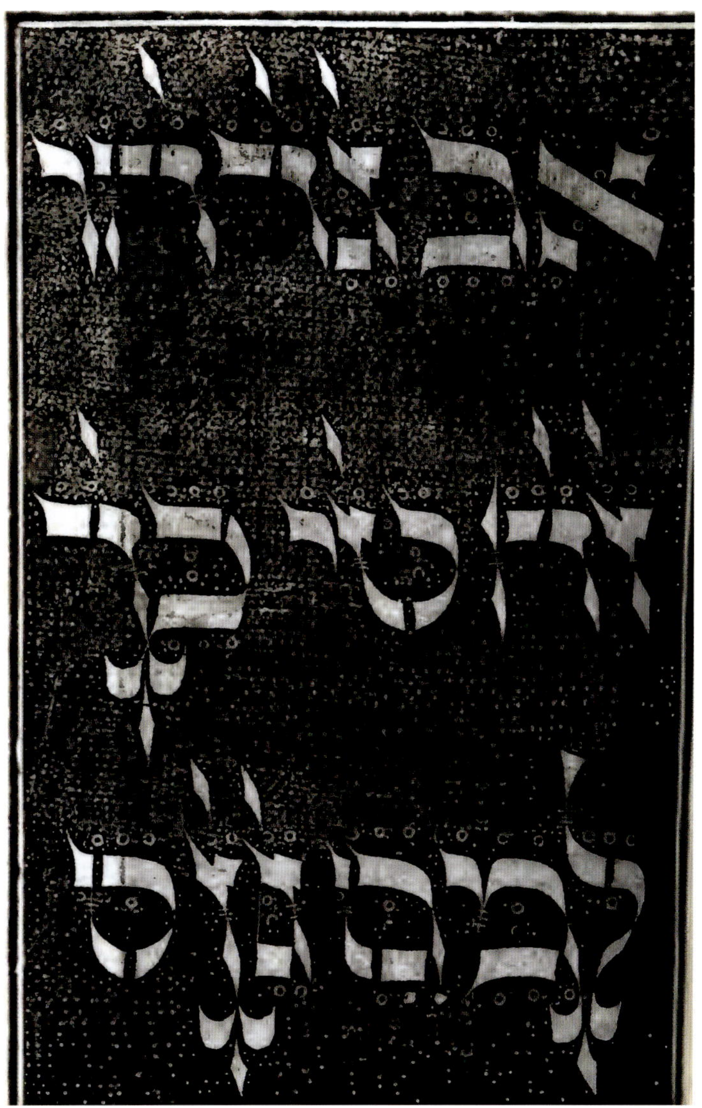

Giovanni Antonio Tagliente
Lo presente libro insegna la vera arte delo excellente scrivere de litere, 1524

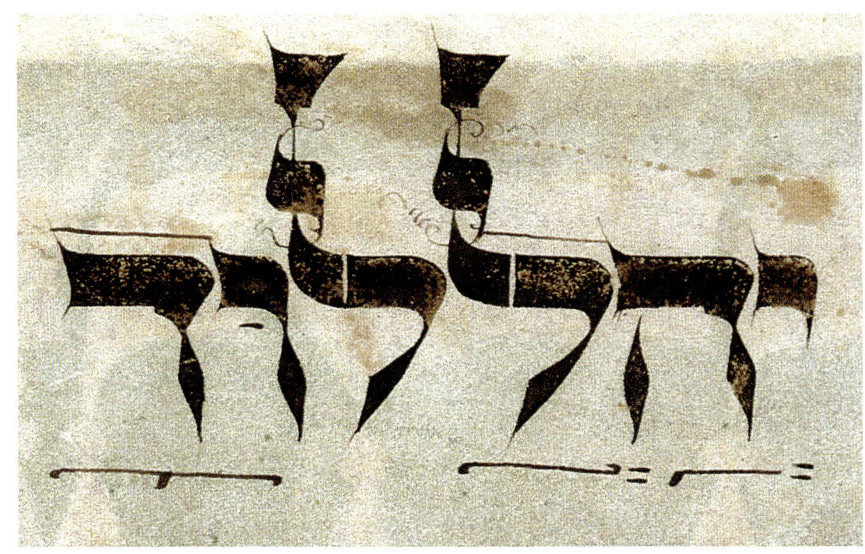

Details from the *Ashkenazi Haggadah*
Germany, fifteenth century
British Library

Ashkenazic forms, in particular, lend themselves to being shaped into decorative lettering. The letter lamed, *being the only ascender in the Hebrew aleph-bet, often received the special attention of the lettering illuminator.*

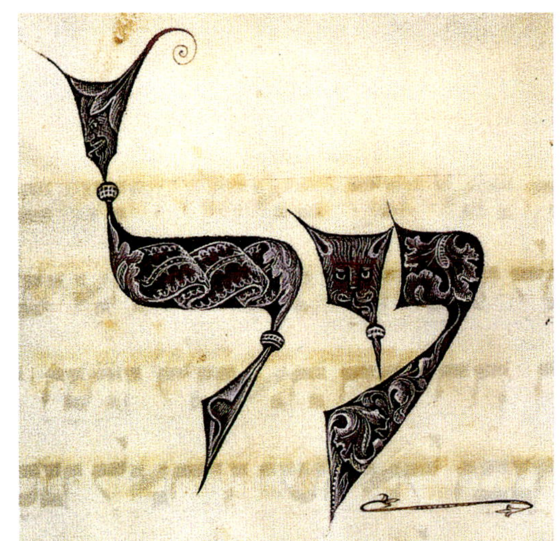

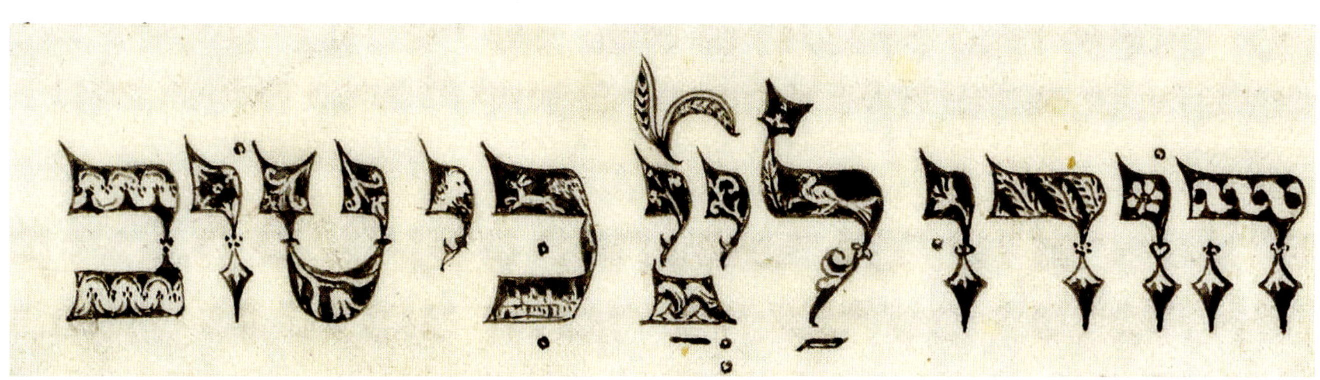

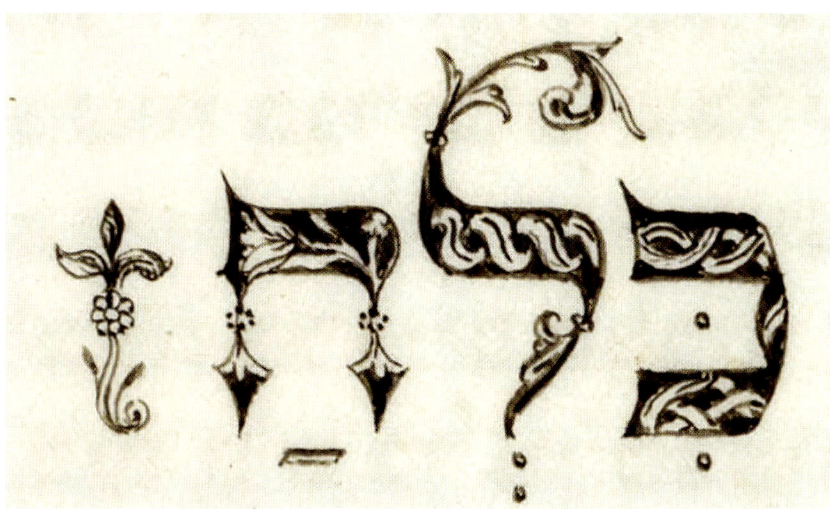

Painting just the outline of the letter allowed for illumination and illustration within the letterform.

Details from the *Herlingen Haggadah*
Vienna, 1730
Braginsky Collection, Zurich. BCB 388.
Photography by Ardon Bar-Hama, Ra'anana, Israel

Developing alongside the more formal square scripts were semi-cursive scripts—scripts that were simpler in form and thus faster to write. In most manuscripts the main text was written in square script, and commentaries were written in semi-cursive. In this manuscript, however, the main text is written in an elegant Italian semi-cursive hand, with only the large initial word in Ashkenazic square script.

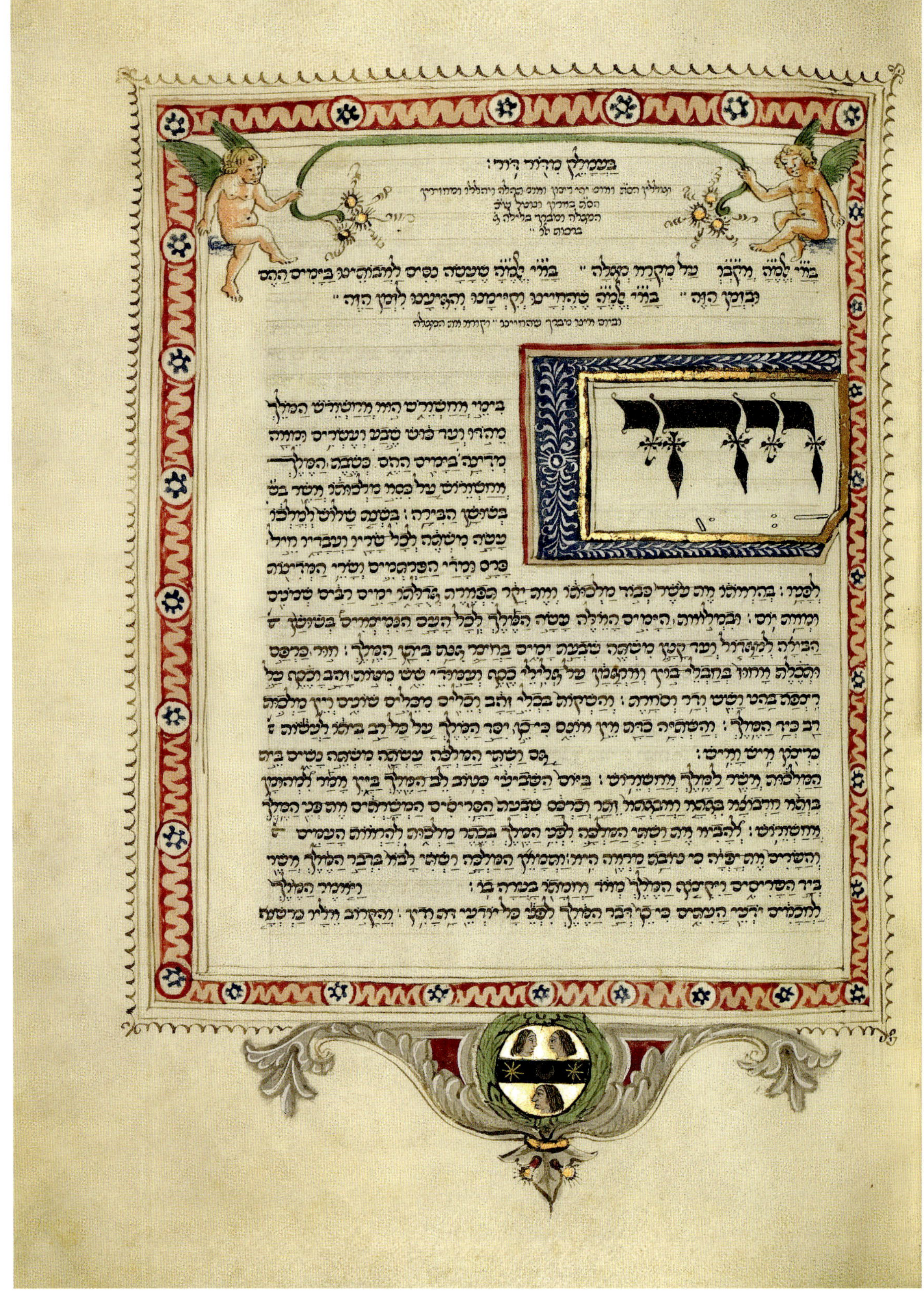

The Rothschild Machzor
Florence, 1492
Library of the Jewish Theological Seminary

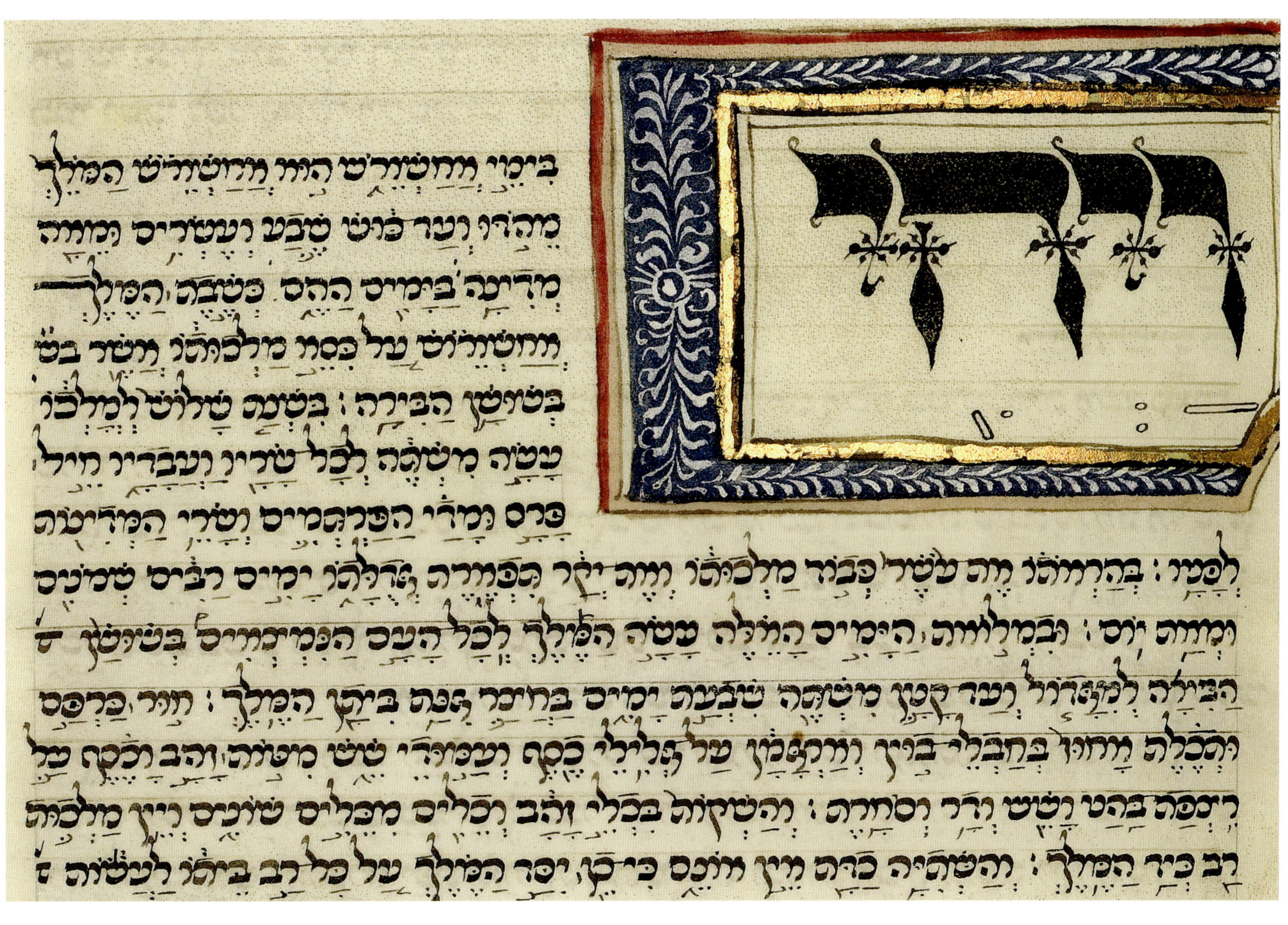

ויהי

בימי אחשורוש הוא אחשורוש המלך
מהדו ועד כוש שבע ועשרים ומאה
מדינה בימים ההם כשבת המלך
אחשורוש על כסא מלכותו אשר
בשושן הבירה בשנת שלוש למלכו
עשה משתה לכל שריו ועבדיו חיל
פרס ומדי הפרתמים ושרי המדינות
לפניו בהראתו את עשר כבוד מלכותו ואת יקר תפארת גדולתו ימים רבים שמונים
ומאת יום ובמלואת הימים האלה עשה המלך לכל העם הנמצאים בשושן
הבירה למגדול ועד קטן משתה שבעת ימים בחצר גנת ביתן המלך חור כרפס
ותכלת אחוז בחבלי בוץ וארגמן על גלילי כסף ועמודי שש מטות זהב וכסף על
רצפת בהט ושש ודר וסחרת והשקות בכלי זהב וכלים מכלים שונים ויין מלכות
רב כיד המלך והשתיה כדת אין אנס כי כן יסד המלך על כל רב ביתו לעשות

The Rothschild Machzor (detail)
Florence, 1492
Library of the Jewish Theological Seminary

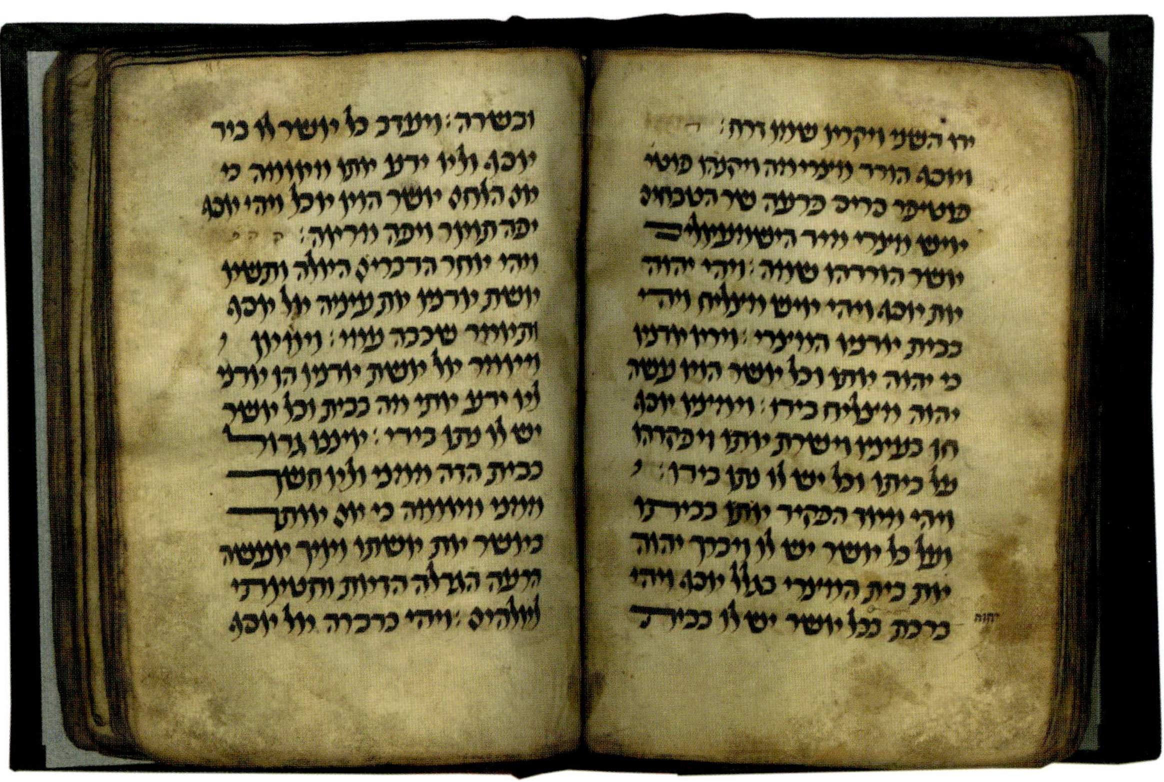

Here we have an impressive Ashkenazic semi-cursive book hand. Note the sharper angles in the letterforms, which provide a different texture compared to the softer curves of the script on the previous page. The arch-like letterforms here mirror forms found in Gothic architecture.

Book of Genesis, manuscript on parchment
Northern France or Germany, c. 1250–1300 CE

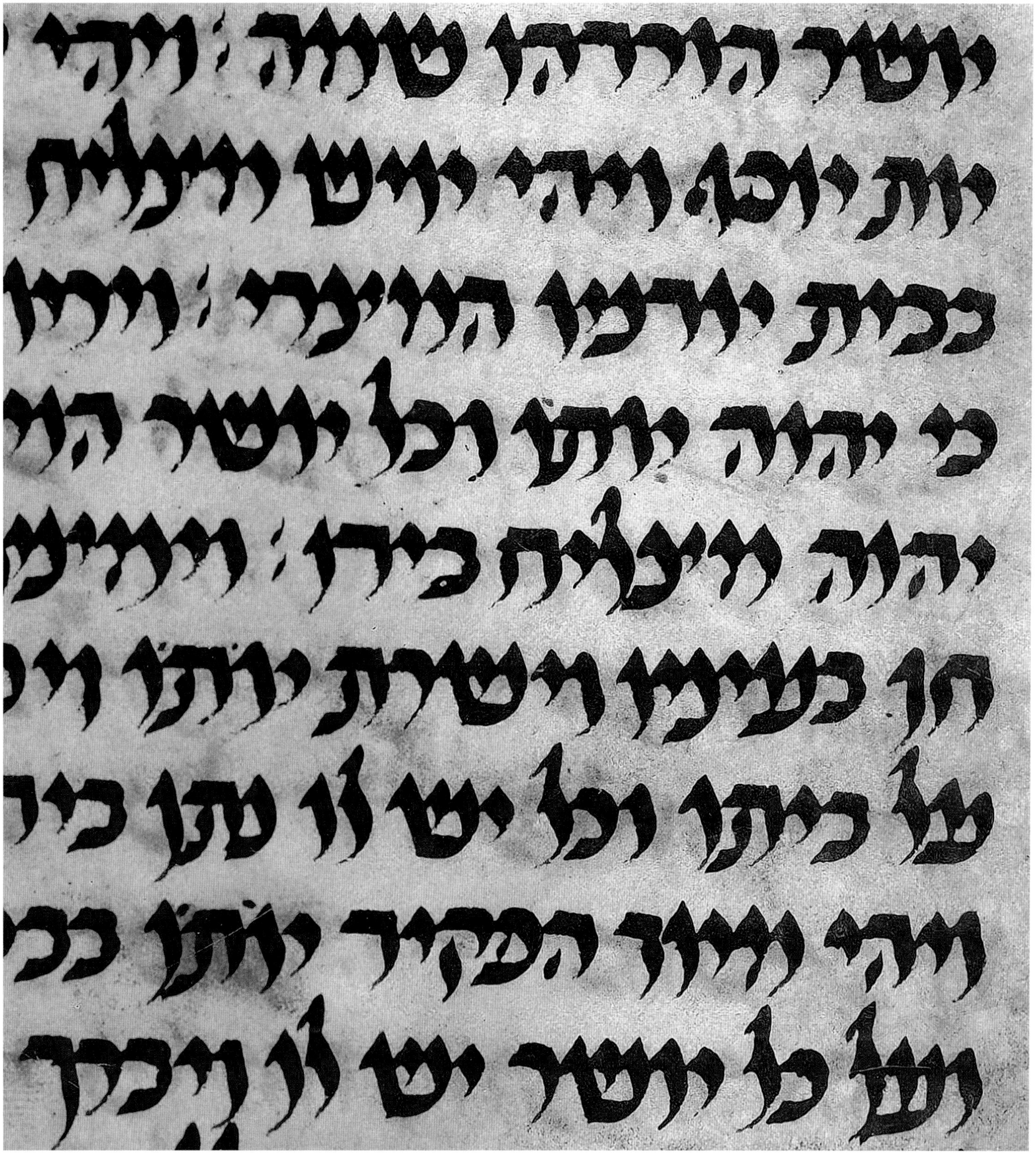

אשר הורדהו שמה׃ ויה
את יוסף ויהי איש מצליח
בבית אדניו המצרי׃ ויר
כי יהוה אתו וכל אשר הו
יהוה מצליח בידו׃ וימצ
חן בעיניו וישרת אתו וי
על ביתו וכל יש לו נתן בי
ויהי מאז הפקיד אתו בב
ועל כל אשר יש לו ויברך

Sefer Mitzvot Katan
1201–1400 CE
Bibliothèque Nationale de France

In this example we see the Ashkenazic formal square script, used for the large, decorated heading, contrasted with the more quickly written semi-cursive used for the body text. The letterforms for the text here are more condensed than those on the previous page, demonstrating an even more pronounced Gothic influence.

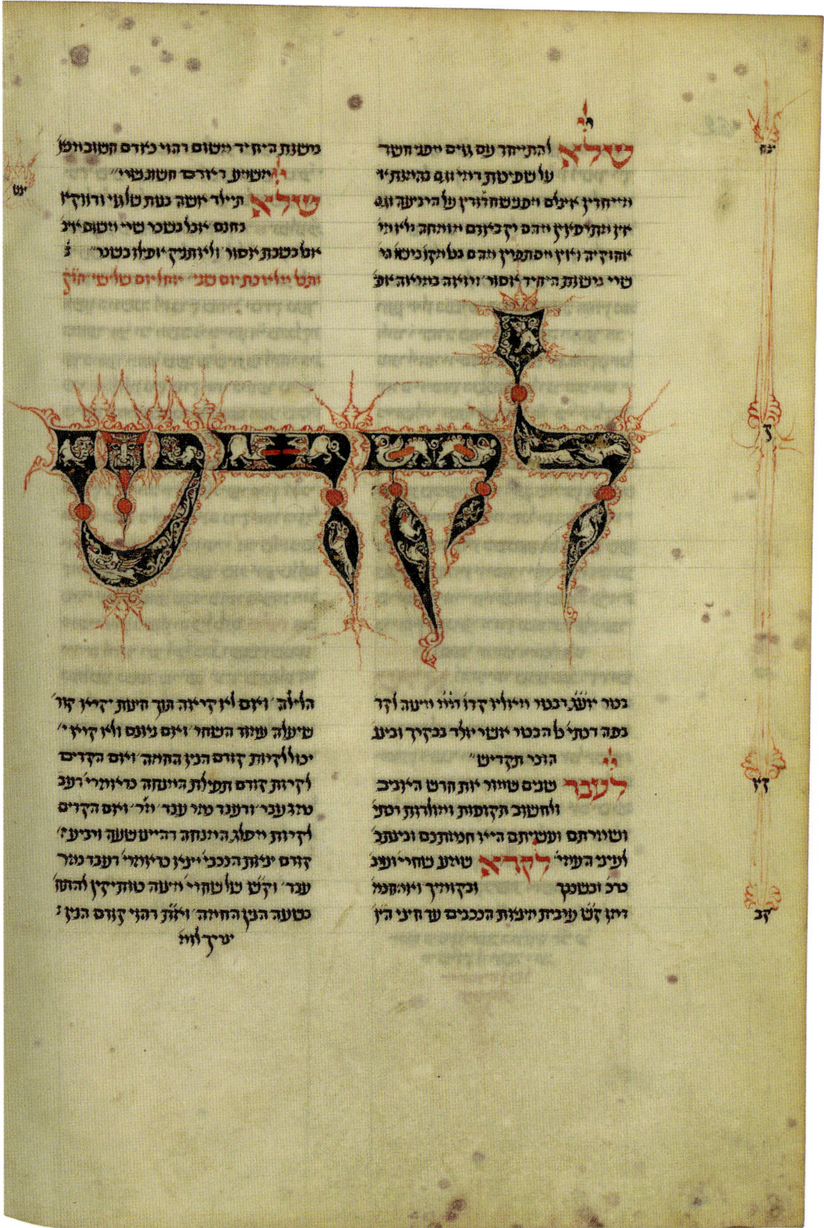

Sefer Mitzvot Katan (enlarged detail)

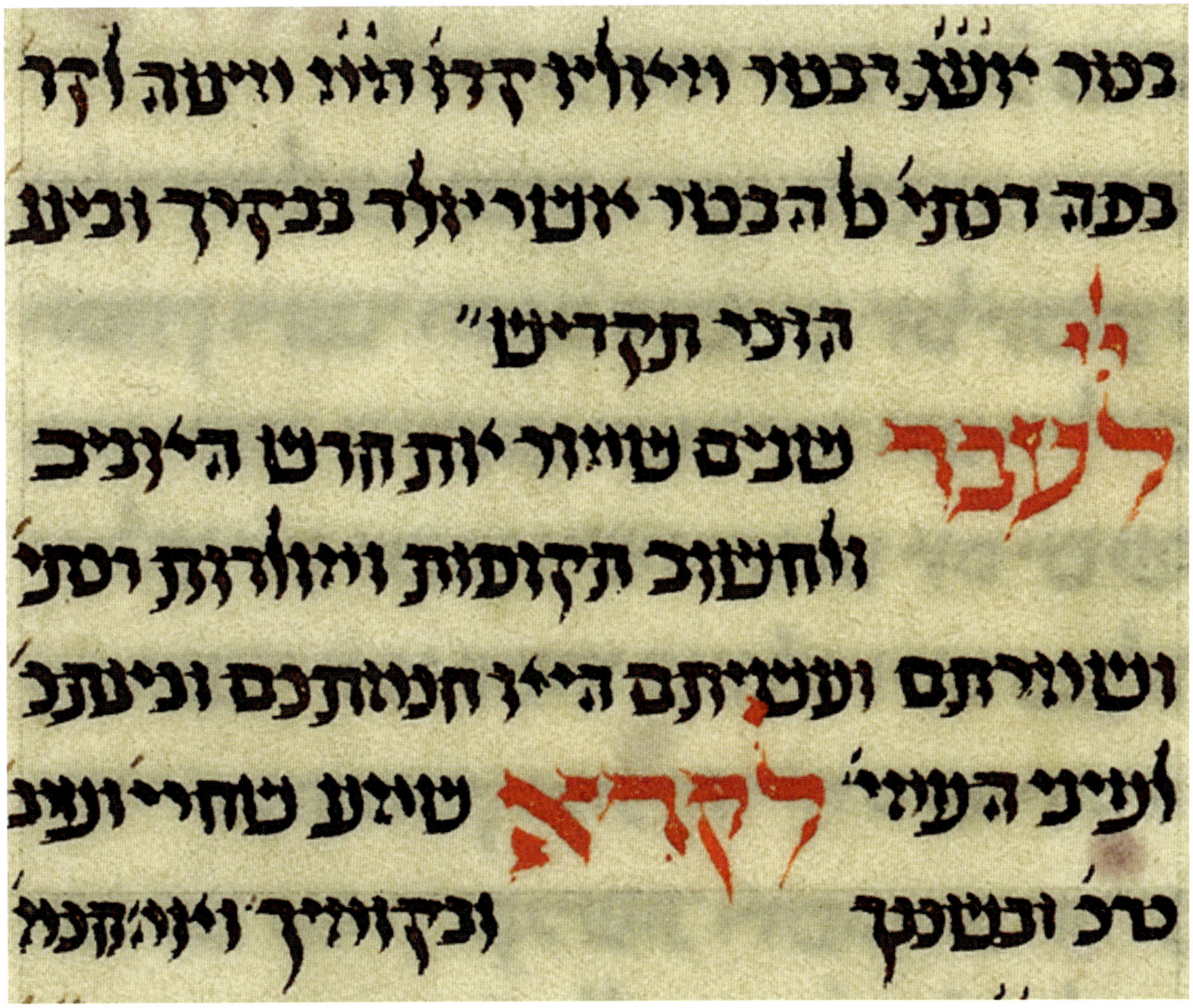

Beauty in Hebrew writing is not just a matter of having beautiful letterforms, but also how those forms string together to produce an interesting rhythm. Here is a Spanish semi-cursive that seems to be influenced by Arabic writing. The rhythm here is produced by an almost hypnotic repetition of form.

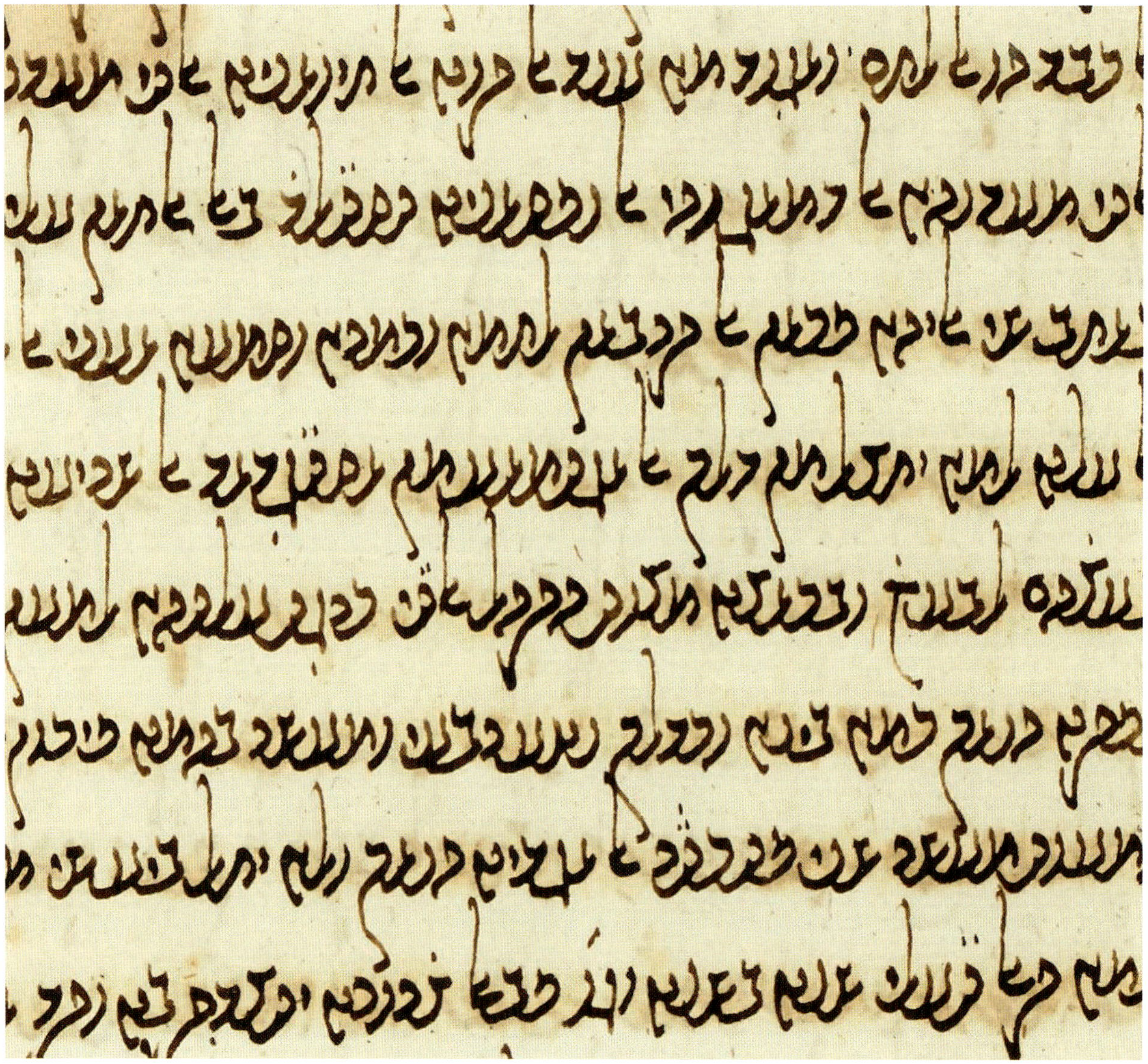

Detail from *Guide to the Perplexed*
Southern Spain, 1479
Bibliothèque Nationale de France

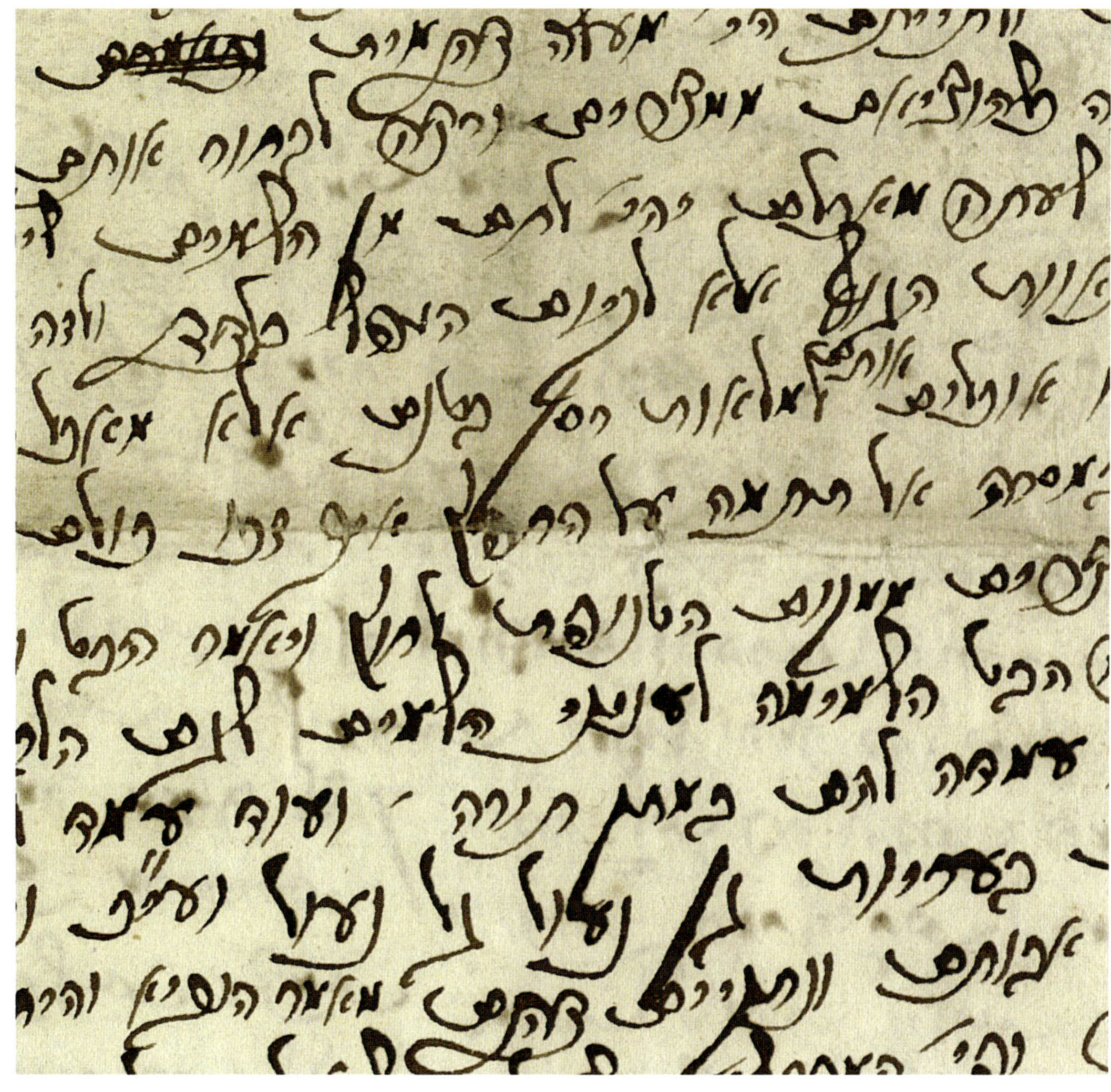

In this example there is a freer sense of movement than in the previous image, almost analogous to a jazz improvisation.

Rosh Av Bet Din be-Kopenhagen (enlarged detail)
Drashot ve-ḥidushim al parashat ha-shavu'a
Eighteenth century
Royal Danish Library, David Simonsen Collection

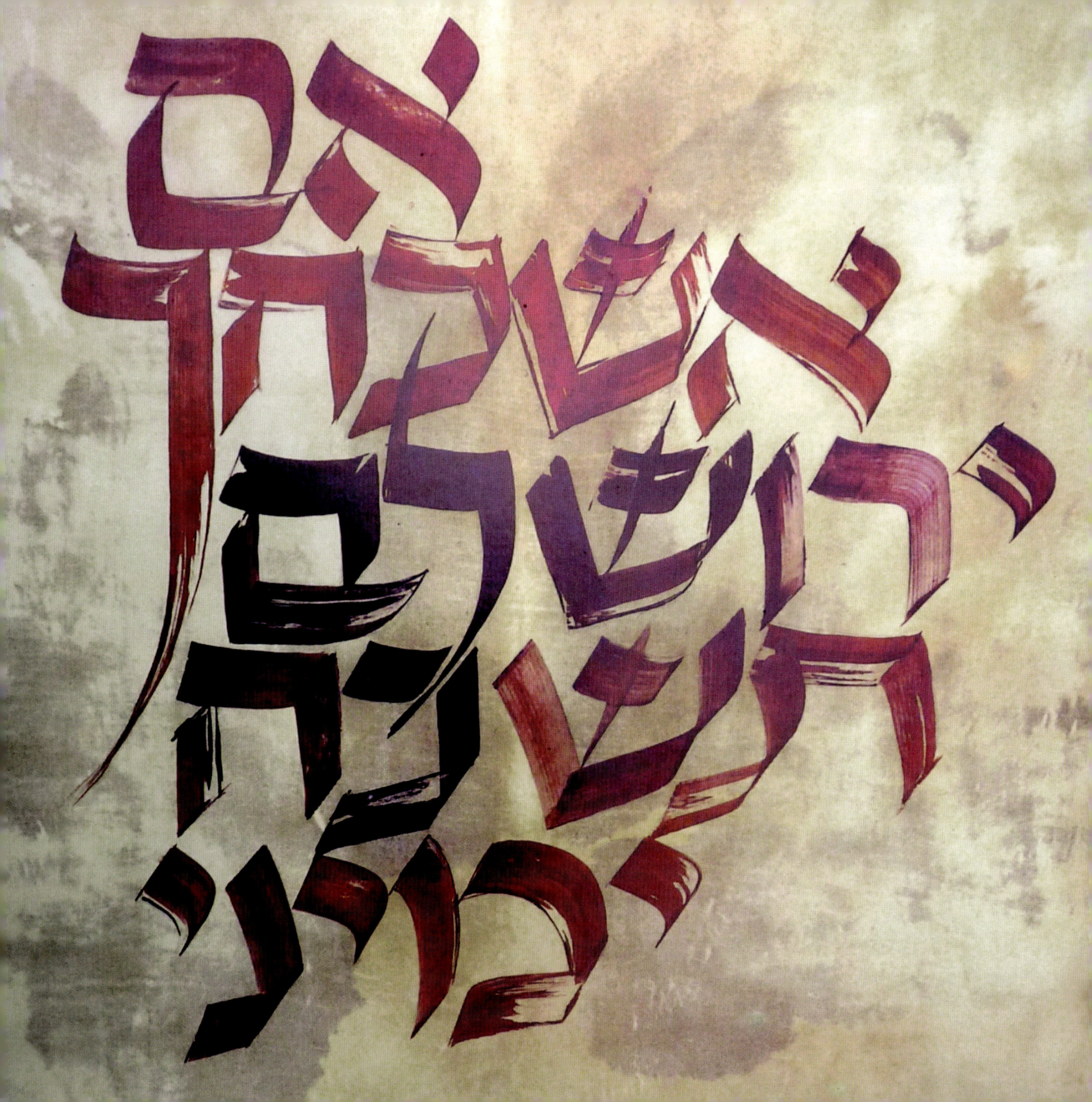
אם
אשכחך
ירושלם
תשכח
ימיני

2

Traditional Calligraphy and Lettering

Calligraphy with a broad-edged pen has traditionally been a craft where the scribe has more or less remained anonymous. Tasked with transcribing texts as clearly and as beautifully as possible, there was little room for experimentation and abstract expression. And yet within these limitations, calligraphers and lettering artists in the twentieth century produced beautiful works, subtly infusing them with personal style and creativity. Many of the works shown in this section were produced for utilitarian purposes and thus are, for the most part, highly legible. They include logos, book covers, and items of Judaica, as well as standalone calligraphic artworks.

Malla Carl
Detail from *If I Forget Thee O Jerusalem*
Late twentieth century

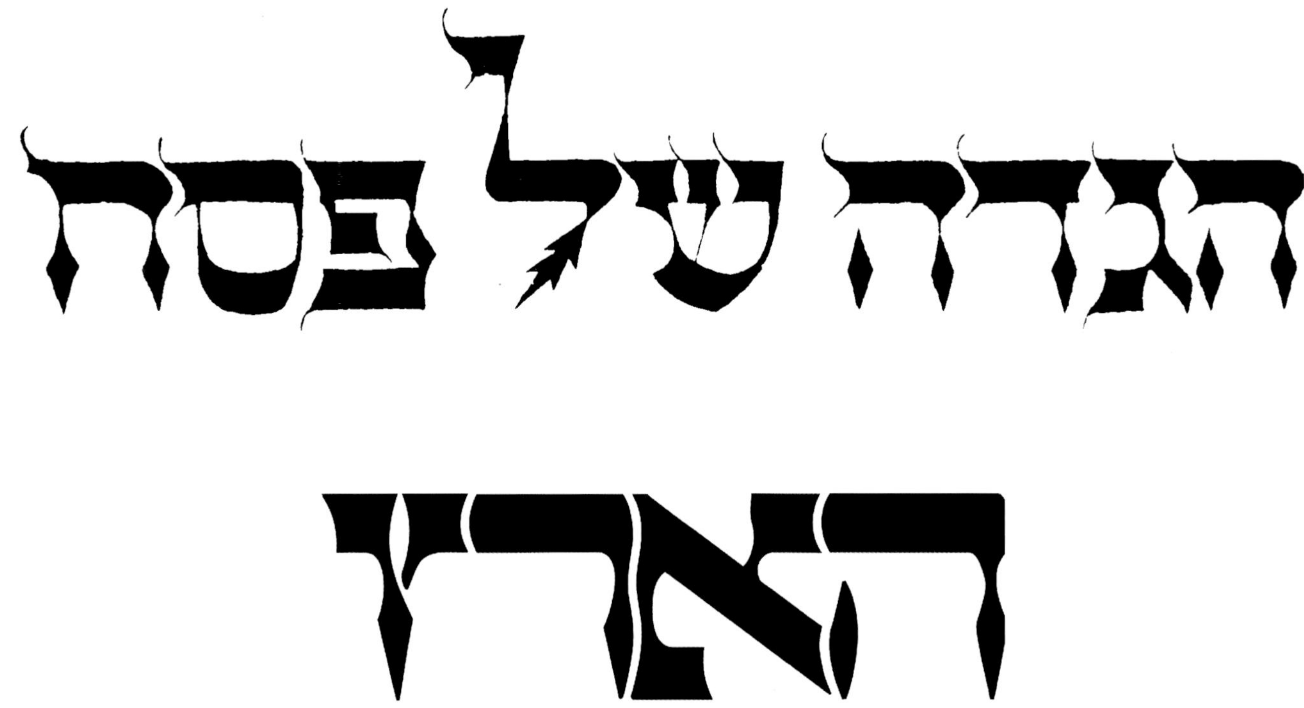

The German-born designer Franzisca Baruch revived the Ashkenazic script for design in the early to mid-twentieth century after she was commissioned to design lettering for a Haggadah *by the artist Jacob Steinhardt, the title for which is shown here. Below that is her logo design for the* Haaretz *newspaper, which is still used today.*

Franzisca Baruch
TOP: Title for Passover *Haggadah*, 1921
BOTTOM: Logo for *Haaretz* newspaper, 1936

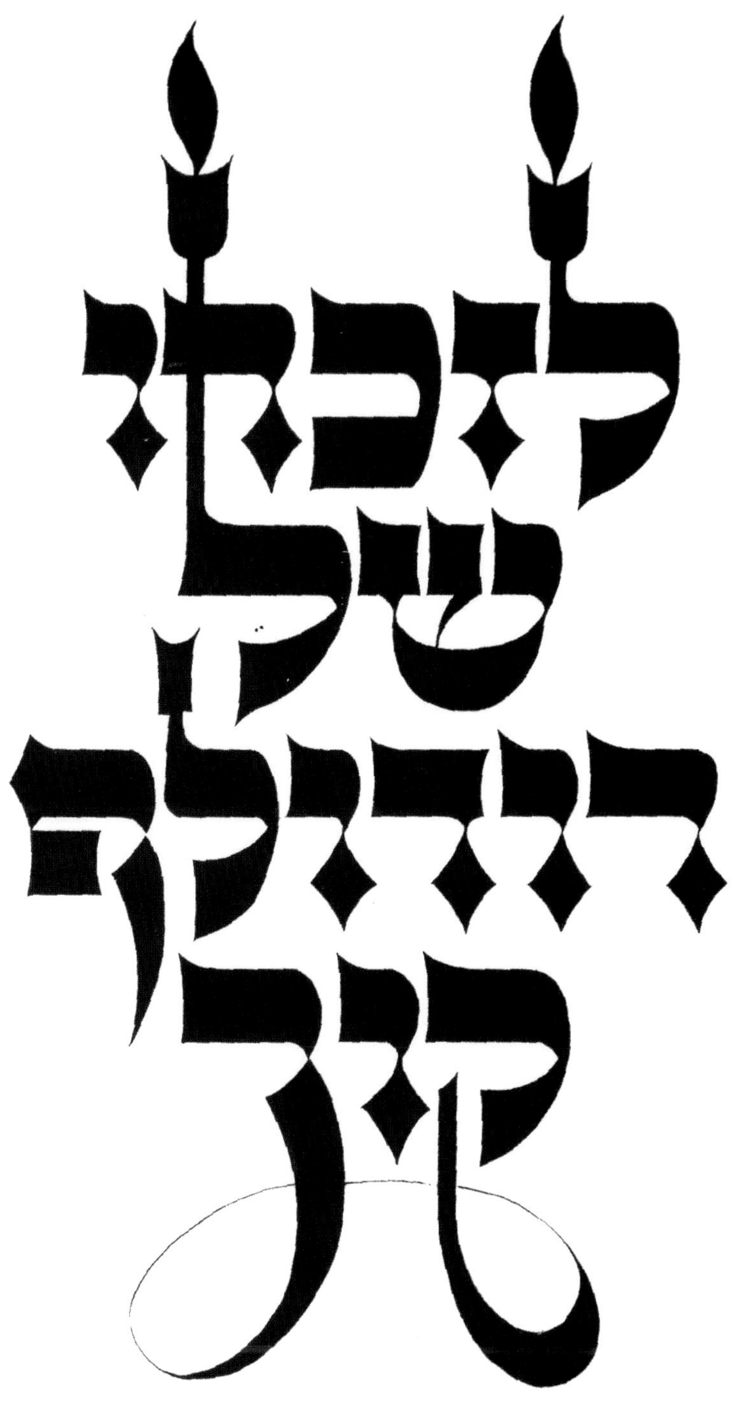

Zev Lipman was a graphic artist who designed many coins, stamps, and branding in Israel in the mid-twentieth century. Here is a highly stylized version of the Ashkenazic script.

Zev Lipman
In Memory of Rudolph Koch
Mid- to late twentieth century

Two more versions of the Ashkenazic script. This page shows a more rounded interpretation. Compare the curviness and movement of the letters here with the upright stability of the letters on the facing page.

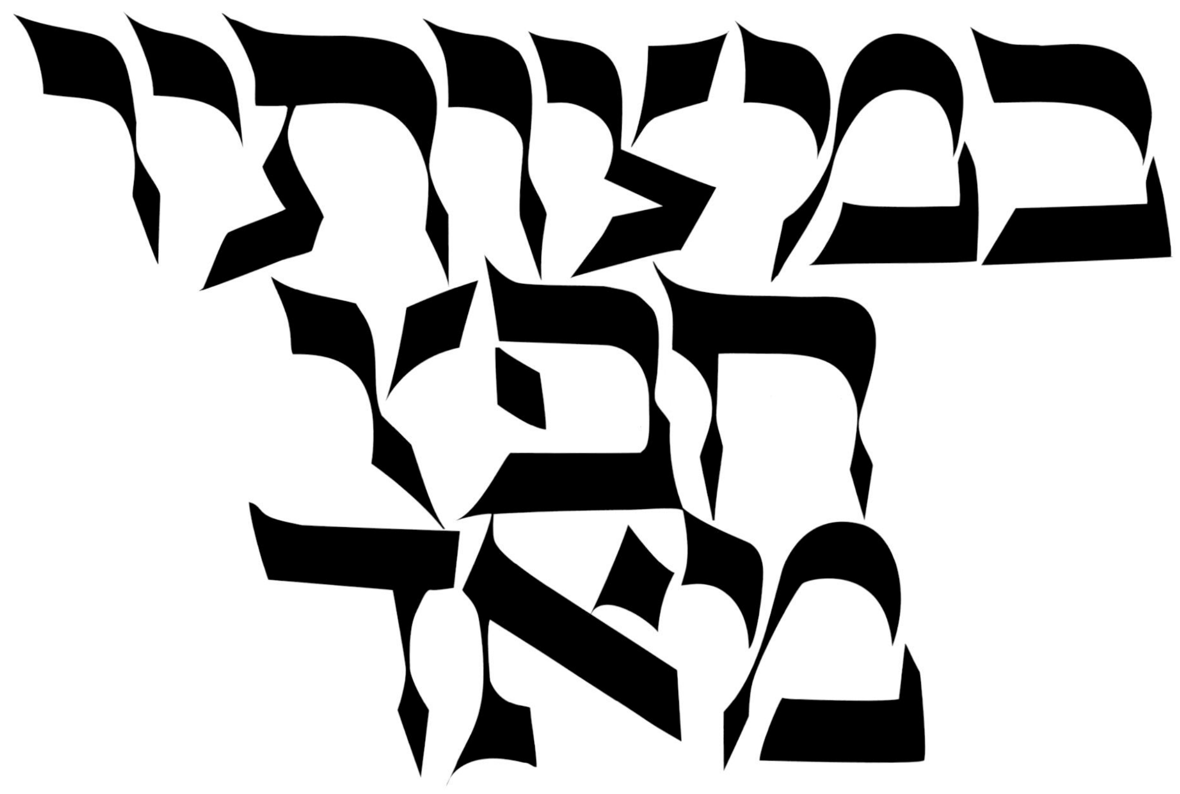

Siegmund Forst
Lettering in cover illustration for *A Lifetime in Arts and Letters*, 1993

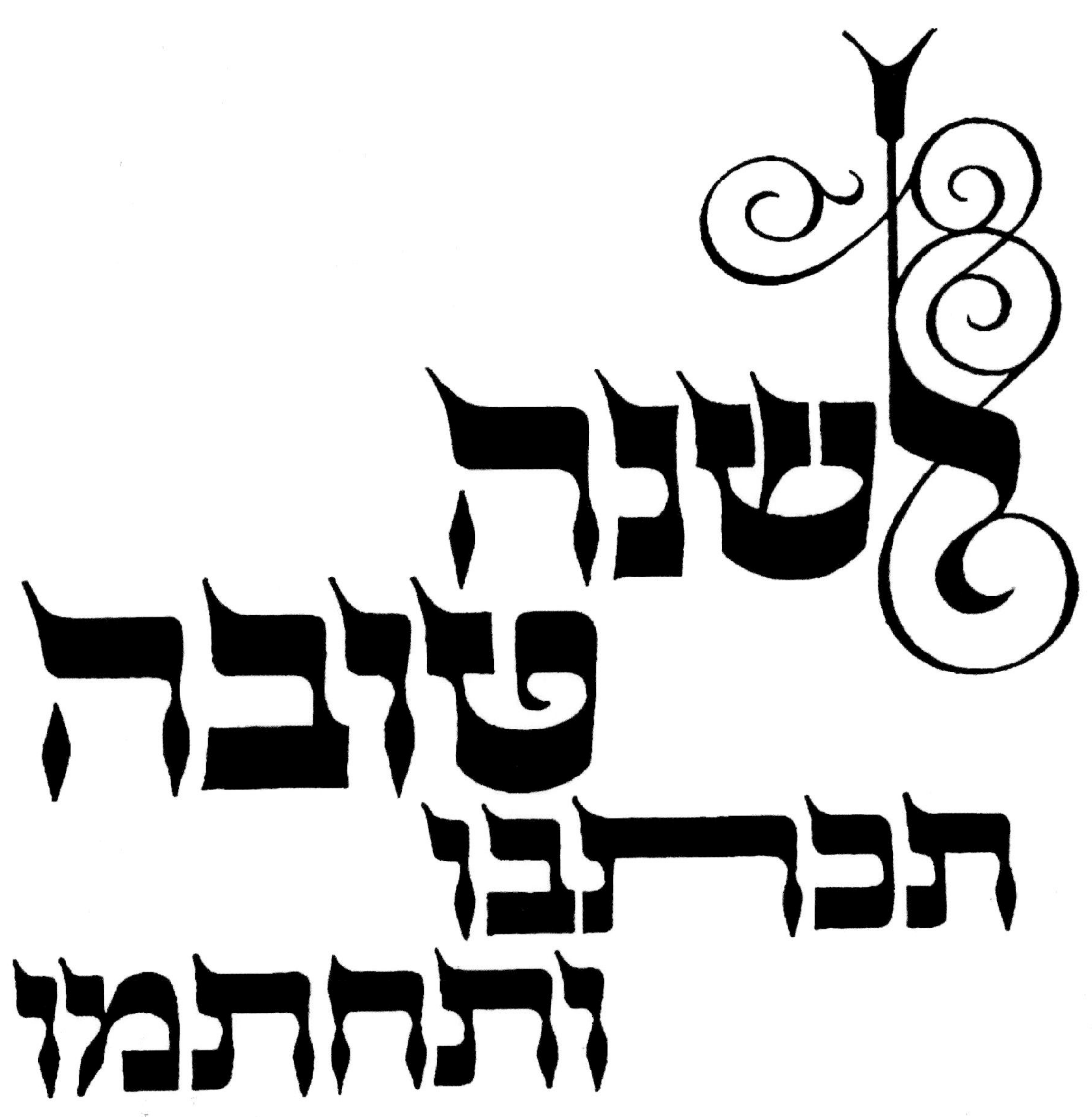

Zev Lipman
Greeting card for New Year
Mid- to late twentieth century

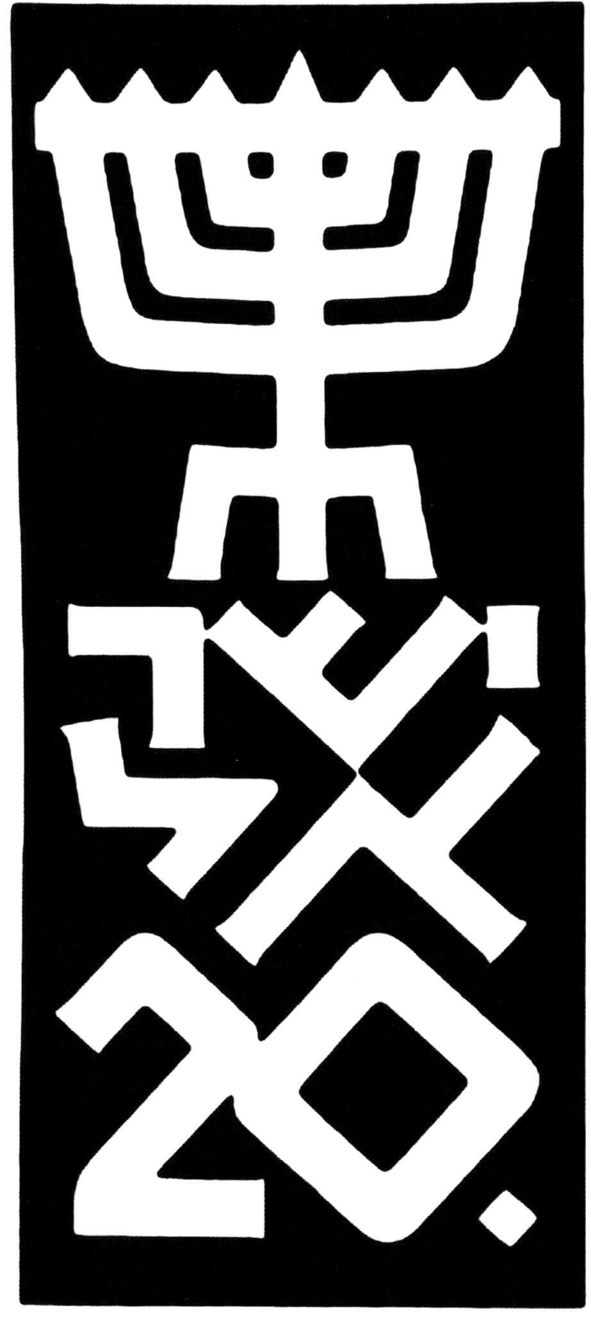

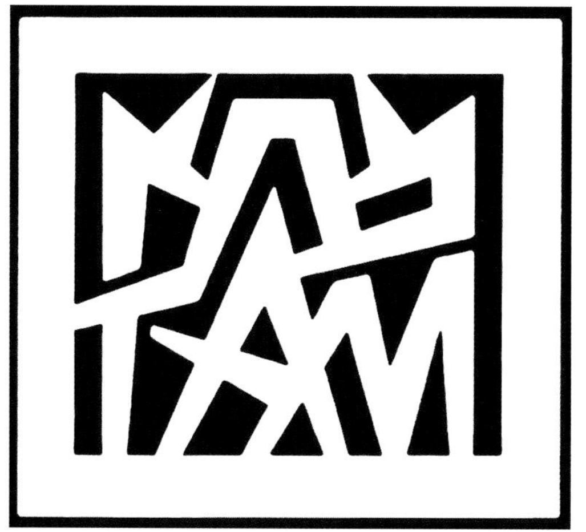

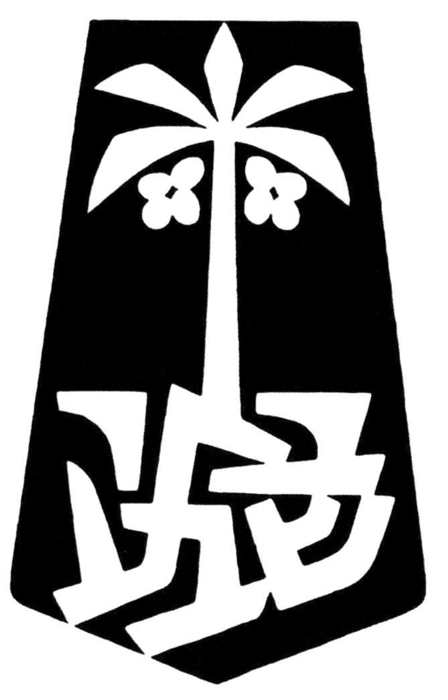

Zev Lipman/Studio Roli
LEFT: Logo proposal for Israel's twentieth anniversary, c. 1968
TOP RIGHT: Logo proposal for Tel Aviv Museum, n.d.
BOTTOM RIGHT: Logo proposal for the city of Beer Sheva, n.d.

This is one of many exemplar pages from the book The Art of Hebrew Lettering, *in which Zev Lipman demonstrates the making of various calligraphic styles. This style he called* Rolit. *The bases of some of the letters show an influence from Arabic calligraphy. The letters have a slight cursive feel, though with a backwards slant. The emphasized words, in red, are written in a more formal Ashkenazic script.*

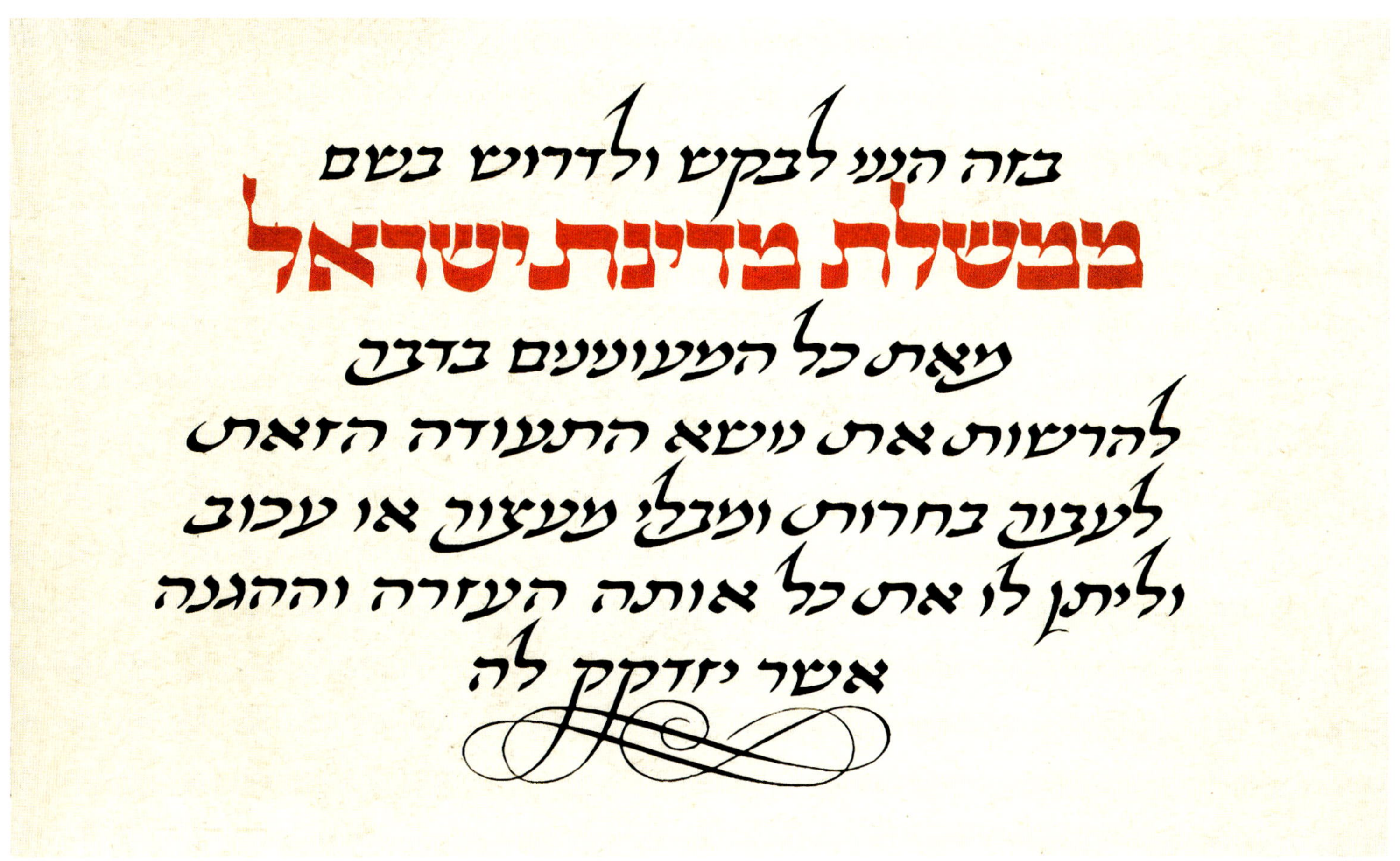

Zev Lipman
Sample calligraphy page in *The Art of Hebrew Lettering* by L. F. Toby, c. 1951

Both examples of Zev Lipman's work show a blending of Ashkenazic and Sephardic styles. Lipman uses Sephardic letterforms but gives the piece an Ashkenazic feel by their sharpness and added decoration, whereas in the next example, Yardeni has created a handsome hybrid letterform.

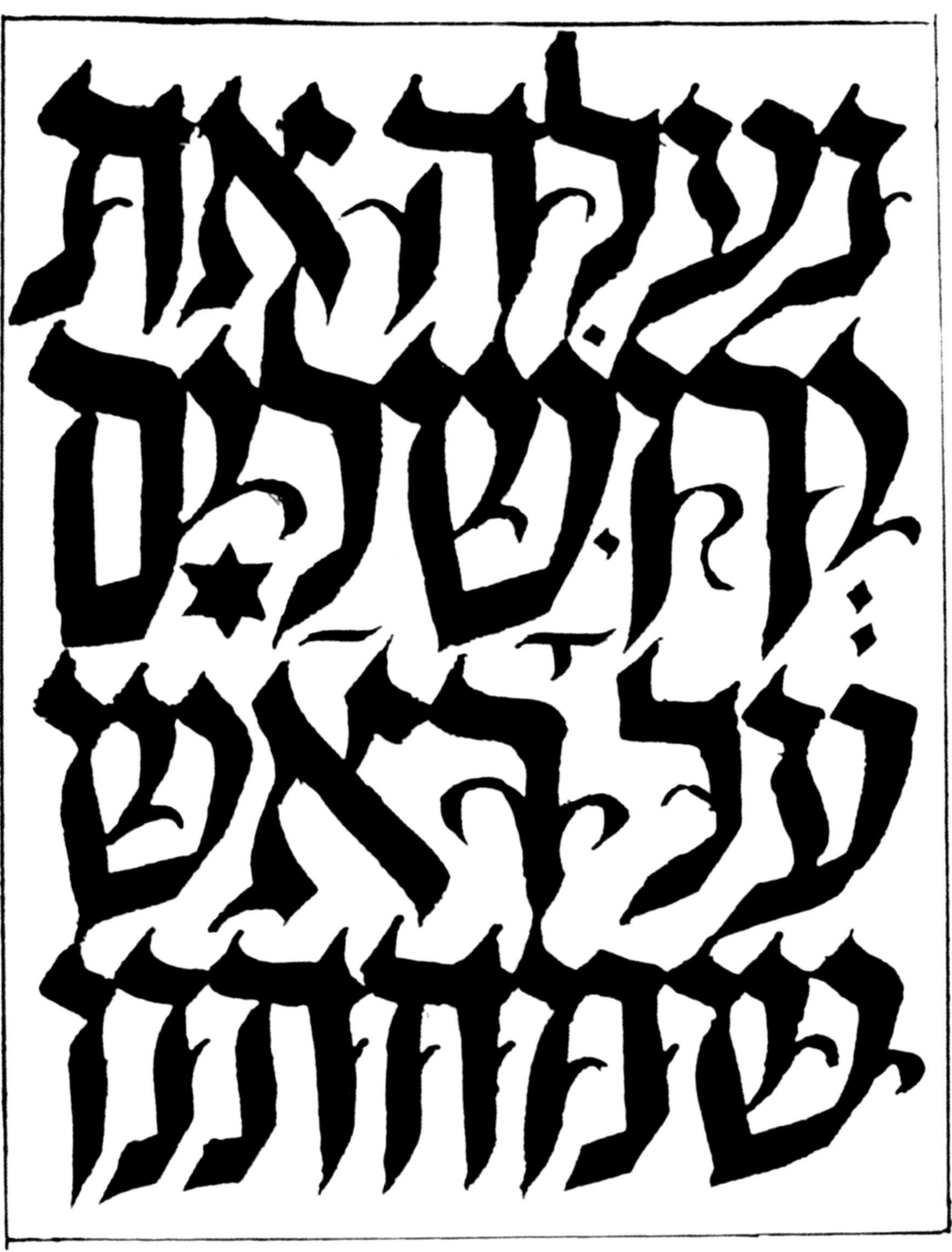

Zev Lipman
I Will Raise Jerusalem above All My Joy
Mid- to late twentieth century

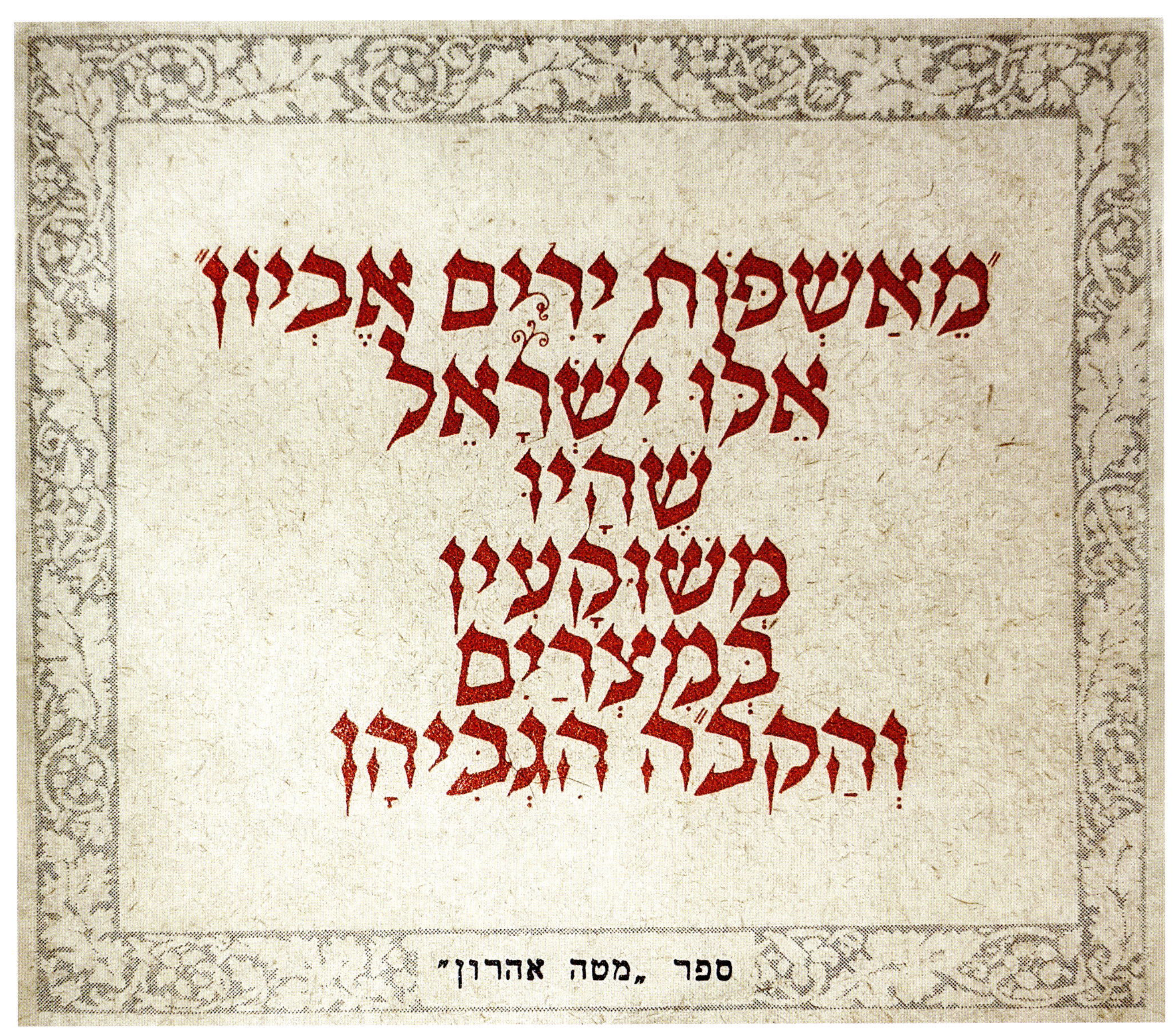

Ada Yardeni
Page from Passover *Haggadah*, 1976

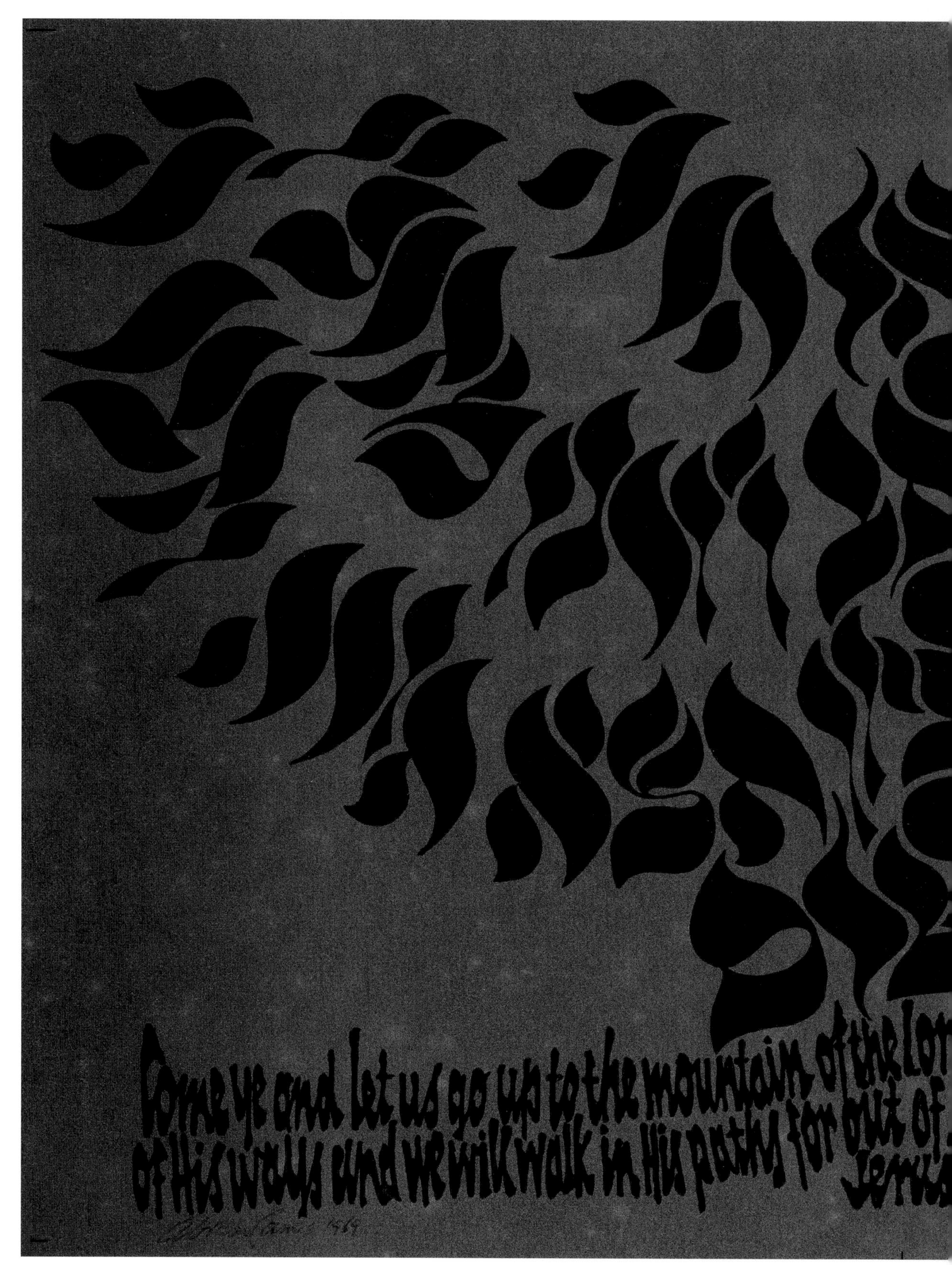

Abram Games
Design for *The Encyclopedia Judaica*, 1969

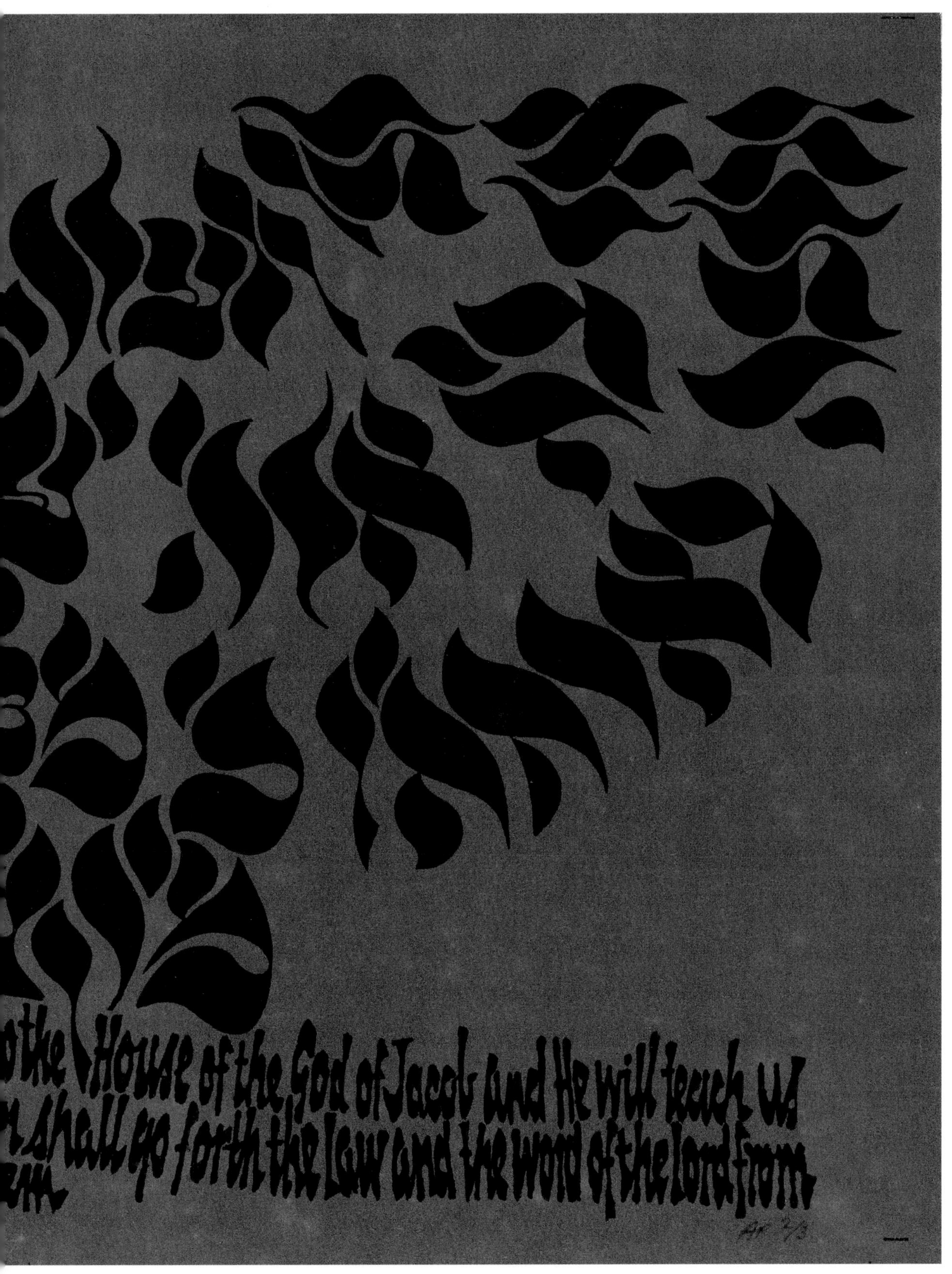
o the House of the God of Jacob and He will teach us
n shall go forth the Law and the word of the Lord from
em

The design of book titles often showcased fine and creative lettering.

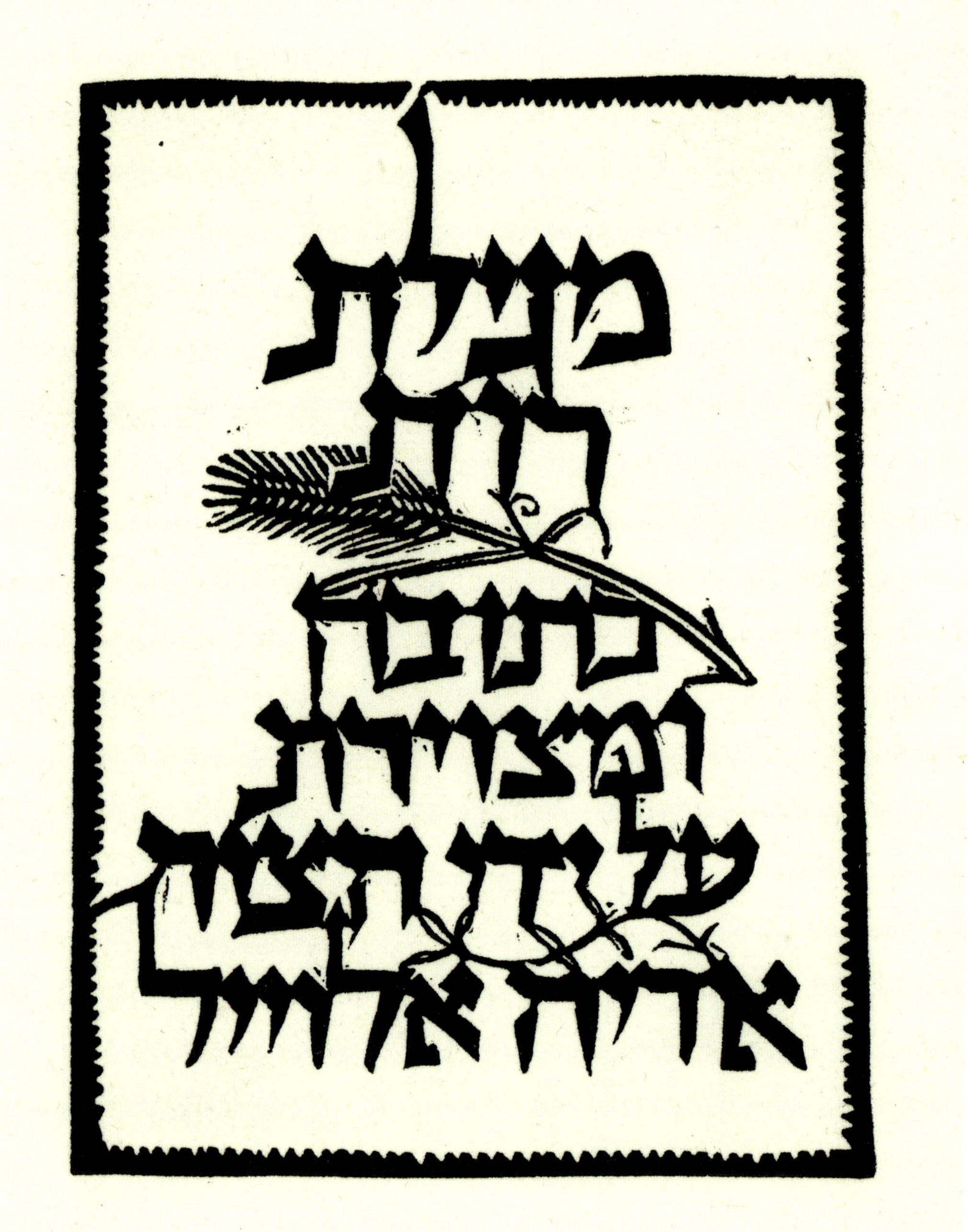

Arieh Allweil
Title page for a fully illustrated *Megillat Ruth*, 1939

Title showcasing highly stylized and decorative Ashkenazic letterforms.

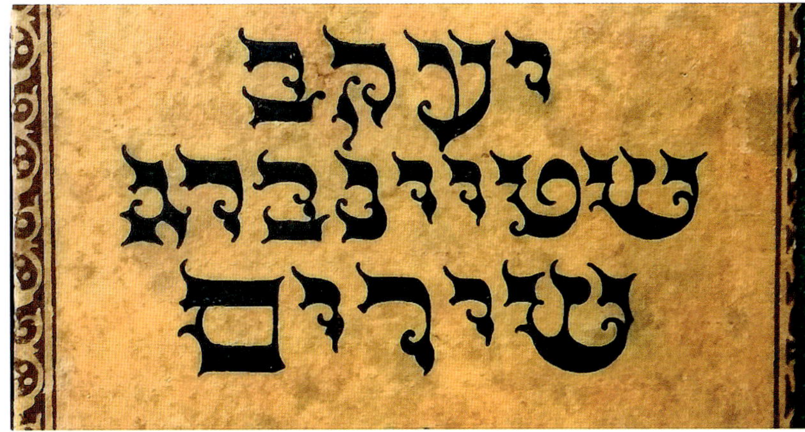

Title showcasing fluid and rounded Ashkenazic letterforms with a semi-cursive spirit.

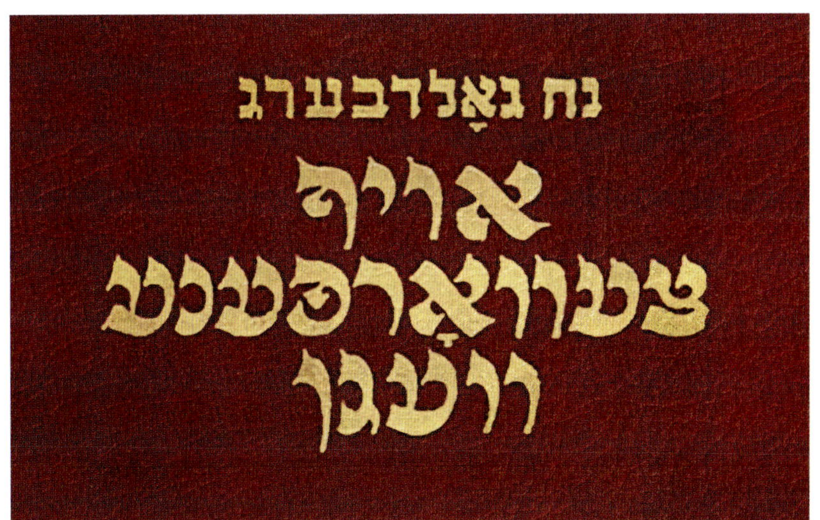

ABOVE: Designer Unknown. Publisher: Avraham Yoseph Shteibel, Leipzig, 1923
BELOW: Designer Unknown. Publisher: Yidbukh, Buenos Aires, 1957

Design of government coins, medals, and stamps was another venue for lettering artists to produce creative work for the public.

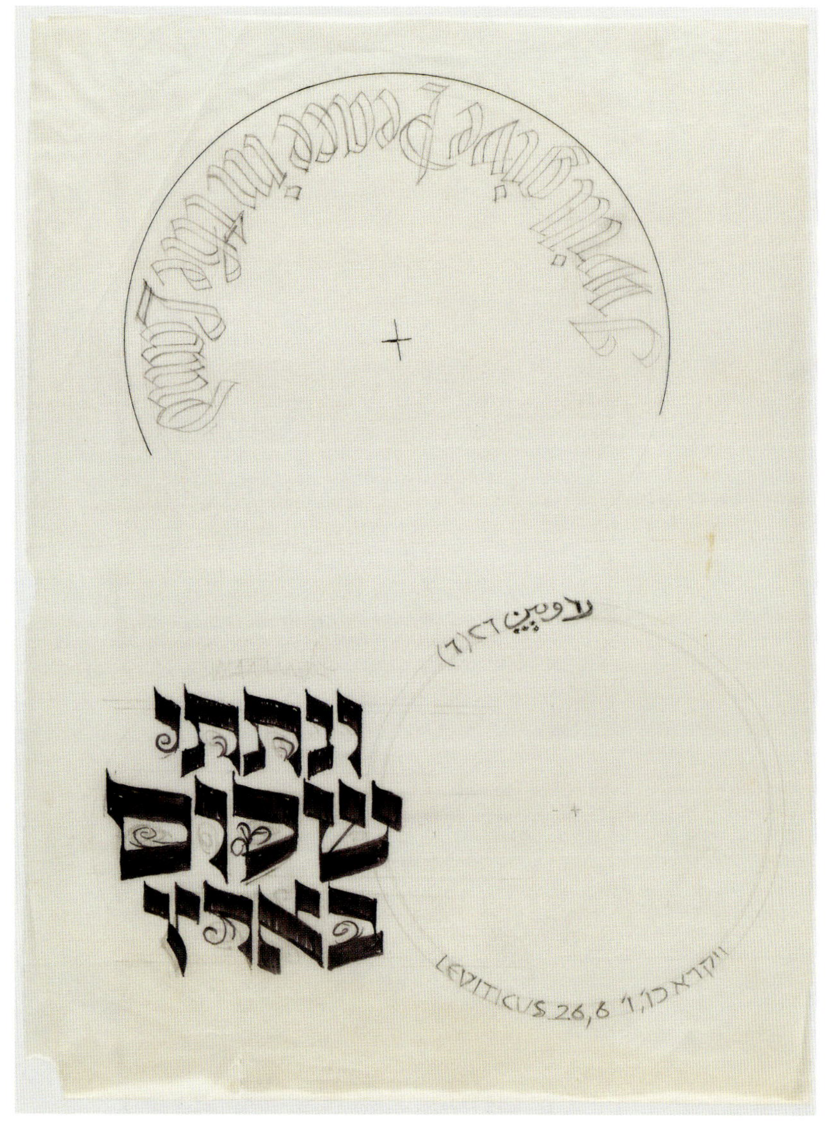

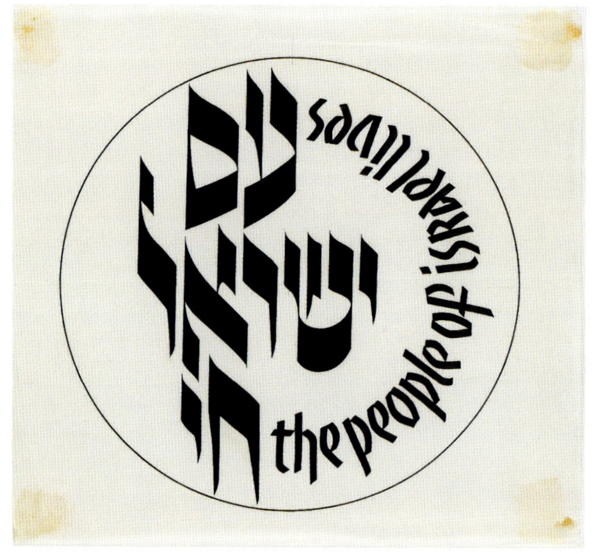

Zvi Narkiss
LEFT: Design sketch for medal commemorating the 1979 peace accord with Egypt
RIGHT: Design sketch for "Am Yisrael Chai" medal
Photo by Ofrit Rosenberg

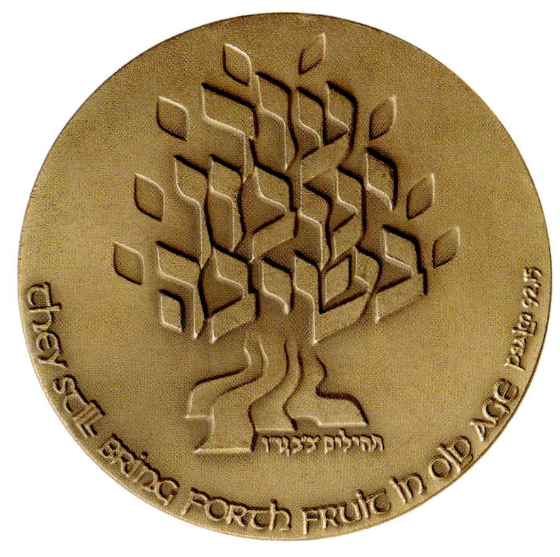

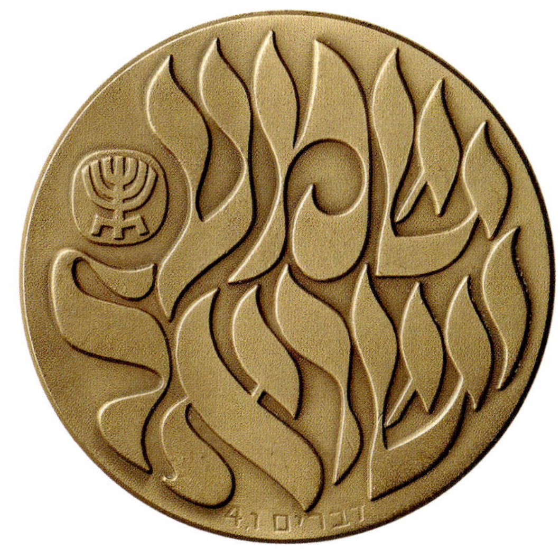

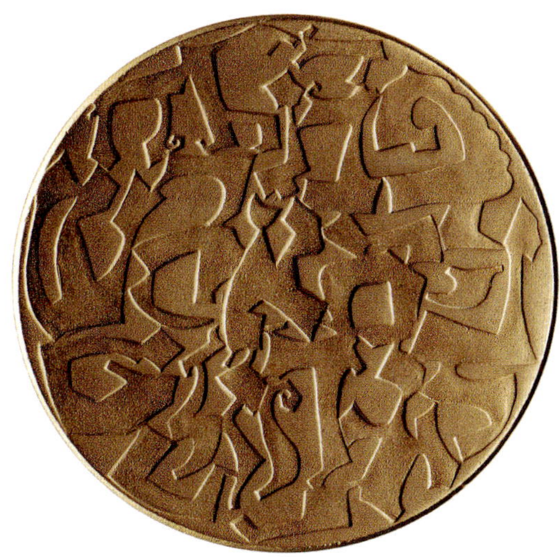

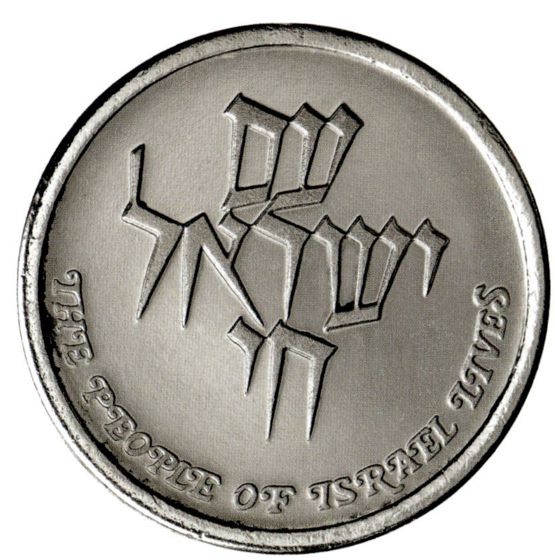

TOP LEFT: Gideon Keich, "They Still Bring Forth Fruit . . . ," 1982
TOP RIGHT: Zvi Narkiss, "Hear O Israel," 1980
BOTTOM LEFT: Ben Shahn, Commemorative medal celebrating the twentieth anniversary of El Al Israel Airlines, 1969
BOTTOM RIGHT: Nathan Karp, "Am Yisrael Chai," 1982

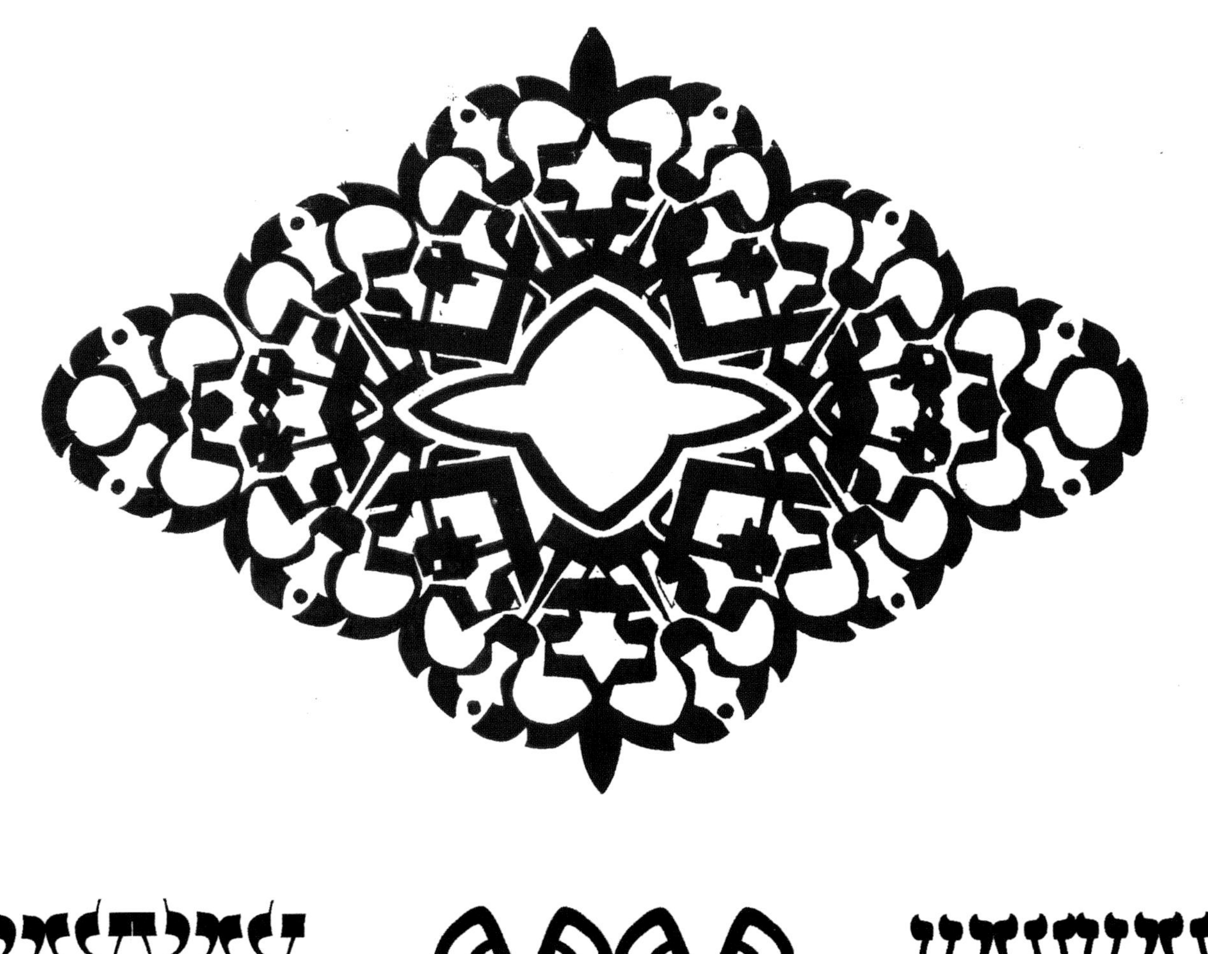

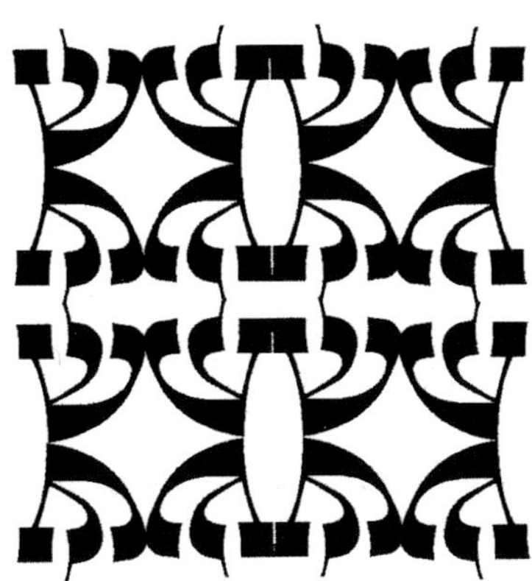

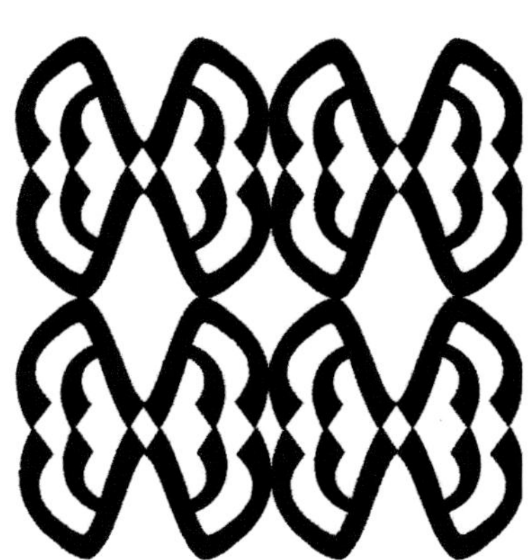

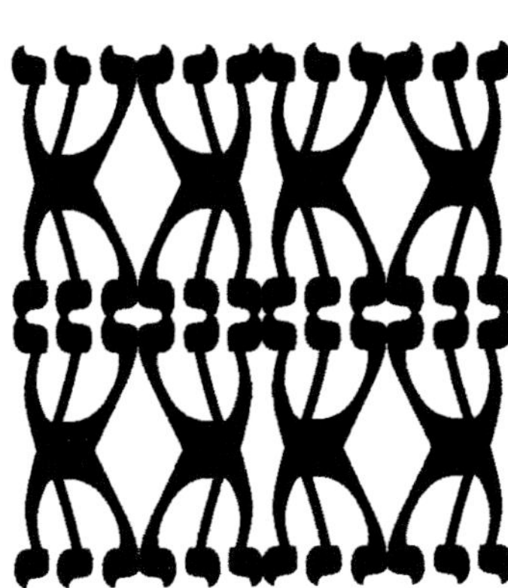

Designer and painter Yaakov Stark used Hebrew letter monograms to create Arabesque-like patterns. Can you guess the letters? Below are more contemporary monograms by Joy Rosenblum.

TOP: Yaakov Stark
Hebrew monogram designs, 1915
Original photo by Elie Posner (edited)
BOTTOM: Joy Rosenblum
Hebrew monogram designs, 1994

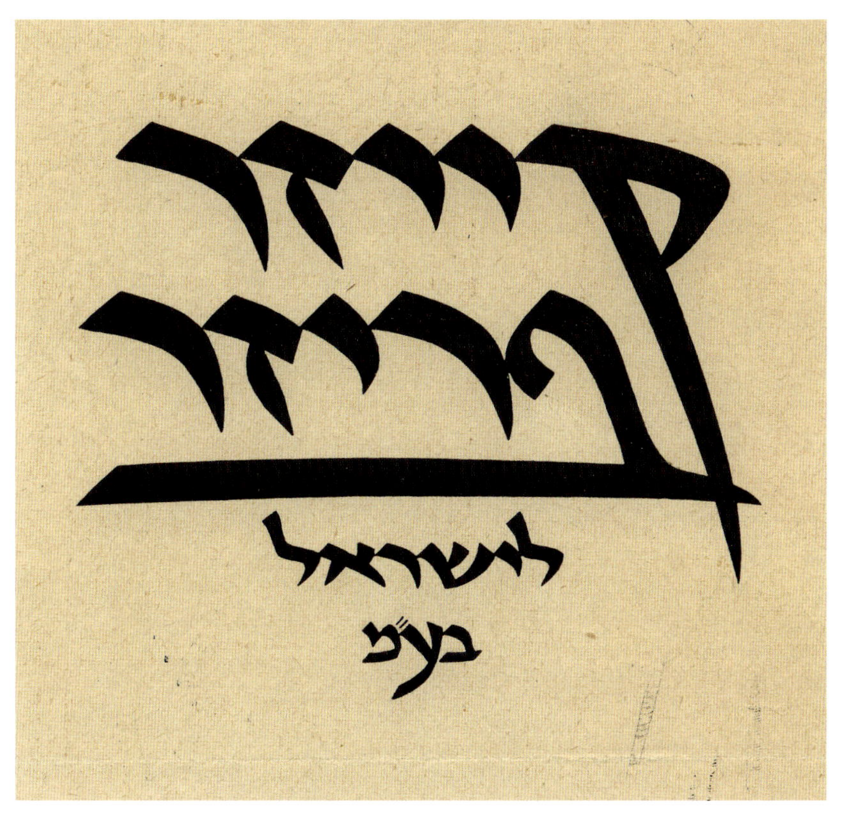

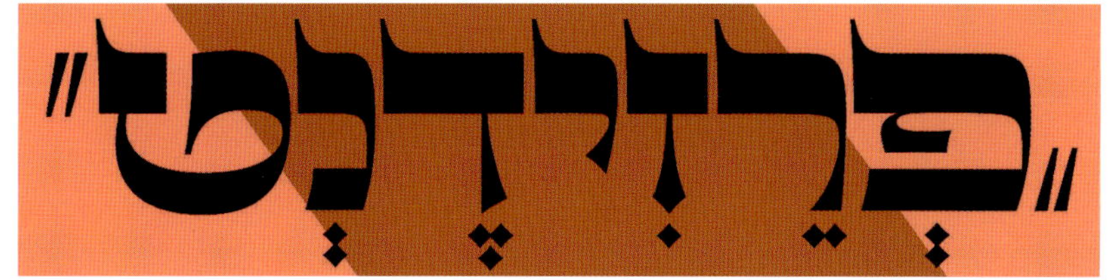

TOP: Ismar David
Detail from invitation announcing the opening of the Kaiser-Fraiser Auto Company, 1951
BOTTOM: Shavit Yaakov
Satirical logo for tobacco company, 2020

The text on the central gate reads, "Peace, peace to those far and near" (from Isaiah 57:19). The text on the side gates reads, "Blessed are you in your goings and blessed are you in your comings" (from Deuteronomy 28:6). The Hebrew letters here function both as the design for the gates as well as the text welcoming travelers.

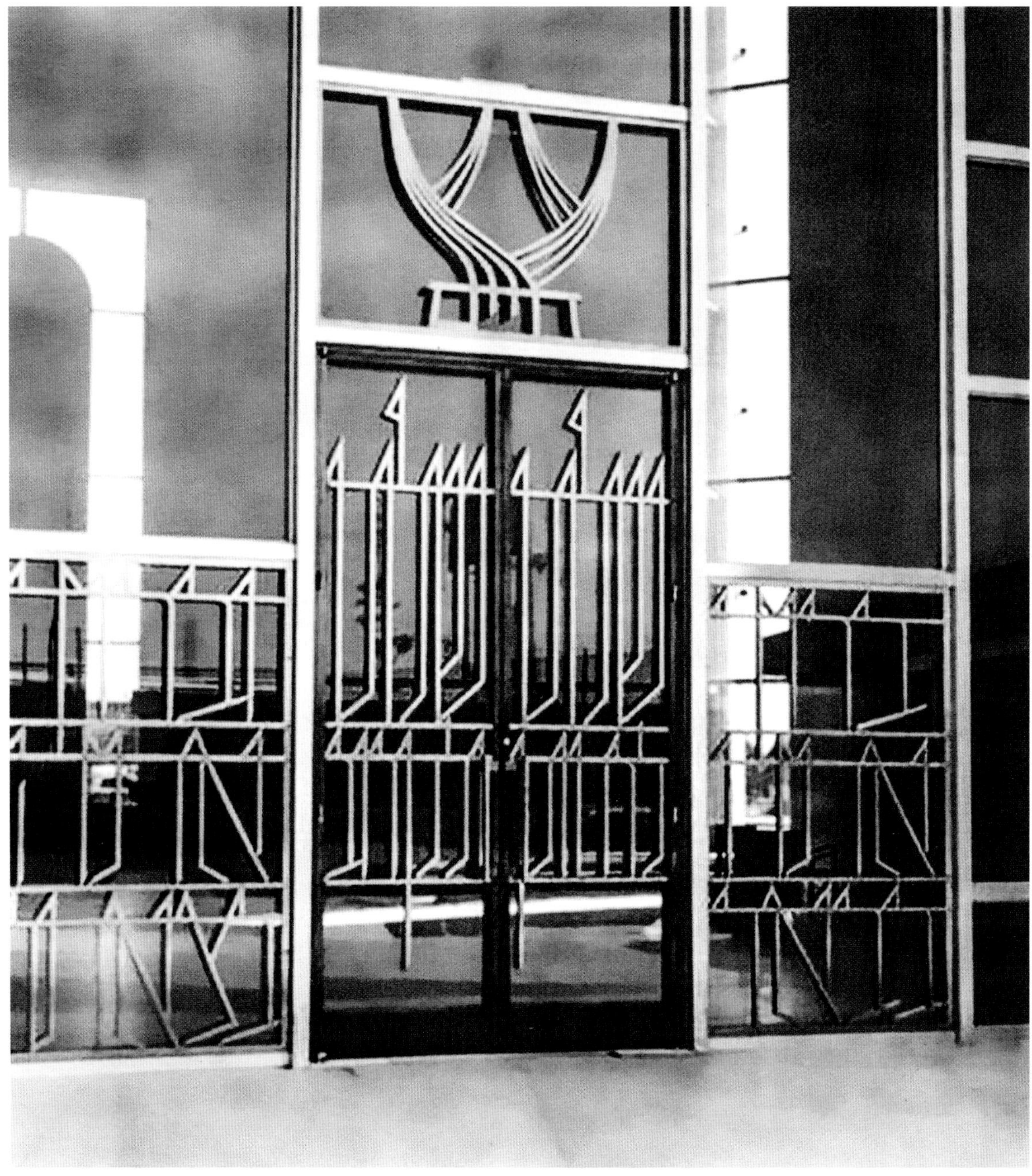

Ludwig Yehudah Wolpert
Bronze gates of the synagogue at Kennedy International Airport, New York, 1968

Here too the tall letters resemble gates. This text, fittingly for the mezuzah that is placed in a doorway, reads, "Blessed are you in your goings and blessed are you in your comings."

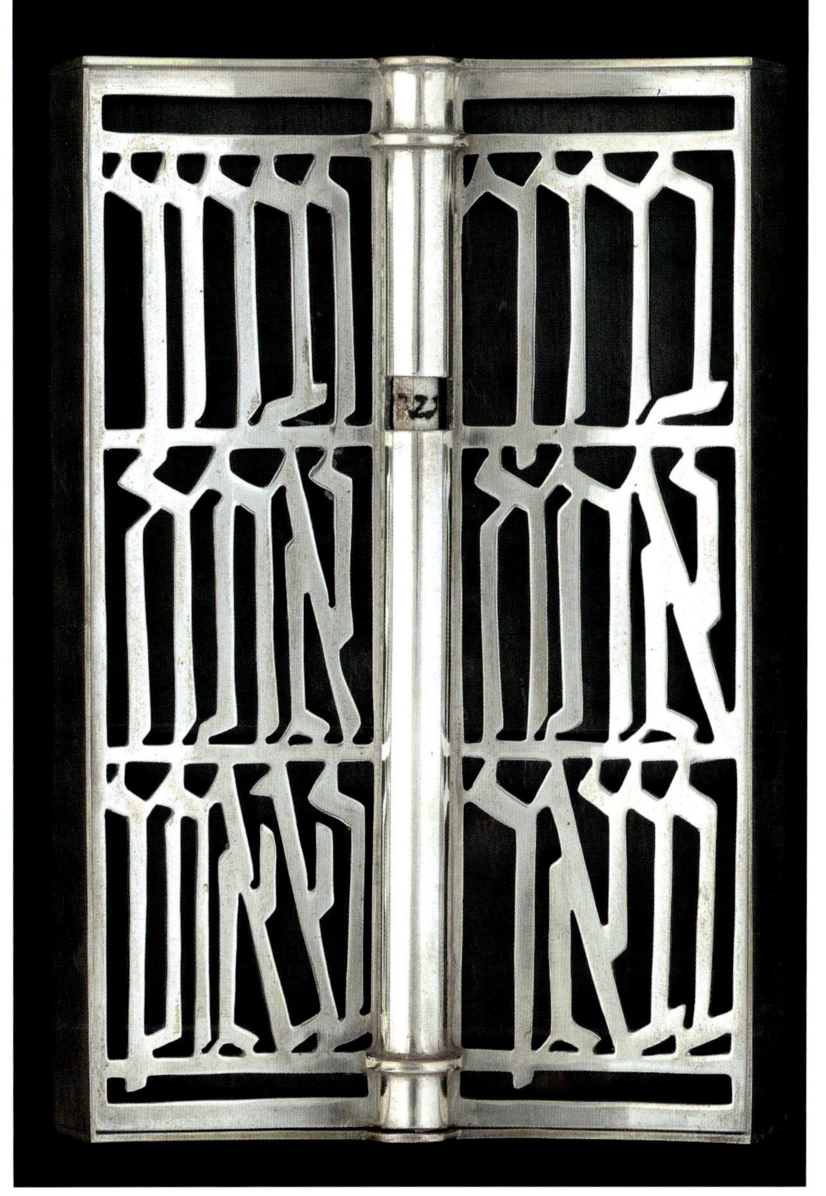

Ludwig Yehudah Wolpert
Mezuzah, 195

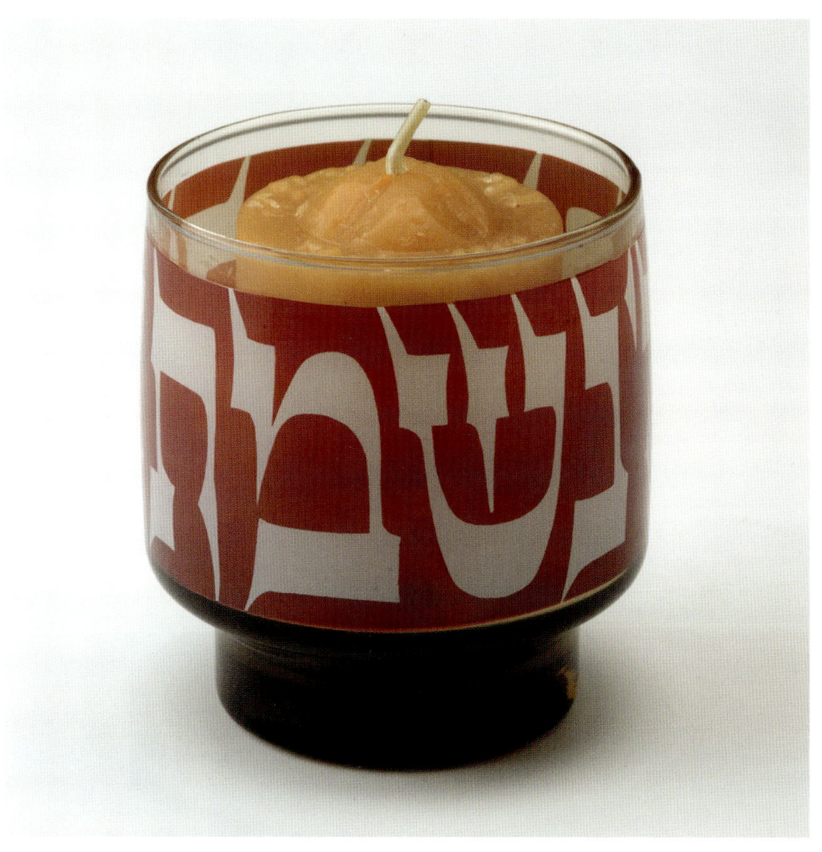

Chava Wolpert Richard used clean, classic Ashkenazic forms in this memorial lamp; these convey a calming feeling of tradition. Fittingly, in the brooch pin designed by Ludwig Wolpert (Chava's father), much less traditional letterforms were used for the word sheheyanu, *which means "renewal."*

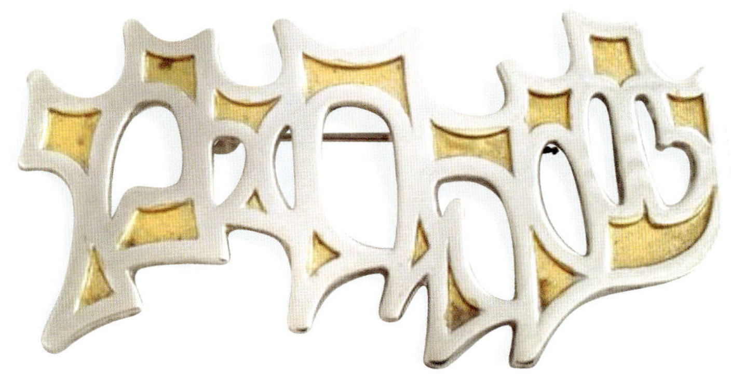

LEFT: Chava Wolpert Richard
Memorial Lamp, c. 1980
RIGHT: Ludwig Yehudah Wolpert
Shecheyanu pin, c. 1970s (?)

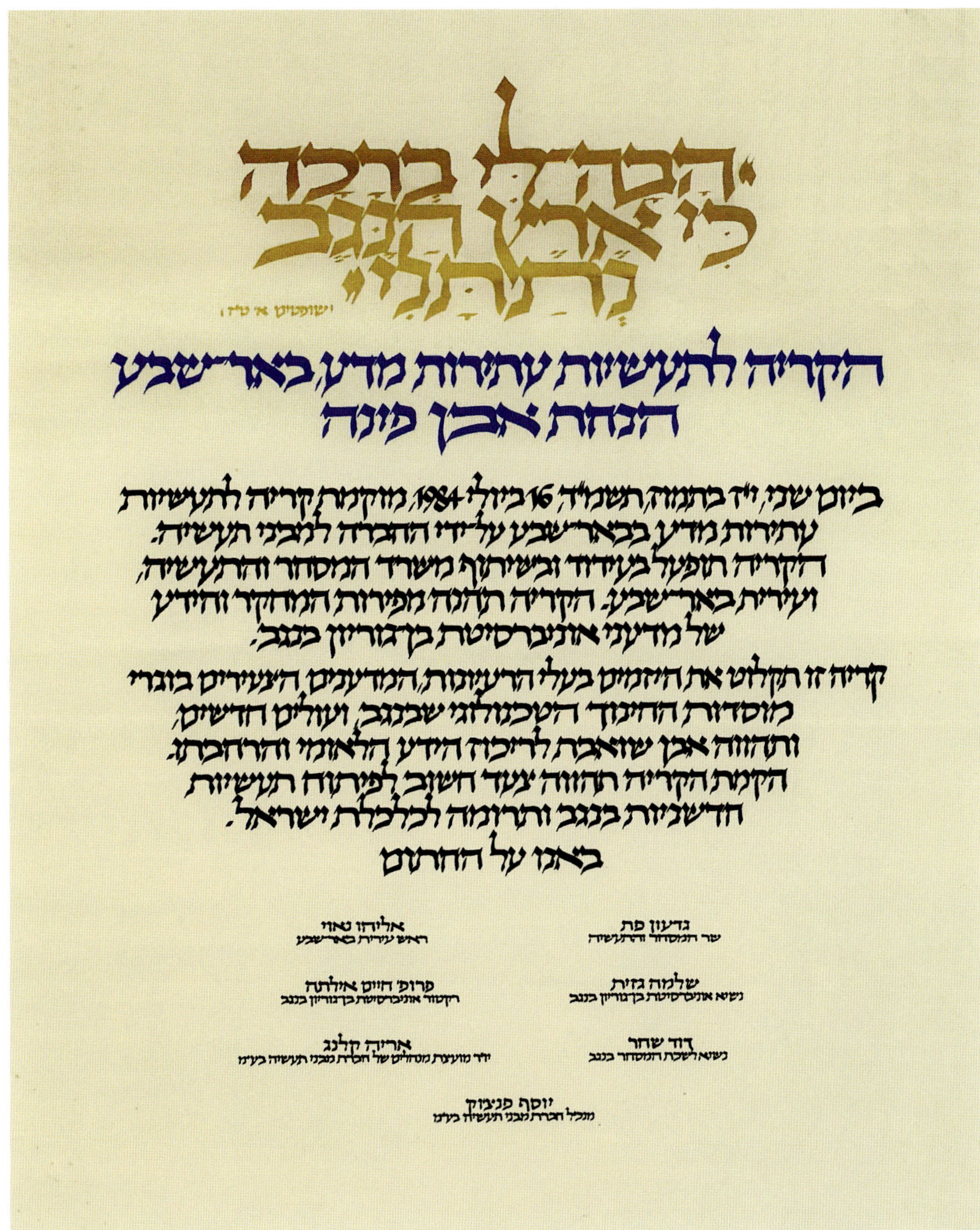

הבה לי ברכה
כי ארץ הנגב
נתתני
(שופטים א׳ ט״ו)

הקריה לתעשיות עתירות מדע, באר-שבע
הנחת אבן פינה

ביום שני, י"ד בתמוז, תשמ"ד, 16 ביולי 1984, מוקמת קריה לתעשיות
עתירות מדע בבאר-שבע על-ידי החברה למבני תעשיה.
הקריה תופעל בעידוד ובשיתוף משרד המסחר והתעשיה,
ועירית באר-שבע. הקריה תהנה מפירות המחקר והידע
של מדעני אוניברסיטת בן-גוריון בנגב.

קריה זו תקלוט את היזמים בעלי הרעיונות, המדענים, הצעירים בוגרי
מוסדות החינוך הטכנולוגי שבנגב, ועולים חדשים,
ותהווה אבן שואבת לריכוז הידע הלאומי והרחבתו.
הקמת הקריה תהווה צעד חשוב לפיתוח תעשיות
חדשניות בנגב ותרומה לכלכלת ישראל.

באנו על החתום

גדעון פת שר המסחר והתעשיה	אליהו נאוי ראש עירית באר-שבע
שלמה גזית נשיא אוניברסיטת בן-גוריון בנגב	פרופ' חיים אילתה רקטור אוניברסיטת בן-גוריון בנגב
דוד שחר נשיא לשכת המסחר בנגב	אריה קלנג יו"ר מועצת מנהלים של חברת מבני תעשיה בע"מ

יוסף פניבזק
מנכ"ל חברת מבני תעשיה בע"מ

Fred Pauker
Cornerstone certificate for Hi-Tech Park in Beer Sheva, 1984

Fred Pauker was a Viennese-born British-Israeli graphic designer. This script, which he developed, shows an influence from the Mizrachi script. One of the characteristics of his script is the diamond-like shape at the head of many of the roof strokes.

Yerachmiel Shechter headed the New Bezalel School in Jerusalem in the mid 1950s and taught calligraphy there. Here and on the following page are works by some of his students.

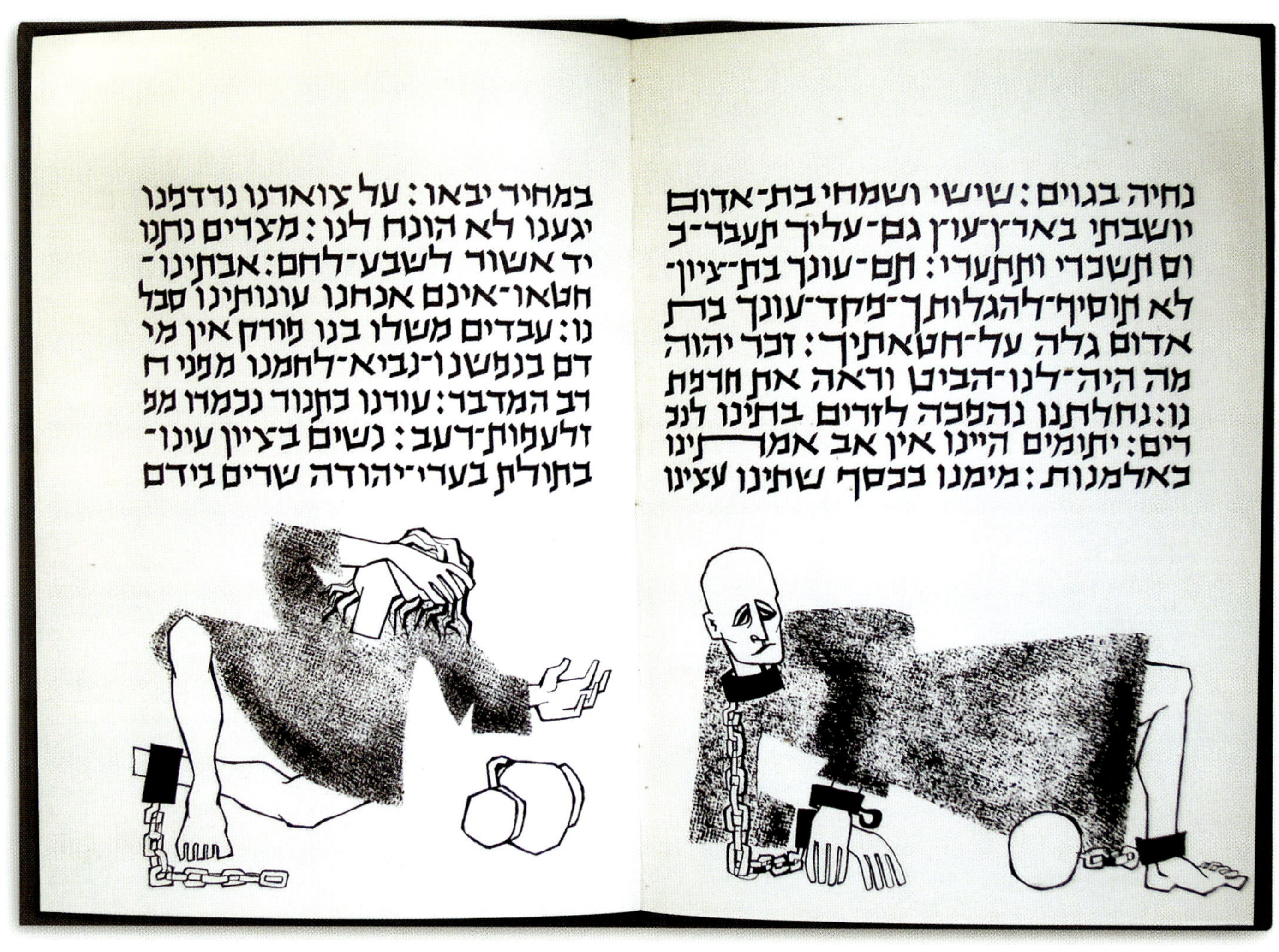

Moshe Chatumi
Book of Lamentations, 1960

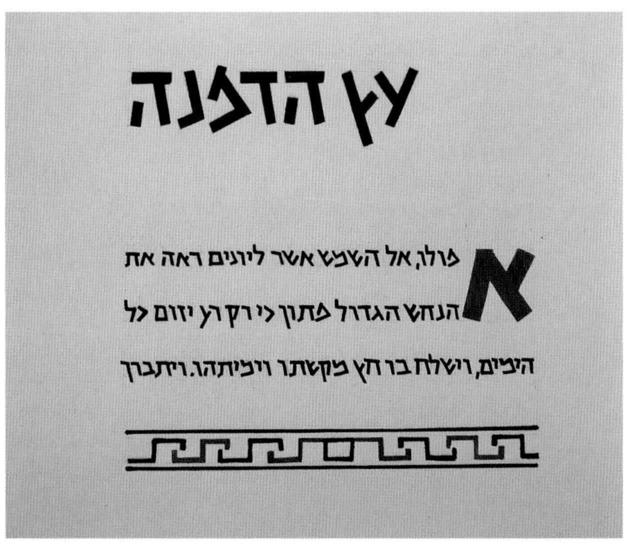

עץ הדפנה

אפולו, אל השמש אשר ליונים ראה את
הנחש הגדול פתון כי רק רע יזום כל
הימים, וישלח בו חץ מקשתו ויכיתהו. ויתבון

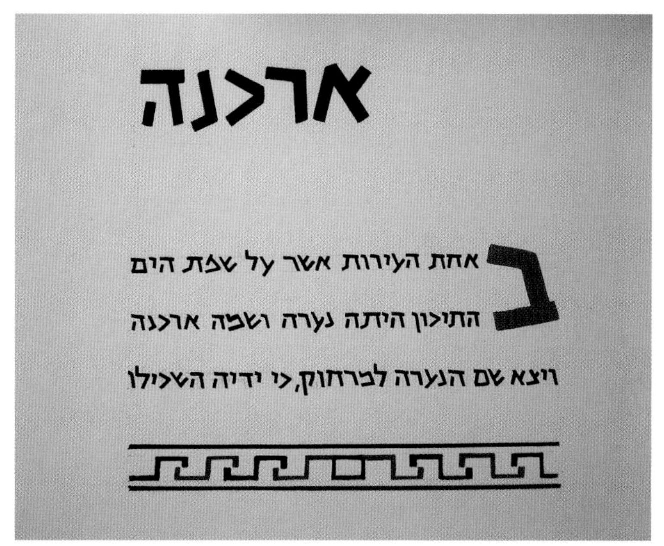

ארכנה

באחת העירות אשר על שפת הים
התיכון היתה נערה ושמה ארכנה
ויצא שם הנערה לברחוק, כי ידיה השכילו

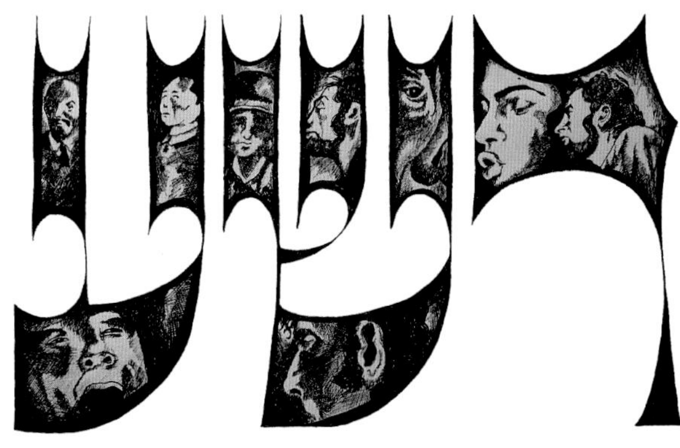

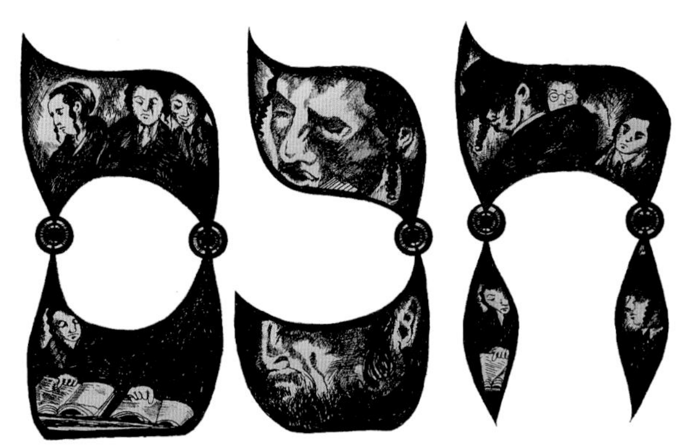

TOP: Arnona Rozin
Selected pages from *Greek Mythologies*, c. 1960 (?)
BOTTOM: *Chaham, Rasha*, by student of Yerachmiel Shechter, c. 1960 (?)

These semi-cursive letters, written in a hypnotically repetitive form, along with the circular composition, nicely express the content of the song "Chad Gadya."

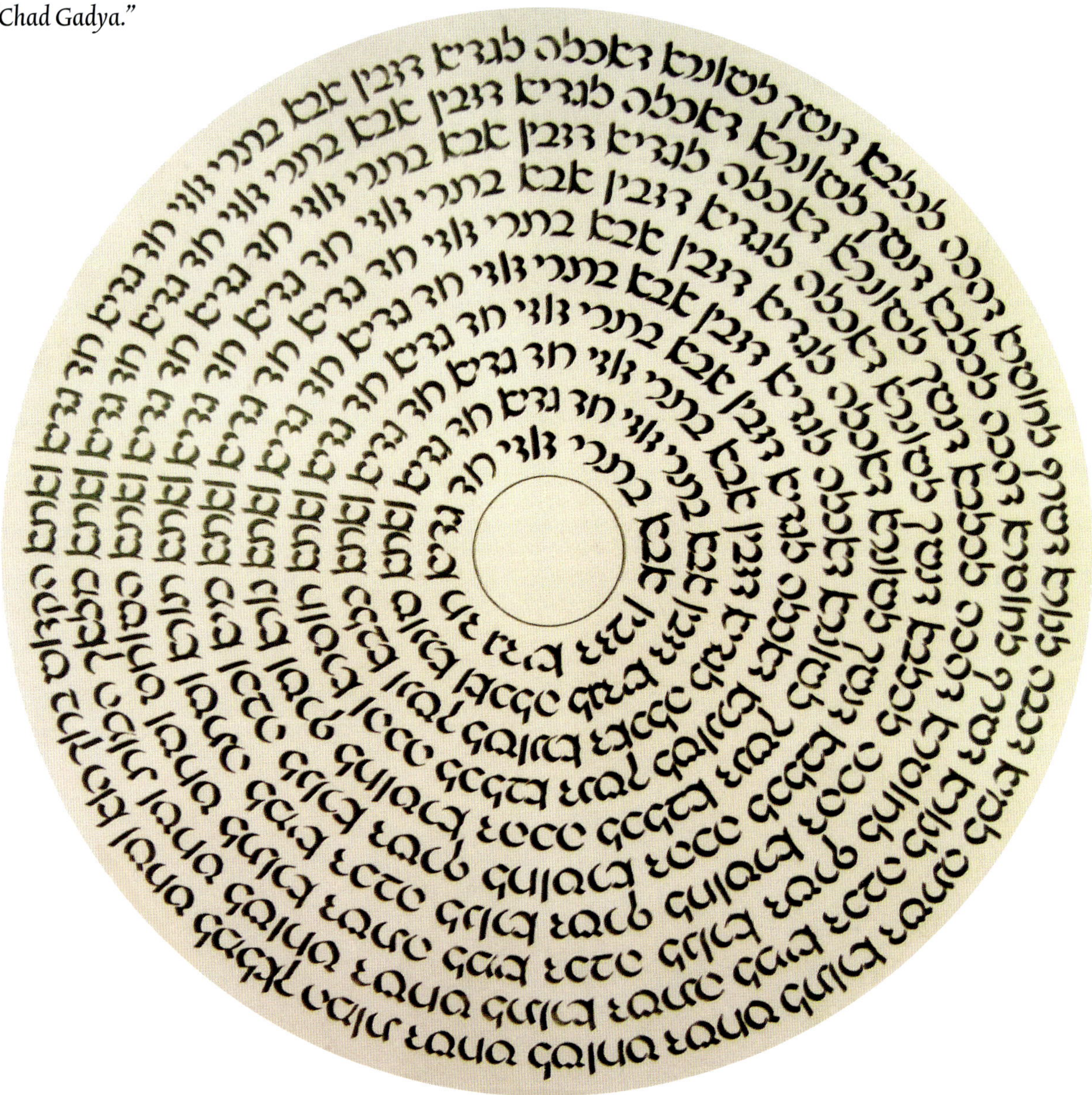

Yerachmiel Shechter
Chad Gadya, 1930s

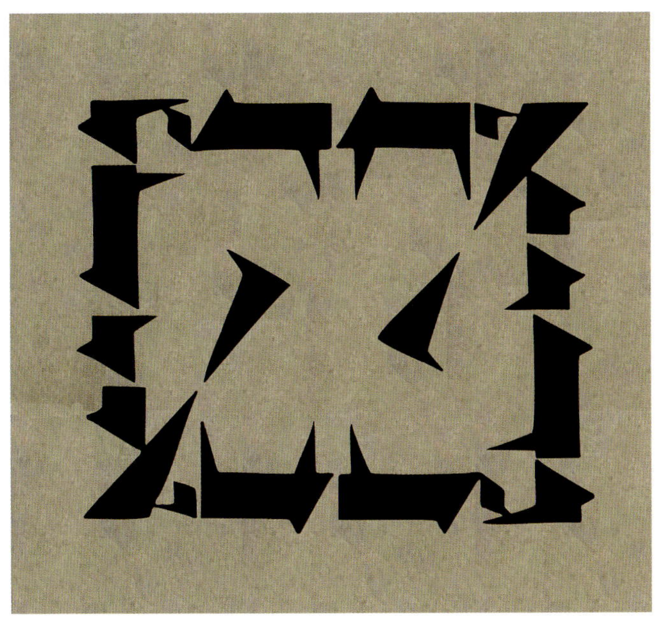

These two pieces show variations on what is known as Yerushalmi script, a script modernized from the writing of the Dead Sea Scrolls and characterized by triangular serifs.

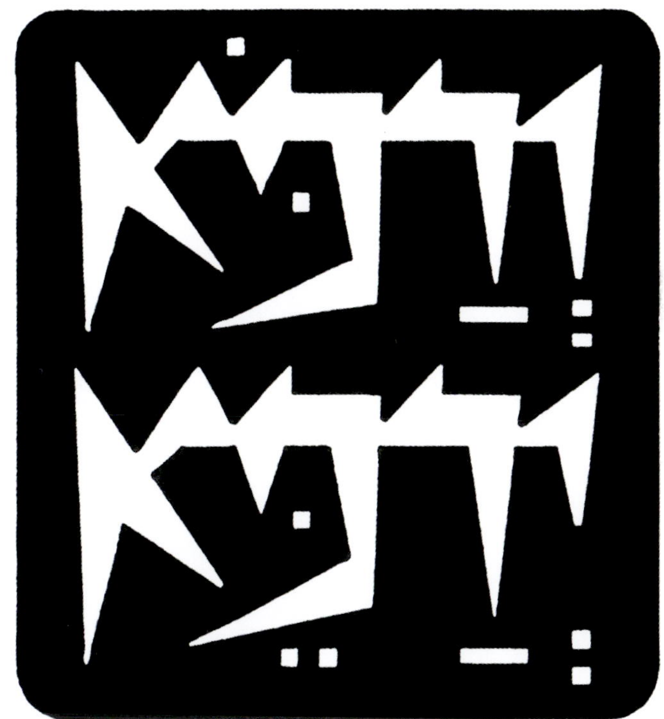

TOP: Yerachmiel Shechter
Chad Gadya, 1930s
BOTTOM: Elly Gross
Design for the Israel Medical Association, 1965–1970

Zvi Narkiss was one of Israel's most influential and prolific type designers. Here is an example of his calligraphic work.

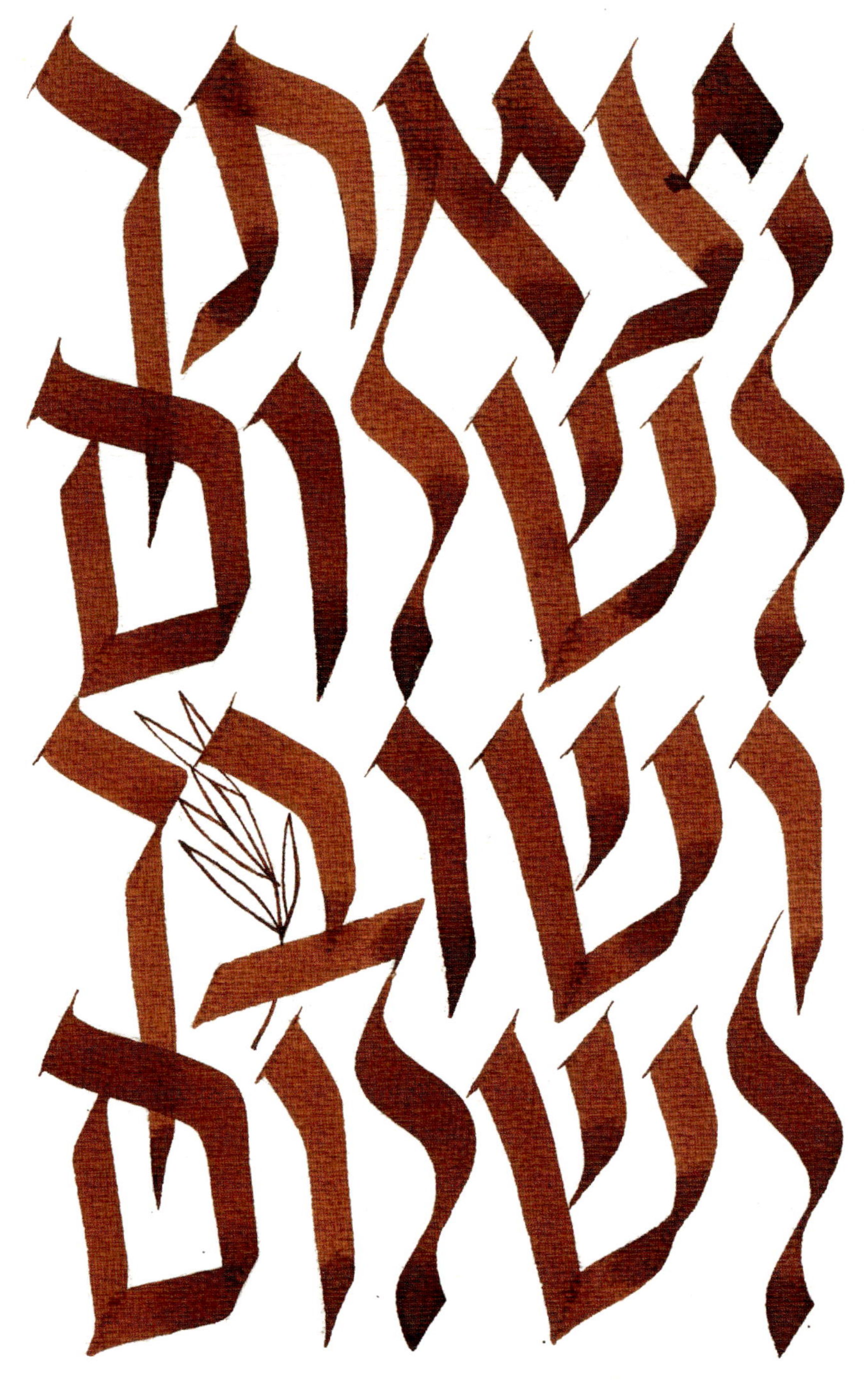

Zvi Narkiss
Traveler's Blessing, c. 1970s (?)

The monoline, skeletal letters for the cover and title page of the Koren Siddur *point to early Hebrew inscriptions. Note too how each stroke of every letter is angled, giving unity to the design.*

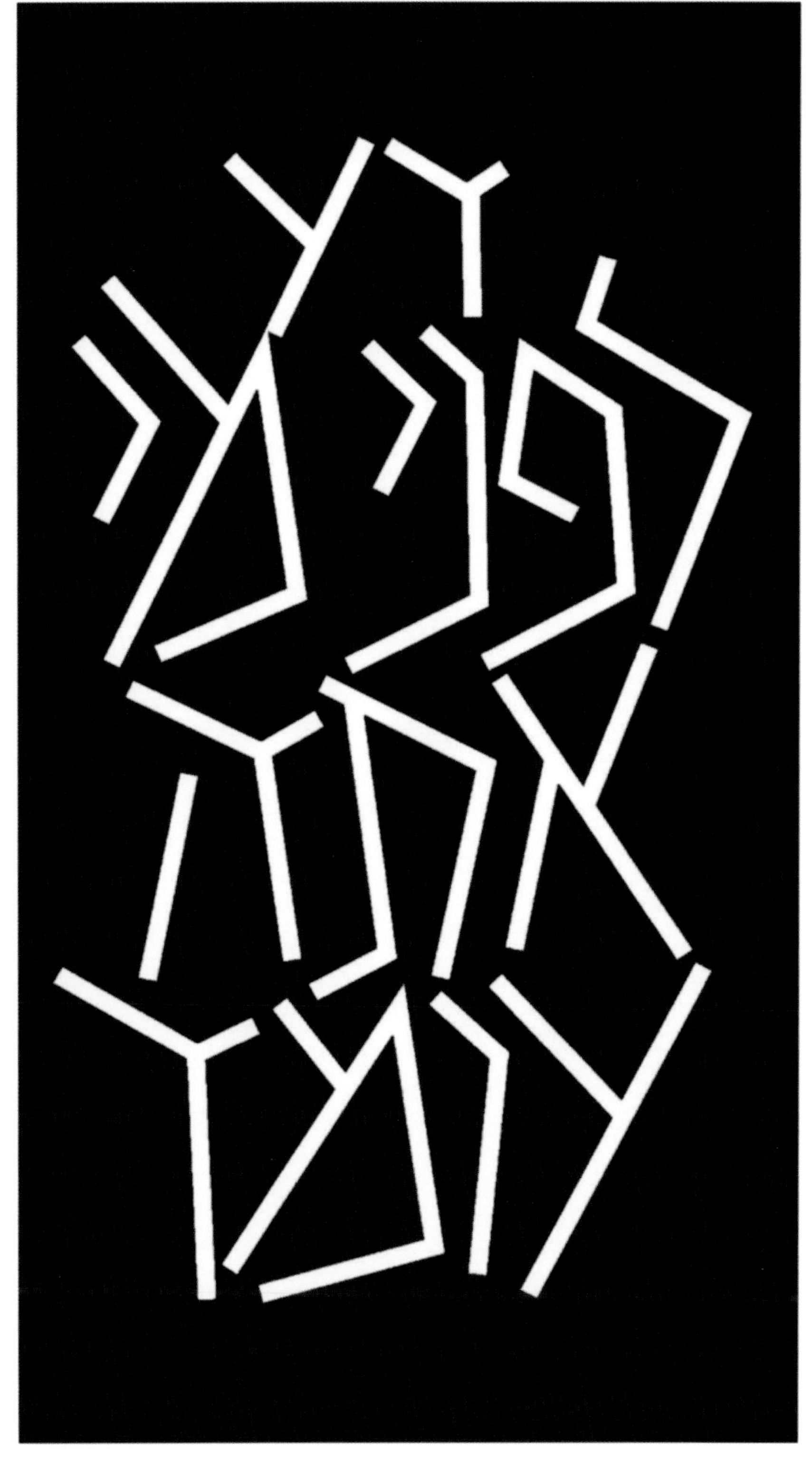

Design for cover of the *Koren Siddur*, 1971

Ismar David was a prolific graphic designer, letterer, and calligrapher, especially noted for his book jacket designs. He designed the very popular David font.

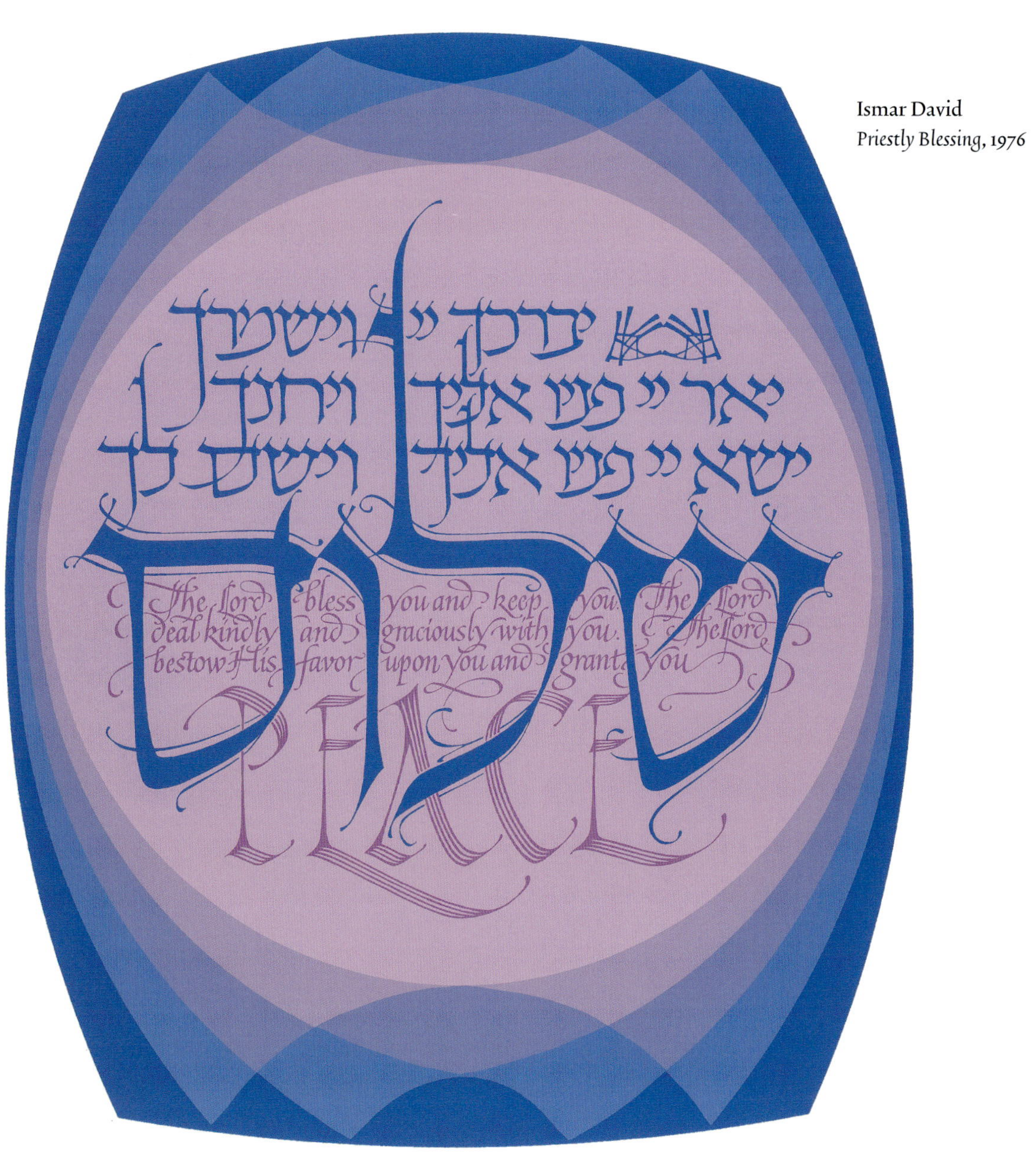

Ismar David
Priestly Blessing, 1976

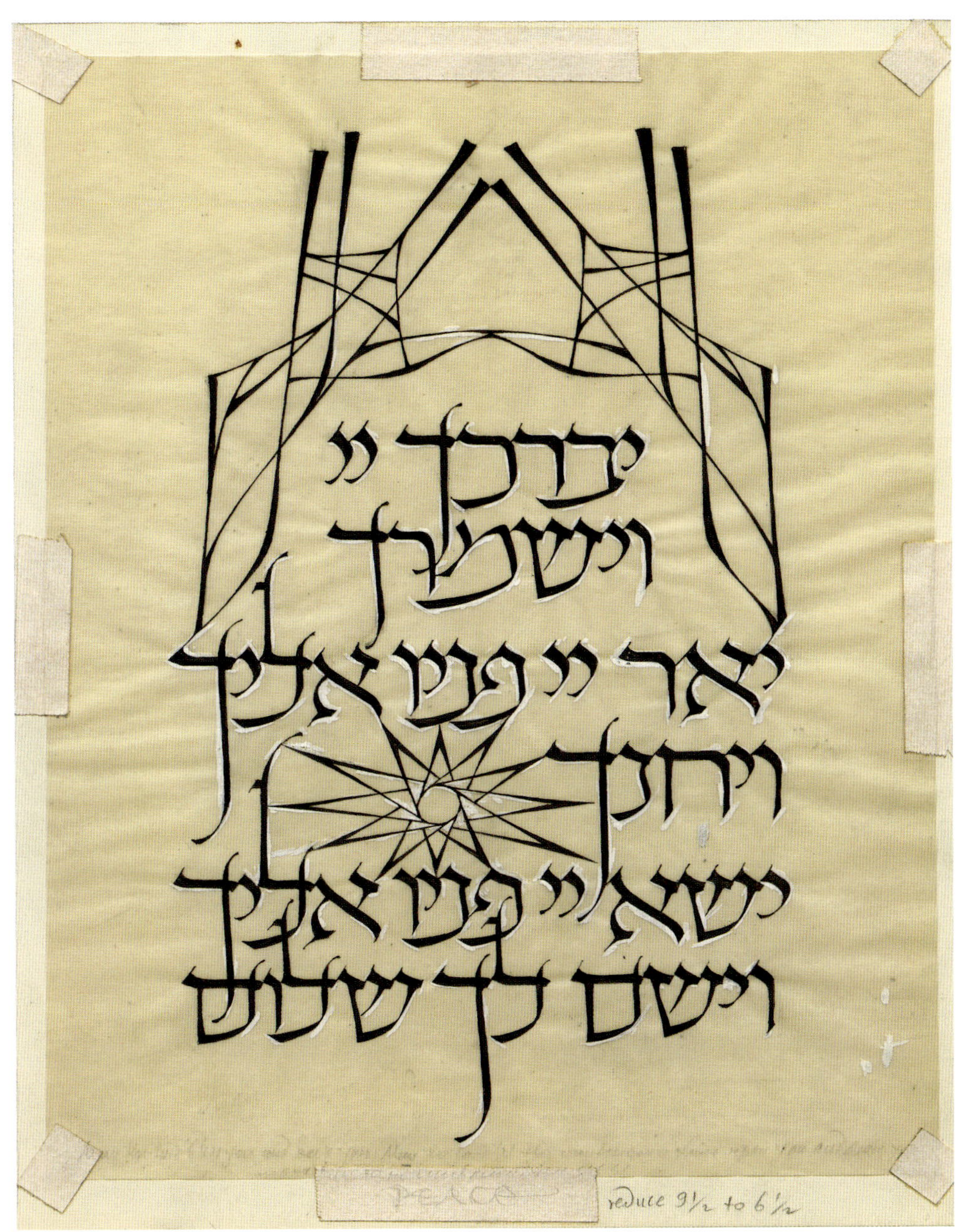

This is an early sketch of Ismar's design for the Priestly Blessing. *One can learn a lot from the areas cleaned with whiteout, which was standard practice for designers submitting hard copy before the digital age.*

Ismar David
Sketch for *Priestly Blessing*, c. 1980

The Ten Commandments often appeared on or above the central ark in many synagogues. In this design, the addition of serifs allows the letters to interconnect, adding strength and visual interest to the composition.

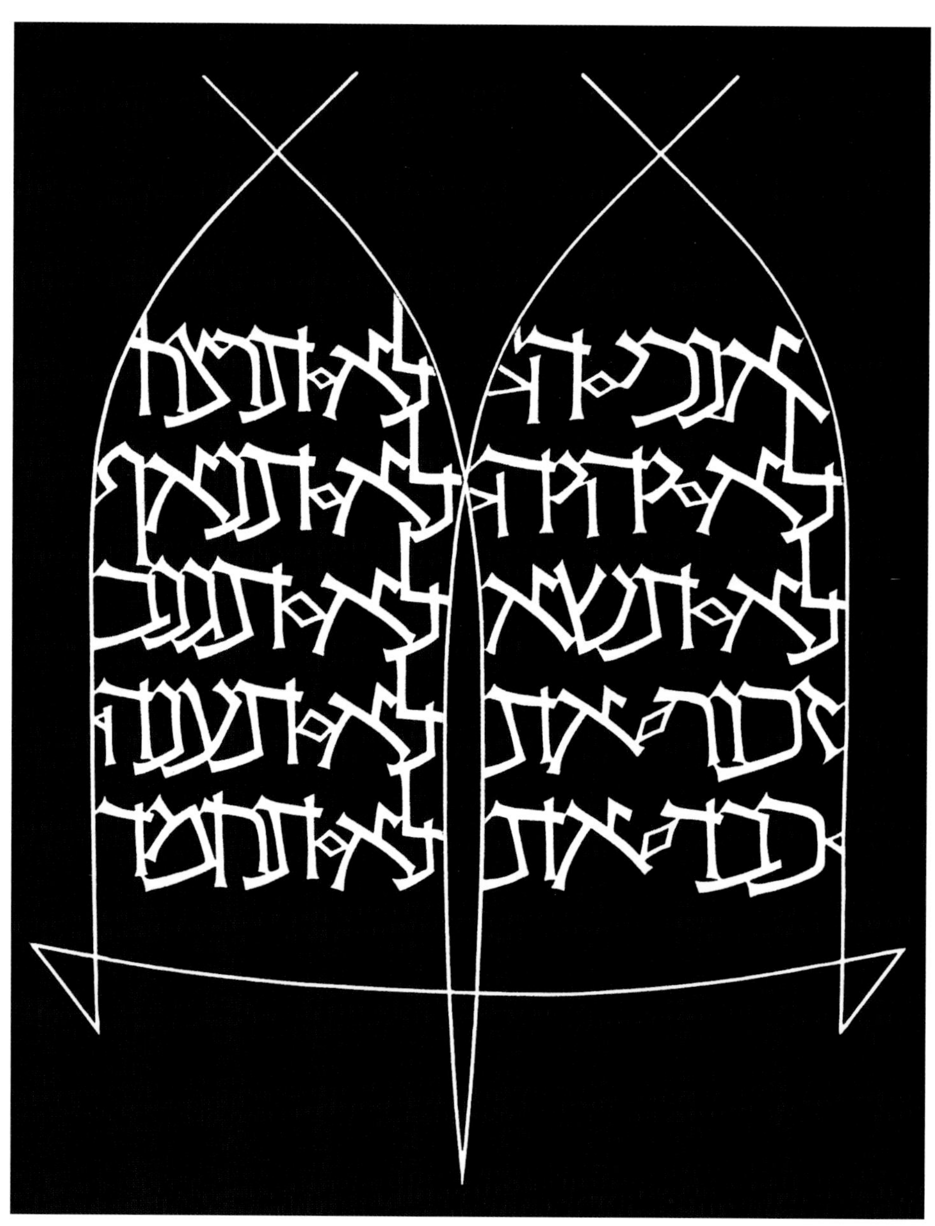

Ismar David
Ten Commandments
Design above the ark at Temple Aaron, St. Paul, Minnesota, 1957

Here different sizes of letters as well as serifs are employed in order to form the lace-like pattern that gives strength to this design, which would be eventually cut out of metal.

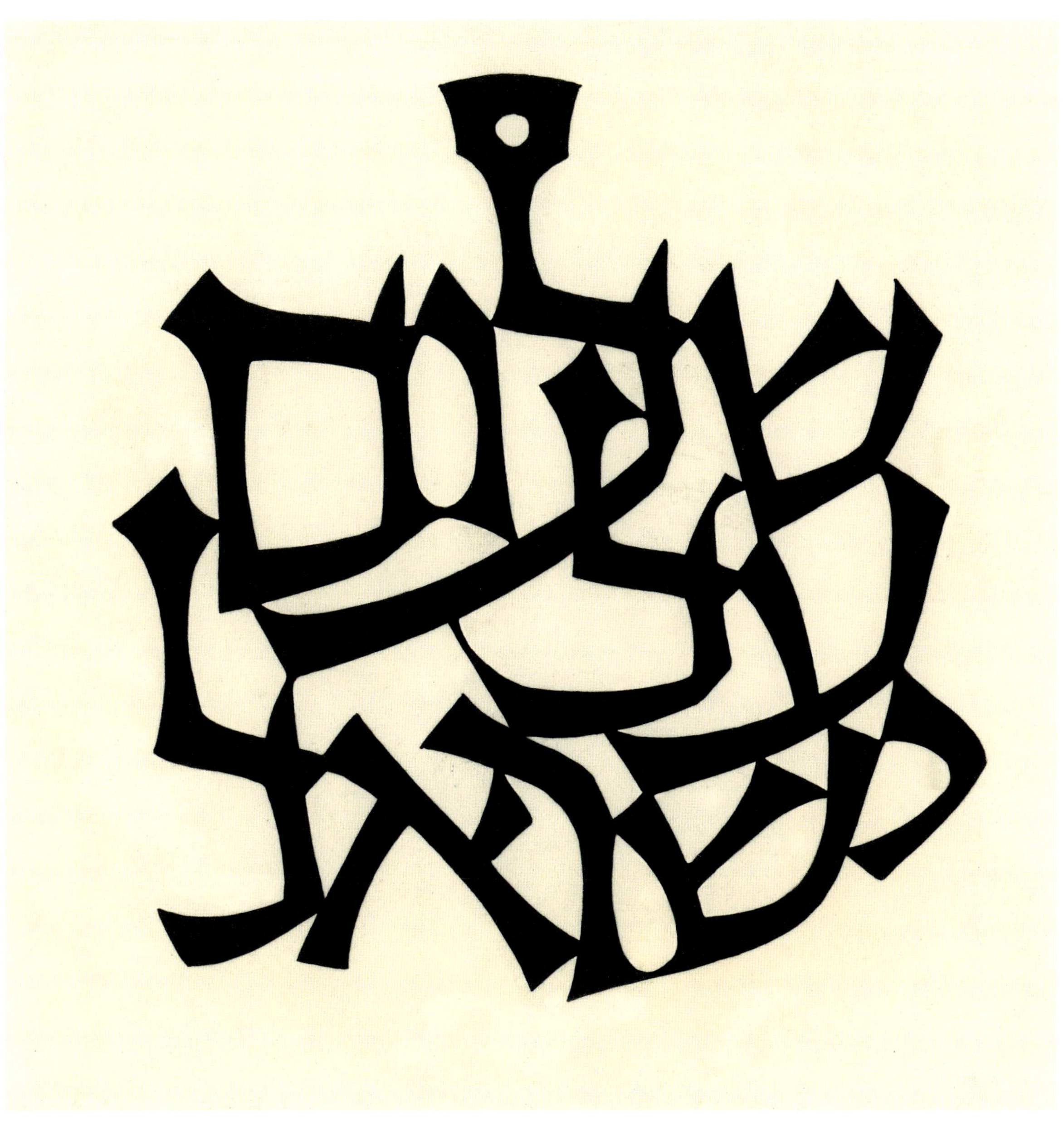

Ismar David
Peace to Israel pendant design, n.d.

The tall vertical letters, as well as the arch design evokes the idea of gates, which fits this title page for the Gates of Jerusalem Haggadah.

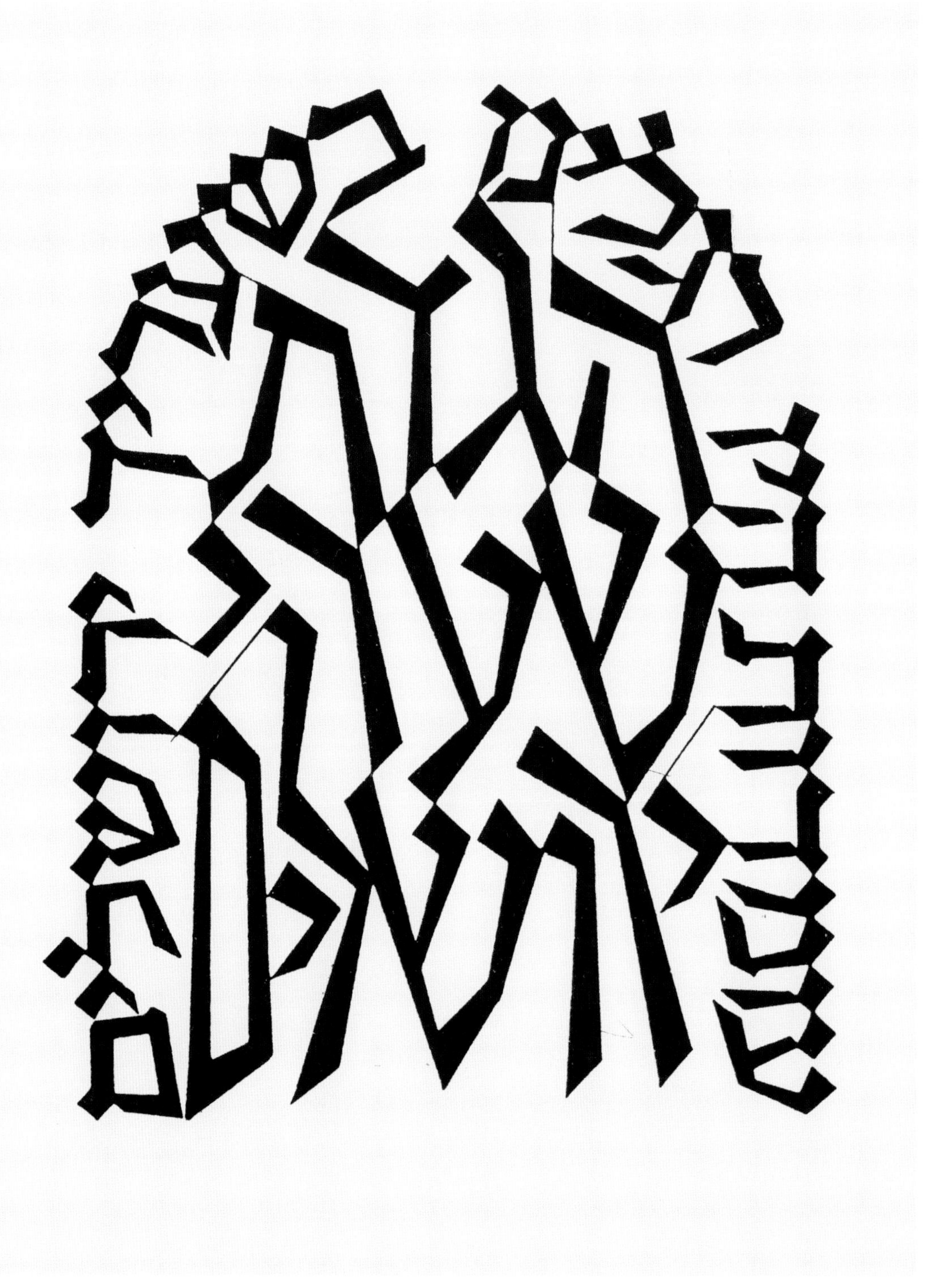

Ada Yardeni
Title page of *Gates of Jerusalem Haggadah*

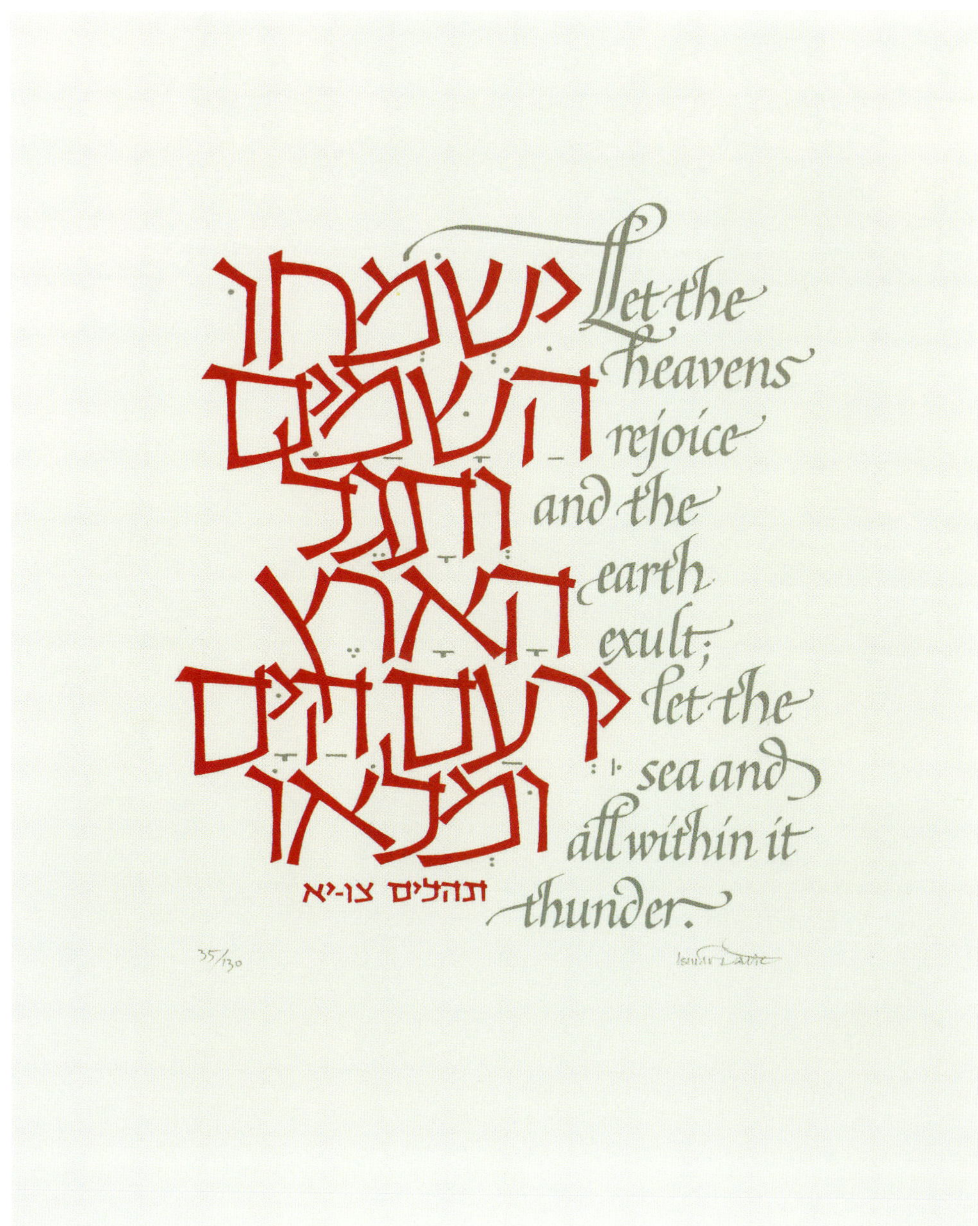

Ismar David
Let the Heavens Rejoice, from Psalm 96, n.d.

In this piece combining two languages, Ismar David emphasizes the Hebrew by making it bolder in color and larger in size. Adding the nikkud *(vocalization marks) in the gray color of the English helps to consolidate the design.*

Lili Wronker was one of the early pioneers of modern Hebrew calligraphy in the United States, beginning already in the 1950s. Here is an example of simple, straightforward forms written boldly and starkly against a highly contrasted background with reversed colors, giving this piece its strength, which fittingly expresses the content of the quote.

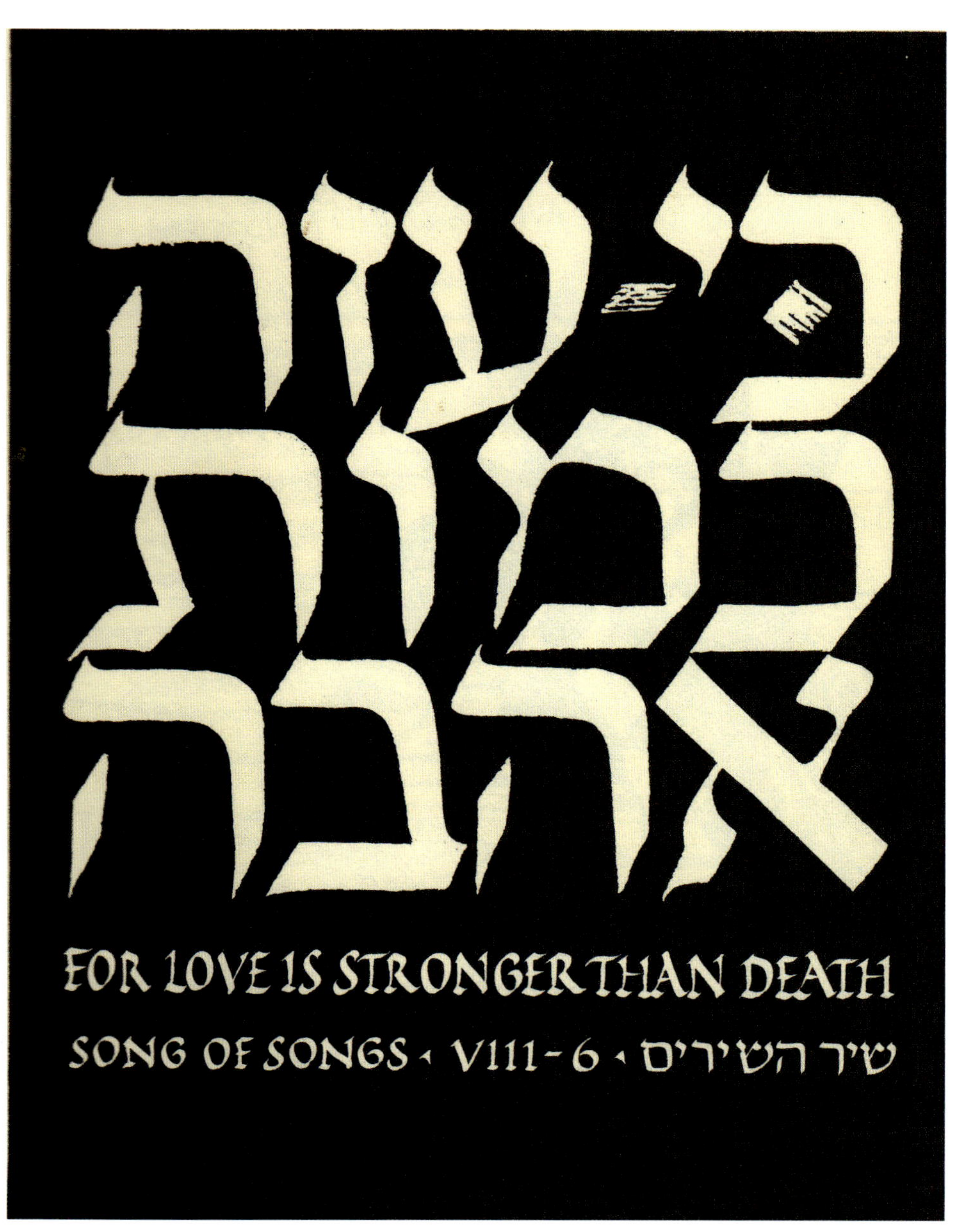

Lili Wronker
For Love Is Stronger than Death
Mid- to late twentieth century

These luscious, drawn, monoline letters were cut in silver for the cover of the memorial book of Ben-Gurion University. Despite packing three different sizes of writing close together, the appearance is one of unity.

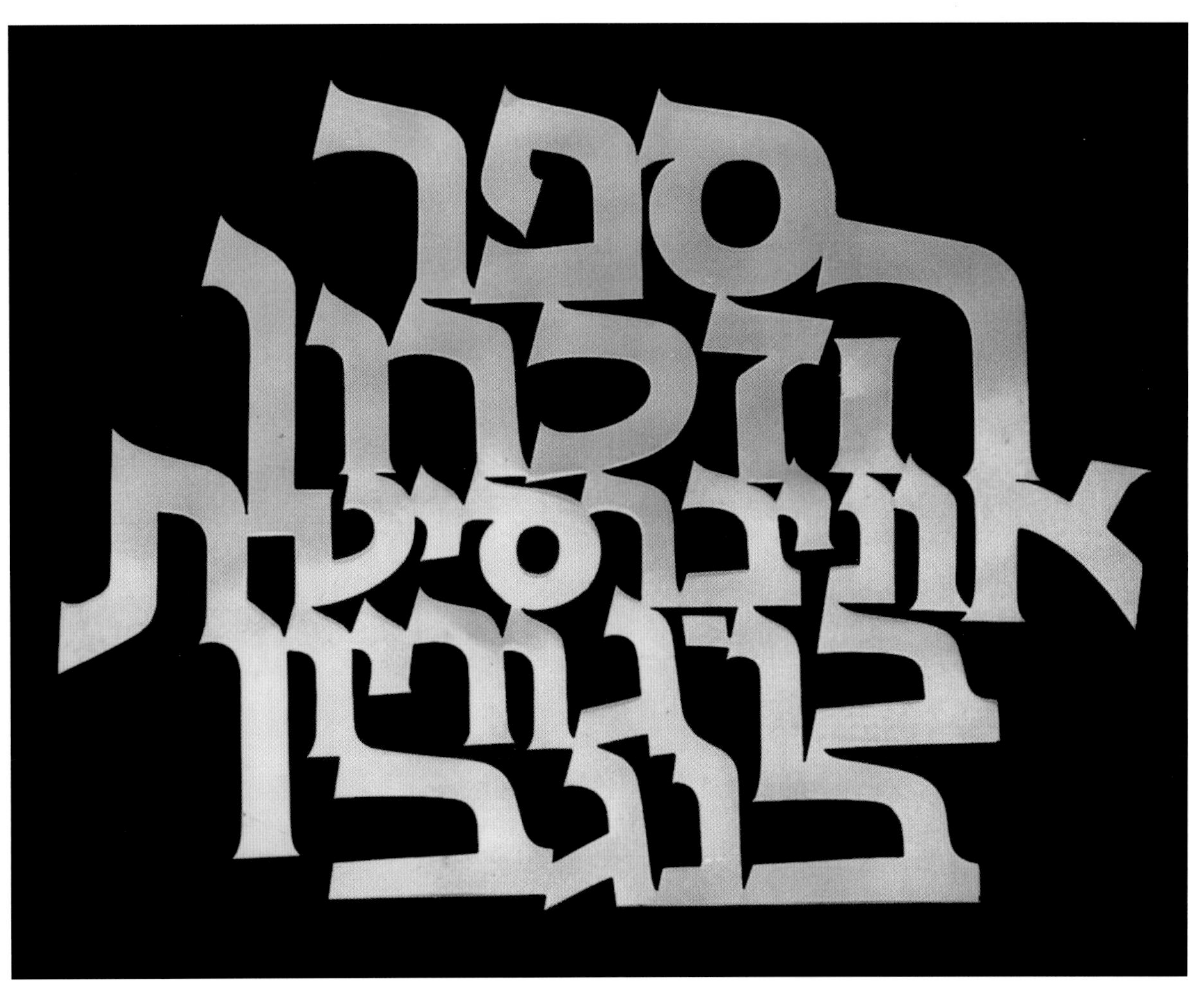

Fred Pauker
Memorial book for Ben-Gurion University, 1984

Micrography has a strong place in the Hebrew scribal tradition, most often as marginal notes and commentary in historical manuscripts. As the script is quite small, less attention is often placed on the elegance of the letterforms. In this piece, though, the micrography is written by Fred Pauker in his beautiful script.

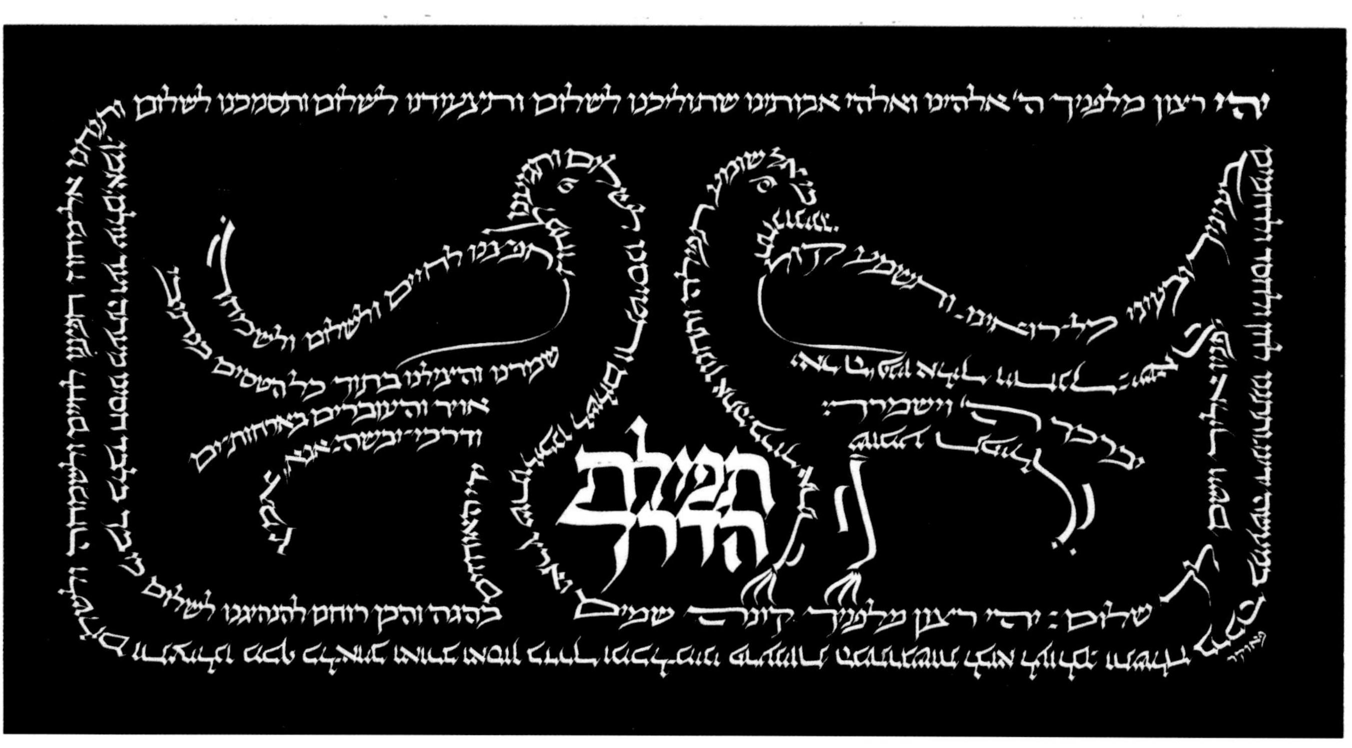

Fred Pauker
Traveler's Prayer, 1975

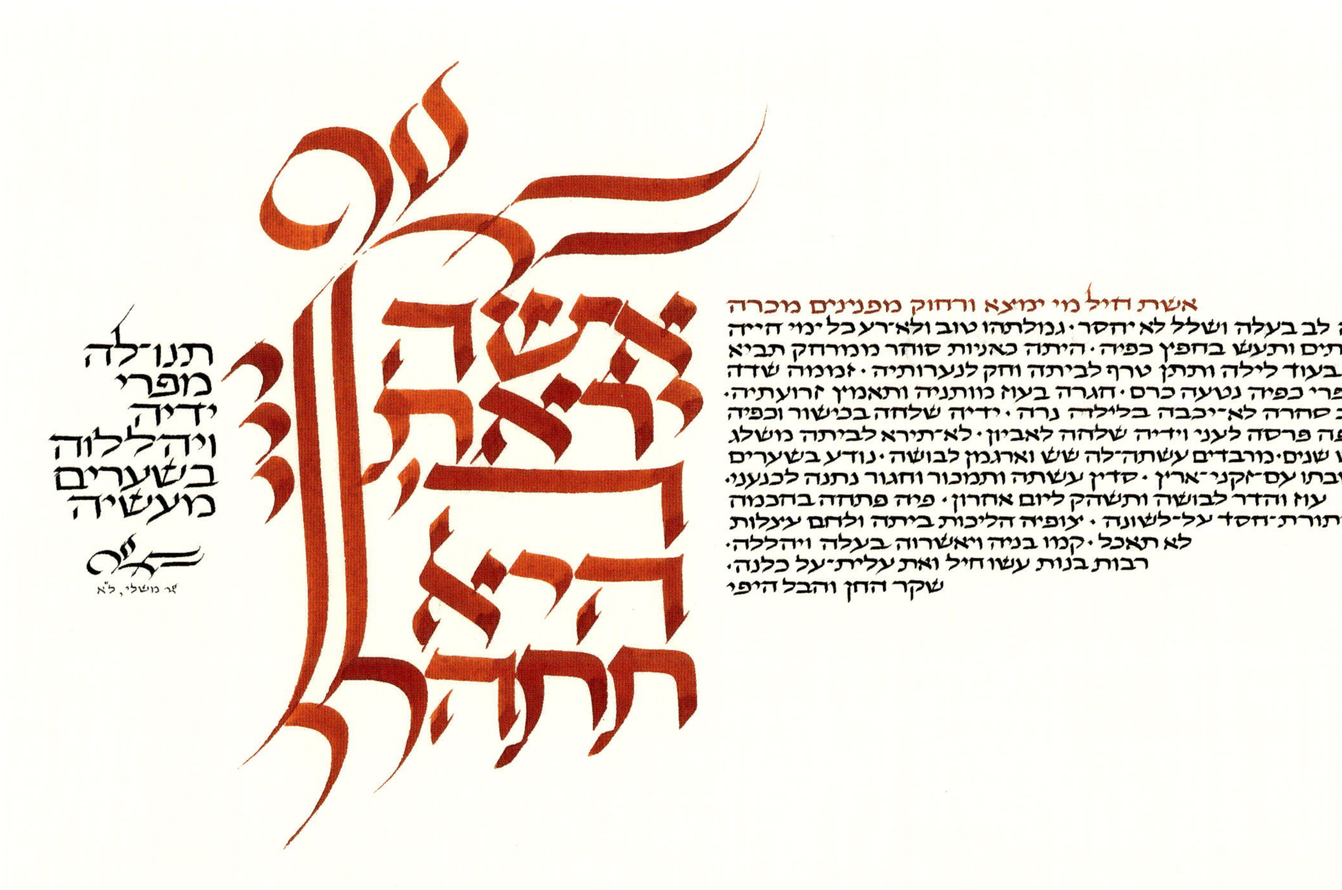

Malla Carl—artist, graphic artist, and calligrapher—nicely balances three different sizes of writing in this piece. Her tall lameds and flourishes also provide a stable border for the large text, which anchors the otherwise open alignment of the two smaller text blocks.

Malla Carl
A Woman of Valor
Late twentieth century

Zvi Narkiss was commissioned to write, design, and illustrate the book Great Is Peace. *The book was printed in a limited, numbered edition to honor the peace treaty between Egypt and Israel. The first three copies were presented to Anwar Sadat, Menachem Begin, and Jimmy Carter.*

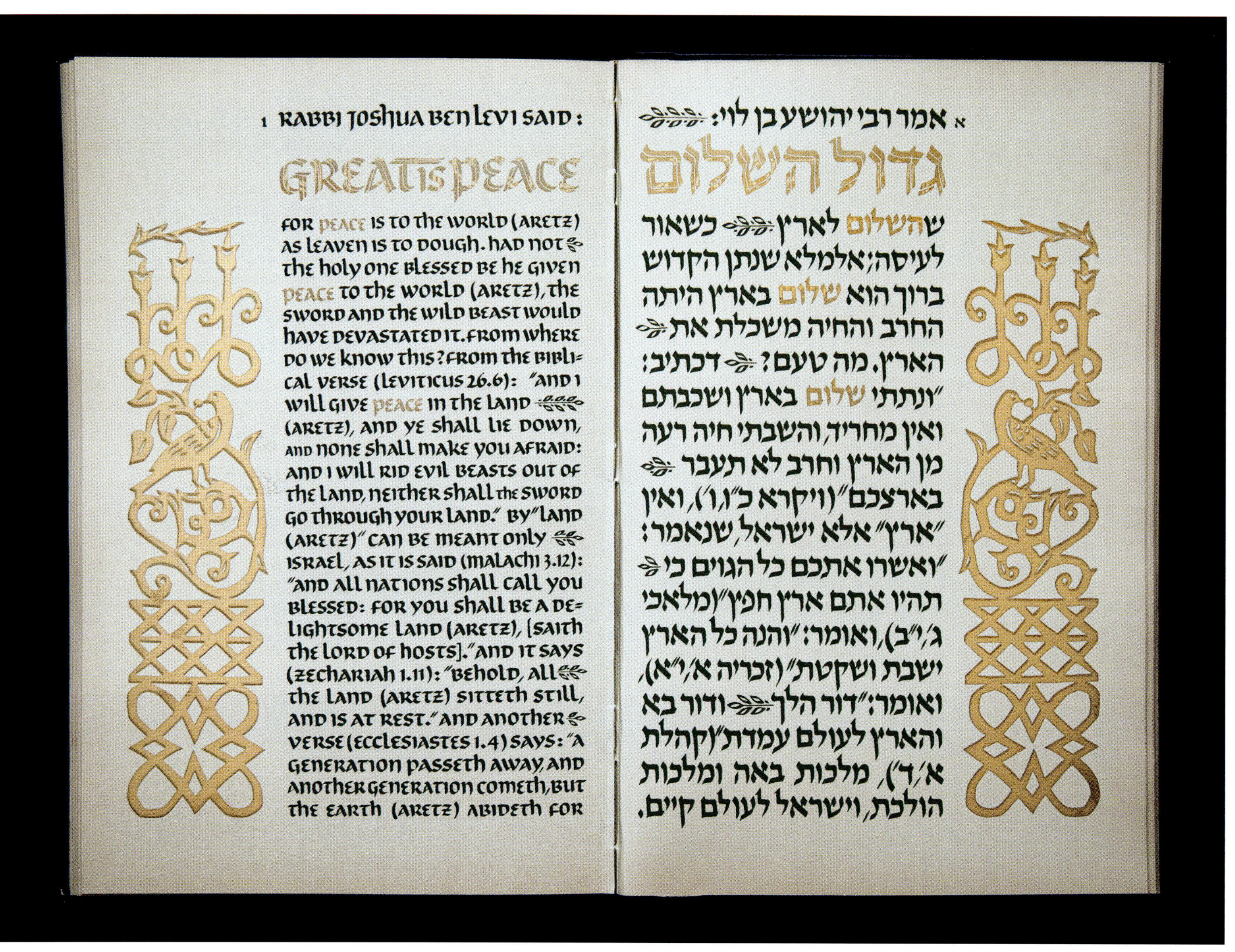

1 RABBI JOSHUA BEN LEVI SAID:

GREAT IS PEACE

FOR PEACE IS TO THE WORLD (ARETZ) AS LEAVEN IS TO DOUGH. HAD NOT THE HOLY ONE BLESSED BE HE GIVEN PEACE TO THE WORLD (ARETZ), THE SWORD AND THE WILD BEAST WOULD HAVE DEVASTATED IT. FROM WHERE DO WE KNOW THIS? FROM THE BIBLICAL VERSE (LEVITICUS 26.6): "AND I WILL GIVE PEACE IN THE LAND (ARETZ), AND YE SHALL LIE DOWN, AND NONE SHALL MAKE YOU AFRAID: AND I WILL RID EVIL BEASTS OUT OF THE LAND, NEITHER SHALL THE SWORD GO THROUGH YOUR LAND." BY "LAND (ARETZ)" CAN BE MEANT ONLY ISRAEL, AS IT IS SAID (MALACHI 3.12): "AND ALL NATIONS SHALL CALL YOU BLESSED: FOR YOU SHALL BE A DELIGHTSOME LAND (ARETZ), [SAITH THE LORD OF HOSTS]." AND IT SAYS (ZECHARIAH 1.11): "BEHOLD, ALL THE LAND (ARETZ) SITTETH STILL, AND IS AT REST." AND ANOTHER VERSE (ECCLESIASTES 1.4) SAYS: "A GENERATION PASSETH AWAY, AND ANOTHER GENERATION COMETH, BUT THE EARTH (ARETZ) ABIDETH FOR

א אמר רבי יהושע בן לוי:

גדול השלום

שהשלום לארץ כשאור לעיסה; אלמלא שנתן הקדוש ברוך הוא שלום בארץ היתה החרב והחיה משכלת את הארץ. מה טעם? דכתיב: "ונתתי שלום בארץ ושכבתם ואין מחריד, והשבתי חיה רעה מן הארץ וחרב לא תעבר בארצכם" (ויקרא כ"ו, ו'), ואין "ארץ" אלא ישראל, שנאמר: "ואשרו אתכם כל הגוים כי תהיו אתם ארץ חפץ" (מלאכי ג', י"ב), ואומר: "והנה כל הארץ ישבת ושקטת" (זכריה א', י"א), ואומר: "דור הלך ודור בא והארץ לעולם עמדת" (קהלת א', ד'), מלכות באה ומלכות הולכת, וישראל לעולם קיים.

Zvi Narkiss
Great Is Peace, 1979
Photograph: Ruth Yehoshua

ד אמר רבי יהושע בן חלפתא:

גדול הוא השלום

שכשברא הקדוש ברוך הוא
את העולם, עשה שלום בין
עליונים לתחתונים. ביום
ראשון ברא מן העליונים ומן
התחתונים, הדא הוא דכתיב:
"בראשית ברא אלהים את
השמים ואת הארץ" (בראשית
א׳, א׳); בשני ברא מן העליונים,
הדא הוא דכתיב: "יהי רקיע
בתוך המים" (שם, ו׳); בג׳ ברא
מן התחתונים שנאמר: "ויאמר
אלהים: יקוו המים מתחת
השמים" (שם, ט׳); בד׳ ברא מן
העליונים, שנאמר: "יהי מארת
ברקיע השמים" (שם, י״ד), בה׳
ברא מן התחתונים, שנאמר:
"ויאמר אלהים: ישרצו המים
[שרץ נפש חיה...]" (שם, כ׳).
בו׳ בא לברוא אדם, אמר: אם

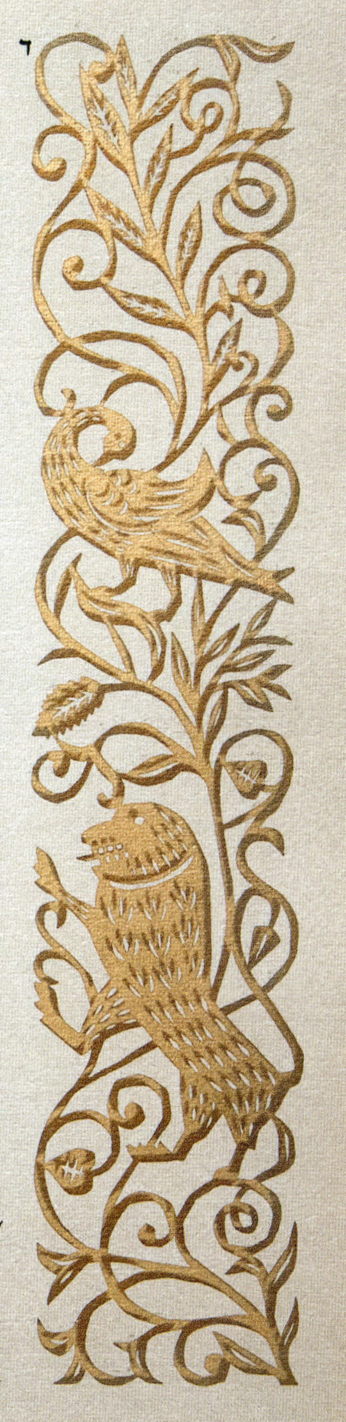

An example of modern illumination and gilding by Barbara Wolff, incorporating strong Ashkenazic letter forms.

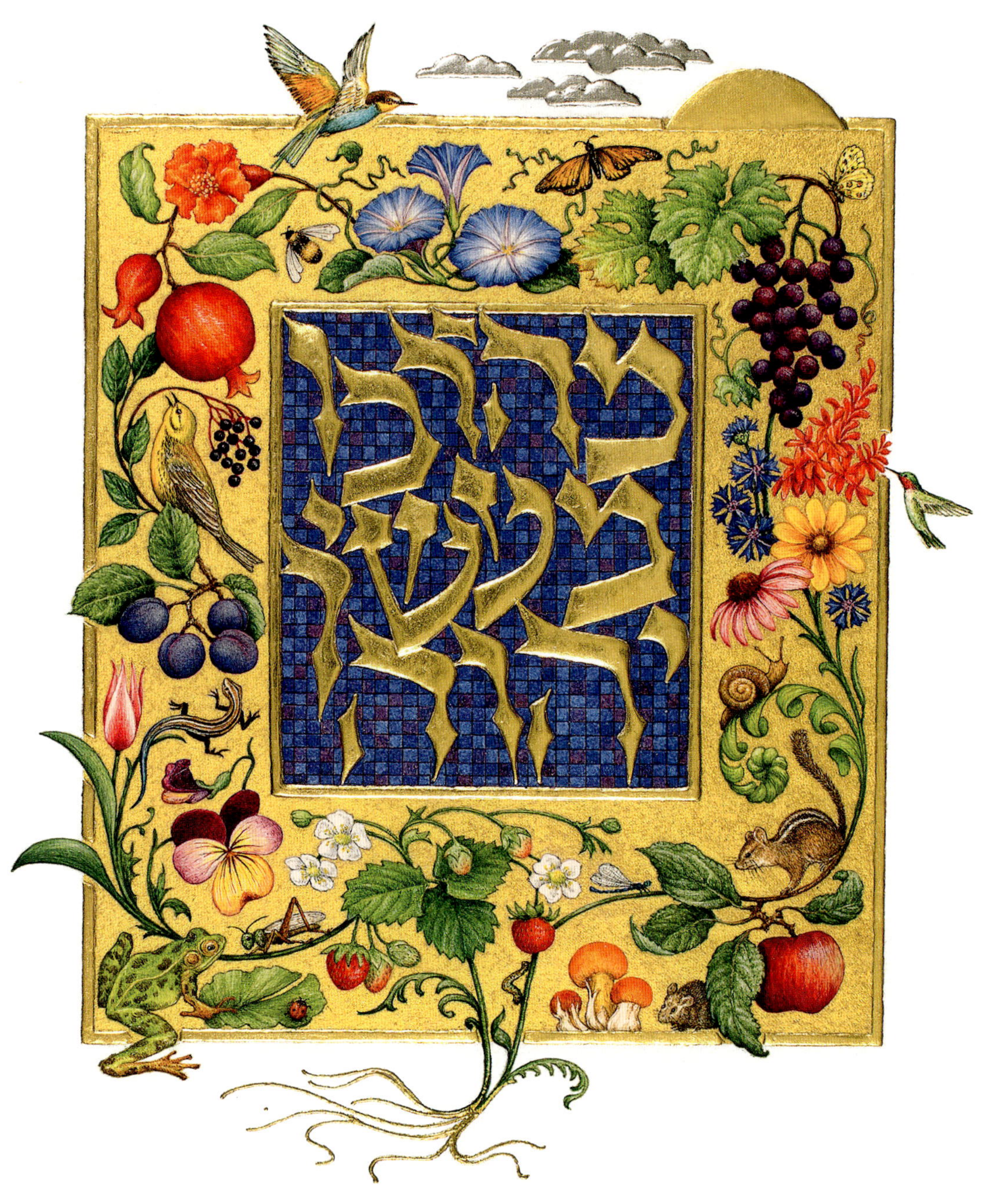

Barbara Wolff
Psalm 104, 2006–7

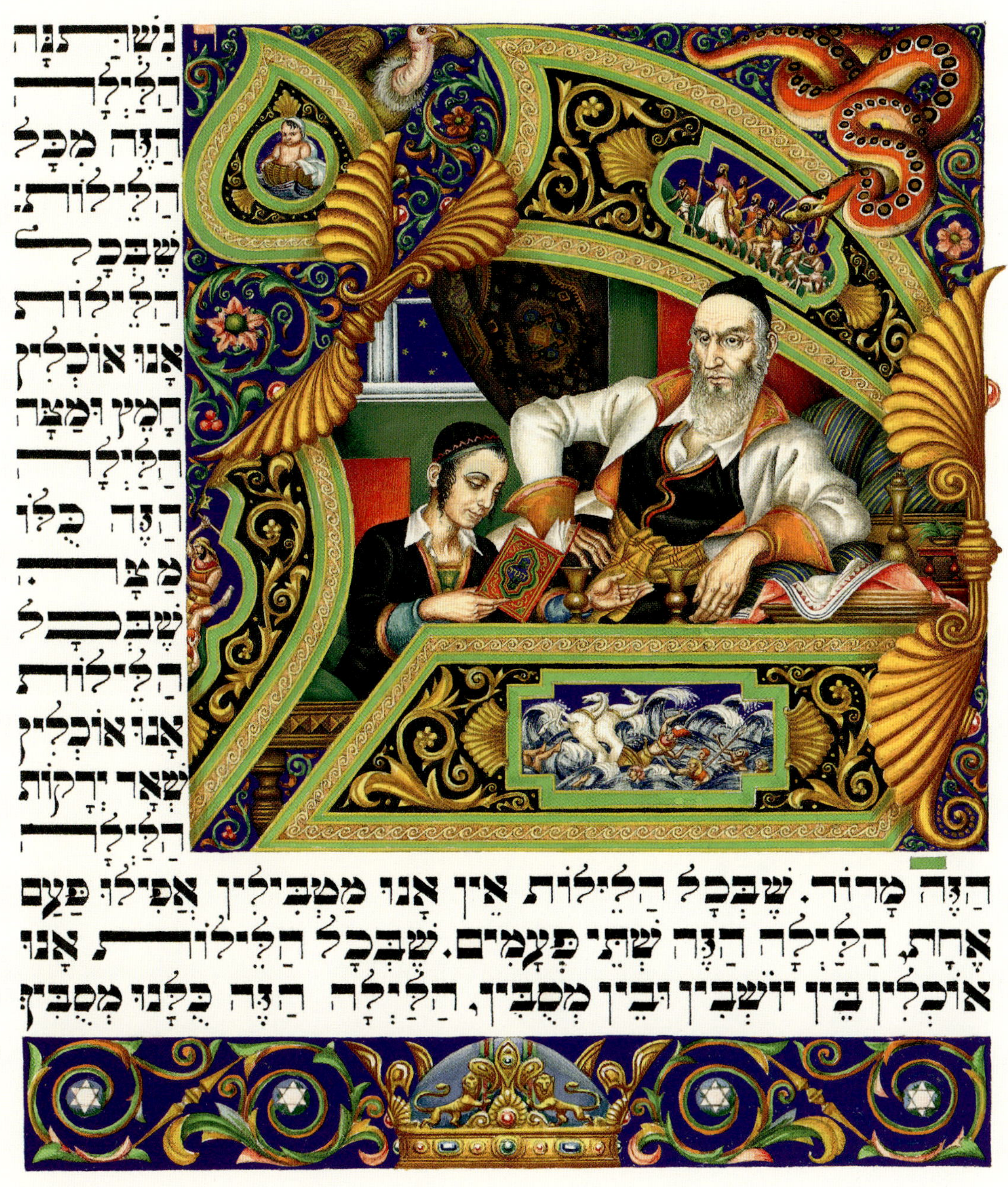

Unique lettering style by Arthur Szyk in his famous Haggadah, which also shows Ashkenazic characteristics. These letters were most likely painted rather than pen-written.

Arthur Szyk
The Four Questions from a Haggadah published in Łódz, 1935

Ruth Lubin calligraphed this illustrated Haggadah, demonstrating a mastery of the Pauker script. The facing page shows an enlarged example from a different manuscript of her writing.

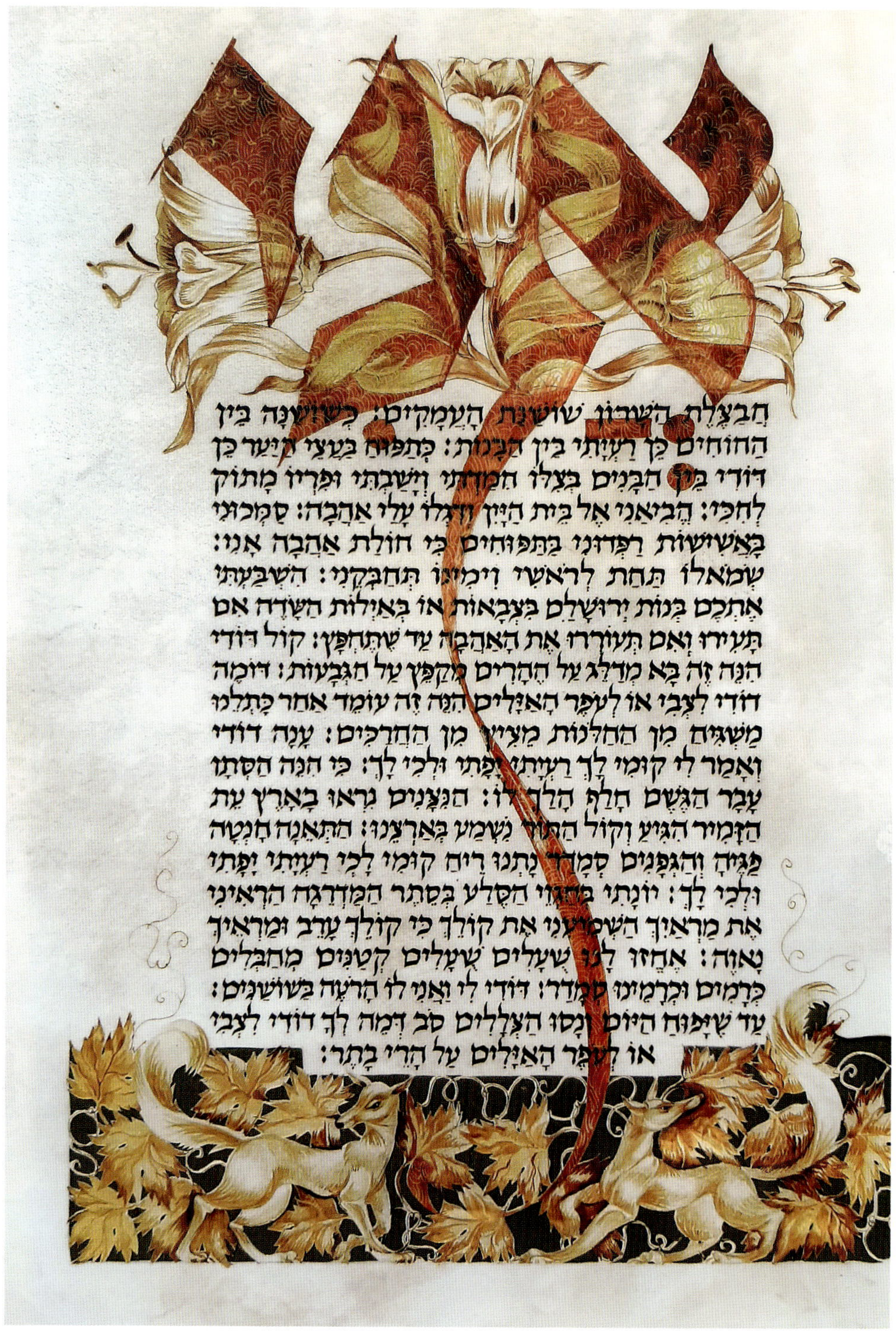

Ruth Lubin, calligrapher
Irina Oblovsky, artist
Passover Haggadah, 2006

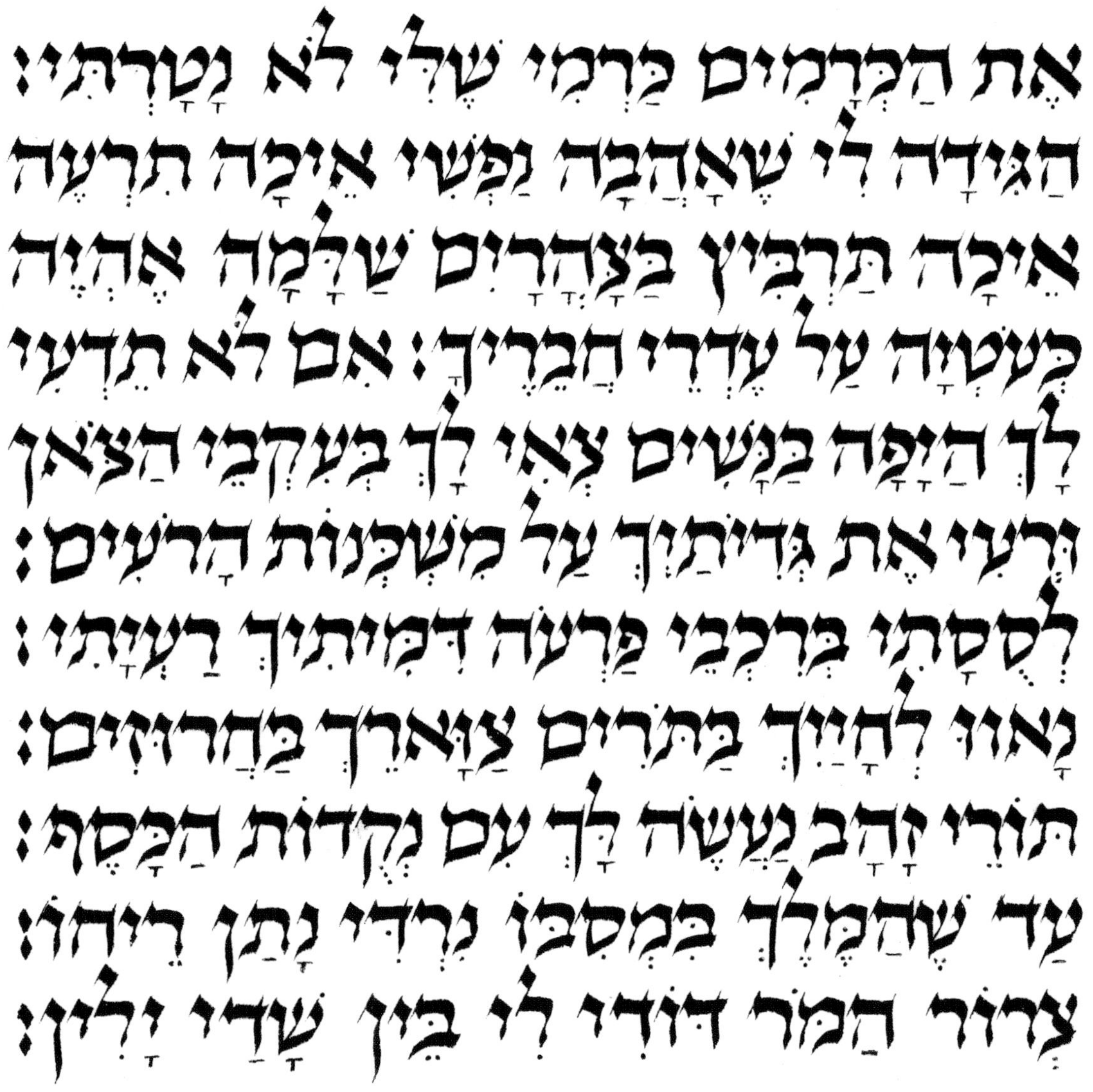

את הכרמים כרמי שלי לא נטרתי:
הגידה לי שאהבה נפשי איכה תרעה
איכה תרביץ בצהרים שלמה אהיה
כעטיה על עדרי חבריך: אם לא תדעי
לך היפה בנשים צאי לך בעקבי הצאן
ורעי את גדיתיך על משכנות הרעים:
לססתי ברכבי פרעה דמיתיך רעיתי:
נאוו לחייך בתרים צוארך בחרוזים:
תורי זהב נעשה לך עם נקדות הכסף:
עד שהמלך במסבו נרדי נתן ריחו:
צרור המר דודי לי בין שדי ילין:

Ruth Lubin
Detail from a *Shir Hashirim (Song of Songs)* book, 2007

The sloped "roofs" of the letters in this delightful script developed by Sharon Binder give an almost italic feel to her lettering.

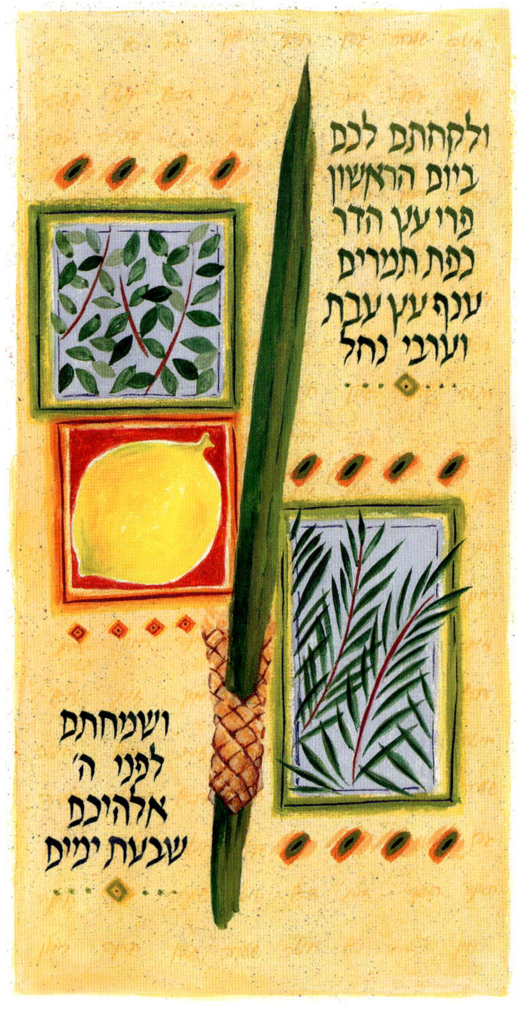

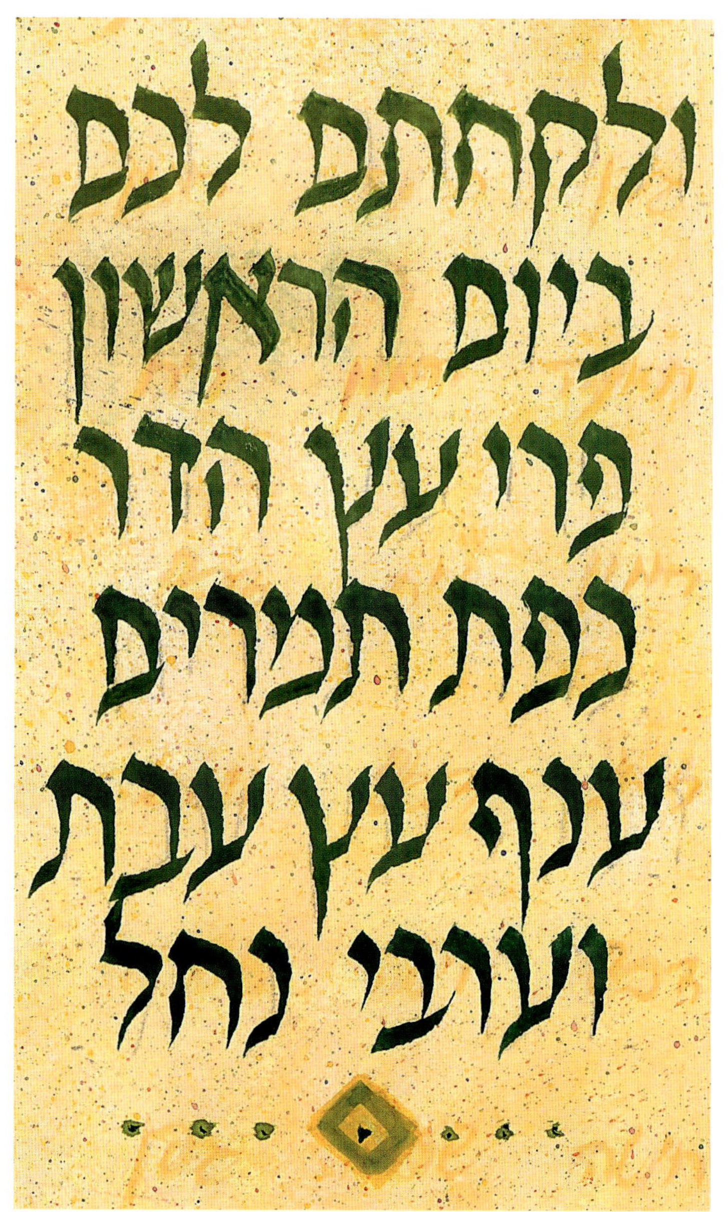

Sharon Binder
The Four Species, 2002

Malla Carl has emulated the moon shape in forming the enlarged red letter heh, representing God's name.

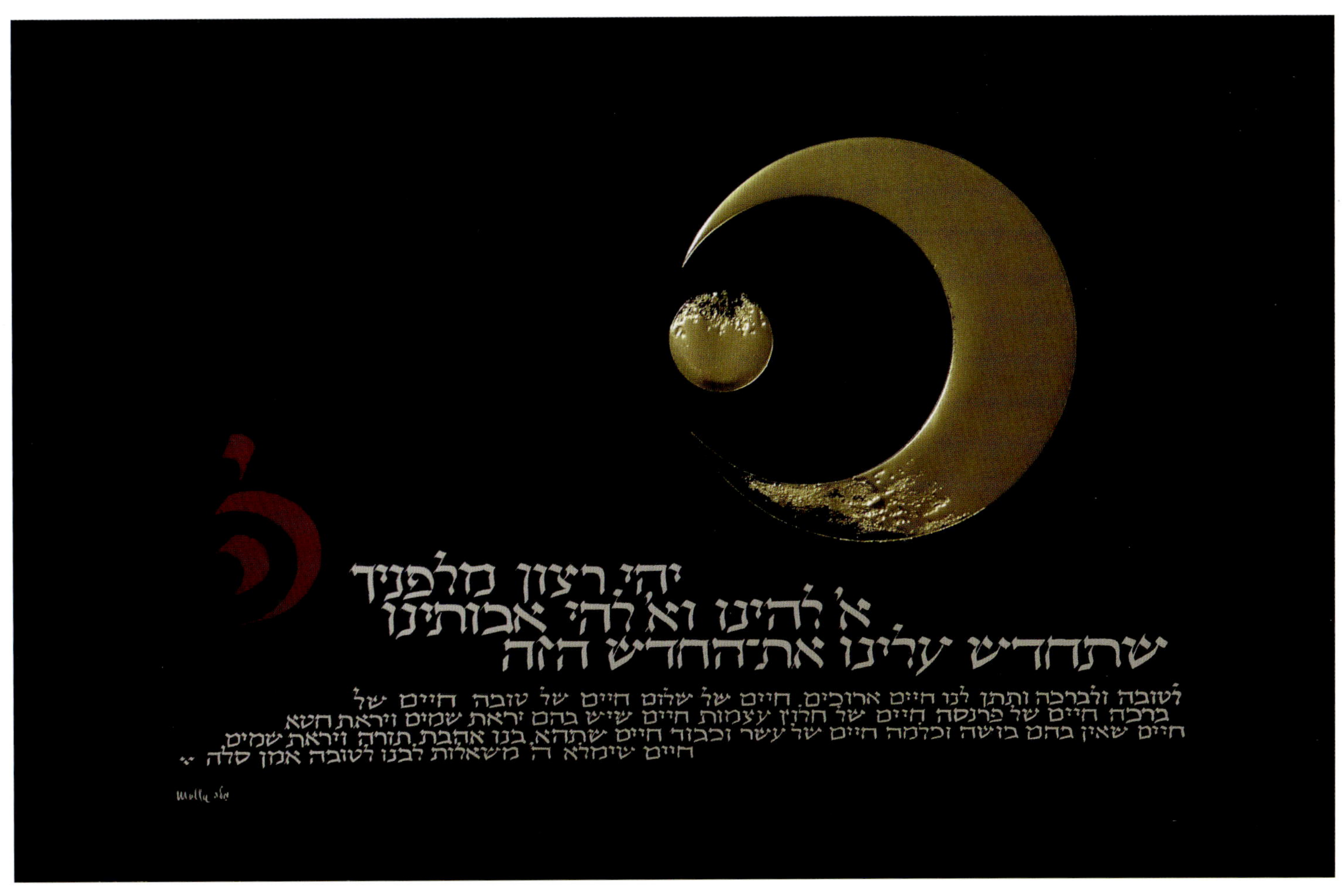

Malla Carl
Prayer for Blessing for the New Month, late twentieth century

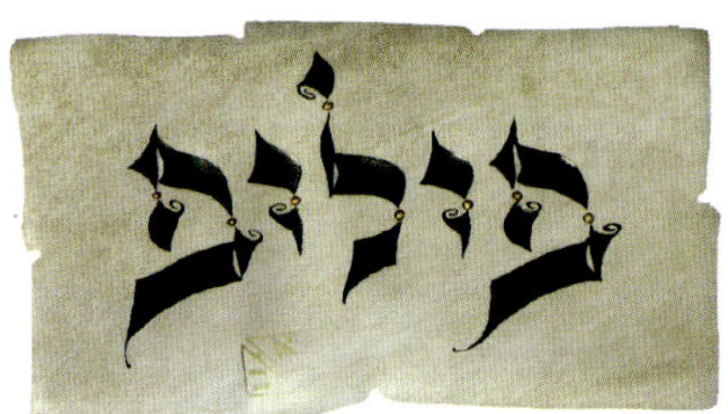

This highly stylized Ashkenazic script emphasizes the shapes of the different strokes by keeping the strokes separate.

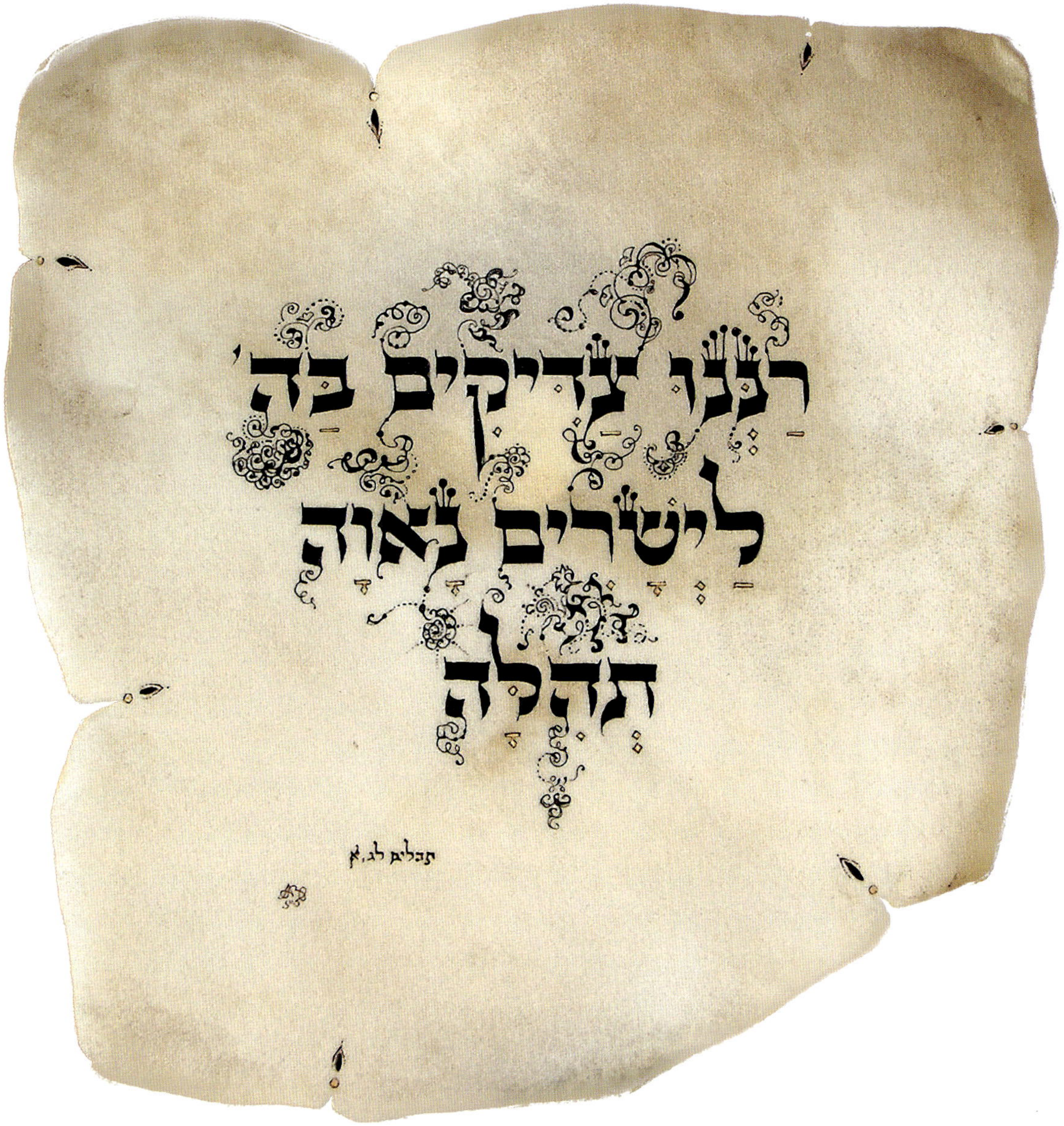

רננו צדיקים בה'
לישרים נאוה
תהלה

תהלים לג, א

Interesting hybrid script, combining medieval Ashkenazic script and the sacred STaM script.

Avraham Borshevsky
LEFT: Philip, 2017
RIGHT: *Psalm 33:1*, 2007

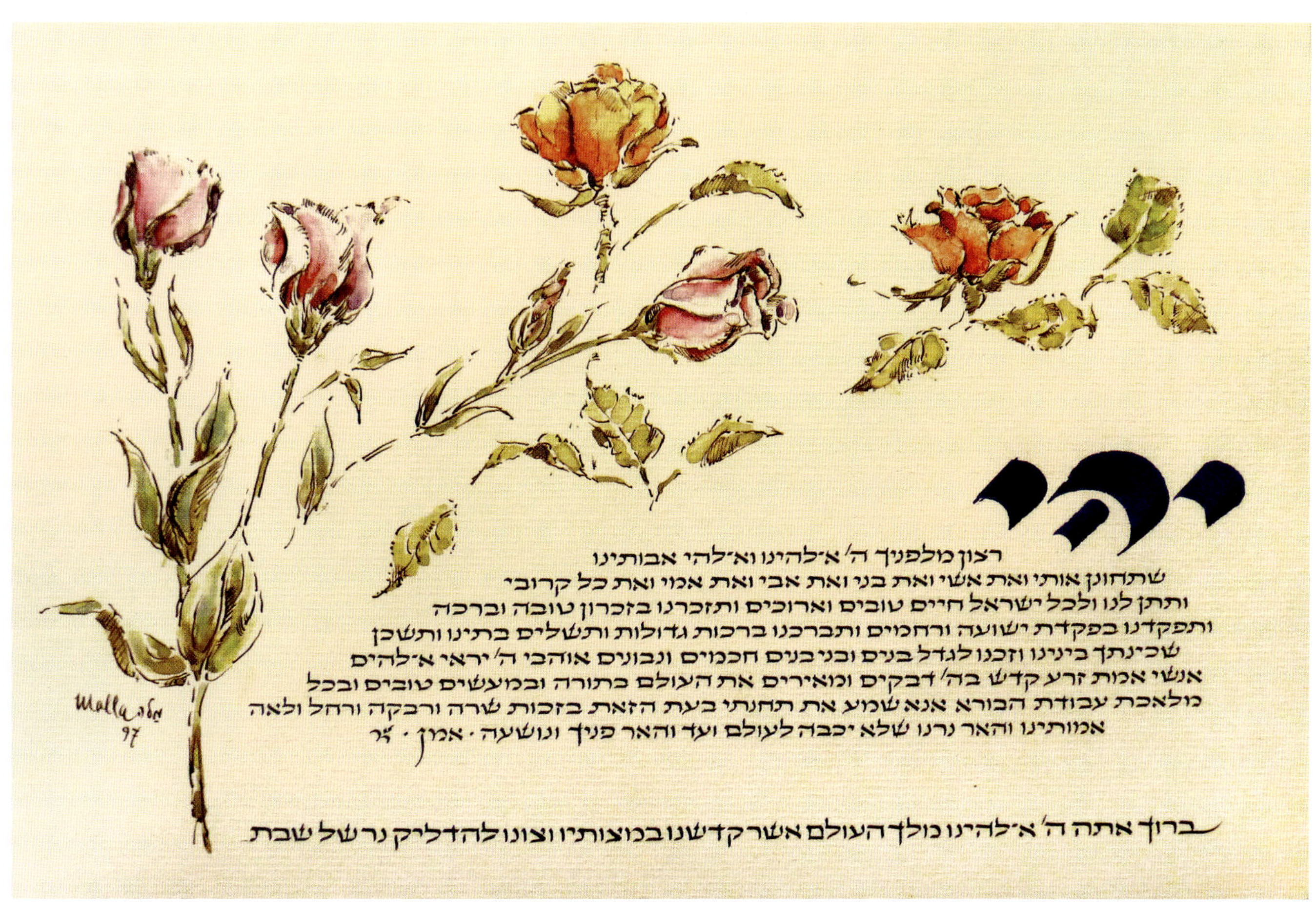

Usually a large initial word is written in a more formal script and the body of the text in a less formal style. Here Malla Carl surprises by flipping it around, drawing the eye in by using a bold semi-cursive for the large initial word

Malla Carl
Prayer After Lighting the Shabbat Candles,
Late twentieth century

Hebrew letters form a strong pattern when written in a roundel, which here contrasts nicely with the delicate, linear floral design.

Sharon Binder
Design for a chuppah, 2016

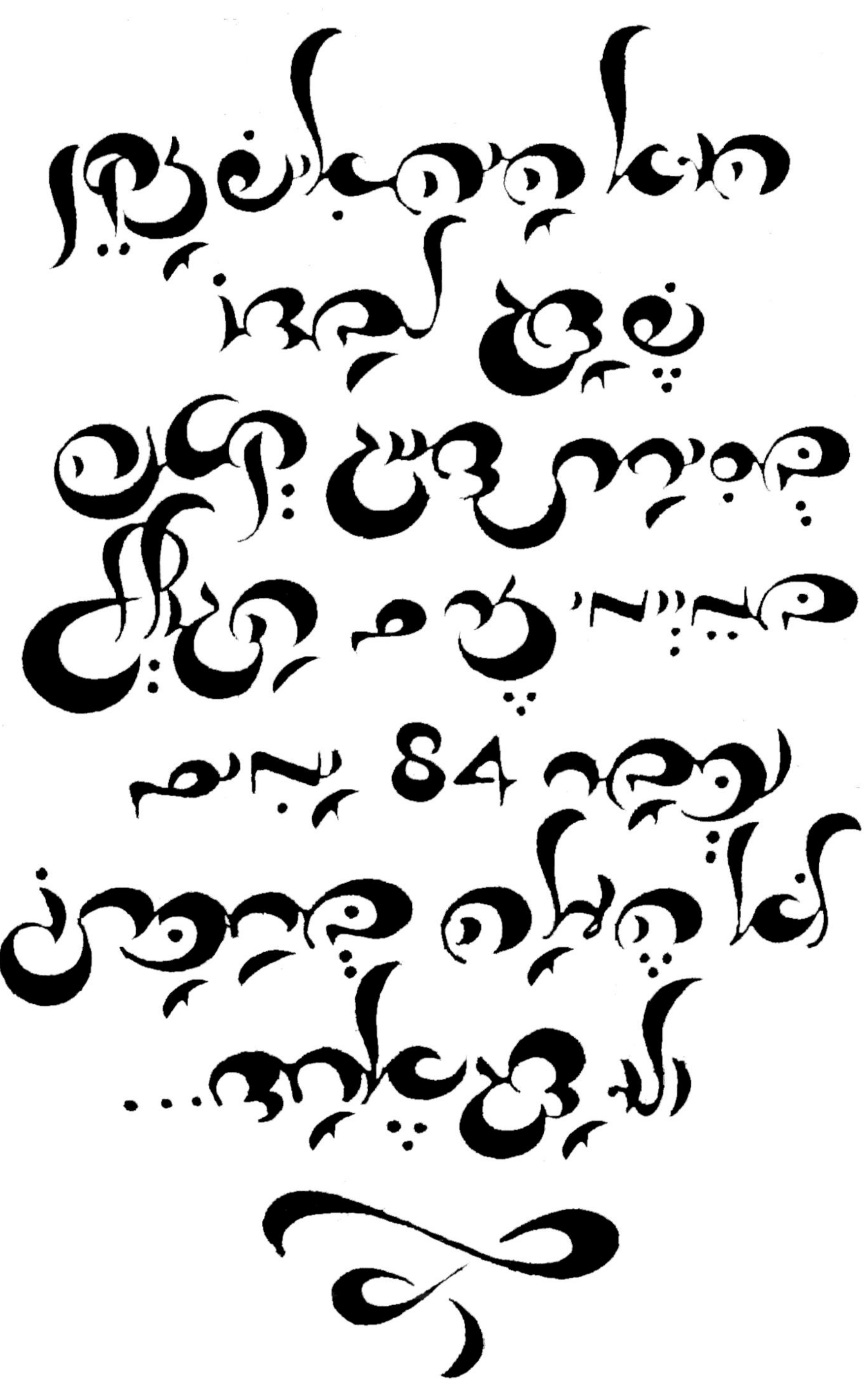

Zina Dorman
The Old Man and the Sea, 2014

This piece was written with a brush using everyday handwriting forms with a bit of a twist. The brush here is allowed to emphasize the thick and thin contrasts within the letters; adding the vocalization marks adds to the emphasis, giving the work an interesting rhythm.

This lively rendition shows an affinity with Ashkenazic writing as it accentuates the strong contrast between the horizontal and vertical strokes.

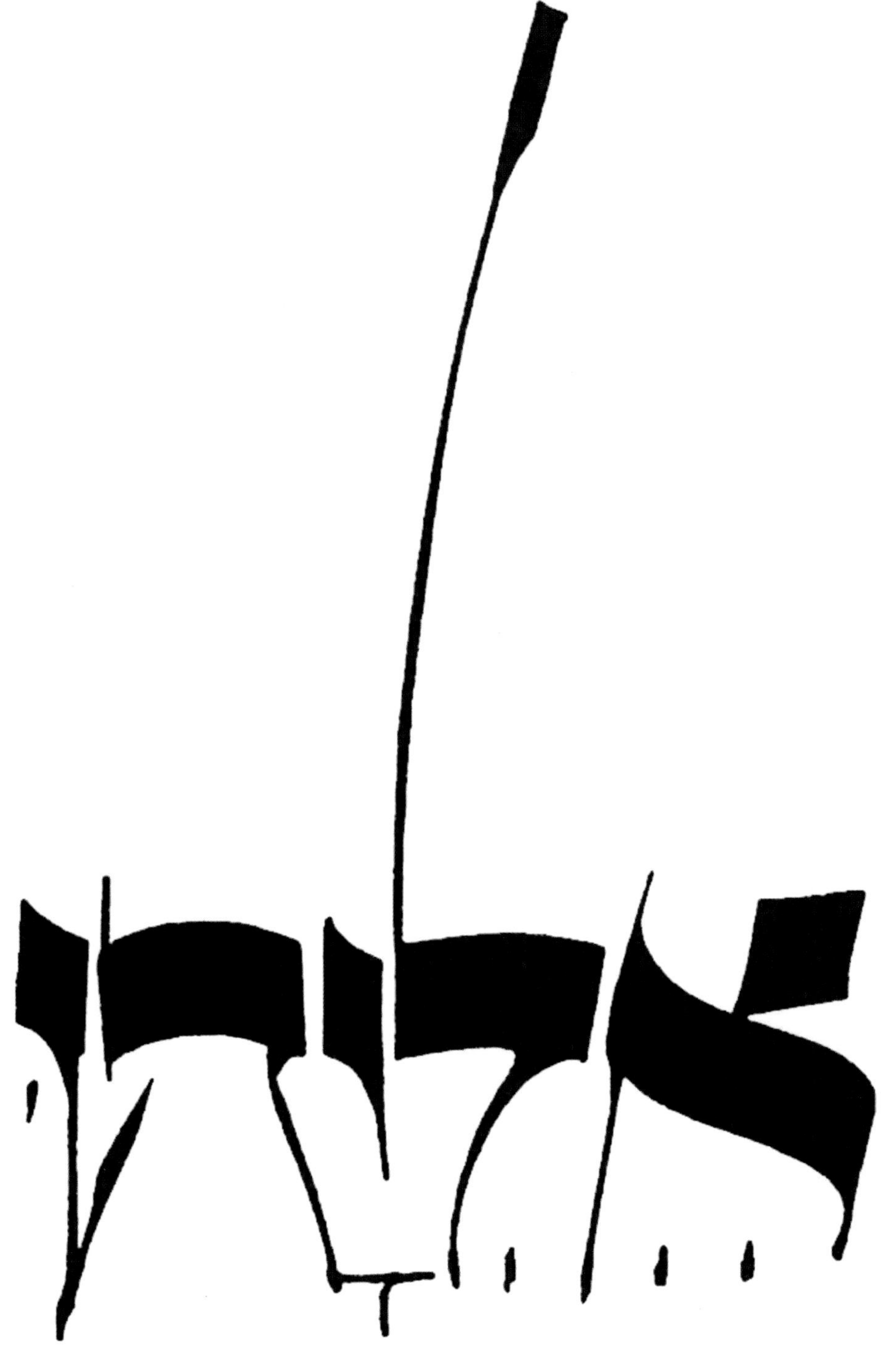

Lynn Broide
Eliyahu
Design for Bar-Mitzvah invitation cover, 1993

Combining Hebrew and English in one composition, with the two elements in such close proximity, is not an easy task. Here is a masterful rendition.

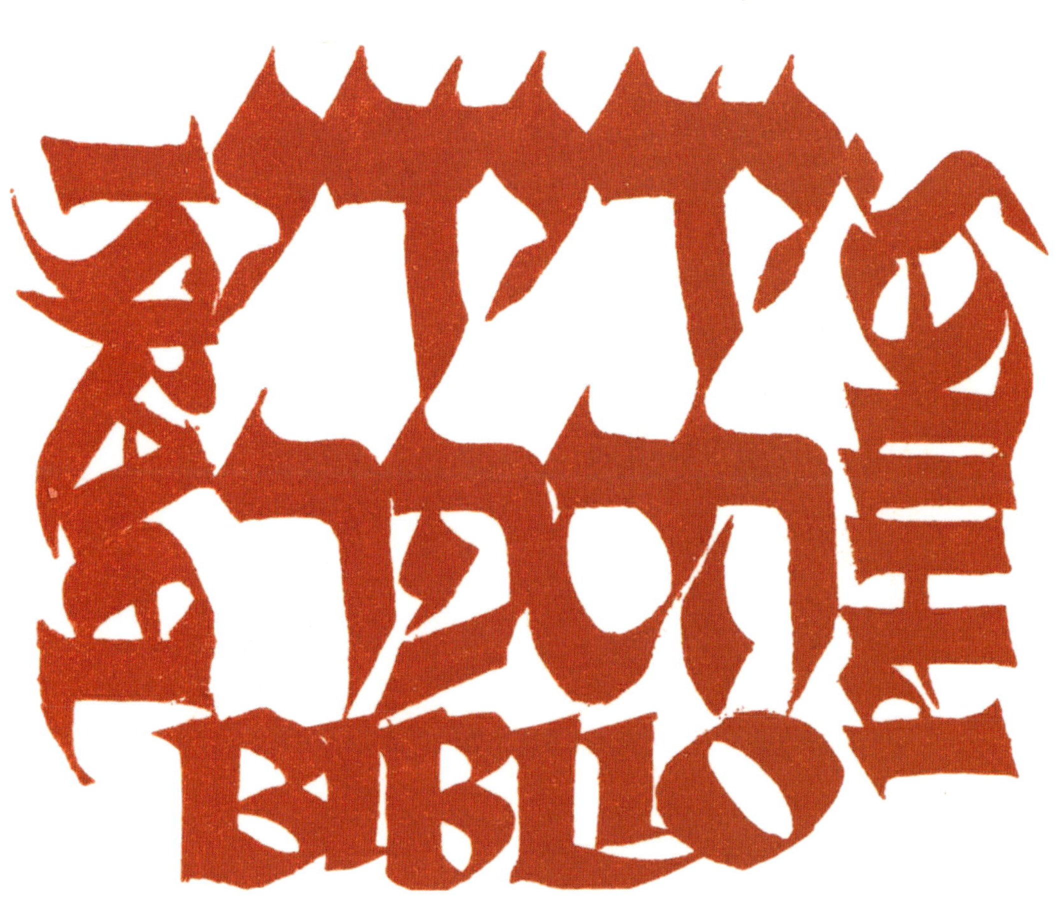

Fred Pauker
Logo for Israel Bibliophiles, 1980–81

Another example of Fred Pauker's strong script. The rough edges to the letters add emotional impact to the title.

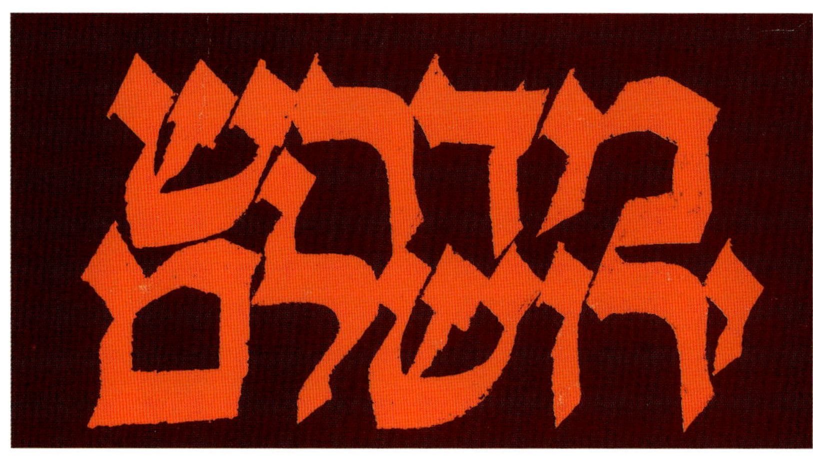

Usually, when Hebrew letters are stretched, they are stretched horizontally. In this work it is the vertical stretching of certain strokes that helps complete the design shape.

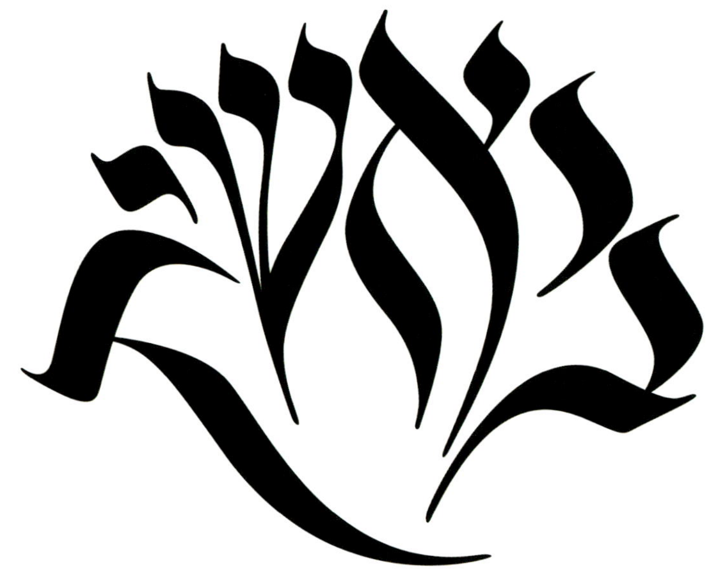

TOP: Fred Pauker
Detail from cover of *Midrash Yerushalayim*, c. 1982

BOTTOM: David Goldstein
Bereshit, 2016

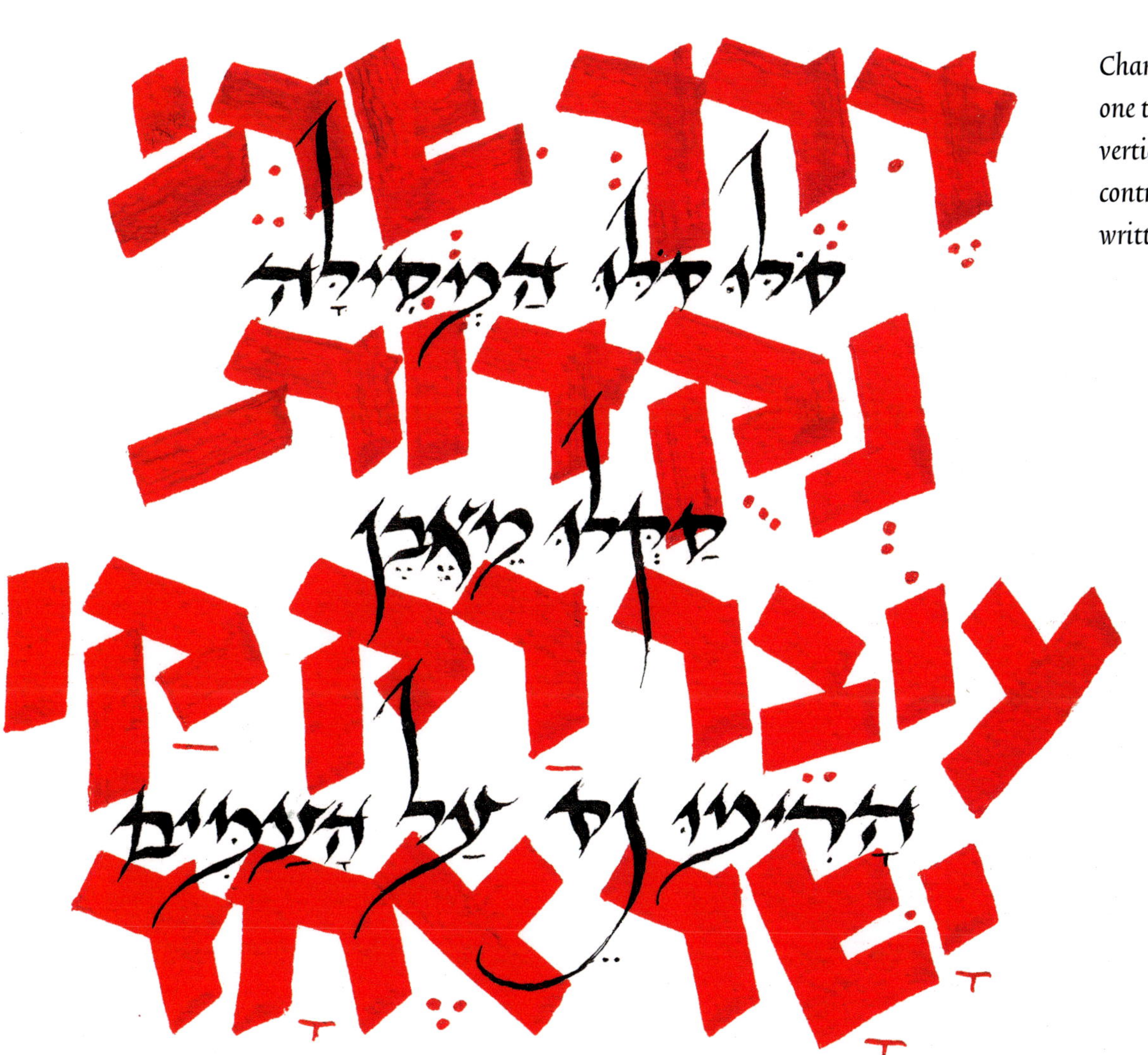

Changing the pen angle for different strokes allows one to get heavy strokes in both the horizontal and vertical direction in the red monoline script, which contrasts nicely with the smaller, more traditionally written black lettering.

David Goldstein
Through Two Points, 2019
With text by Yehuda Amichai

A flowing roundel with concentric circles, each of differently sized lettering, can give a three-dimensional effect.

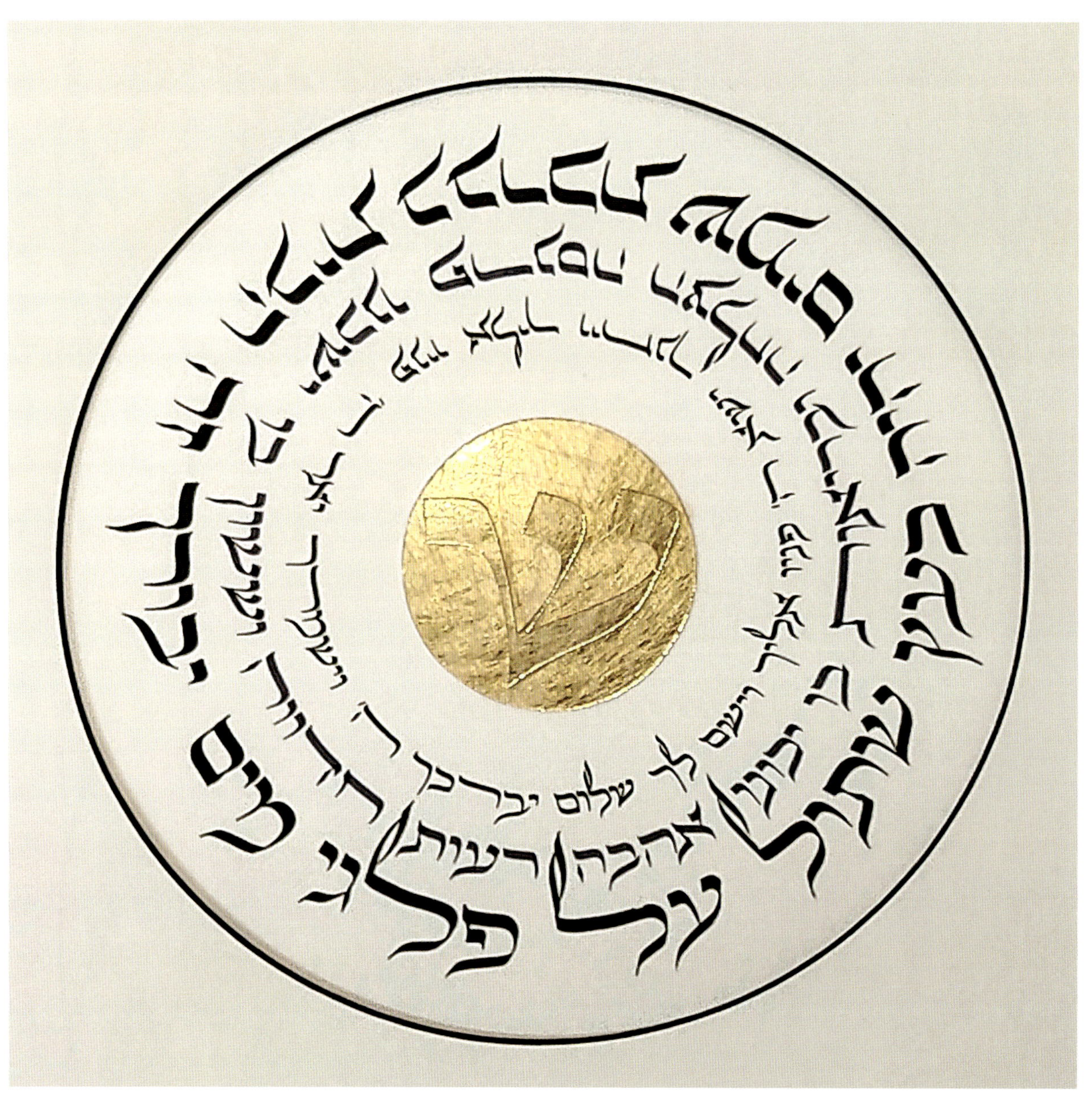

Akiva Roszkowski
Home Blessing, 2019

Contemporary Hebrew handwriting letterforms elegantly designed.

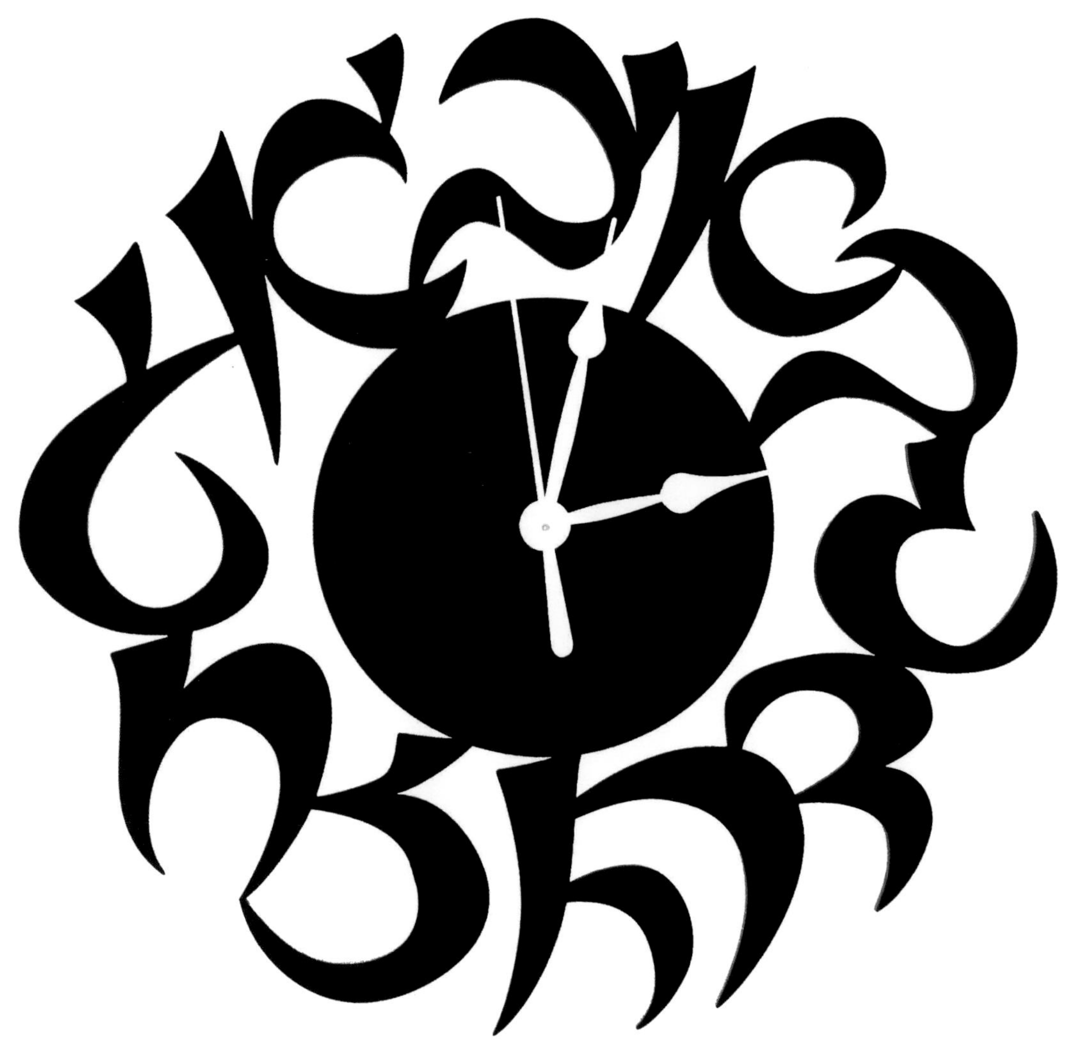

Melanie Dankowicz
Hebrew Clock, 2012

Lettering carved on buildings is another venue for creative Hebrew shapes, here in the form of arches. Notice how the right arm of the aleph *is designed in order to match the "heel" of the* dalet.

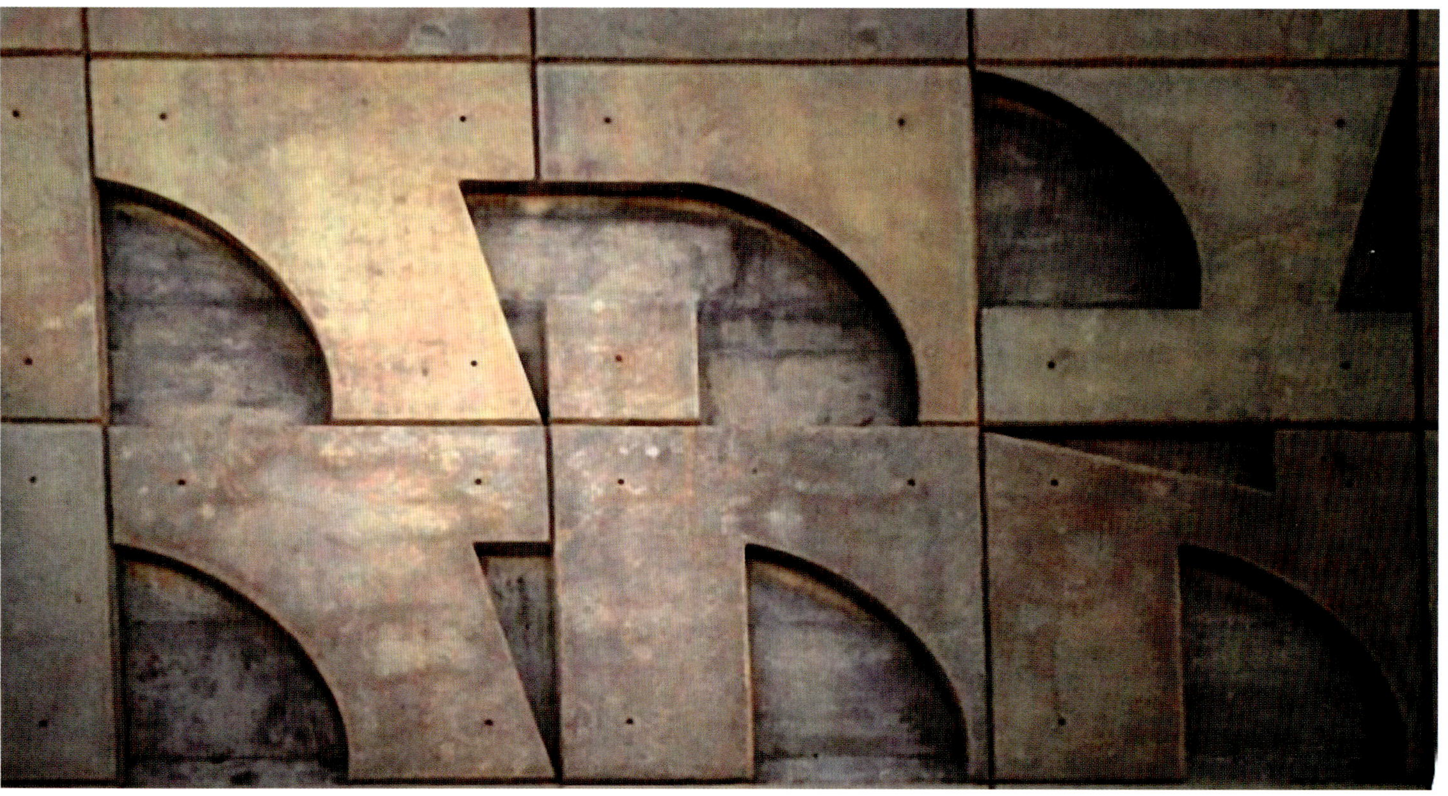

Lettering on the building of the Officer's Training School
Lettering designer unknown
Building constructed in the 1960s

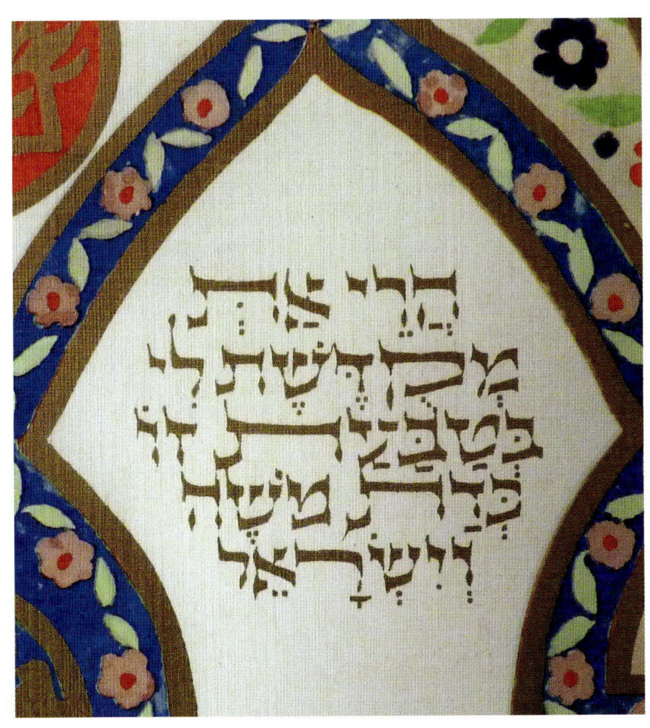

Joseph Hirsch was an Israeli artist and graphic designer who also studied lettering under Yerachmiel Shechter. He designed the Hebrew lettering for street signs in the Jewish quarter of the old city in Jerusalem. These letters show Ashkenazic roots but with a more modern spirit. One can also see related forms in the detail from a marriage certificate Hirsch designed for the Rodeph Shalom Congregation of Philadelphia.

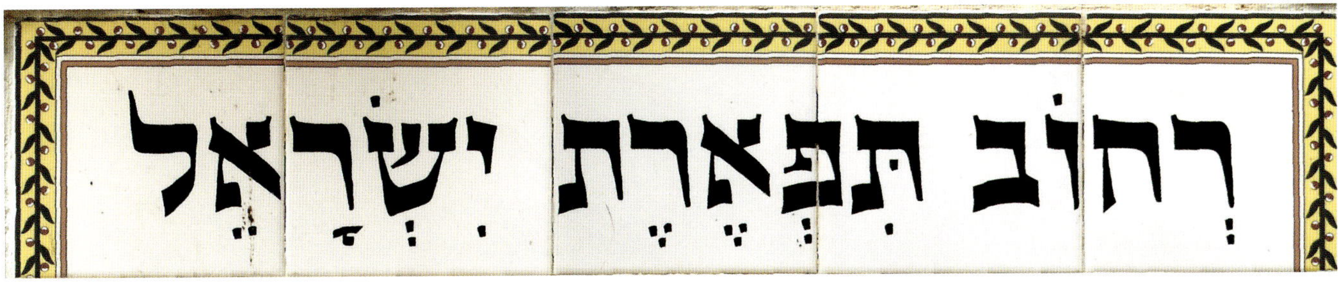

Joseph Hirsch
TOP: Lettering detail from part of a ketubah design, n.d.
BOTTOM: Lettering for street sign in the Jewish quarter, Jerusalem, designed in 1968

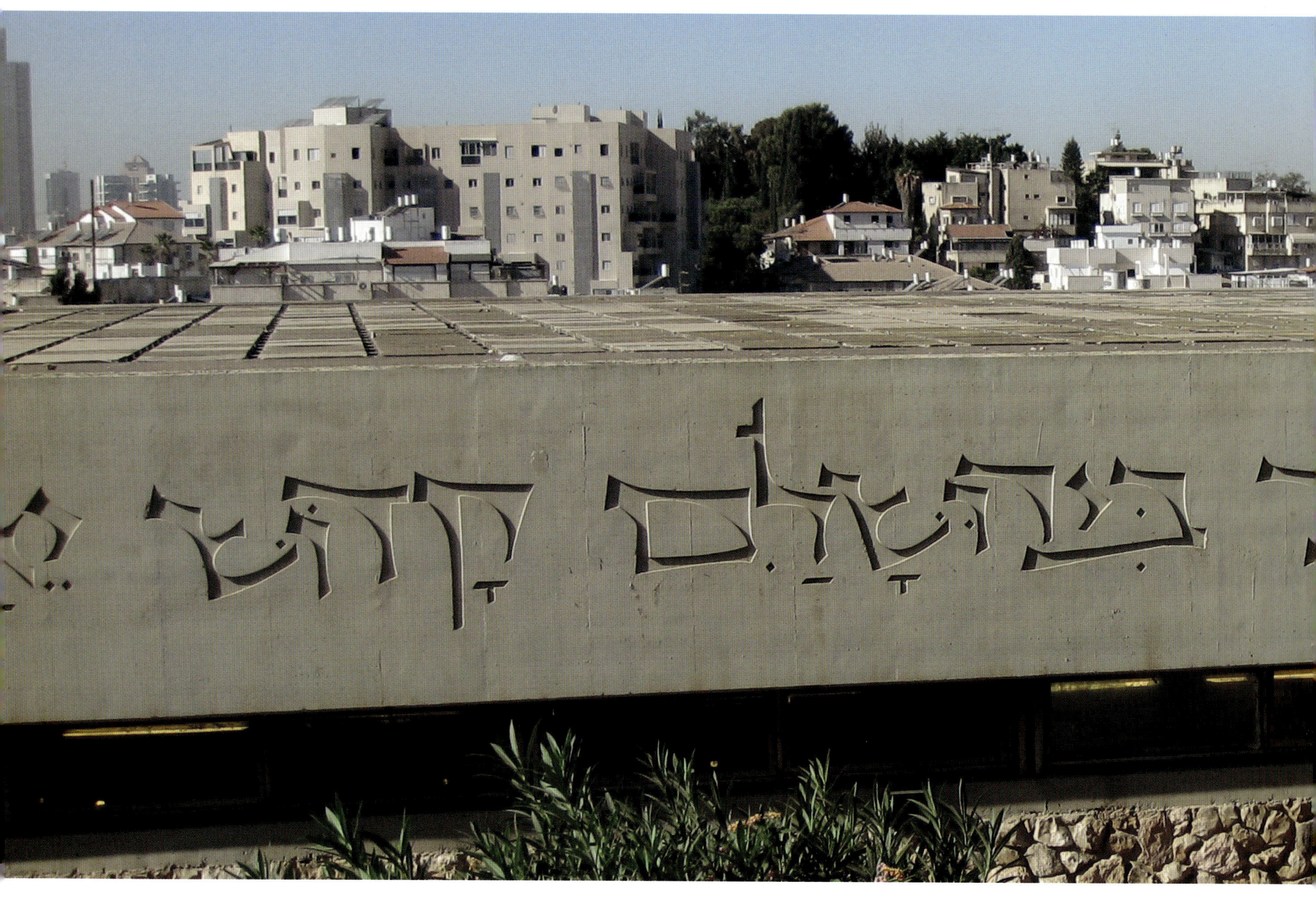

Carved lettering on the building of the Ponevezh Yeshivah, Bnei Brak, second half of twentieth century

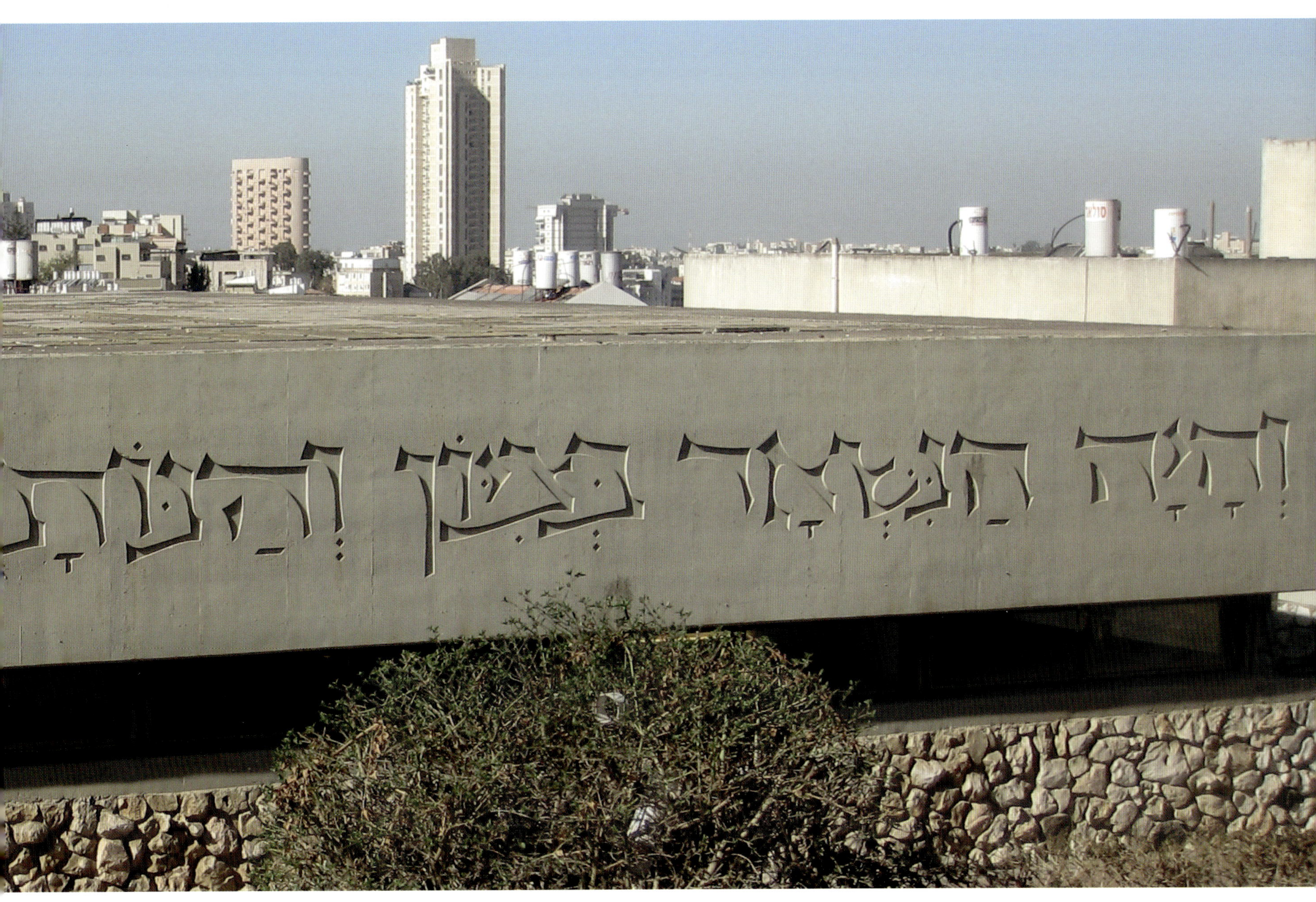

Unfortunately, I was not successful in finding out who designed these beautifully unconventional letters.

The ketubah—the Jewish marriage contract—often showcased fine Hebrew calligraphy and was usually produced on a single page. Here, however, is an unusual "book format" ketubah. Notice the phrase Ani l'dodi v'dodi li within the enlarged white initial bet. The phrase is also spelled out by the decorated letters within the text.

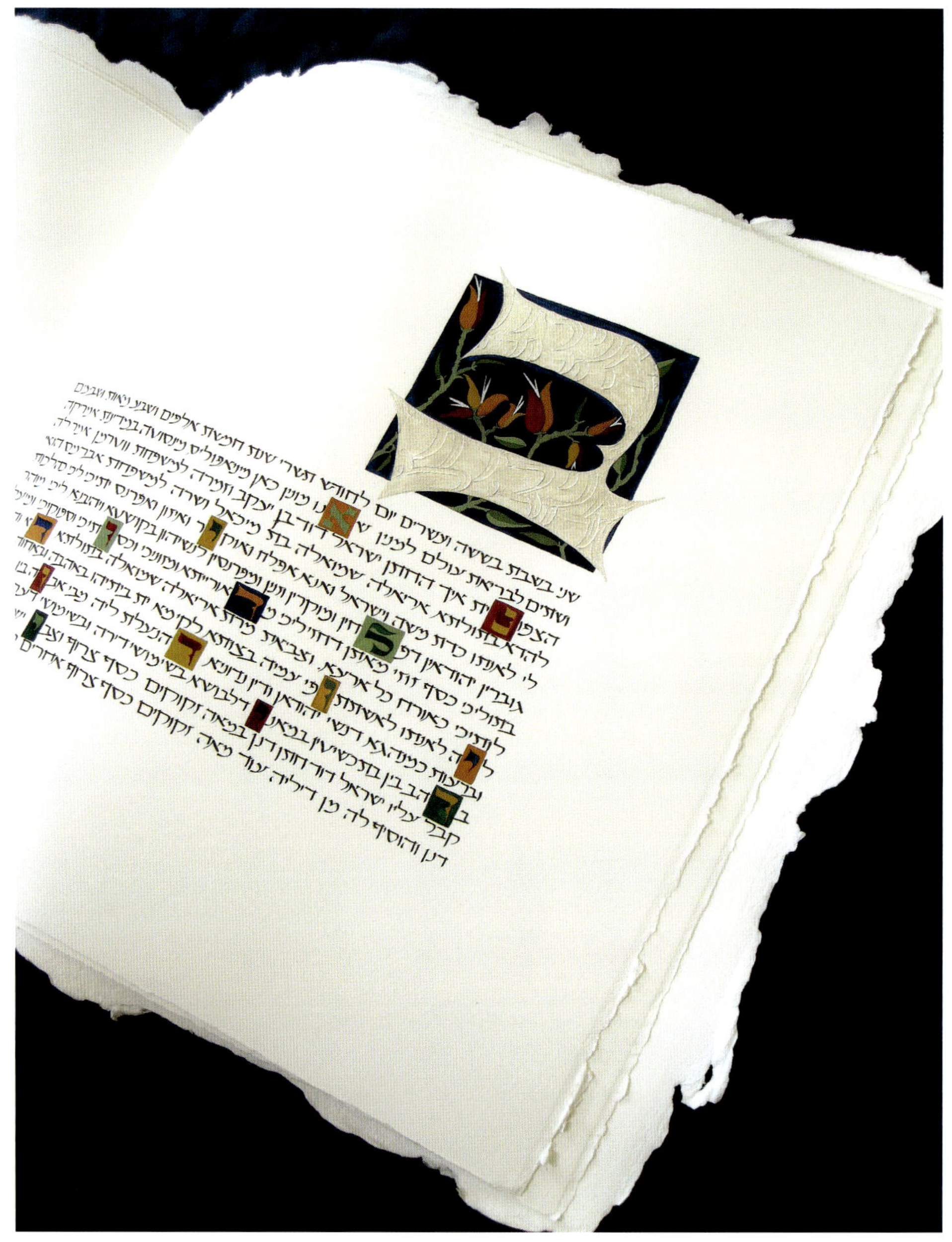

Karen Ness
Ketubah, 2011

The long, curved ending on some of the letters, such as on the bet and aleph of the enlarged initial word, gives movement and a slightly Arabic feel to the lettering.

Ted Scott Kadin
Ketubah, 2010

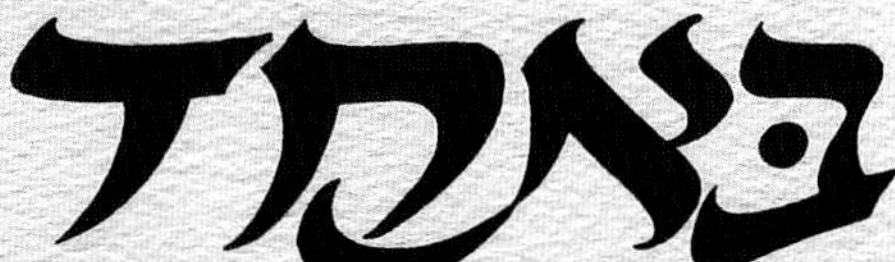

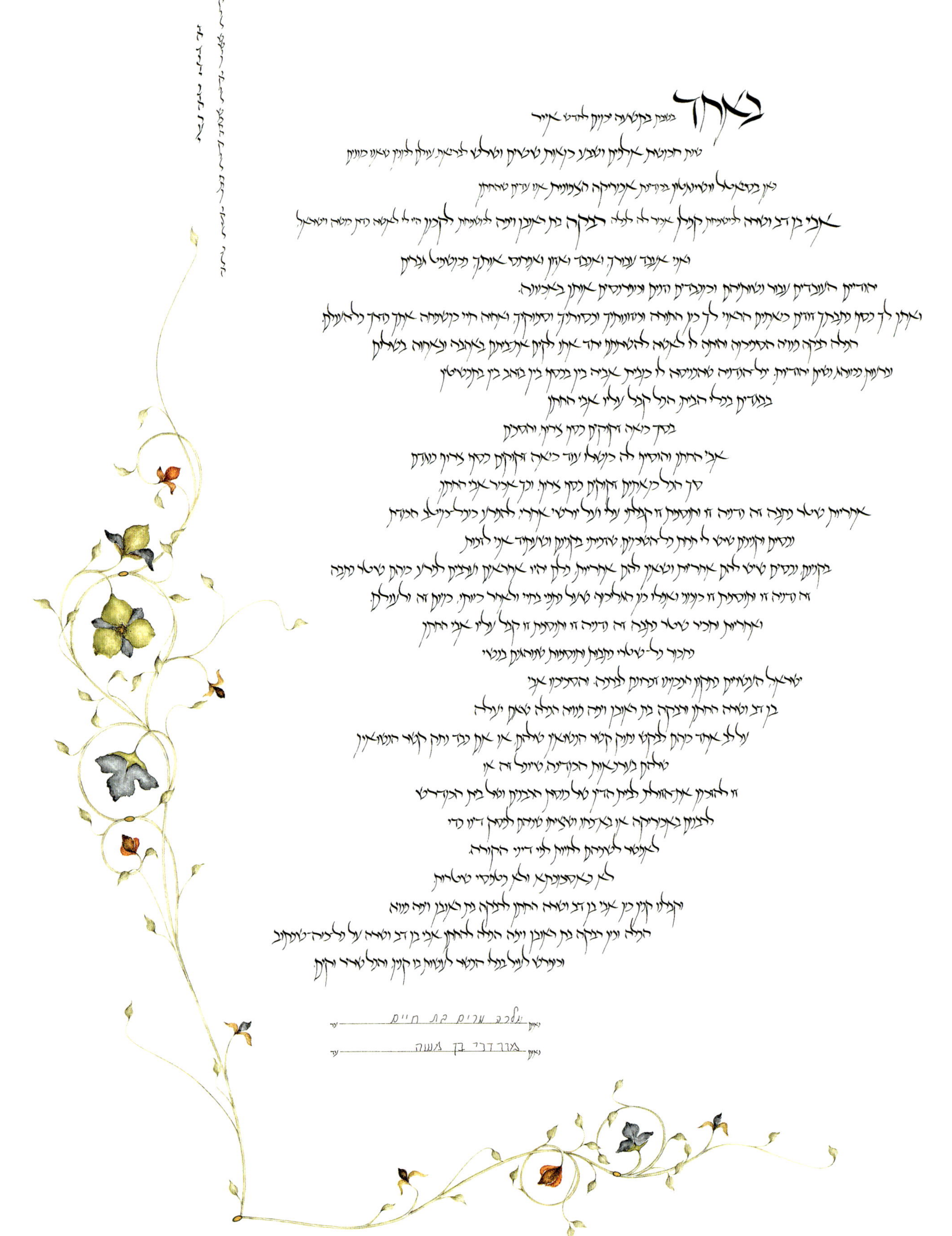

באחד בשבת בשבעה ימים לחדש אייר
שנת חמשת אלפים ושבע מאות ששים ושלש לבריאת
כאן בסיאטל וושינגטון במדינת אמריקה הצפונית אנו עדים שהחתן
דב ושרה למשפחת קהלן אמר לה לכלה רבקה בת ראובן ויפה למשפחת לוי

The liveliness of the writing gives a spirit of dancing, which matches the free-form movement in the layout of the ketubah text, shown on the facing page. Although the forms are technically "square forms," the (apparent) speed with which they were written gives them a cursive feel.

Gina Jonas
FACING PAGE: *Ketubah*, 2003
ABOVE: Enlarged detail of the writing

Although these letterforms are the same as those used for sacred objects, such as the Torah scroll, the artist here gives a certain "bounce" to the forms, which make them more fitting for a marriage contract.

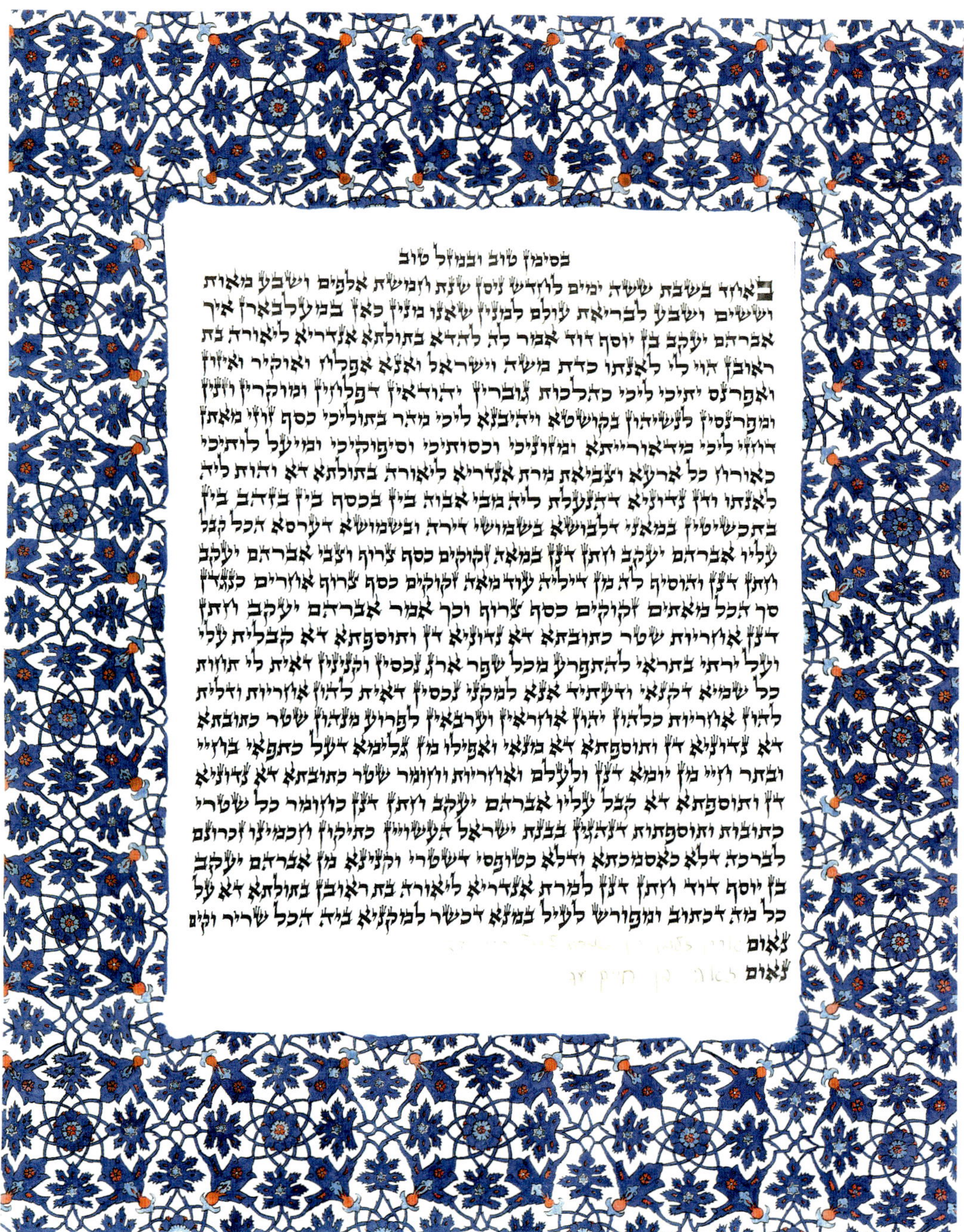

בסימן טוב ובמזל טוב

באחד בשבת ששה ימים לחדש ניסן שנת חמשת אלפים ושבע מאות
וששים ושבע לבריאת עולם למנין שאנו מונין כאן במעלבארן איר
אברהם יעקב בן יוסף דוד אמר לה להדא בתולתא אנדריא ליאורה בת
ראובן הוי לי לאנתו כדת משה וישראל ואנא אפלח ואוקיר ואיזון
ואפרנס יתיכי ליכי כהלכות גוברין יהודאין דפלחין ומוקרין וזנין
ומפרנסין לנשיהון בקושטא ויהיבנא ליכי מהר בתוליכי כסף זוזי מאתן
דחזי ליכי מדאורייתא ומזוניכי וכסותיכי וסיפוקיכי ומיעל לותיכי
כאורח כל ארעא וצביאת מרת אנדריא ליאורה בתולתא דא והות ליה
לאנתו ודן נדוניא דהנעלת ליה מבי אבוה בין בכסף בין בזהב בין
בתכשיטין במאני דלבושא בשמושי דירה ובשמושא דערסא הכל קבל
עליו אברהם יעקב חתן דנן במאה זקוקים כסף צרוף וצבי אברהם יעקב
חתן דנן והוסיף לה מן דיליה עוד מאה זקוקים כסף צרוף אחרים כנגדן
סך הכל מאתים זקוקים כסף צרוף וכך אמר אברהם יעקב חתן
דנן אחריות שטר כתובתא דא נדוניא דן ותוספתא דא קבלית עלי
ועל ירתי בתראי להתפרע מכל שפר ארג נכסין וקנינין דאית לי תחות
כל שמיא דקנאי ודעתיד אנא למקני נכסין דאית להון אחריות ודלית
להון אחריות כלהון יהון אחראין וערבאין לפרוע מנהון שטר כתובתא
דא נדוניא דן ותוספתא דא מנאי ואפילו מן גלימא דעל כתפאי בחיי
ובתר חיי מן יומא דנן ולעלם ואחריות וחומר שטר כתובתא דא נדוניא
דן ותוספתא דא קבל עליו אברהם יעקב חתן דנן כחומר כל שטרי
כתובות ותוספתות דנהגין בבנת ישראל העשויין כתיקון חכמינו זכרונם
לברכה דלא כאסמכתא ודלא כטופסי דשטרי וקנינא מן אברהם יעקב
בן יוסף דוד חתן דנן למרת אנדריא ליאורה בת ראובן בתולתא דא על
כל מה דכתוב ומפורש לעיל במנא דכשר למקניא ביה הכל שריר וקים
נאום
נאום

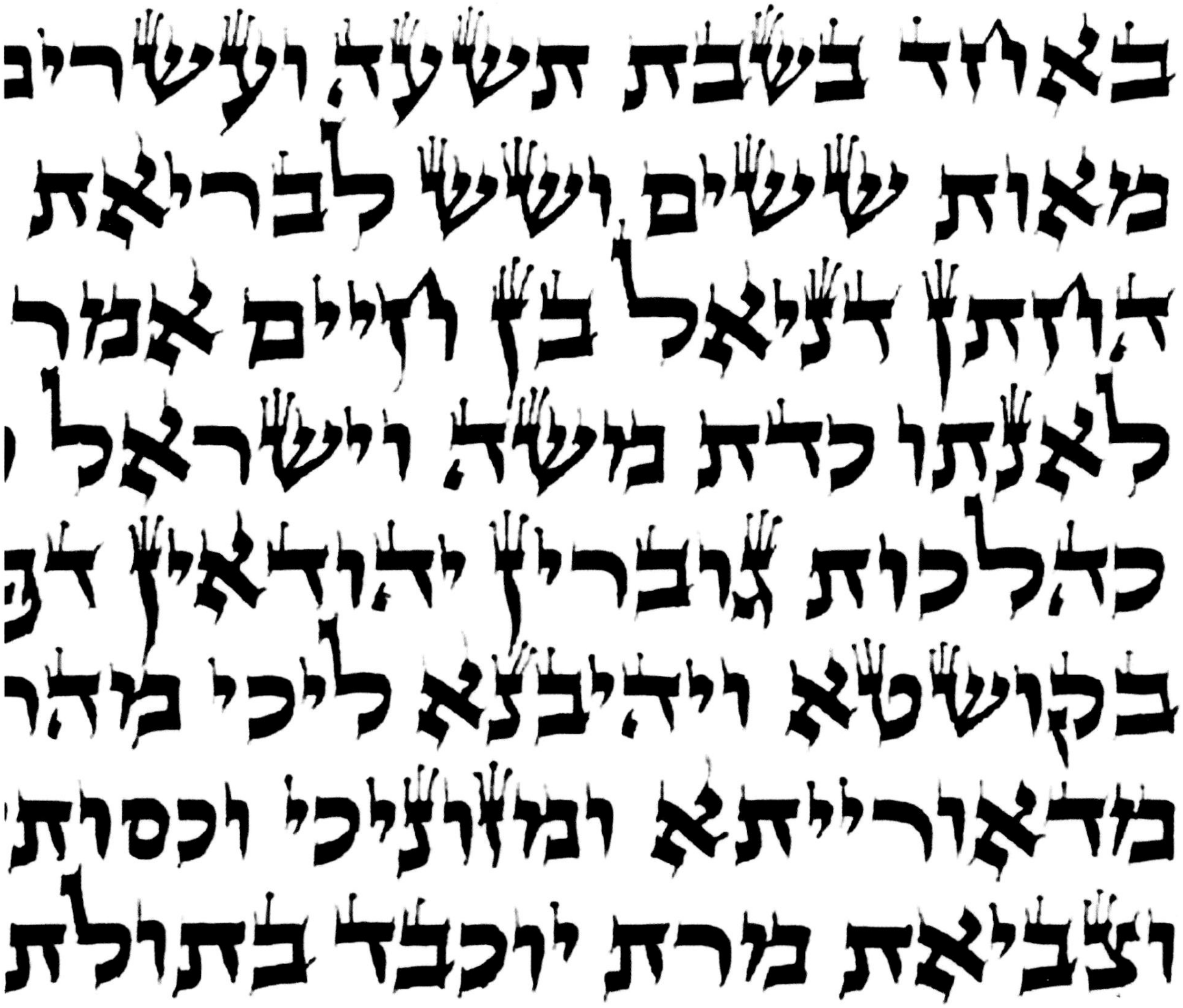

באחד בשבת תשעה ועשרי

מאות ששים ושש לבריאת

החתן דניאל בן חיים אמר

לאנתו כדת משה וישראל

כהלכות גוברין יהודאין ד

בקושטא ויהיבנא ליכי מהר

מדאורייתא ומזוניכי וכסות

וצביאת מרת יוכבד בתולת

Josh Baum
FACING PAGE: *Ketubah*, 2007
ABOVE: Enlarged detail of writing, 2006

אני ישנה ולבי ער קול דודי דופק
פתחי לי אחתי רעיתי יונתי תמתי
שראשי נמלא טל קווצותי רסיסי לי
פשטתי את כתנתי איככה אלבשני
רחצתי את רגלי איככה אטנפם :
דודי שלח ידו מן החר ומעי המו
קמתי אני לפתח לדודי וידי נטפו
ואצבעתי מור עבר על כפות המנ
פתחתי אני לדודי ודודי חמק עב
נפשי יצאה בדברו בקשתיהו ול

Letters based on, and modernized from, a study of Italian semi-cursive forms.

Izzy Pludwinski
Page from a *Song of Songs (Shir Hashirim)* book, 2020

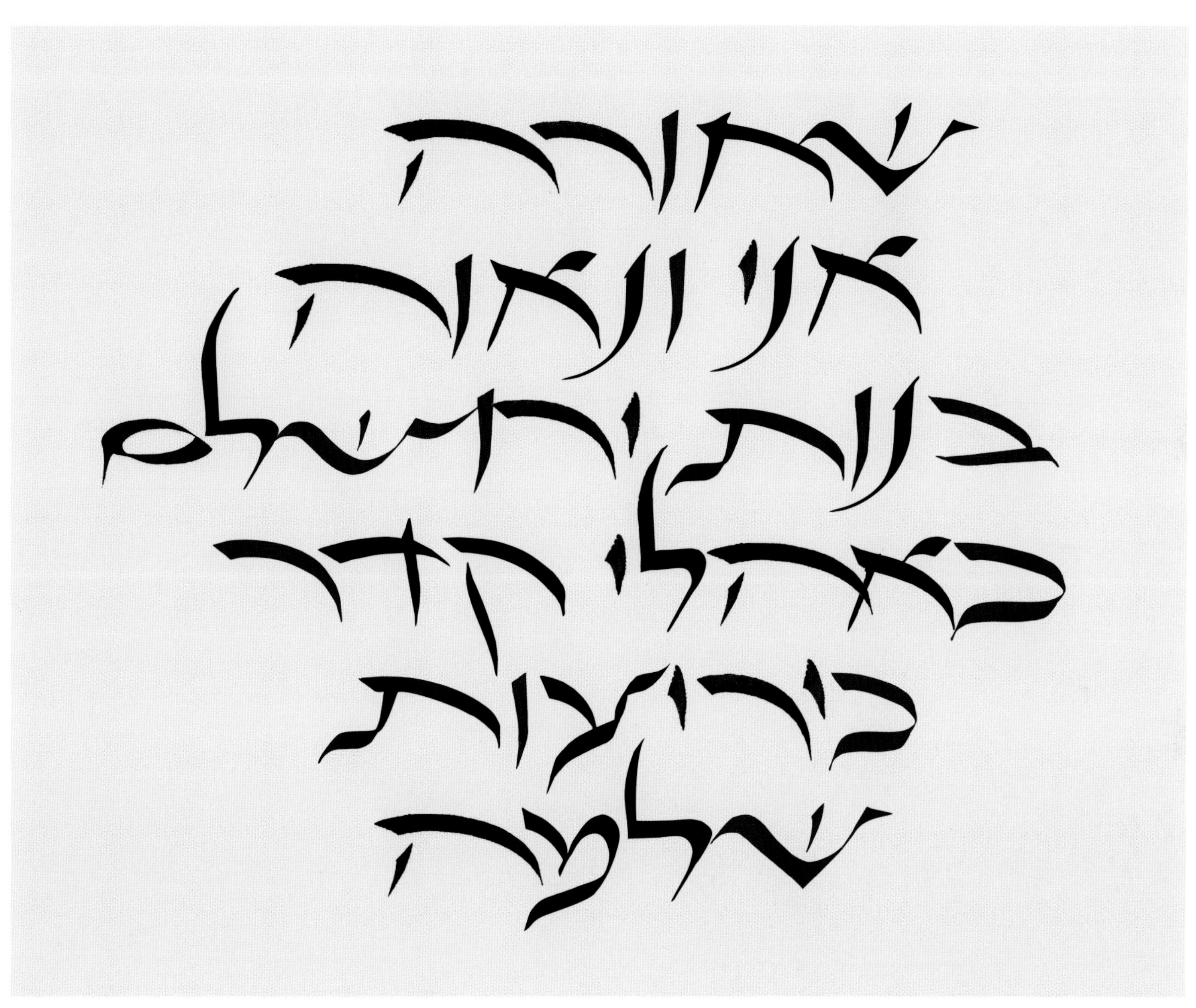

These letters were designed to be gilded for chapter openings for an edition of the Song of Songs.

Izzy Pludwinski
I Am Dark and Beautiful . . . , 2018

The field of Hebrew typography is too vast a subject to be represented properly in this book. Here are two digital fonts that came directly out of calligraphic trials.

Shir, shown here, is an experiment at a non-monorythmic font, incorporating mostly handwritten forms.

יִשָּׁקֵנִי מִנְּשִׁיקוֹת פִּיהוּ כִּי-טוֹבִים דֹּדֶיךָ מִיָּיִן: לְרֵיחַ
שְׁמָנֶיךָ טוֹבִים שֶׁמֶן תּוּרַק שְׁמֶךָ עַל-כֵּן עֲלָמוֹת
אֲהֵבוּךָ: מָשְׁכֵנִי אַחֲרֶיךָ נָּרוּצָה הֱבִיאַנִי הַמֶּלֶךְ
חֲדָרָיו נָגִילָה וְנִשְׂמְחָה בָּךְ נַזְכִּירָה דֹדֶיךָ מִיַּיִן
מֵישָׁרִים אֲהֵבוּךָ: שְׁחוֹרָה אֲנִי וְנָאוָה בְּנוֹת יְרוּשָׁלָםִ
כְּאָהֳלֵי קֵדָר כִּירִיעוֹת שְׁלֹמֹה: אַל-תִּרְאוּנִי שֶׁאֲנִי
שְׁחַרְחֹרֶת שֶׁשֱּׁזָפַתְנִי הַשָּׁמֶשׁ בְּנֵי אִמִּי נִחֲרוּ-בִי

Izzy Pludwinski
Digital font *Shir* used for a limited edition of the *Song of Songs*, 1999

This font, Ashkanizzy, *is based on an informal Square Ashkenazic calligraphic script and was developed for a commissioned, special edition of* Chumash *(Pentateuch).*

כַדָּהּ וַתָּעַל׃ יז וַיָּרָץ הָעֶבֶד לִקְרָאתָהּ וַיֹּאמֶר הַגְמִיאִינִי
נָא מְעַט מַיִם מִכַּדֵּךְ׃ יח וַתֹּאמֶר שְׁתֵה אֲדֹנִי וַתְּמַהֵר
וַתֹּרֶד כַּדָּהּ עַל יָדָהּ וַתַּשְׁקֵהוּ׃ יט וַתְּכַל לְהַשְׁקֹתוֹ
וַתֹּאמֶר גַּם לִגְמַלֶּיךָ אֶשְׁאָב עַד אִם כִּלּוּ לִשְׁתֹּת׃
כ וַתְּמַהֵר וַתְּעַר כַּדָּהּ אֶל הַשֹּׁקֶת וַתָּרָץ עוֹד אֶל
הַבְּאֵר לִשְׁאֹב וַתִּשְׁאַב לְכָל גְּמַלָּיו׃ כא וְהָאִישׁ
מִשְׁתָּאֵה לָהּ מַחֲרִישׁ לָדַעַת הַהִצְלִיחַ יהוה דַּרְכּוֹ
אִם לֹא׃ כב וַיְהִי כַּאֲשֶׁר כִּלּוּ הַגְּמַלִּים לִשְׁתּוֹת וַיִּקַּח
הָאִישׁ נֶזֶם זָהָב בֶּקַע מִשְׁקָלוֹ וּשְׁנֵי צְמִידִים עַל יָדֶיהָ
עֲשָׂרָה זָהָב מִשְׁקָלָם׃ כג וַיֹּאמֶר בַּת מִי אַתְּ הַגִּידִי נָא
לִי הֲיֵשׁ בֵּית אָבִיךְ מָקוֹם לָנוּ לָלִין׃ כד וַתֹּאמֶר אֵלָיו

Izzy Pludwinski
Digital font *Ashkanizzy*, designed for a Pentateuch, 2014

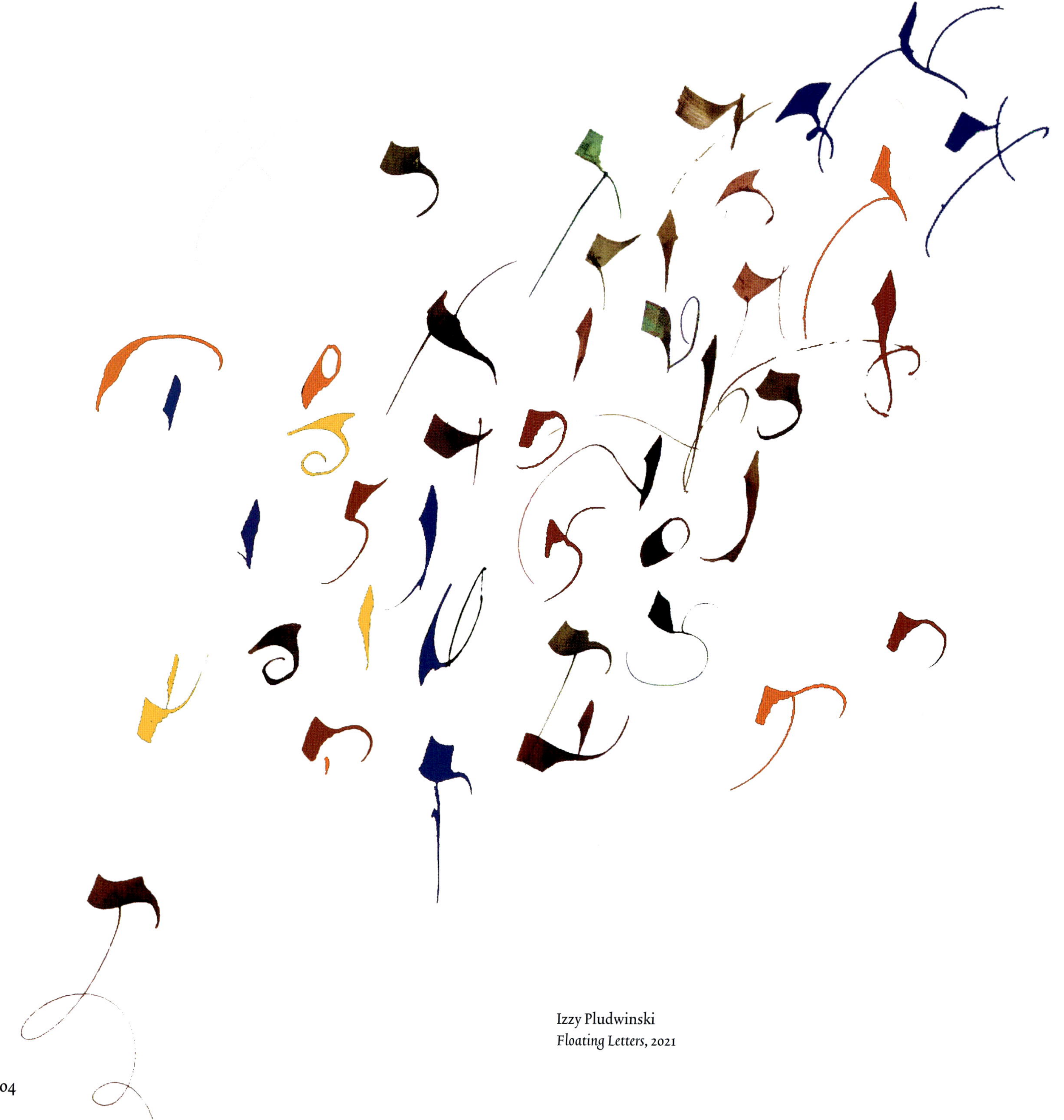

Izzy Pludwinski
Floating Letters, 2021

3

Aleph-bets & Letters

Many calligraphers, typographers, and lettering artists enjoy playing and experimenting with individual letters or entire aleph-bets for their own sake, releasing them from words and literal content, focusing solely on producing interesting compositions.

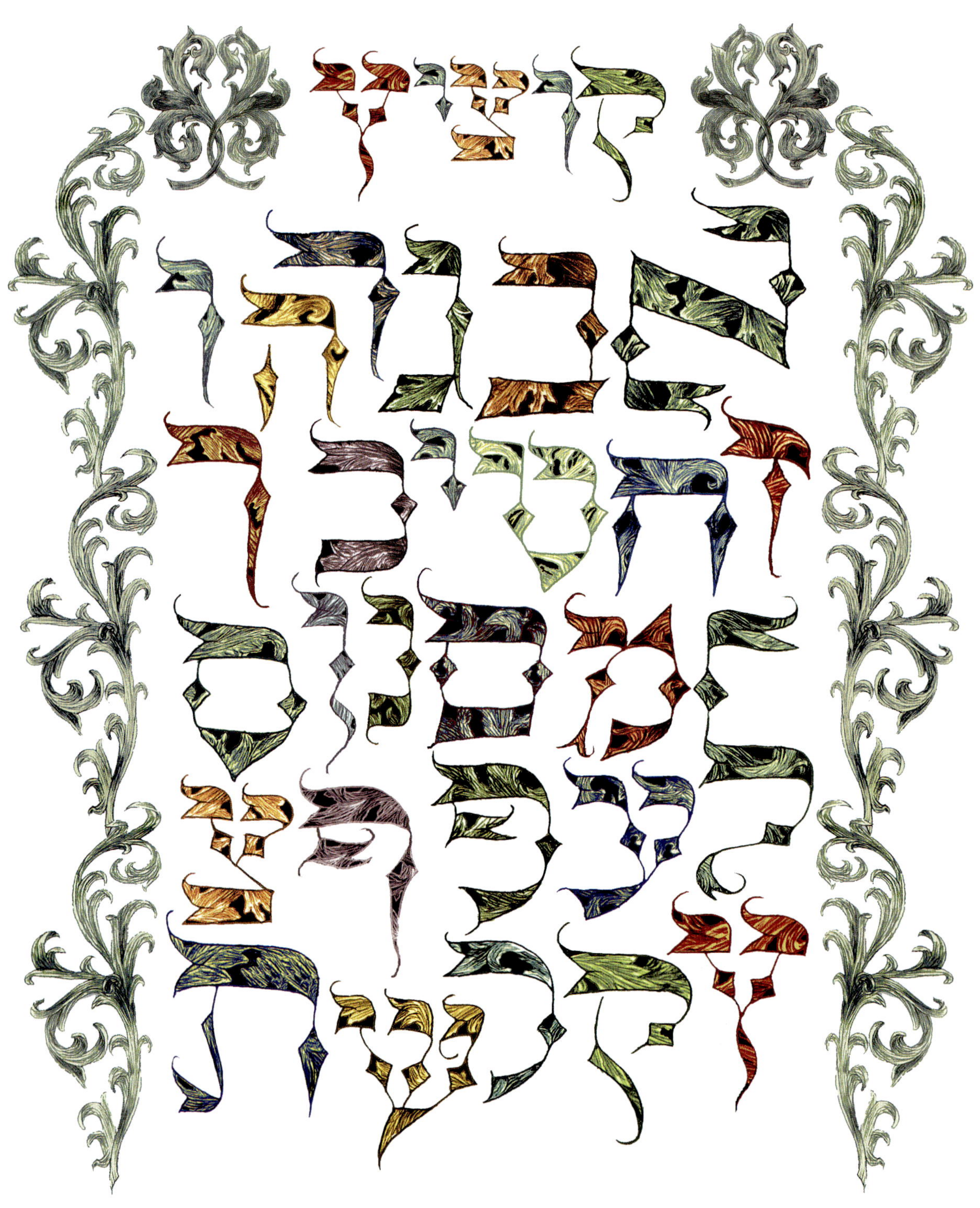

Ilene Winn-Lederer
Acanthus Hebrew Aleph-bet, 2012

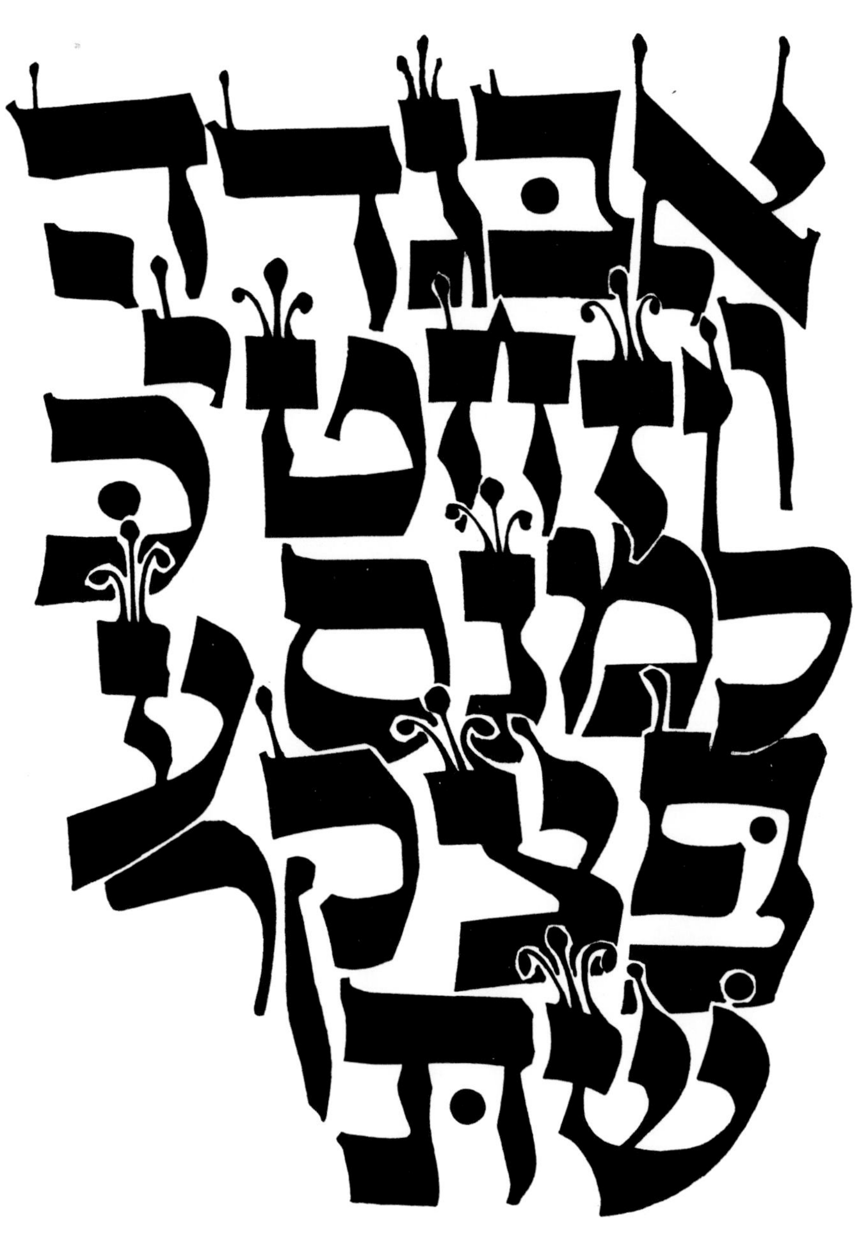

Lawrence Kushner
Hebrew Aleph-bet, c. 1975

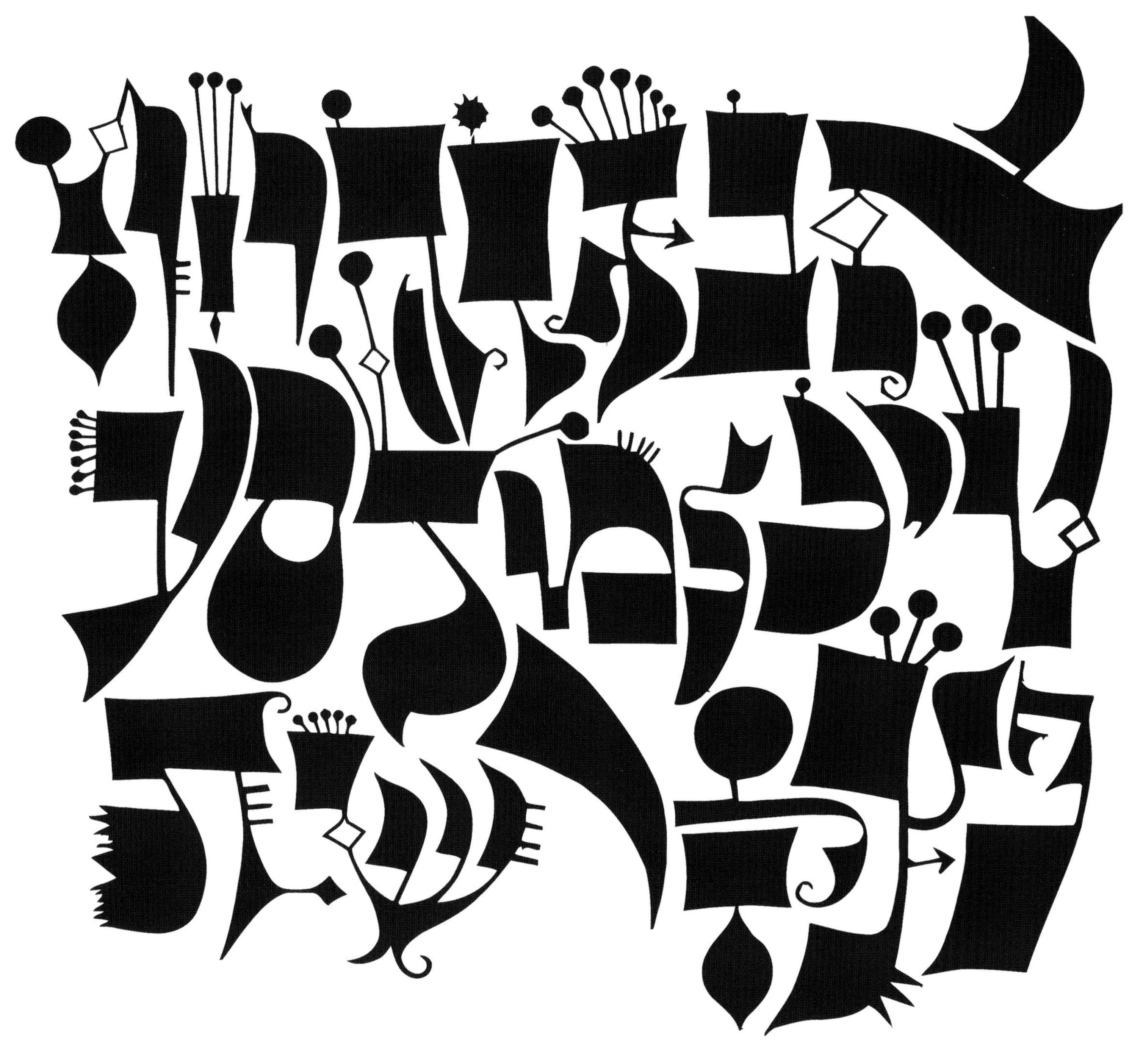

Josh Baum
Hebrew Aleph-bet, 2002

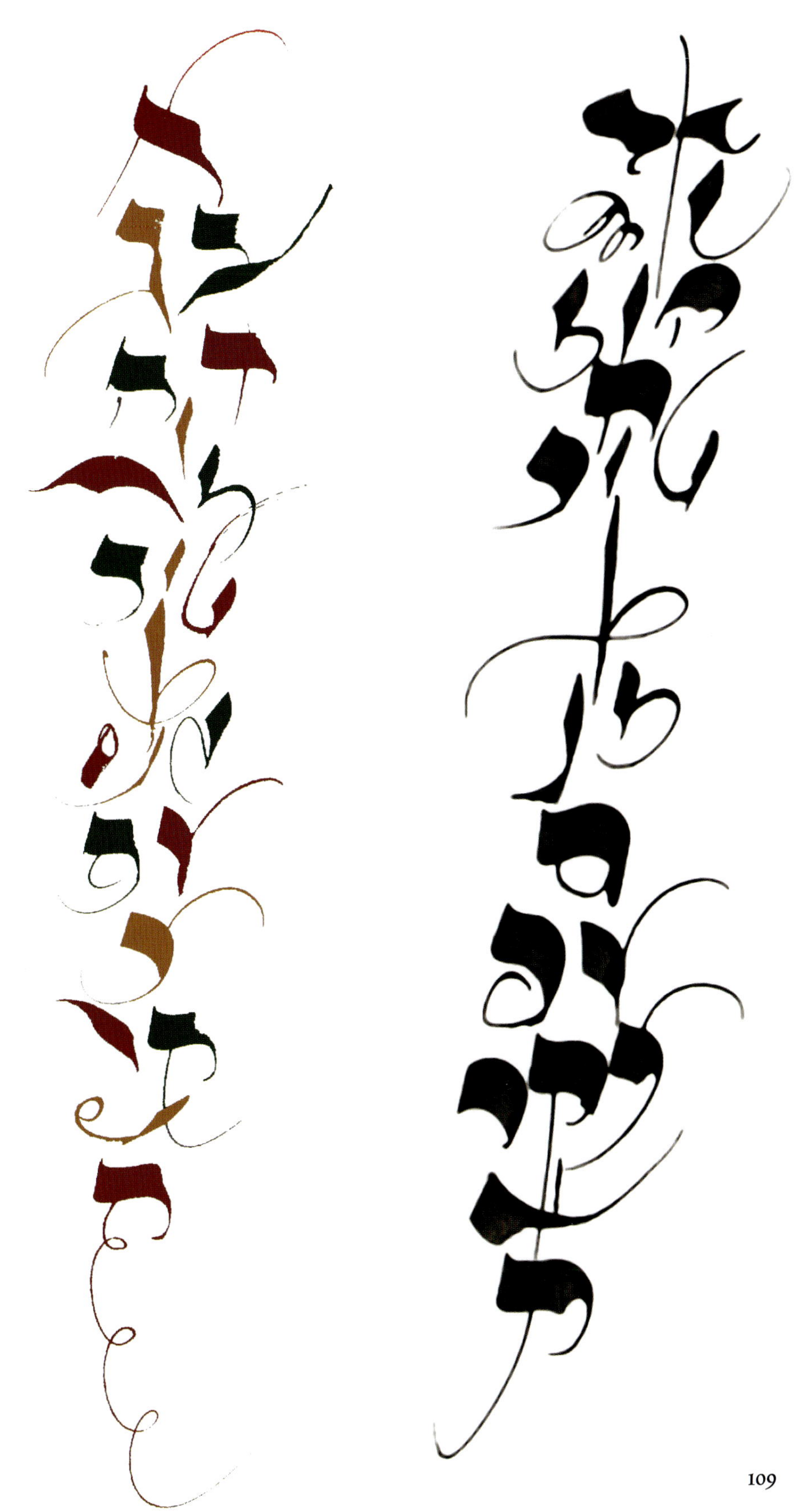

Izzy Pludwinski
Hebrew Aleph-bets, 2016

Izzy Pludwinski
Hebrew Aleph-bet, 2022

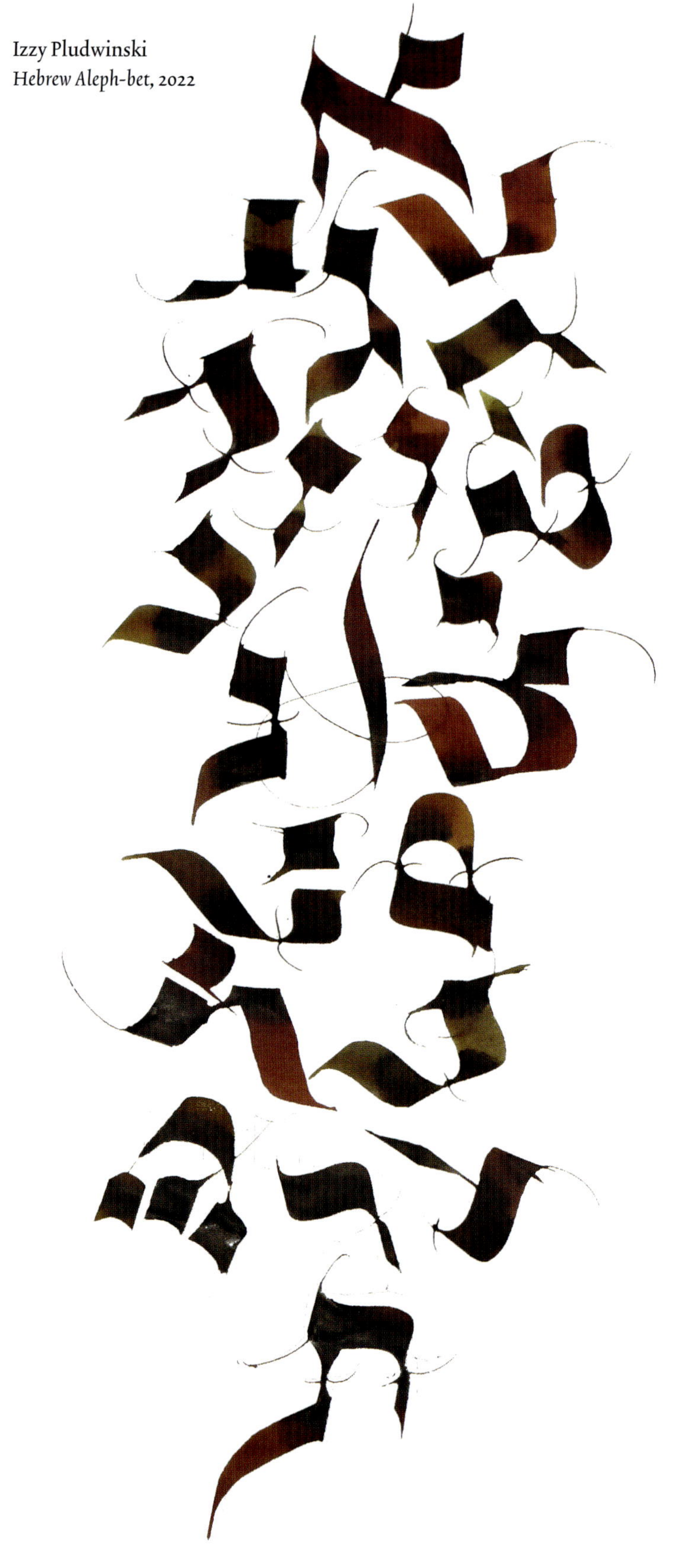

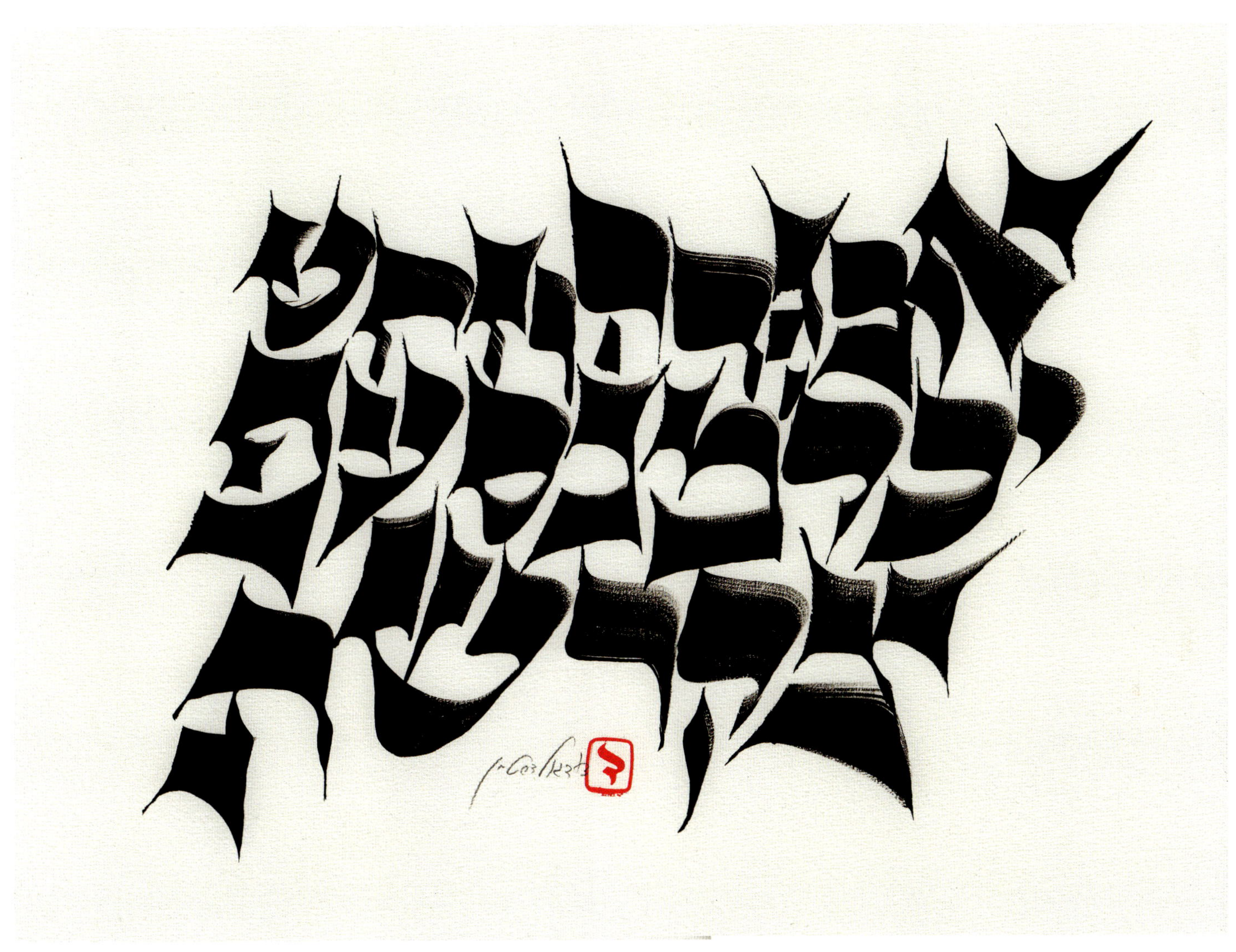

David Goldstein
Hebrew Aleph-bet, 2021

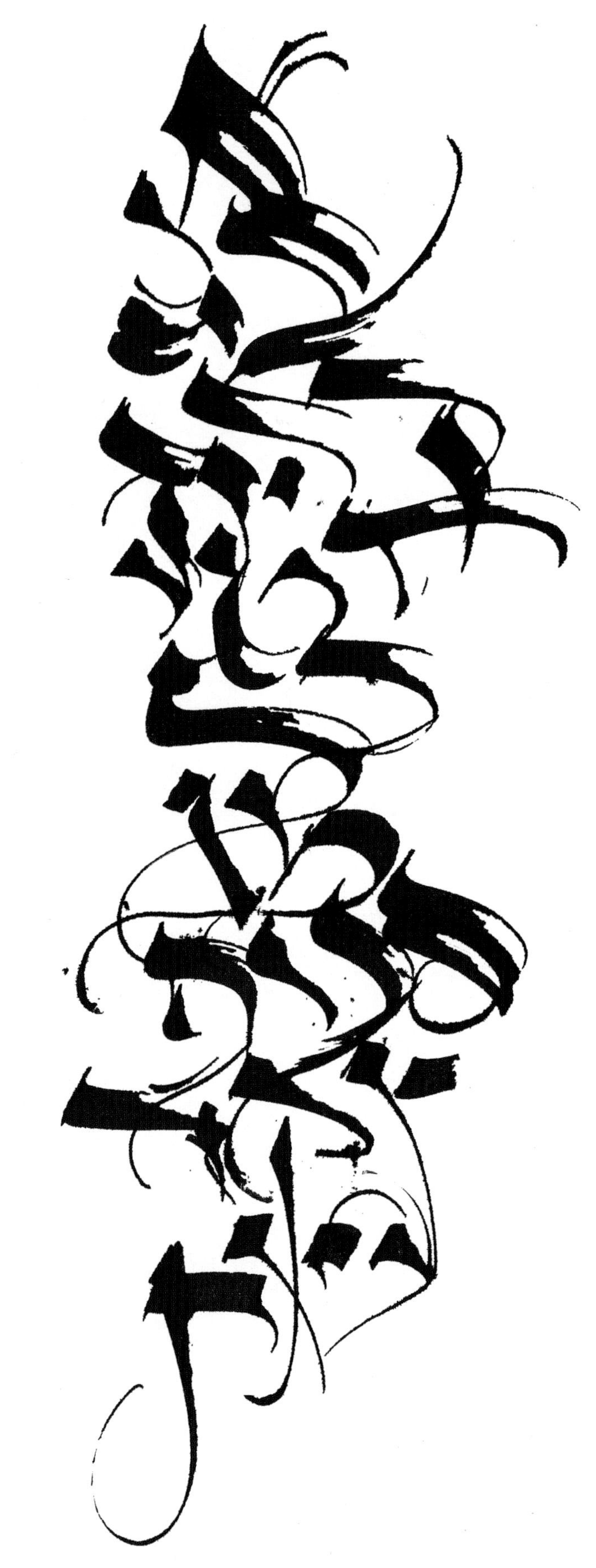

David Goldstein
Aleph-bet, 2020

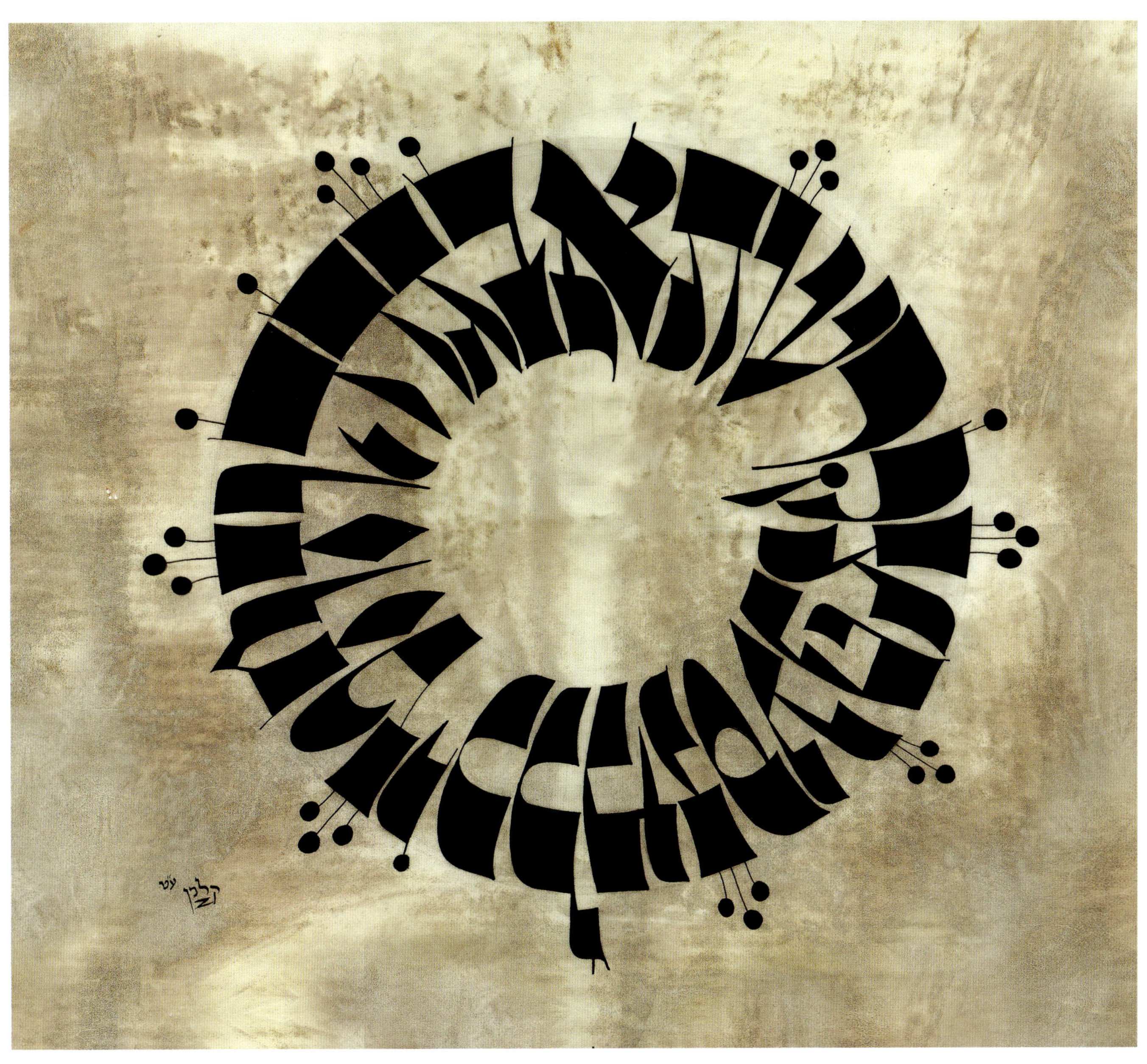

Kalman Gavriel
Alef-bet Circle, 2018

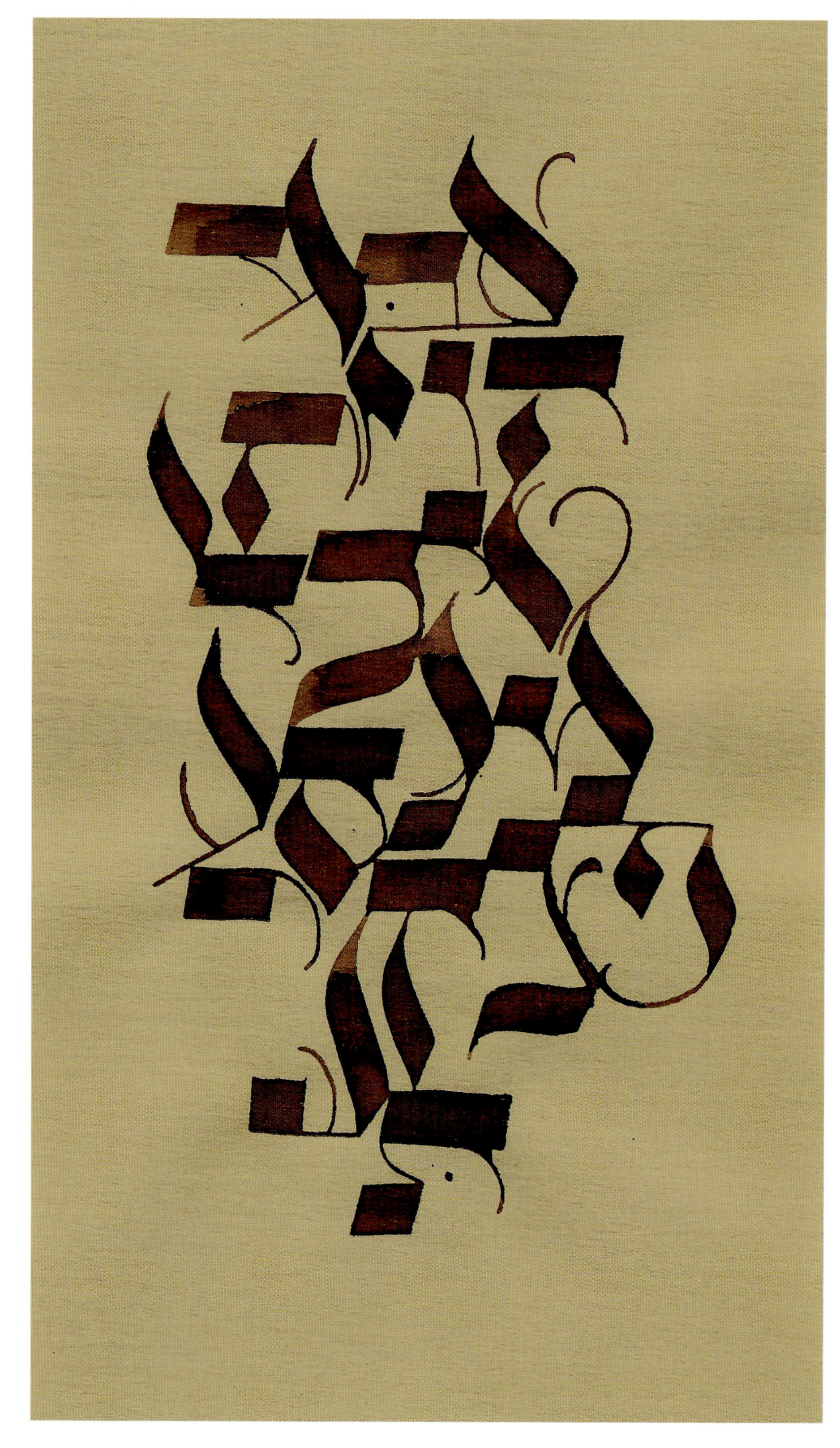

Elhanan Ben Uri
Alef-bet, 2019

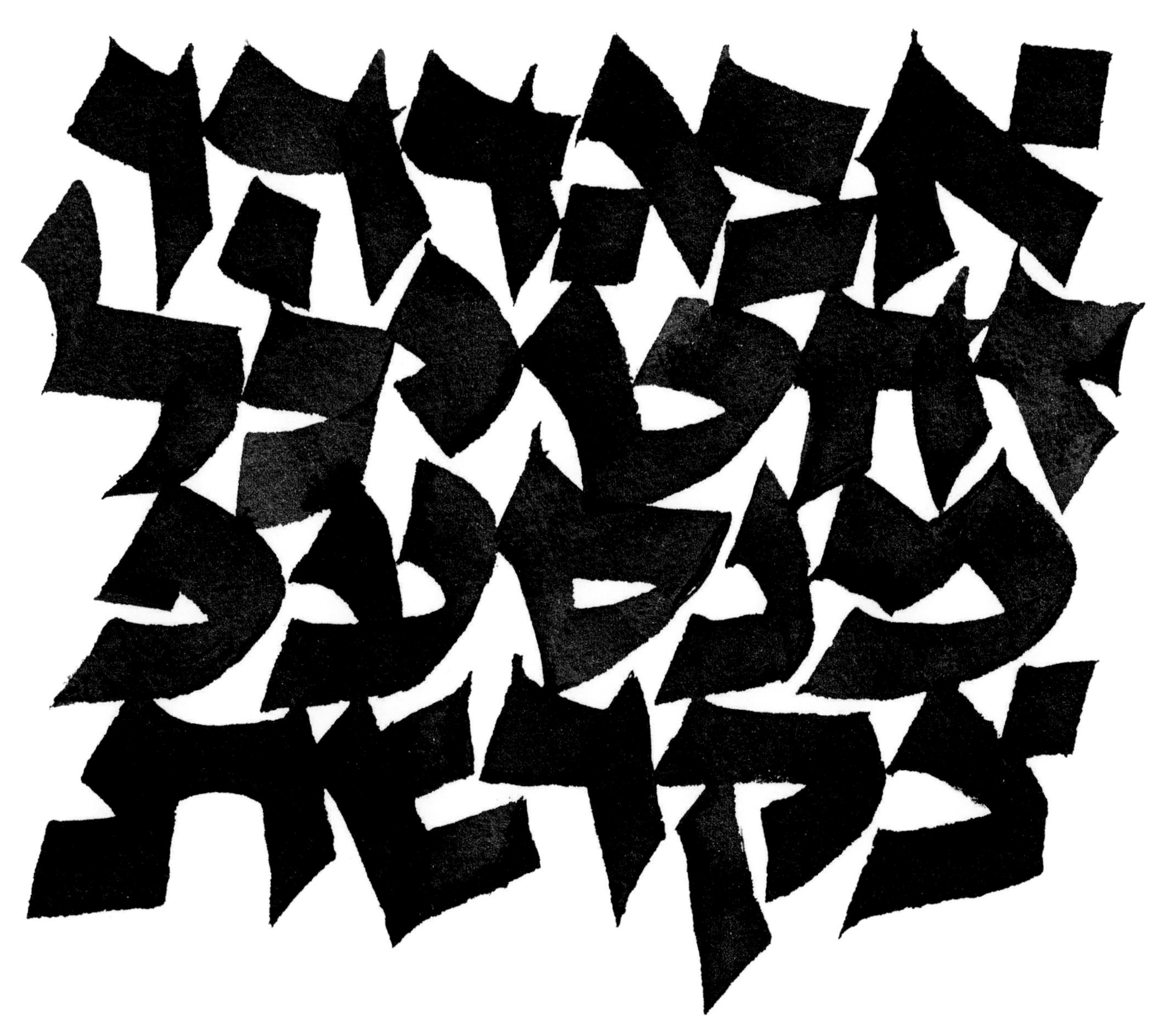

David Goldstein
Hebrew Aleph-bet, 2021

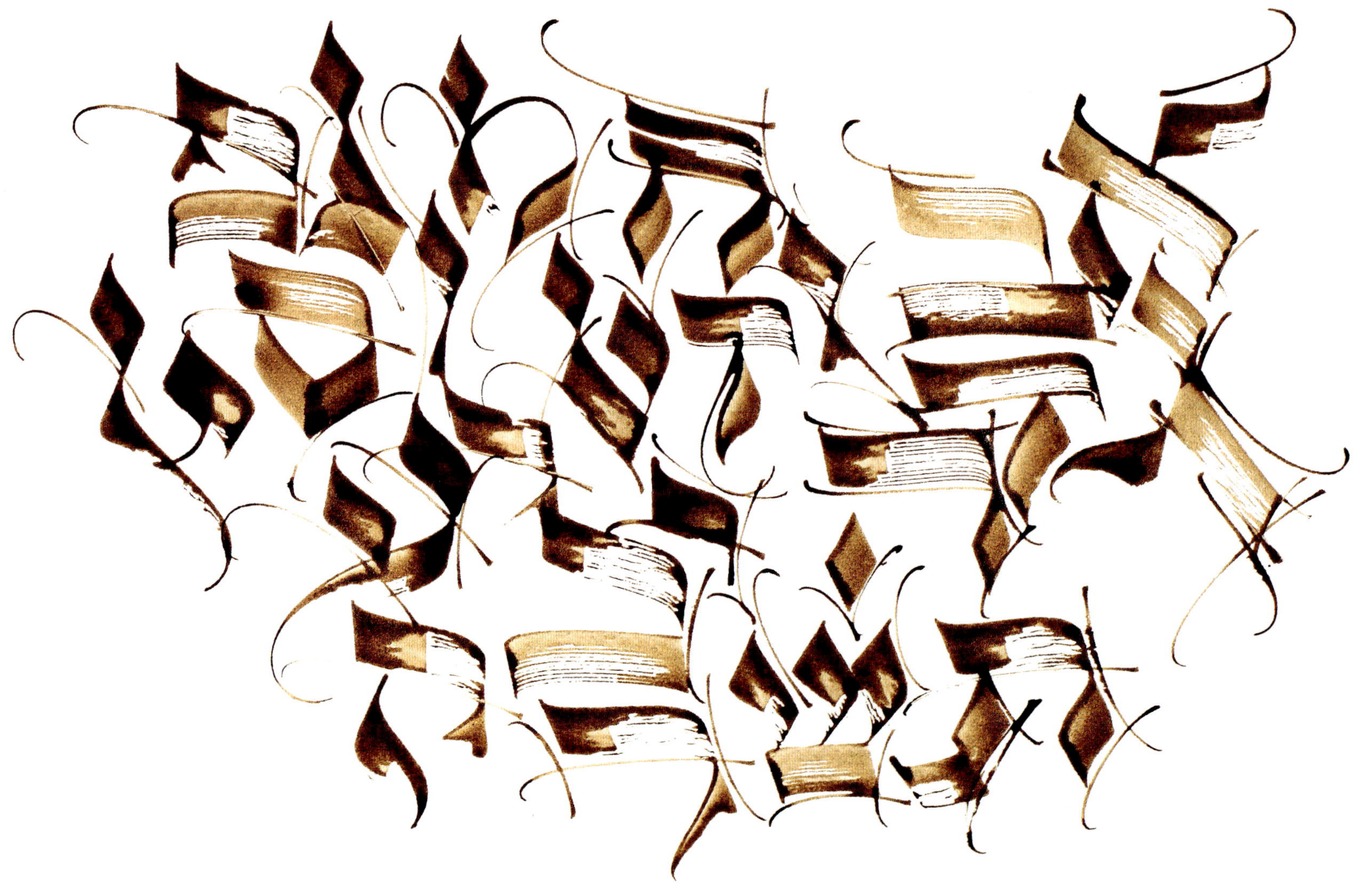

Michel D'Anastasio
Aleph-bet, 2012

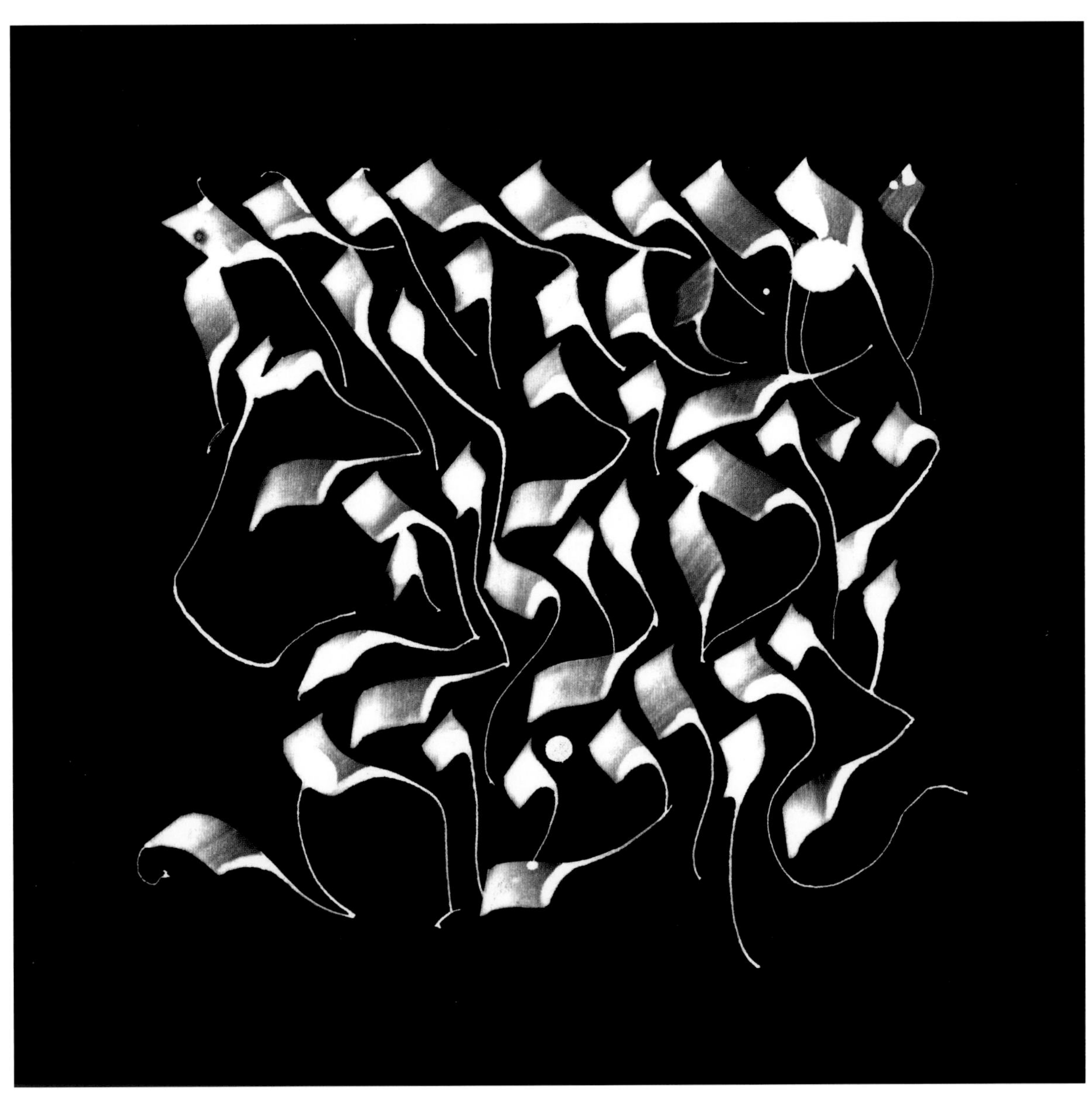

Shiri Lanzer
Aleph-bet, 2014

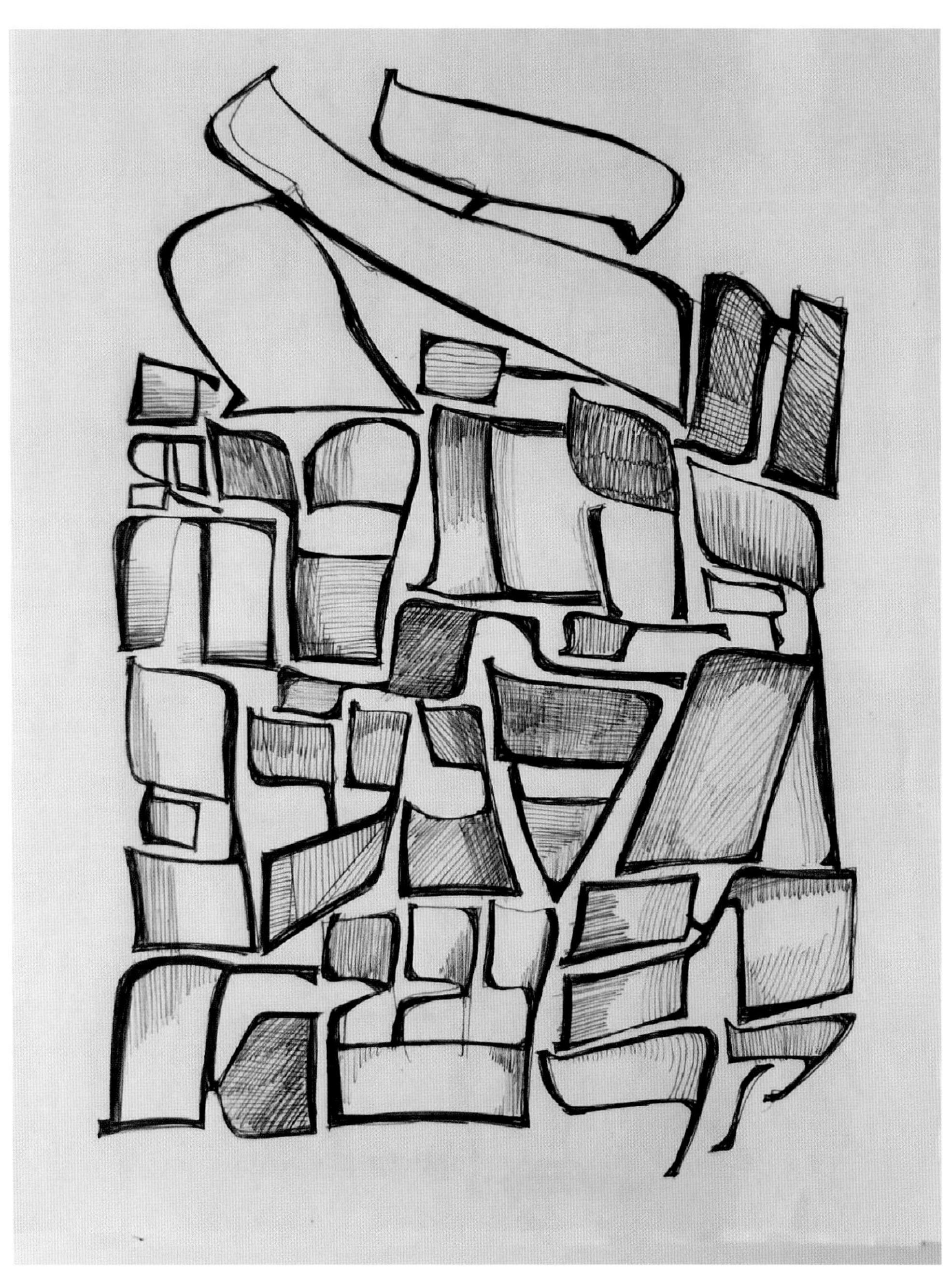

Lynn Broide
Aleph-bet, c. 2019

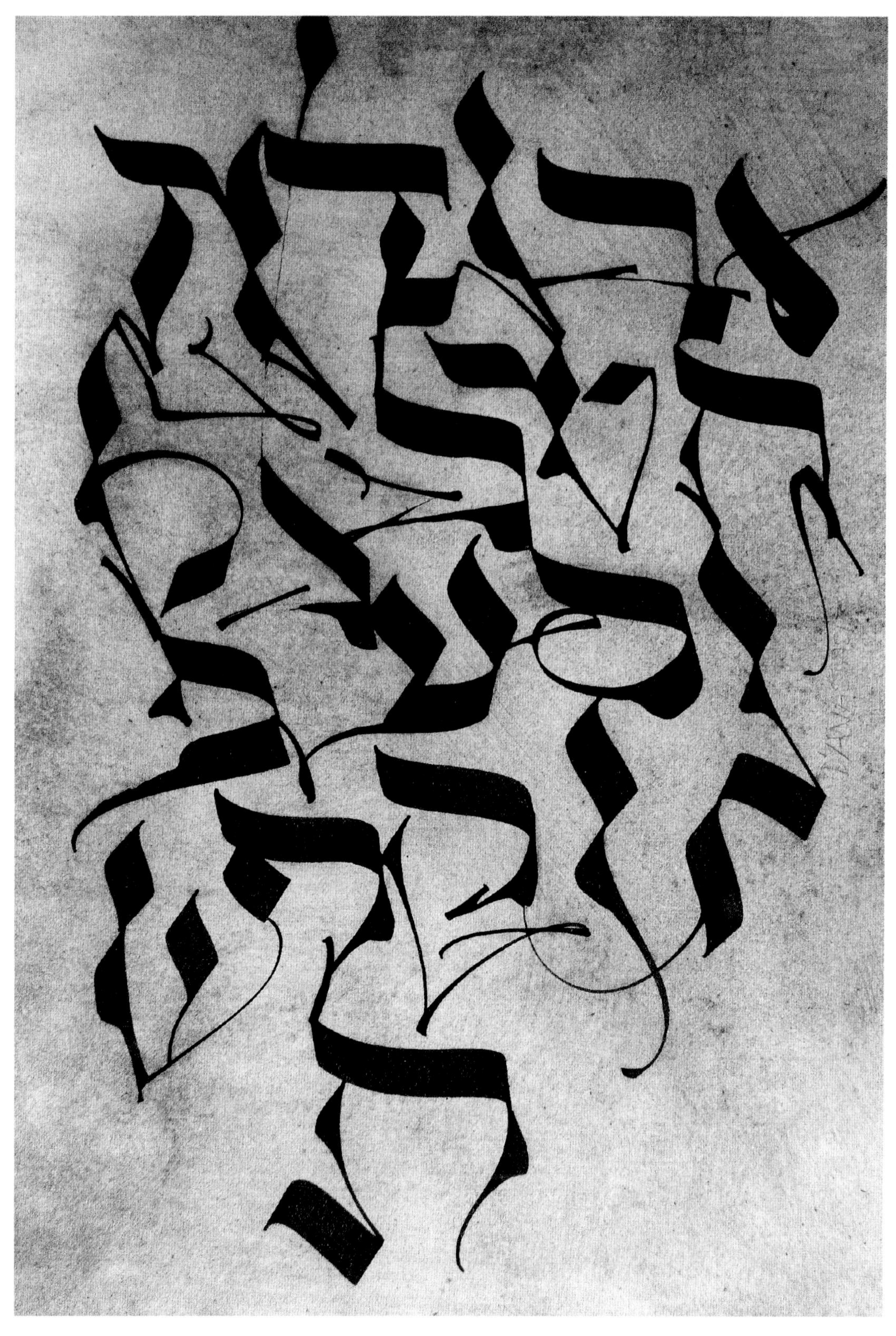

Michel D'Anastasio
Hebrew Aleph-bet, 2016

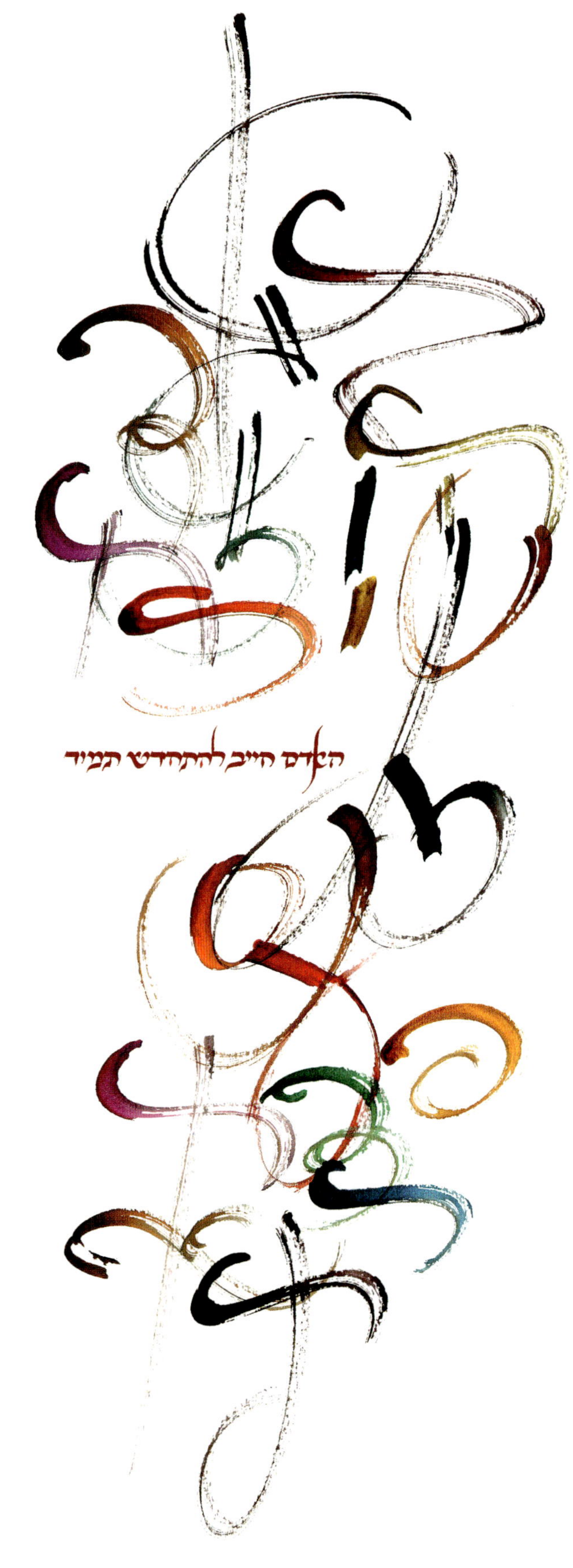

Izzy Pludwinski
Cursive Hebrew Aleph-bet, 1995

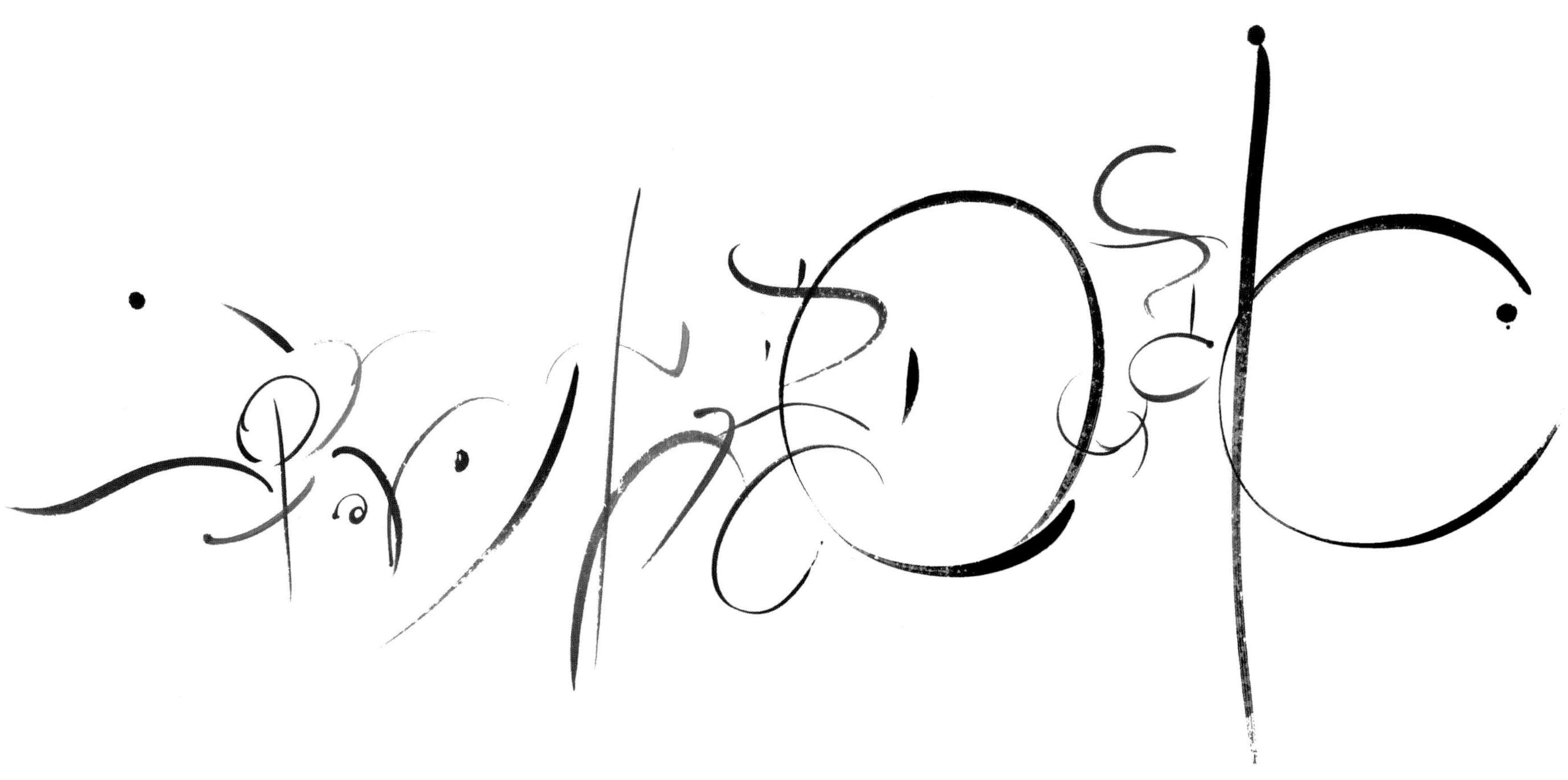

Izzy Pludwinski
Brush Aleph-bet, 2007

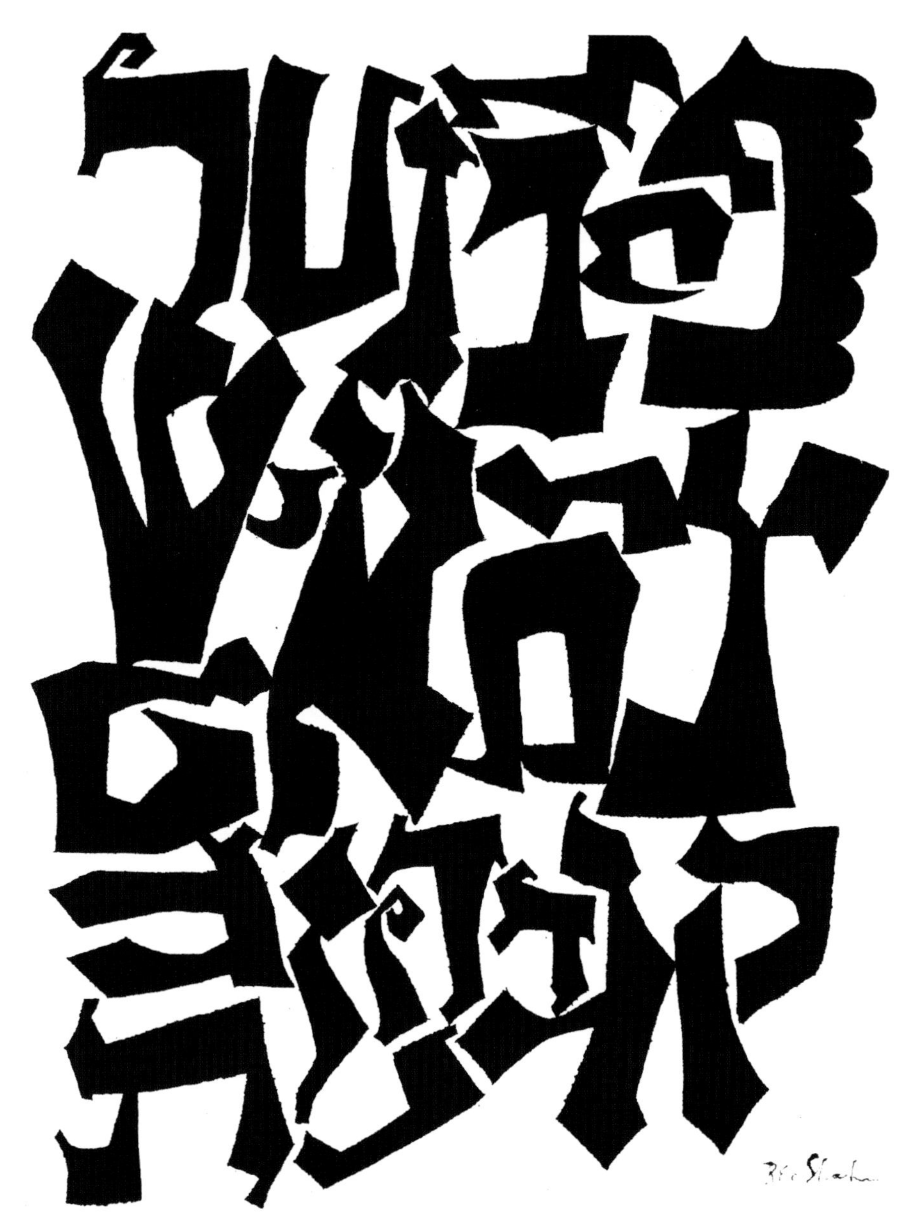

Ben Shahn
Aleph-bet, 1954

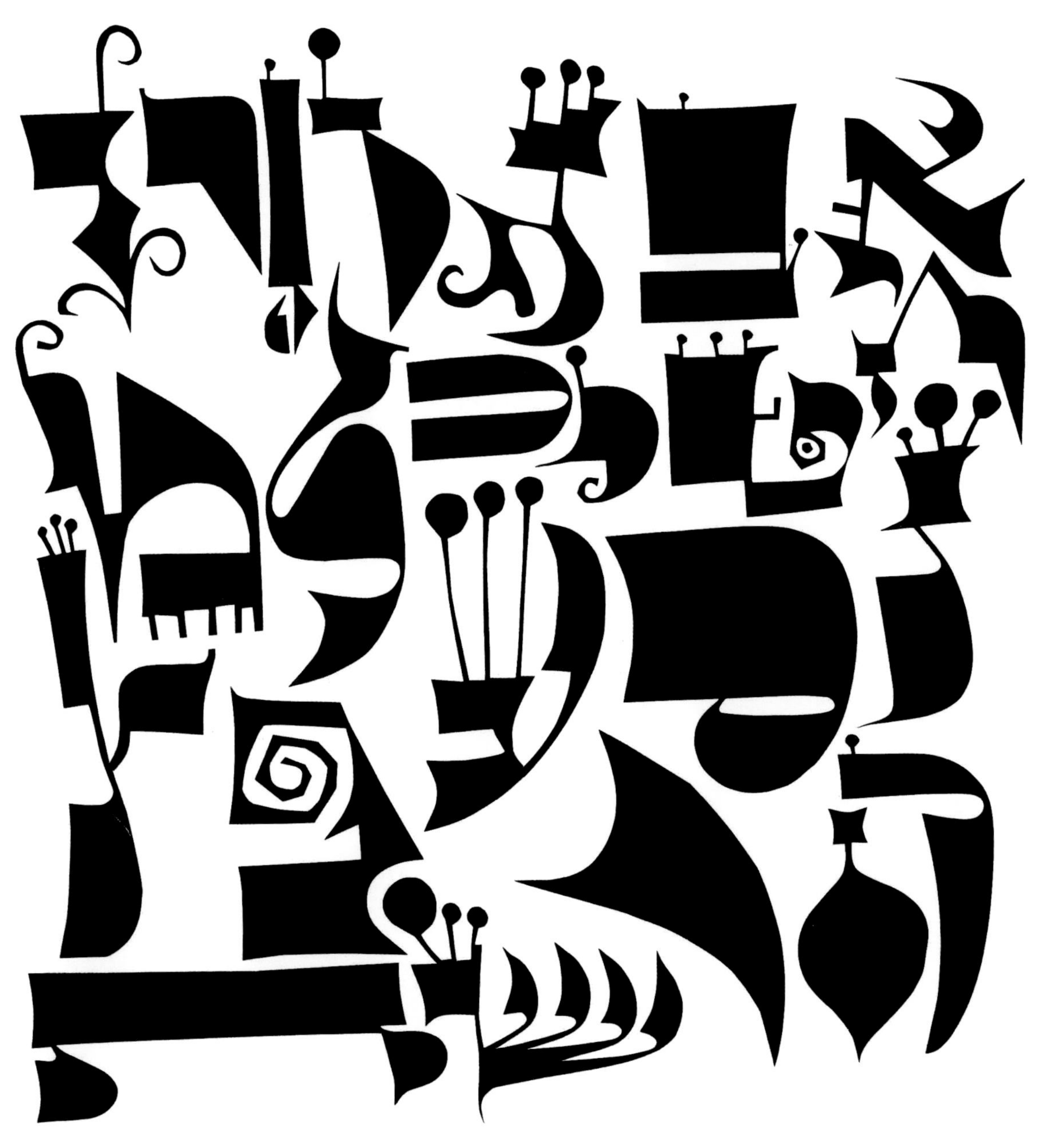

Josh Baum
Aleph-bet, 2002

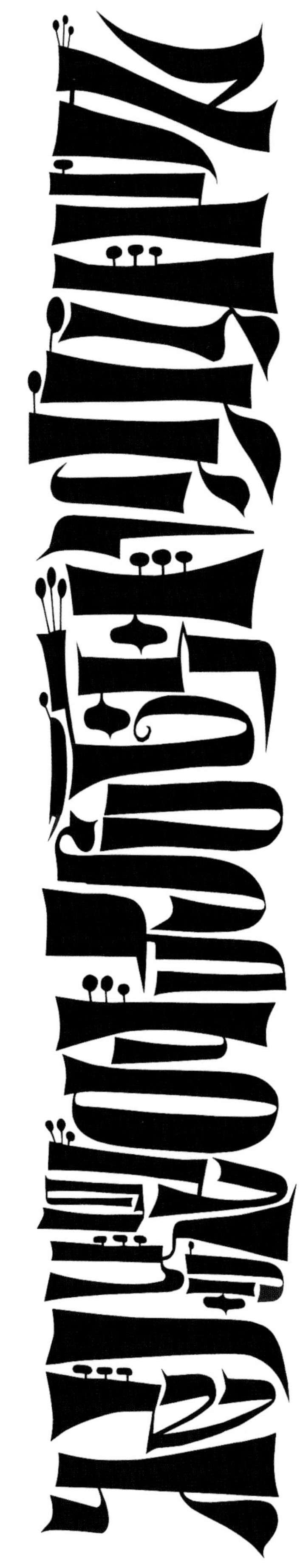

Josh Baum
Squashed Aleph-bet, 2003

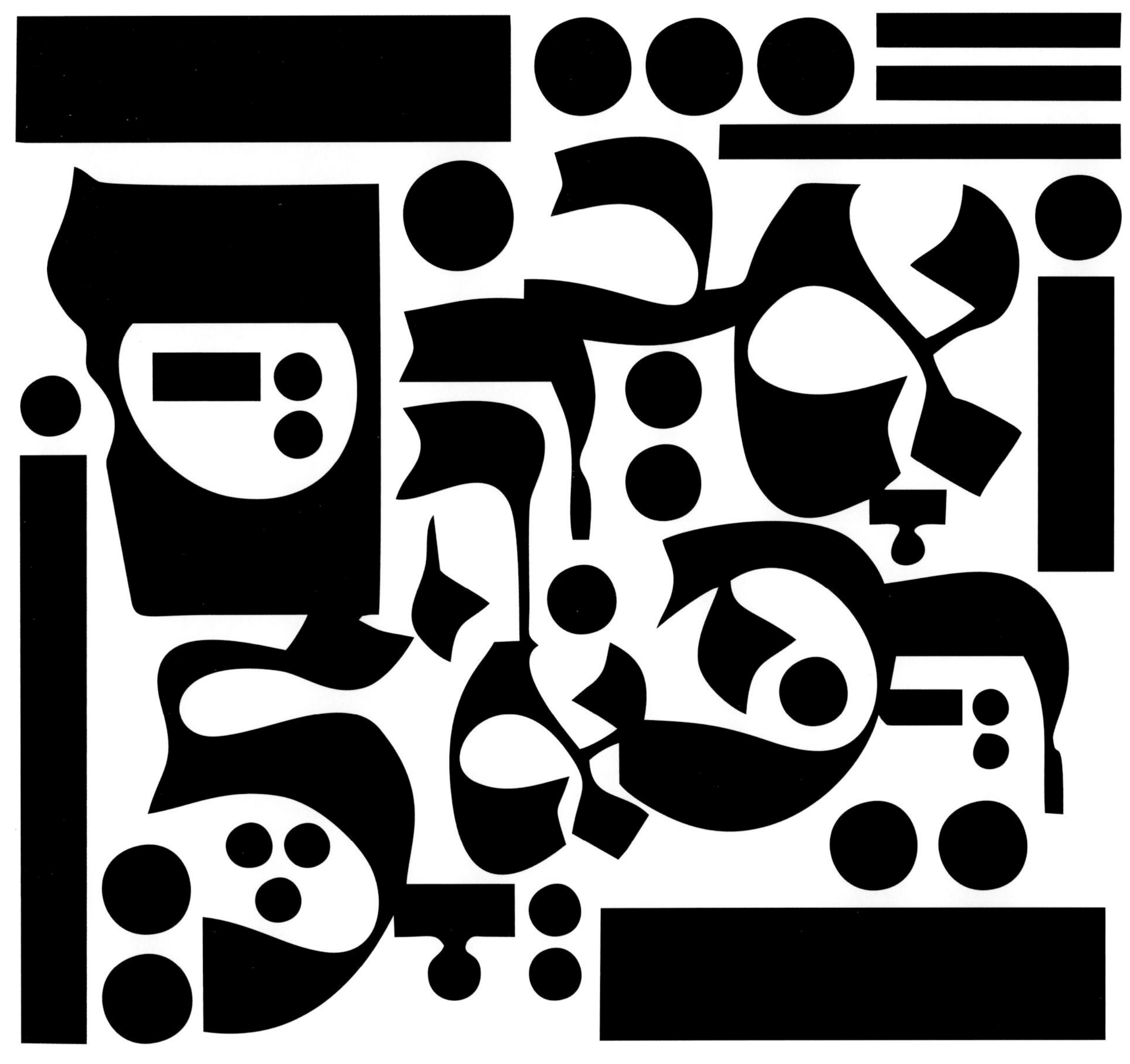

Alan Rafael Najman
Aleph-bet, 2010

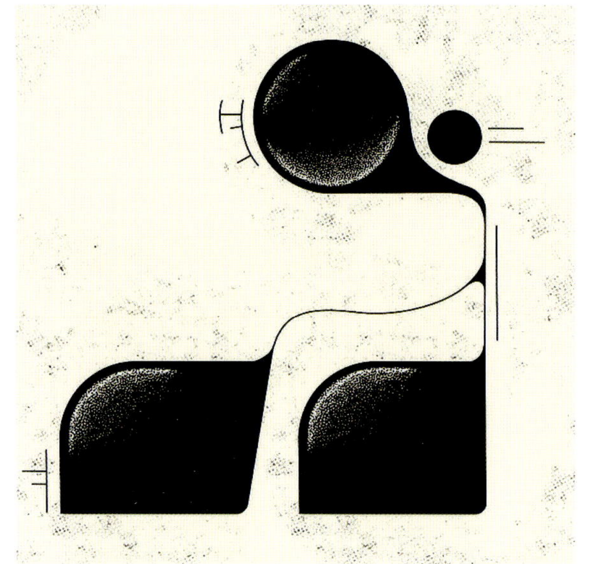

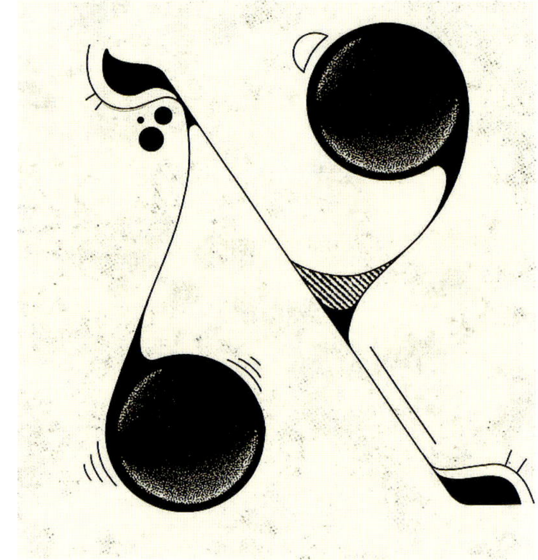

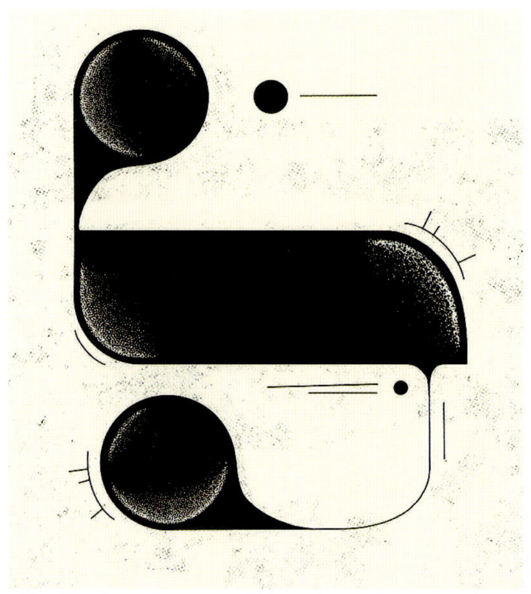

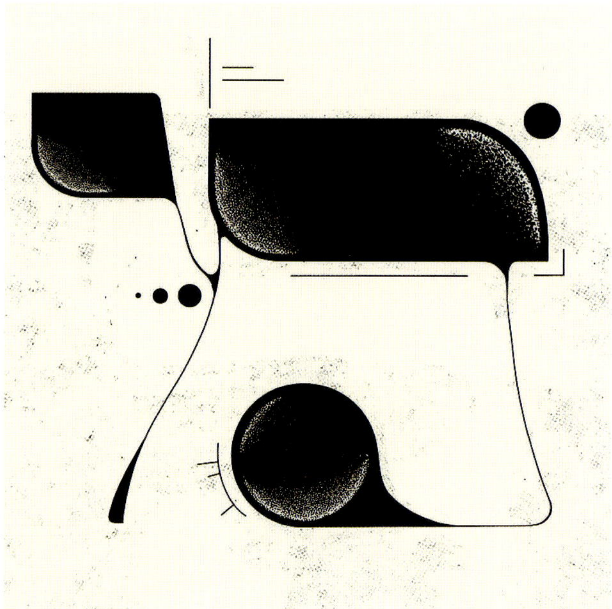

Tal Becker
Hebrew Letters, 2020

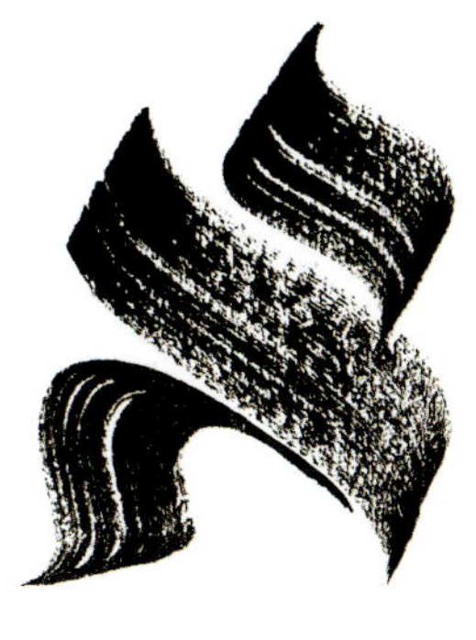
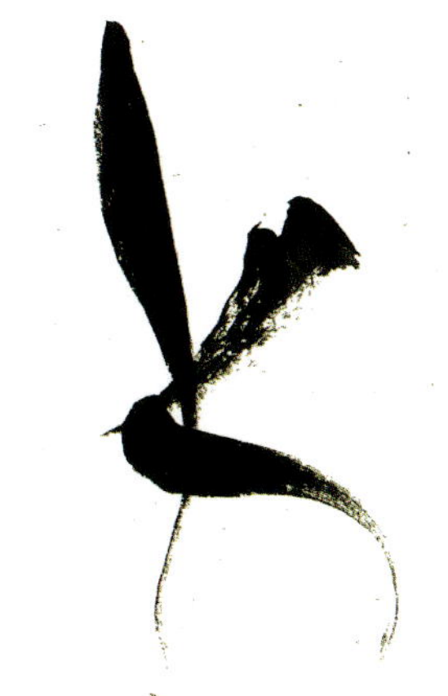
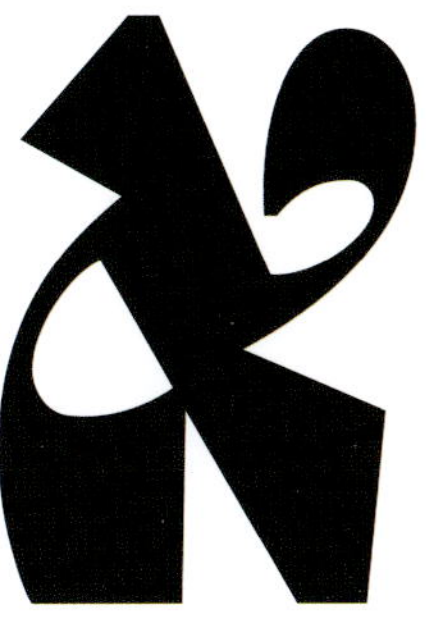
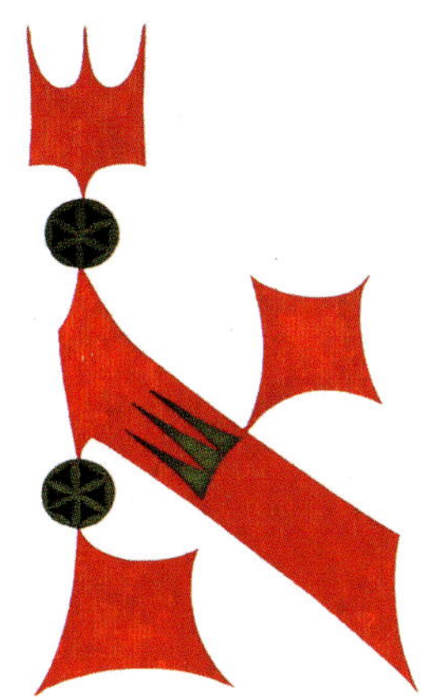
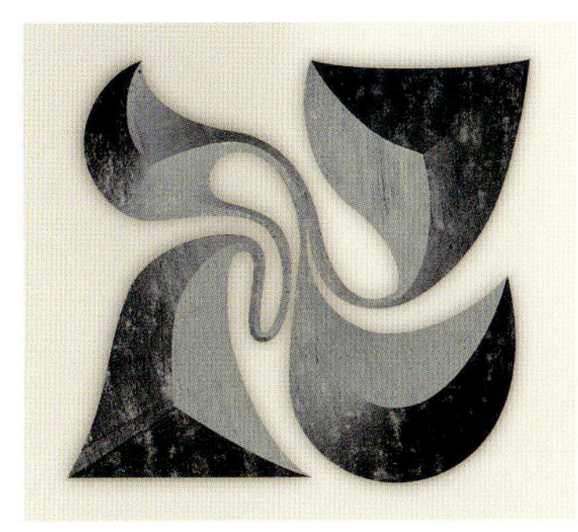
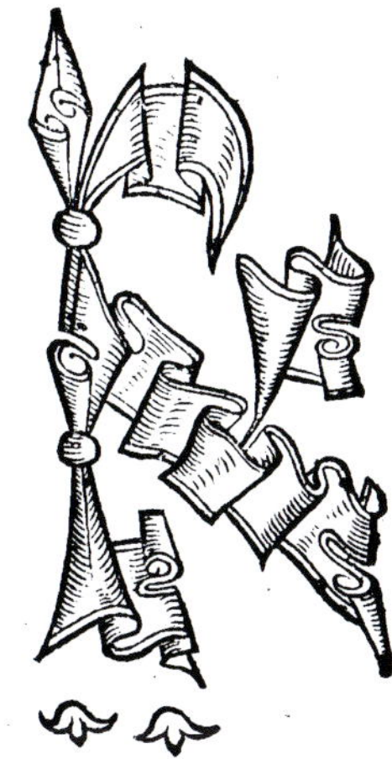
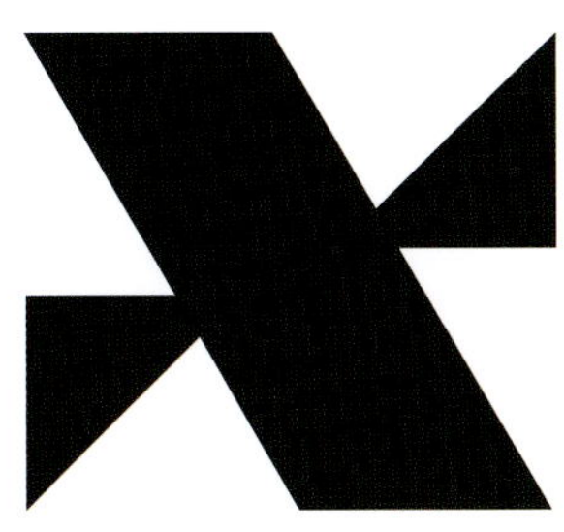
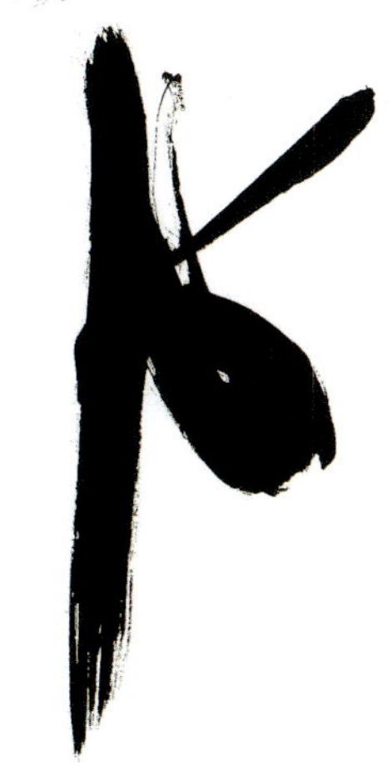
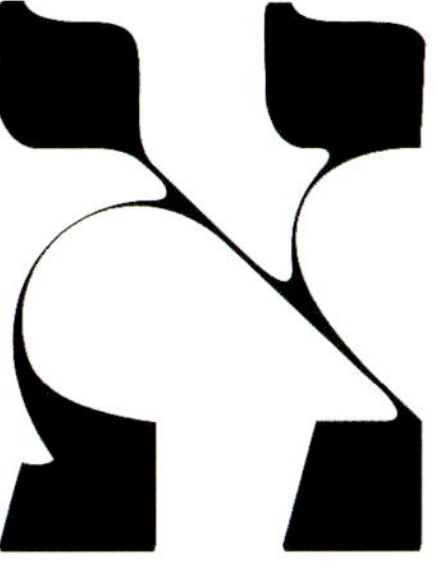

Alephs, LEFT TO RIGHT:
TOP: Guy Tamam, Izzy Pludwinski, Ben Natan
MIDDLE: Fred Pauker, Sagi Carmi, *Aleph-lamed* ligature from the Amsterdam Mahzor, *1670*
BOTTOM: Ben Natan, Izzy Pludwinski, Moshik Nadav

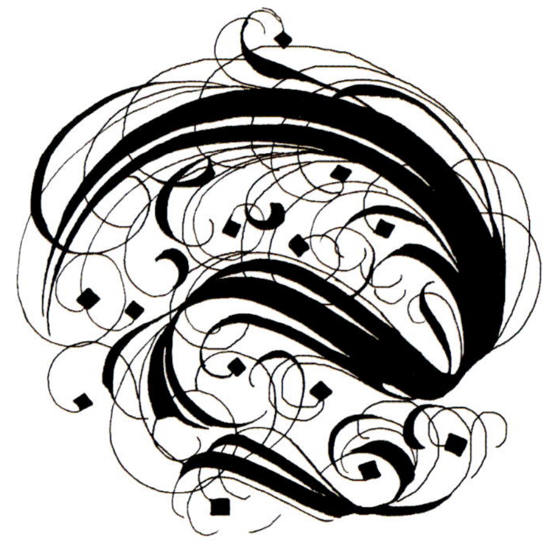

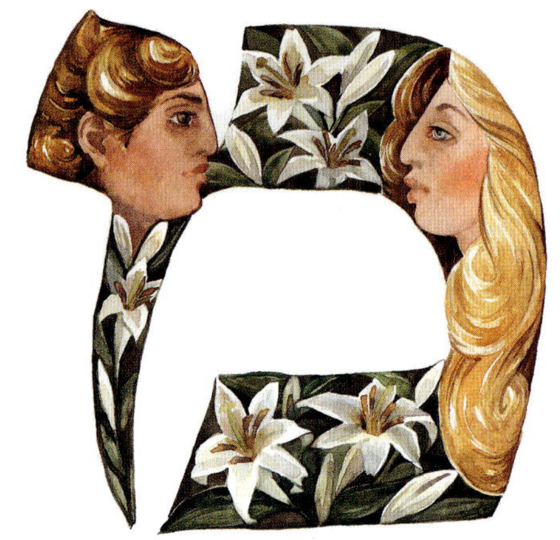

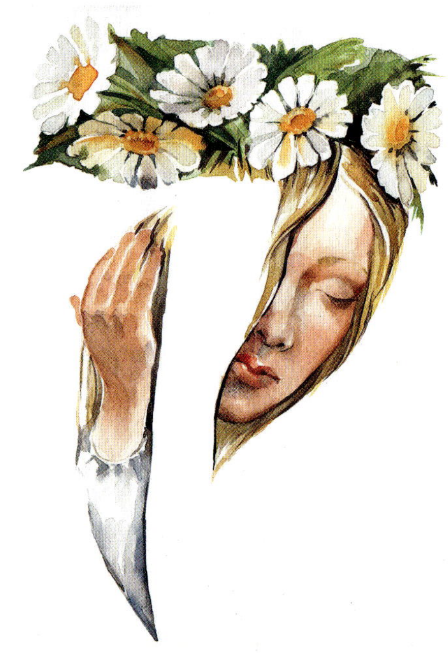

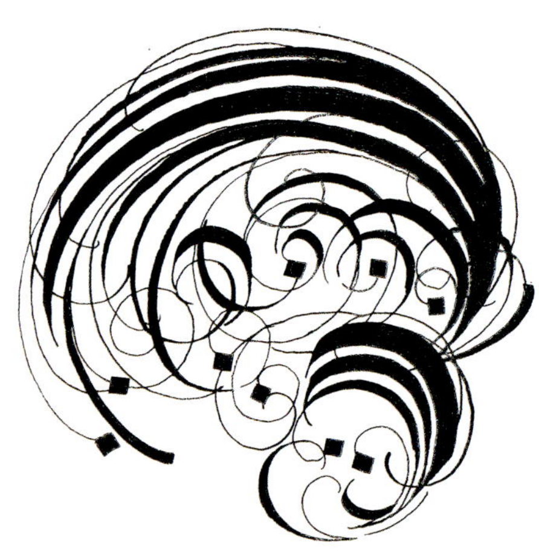

COLORED LETTERS: Anna Zakai
Illustrated Letters from Shir Hashirim, 2015–2016
BLACK-AND-WHITE LETTERS: Zina Dorman
Hebrew Initial Letters, 2015

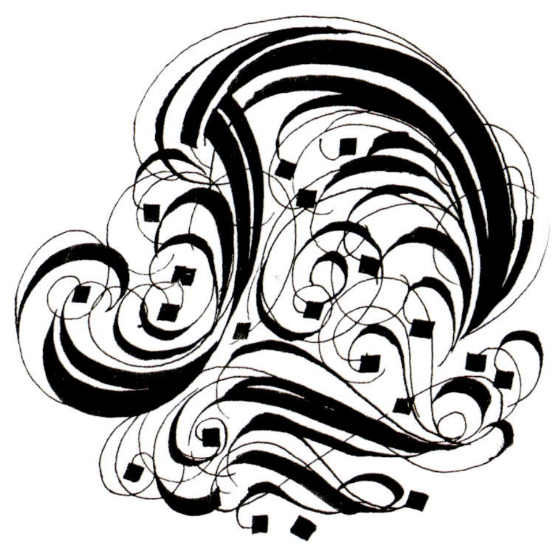

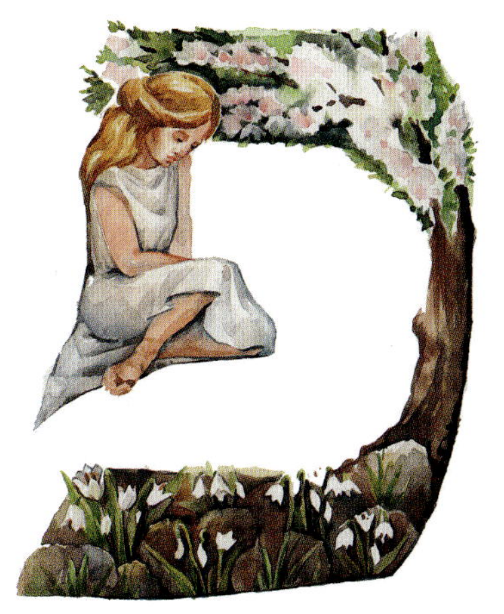

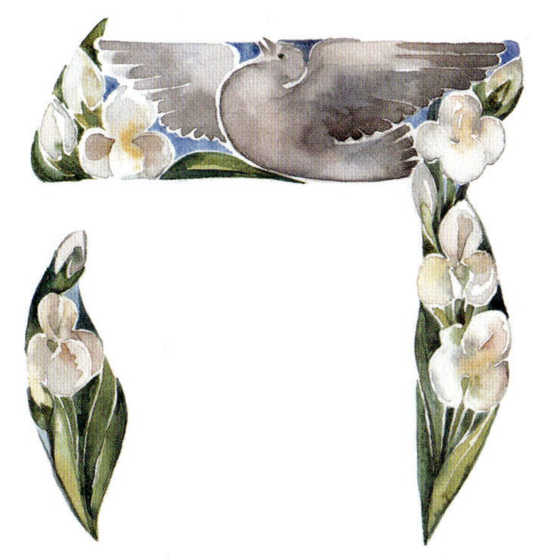

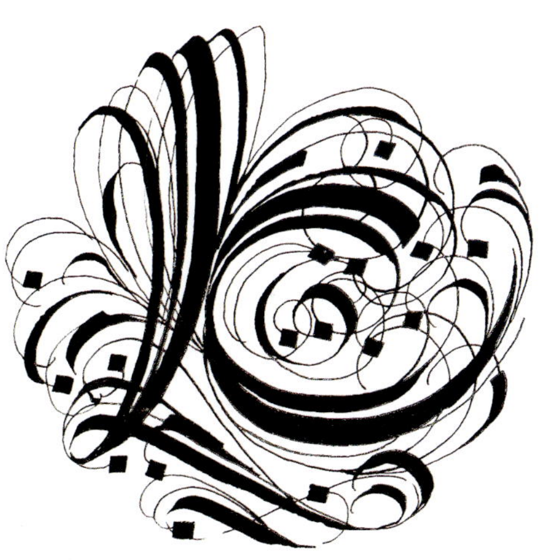

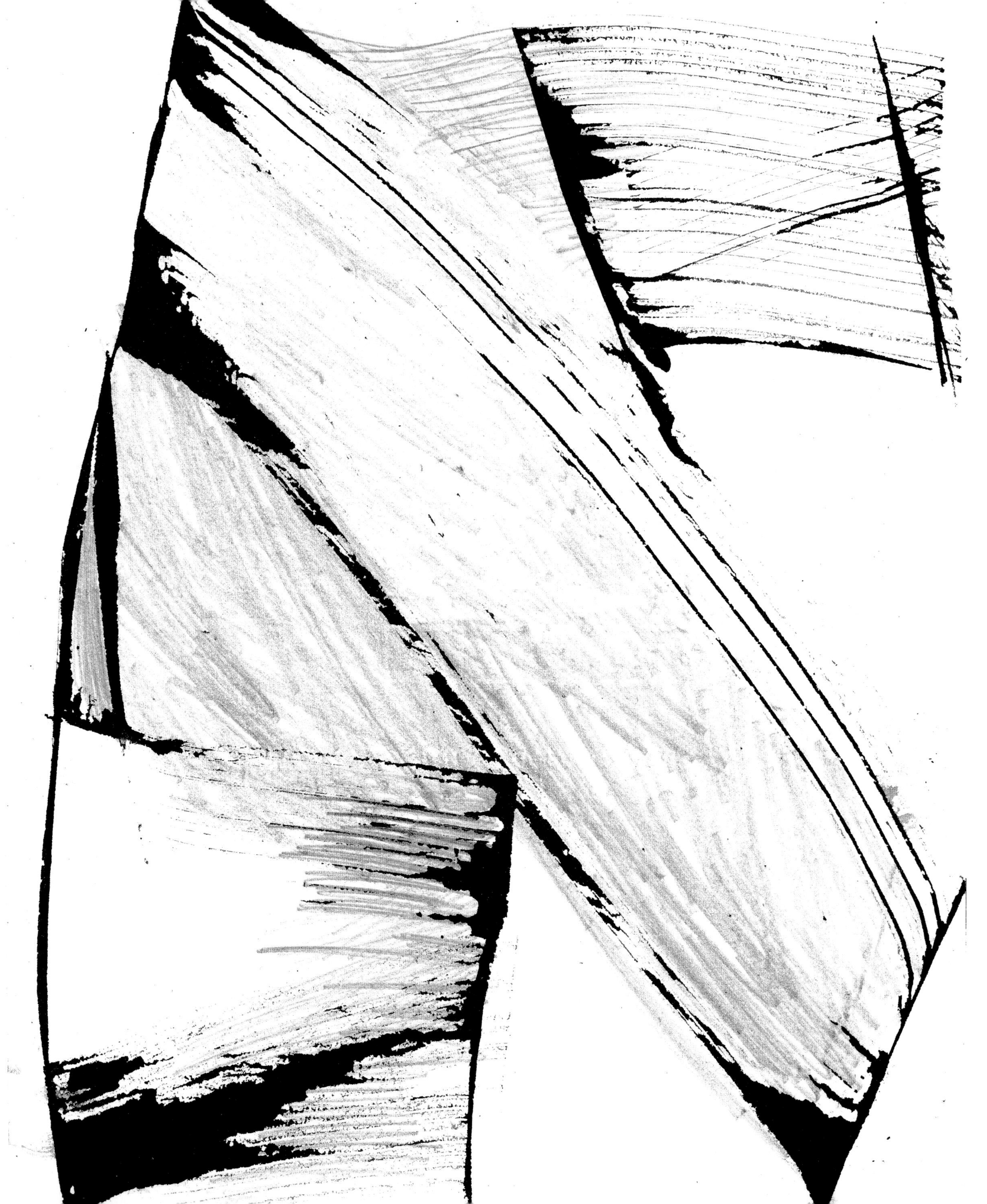

4
Stretching the Boundaries

When is an *aleph* no longer an *aleph*? How important is legibility? As it entered the latter part of the twentieth century, calligraphy took on a new direction as its practical applications were heavily replaced by more modern methods of reproduction. This was intensified by the digital revolution and the ease with which new fonts could be created. Released from the need for legibility, calligraphy often evolved into an expressive art form, encouraging experimentation and the testing of limits. Rather than merely transmitting texts in an anonymous manner, calligraphers began giving personal and creative interpretations to the texts they were using.

Lynn Broide
Aleph, c. 2010

Although not beautiful in the classic sense, the lettering for the covers of these books and journals by Yiddish designers of the early twentieth century shows a rebellious attitude towards traditional letter forms.

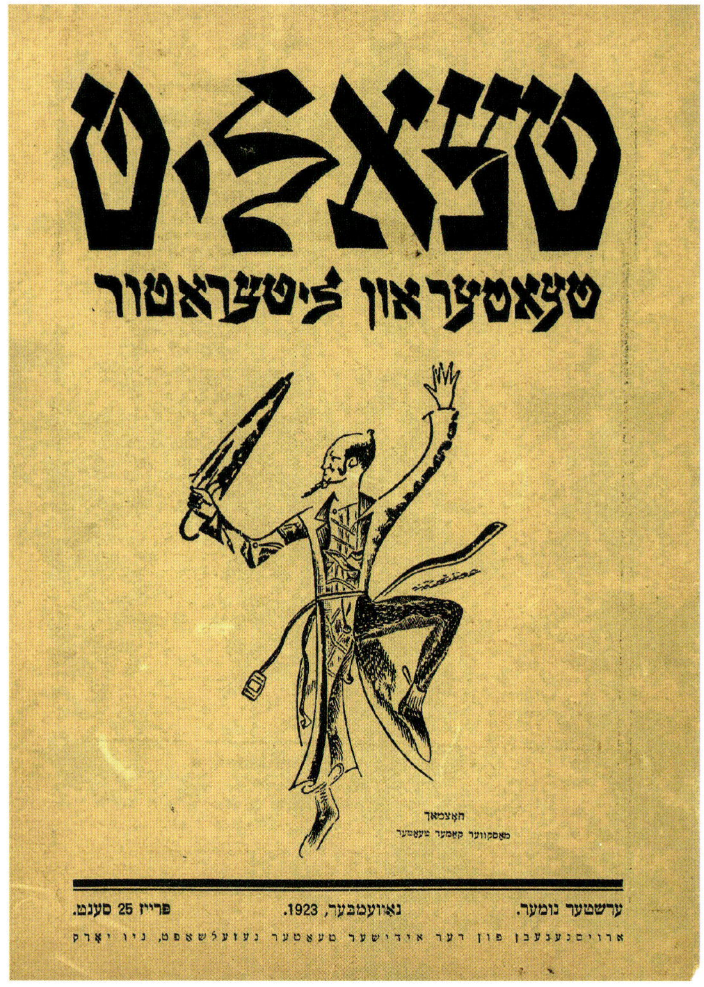

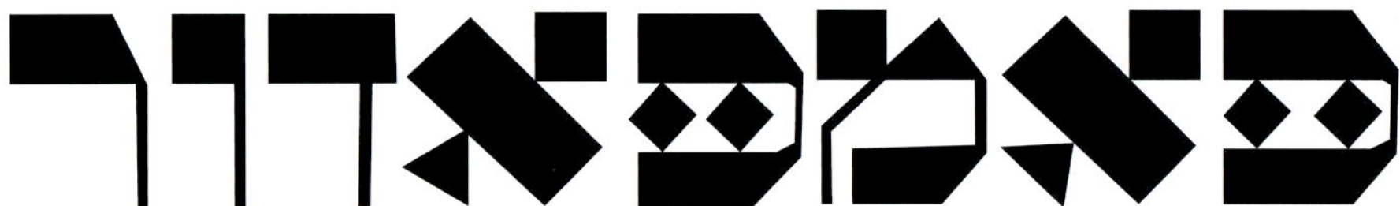

TOP: *Tealit*
Yiddish journal of theater and literature, 1923
Cover designer unknown
BOTTOM: *Pompadour*
Lettering from book cover
Designer unknown
Publisher: Literarisher Farlag, New York, 1918

אַלבּאַטראָס

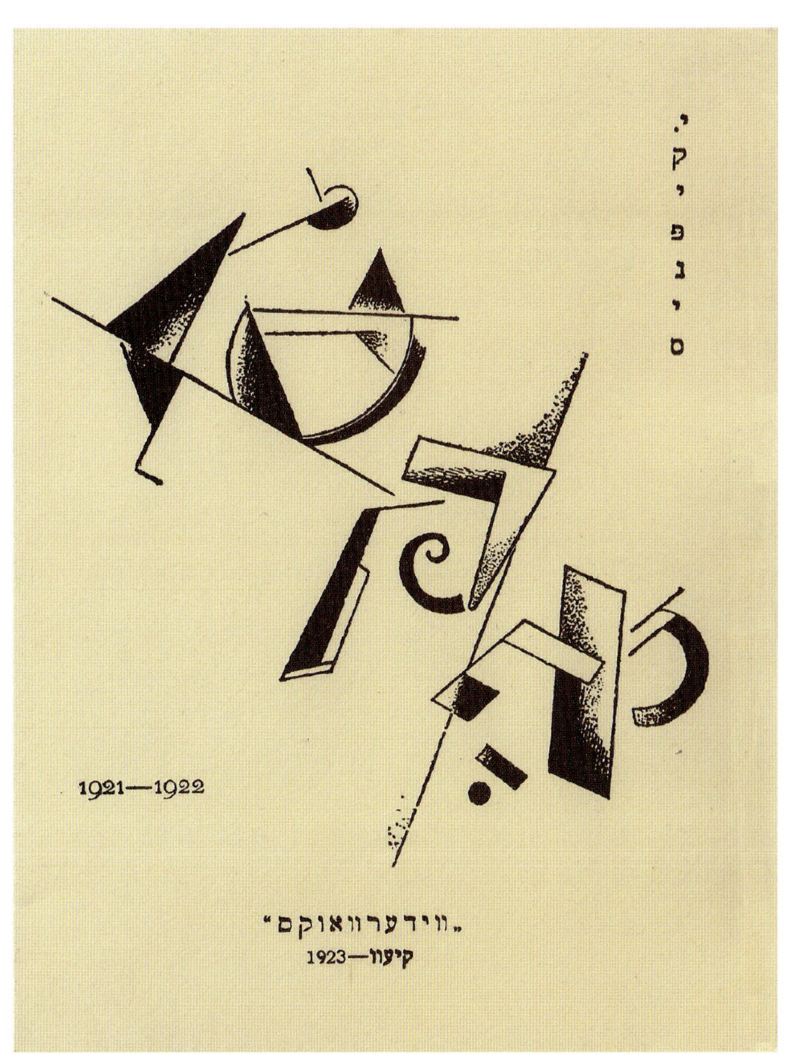

TOP: Henryk Berlewi
Lettering on cover of *Albatross*, a journal for new writing and graphic arts, Berlin, 1923
BOTTOM: Designer unknown
Cover for *Oksn*, a book by Y. Kipnis, 1923

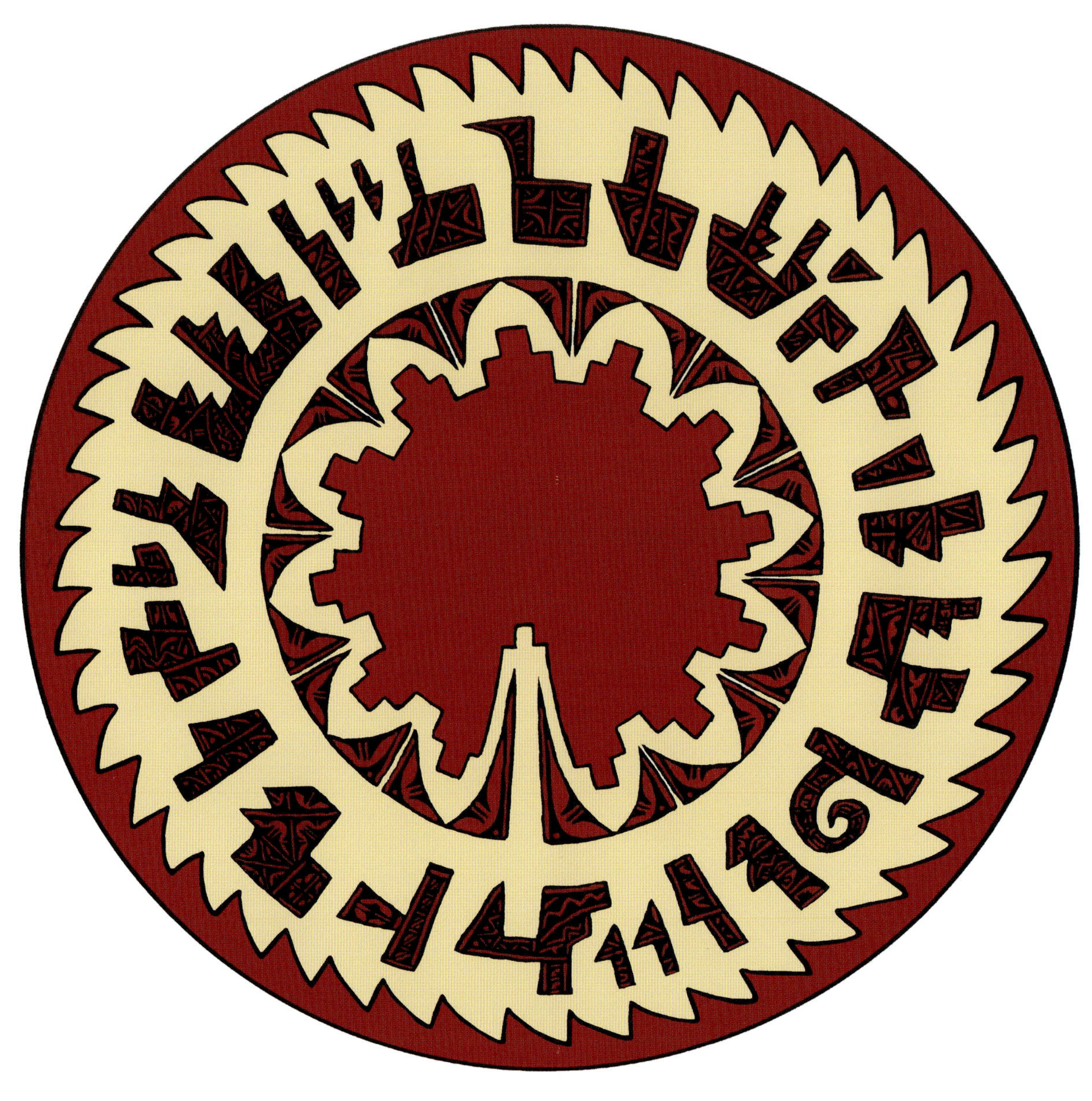

In this design, based on the style of Pueblo pottery, calligrapher/artist David Moss plays with figure-ground relationships, here emphasizing the negative spaces. He consciously makes us work to recognize the letters in order to read this quote from Psalm 105. He does something similar in his "Mizrach Plaque" on the following page.

David Moss
"Psalm 105:4" from *A Pueblo Portfolio*, 2004

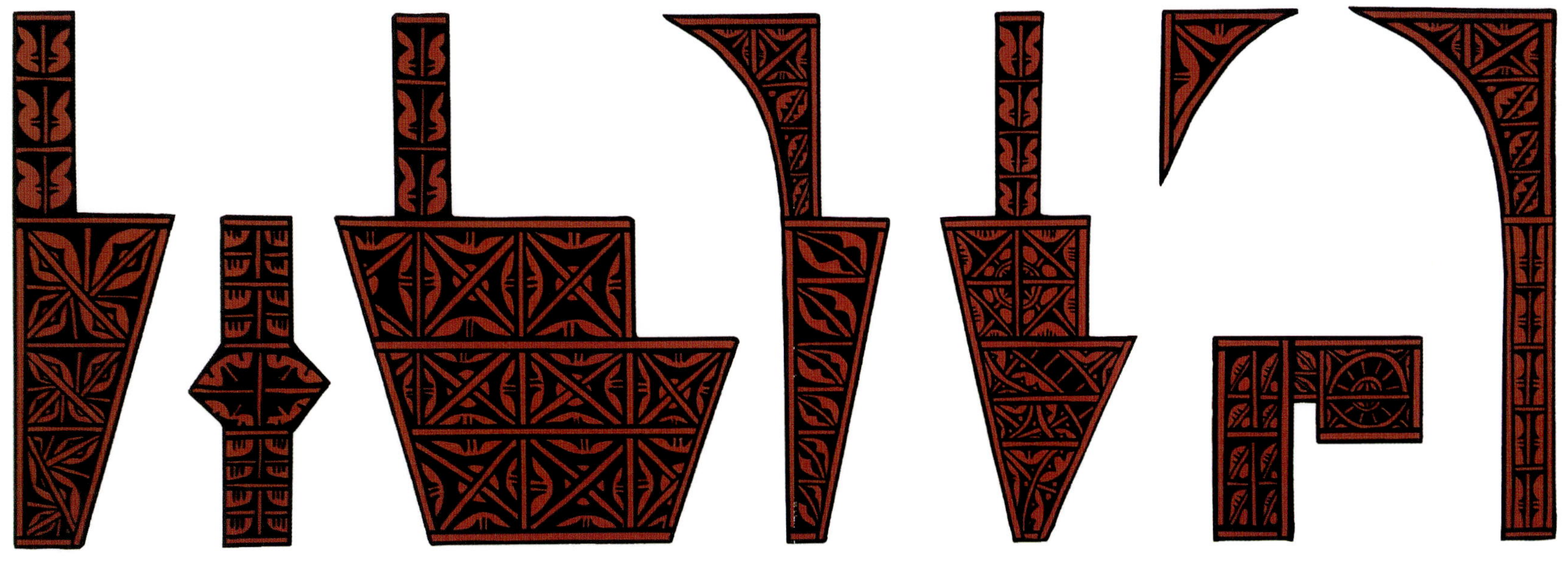

David Moss
"Mizrach Plaque," from *A Pueblo Portfolio*, 2004

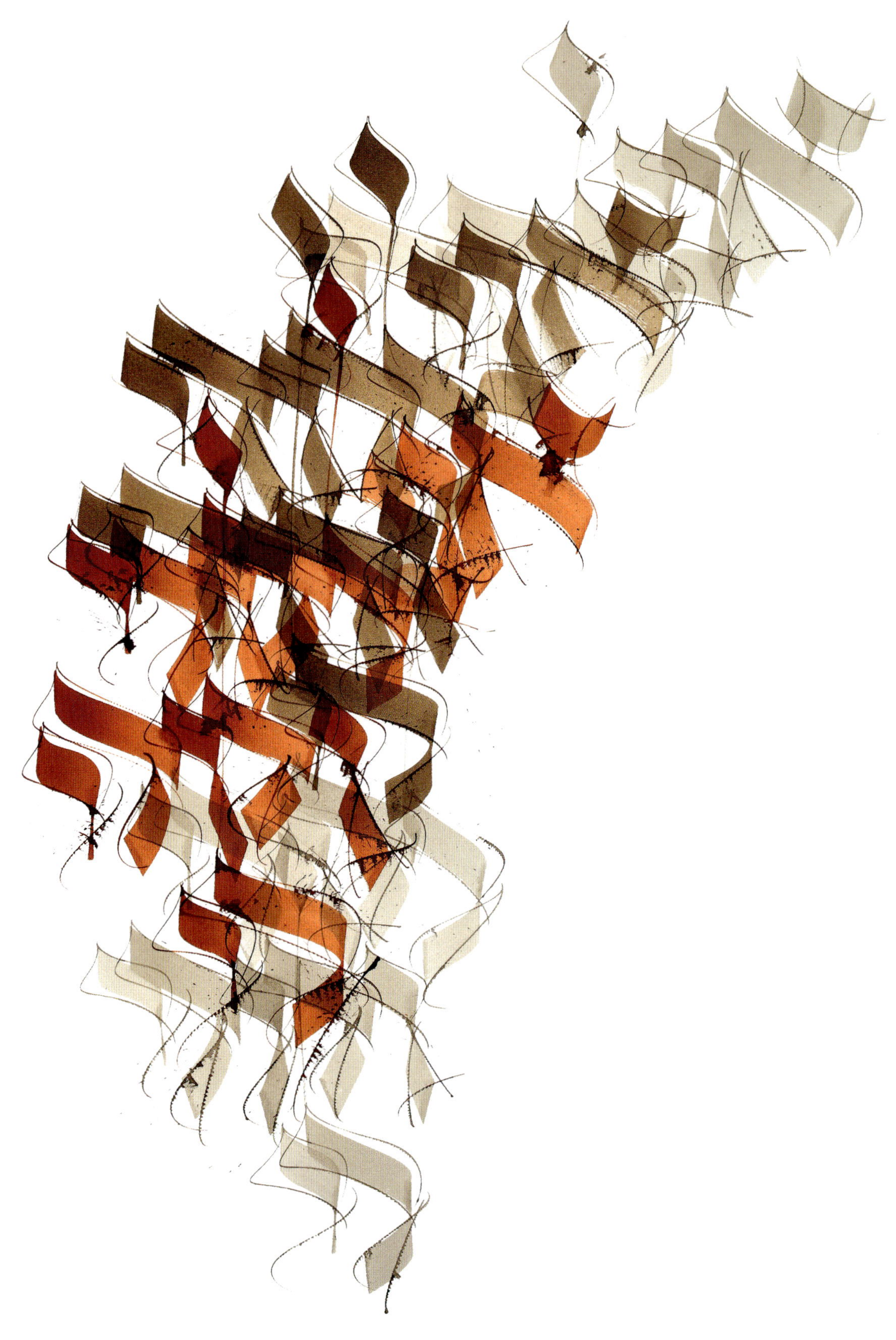

Michel D'Anastasio
I Am My Beloved's, 2020

Michel D'Anastasio
Adam, Adamah, Adom, 2011

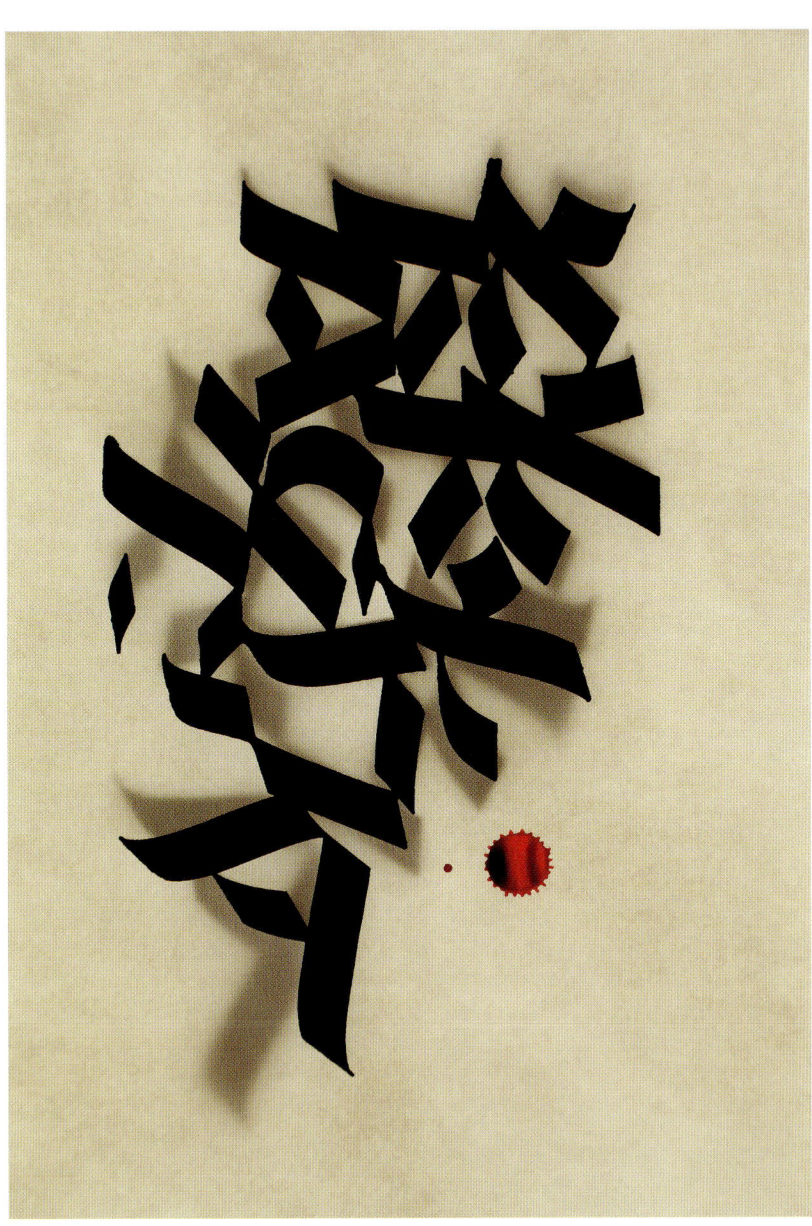

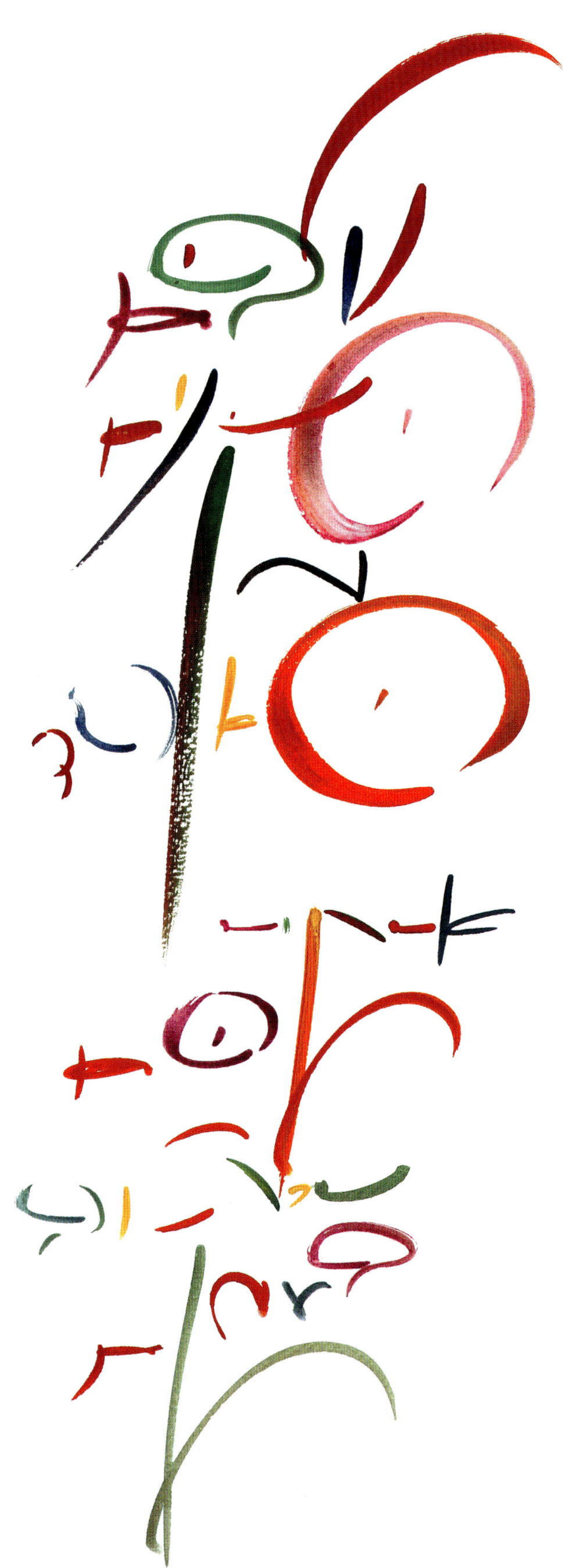

Izzy Pludwinski
Two Are Better Than One, 2002

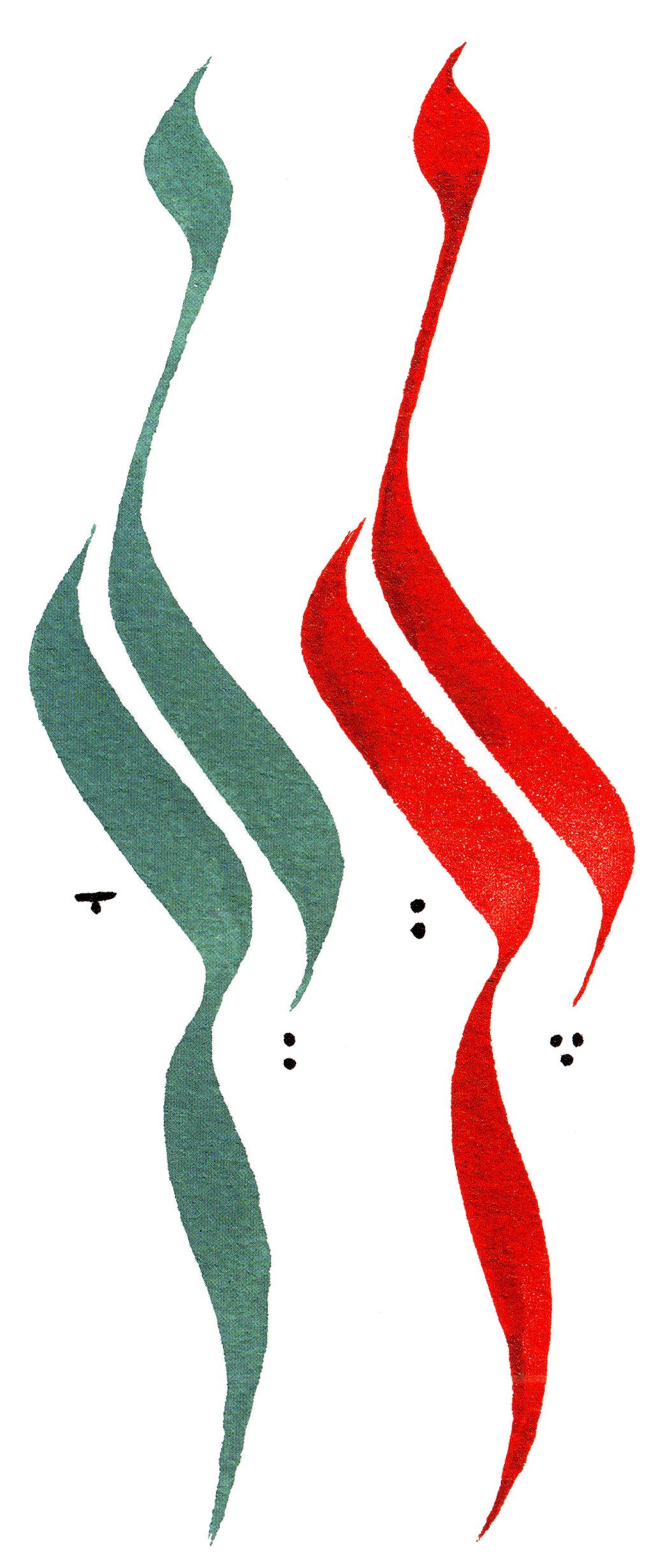

David Goldstein
Lech Lecha, 2017

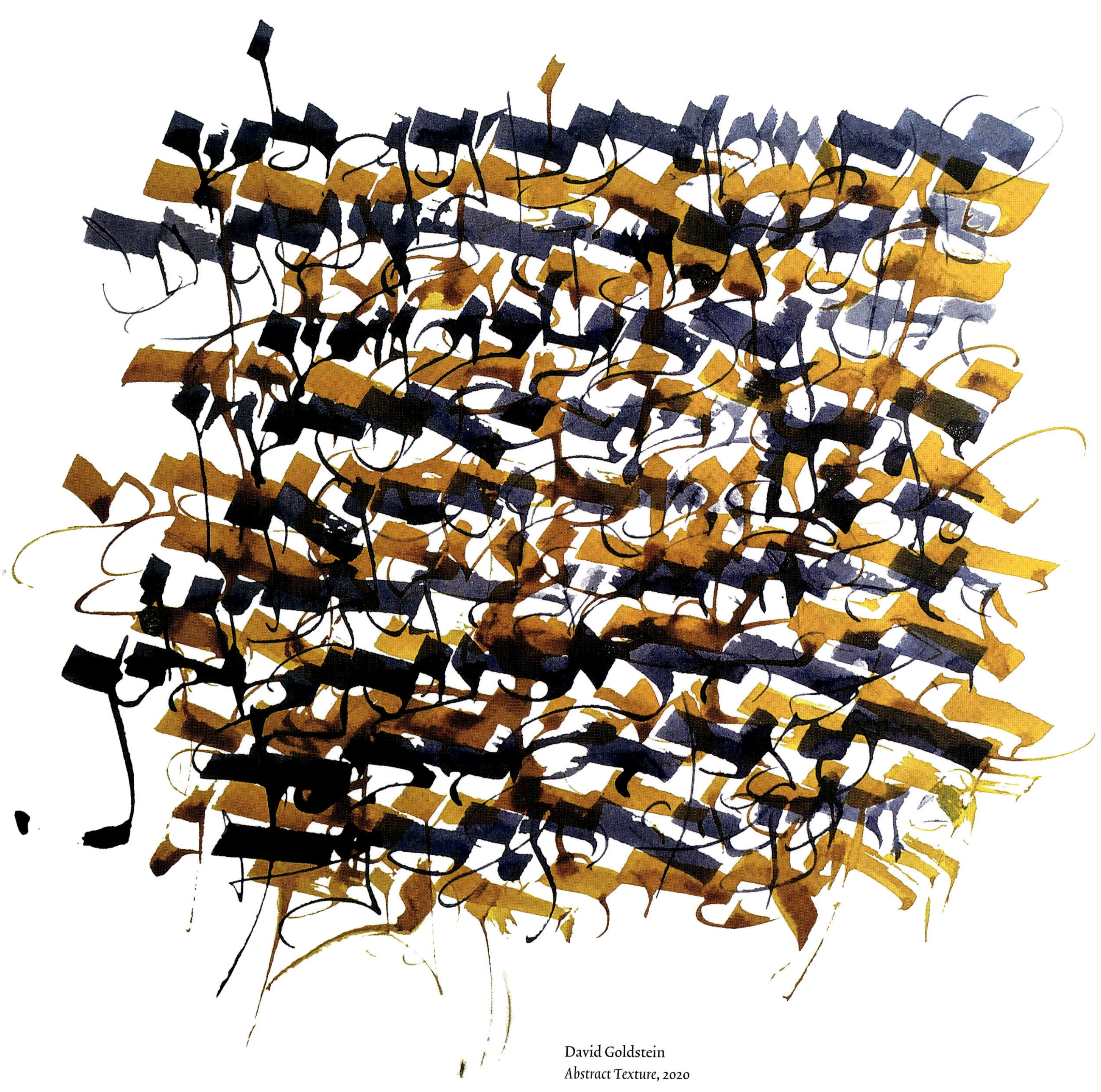

David Goldstein
Abstract Texture, 2020

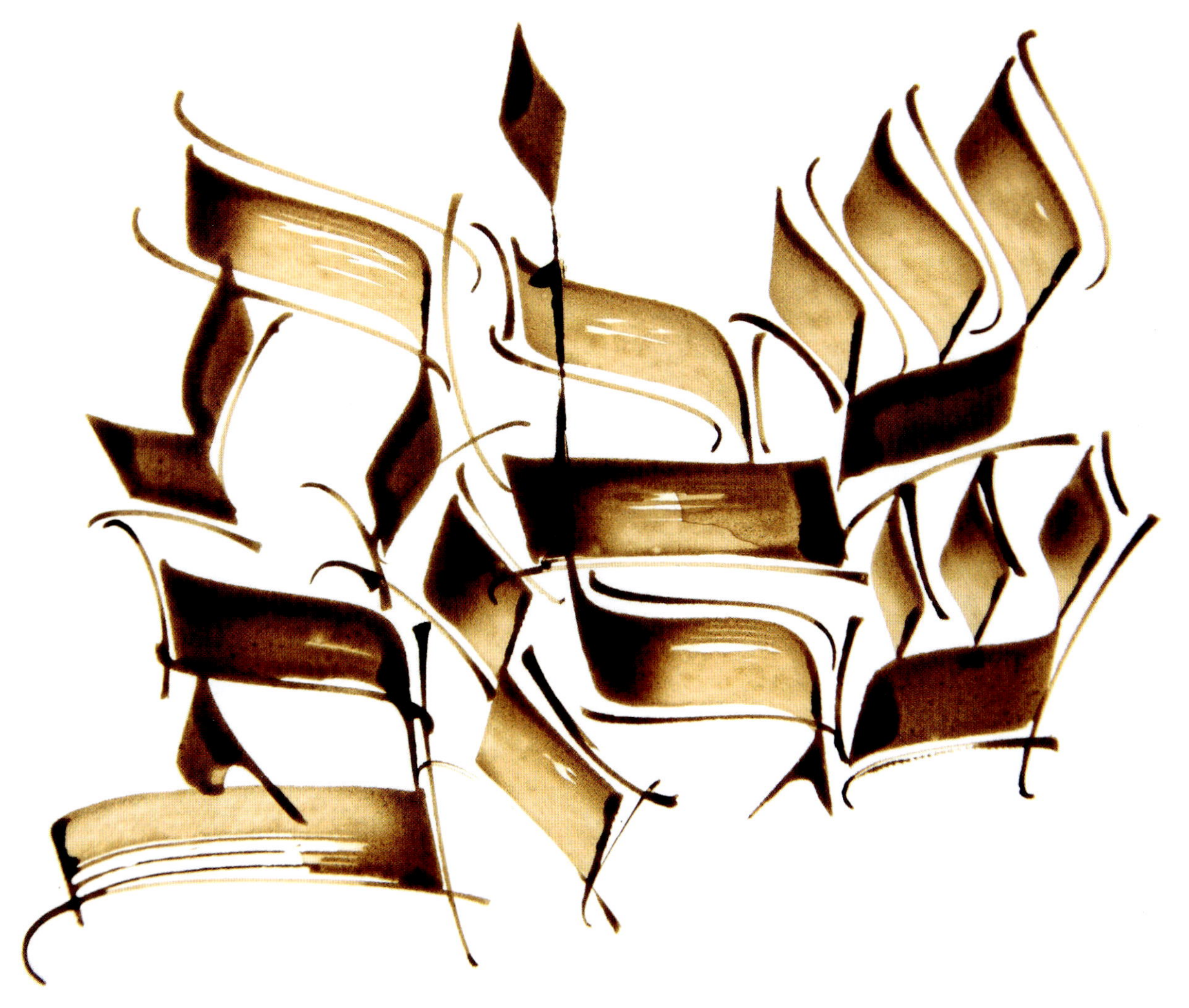

Michel D'Anastasio
Shabbat Shalom, 2012

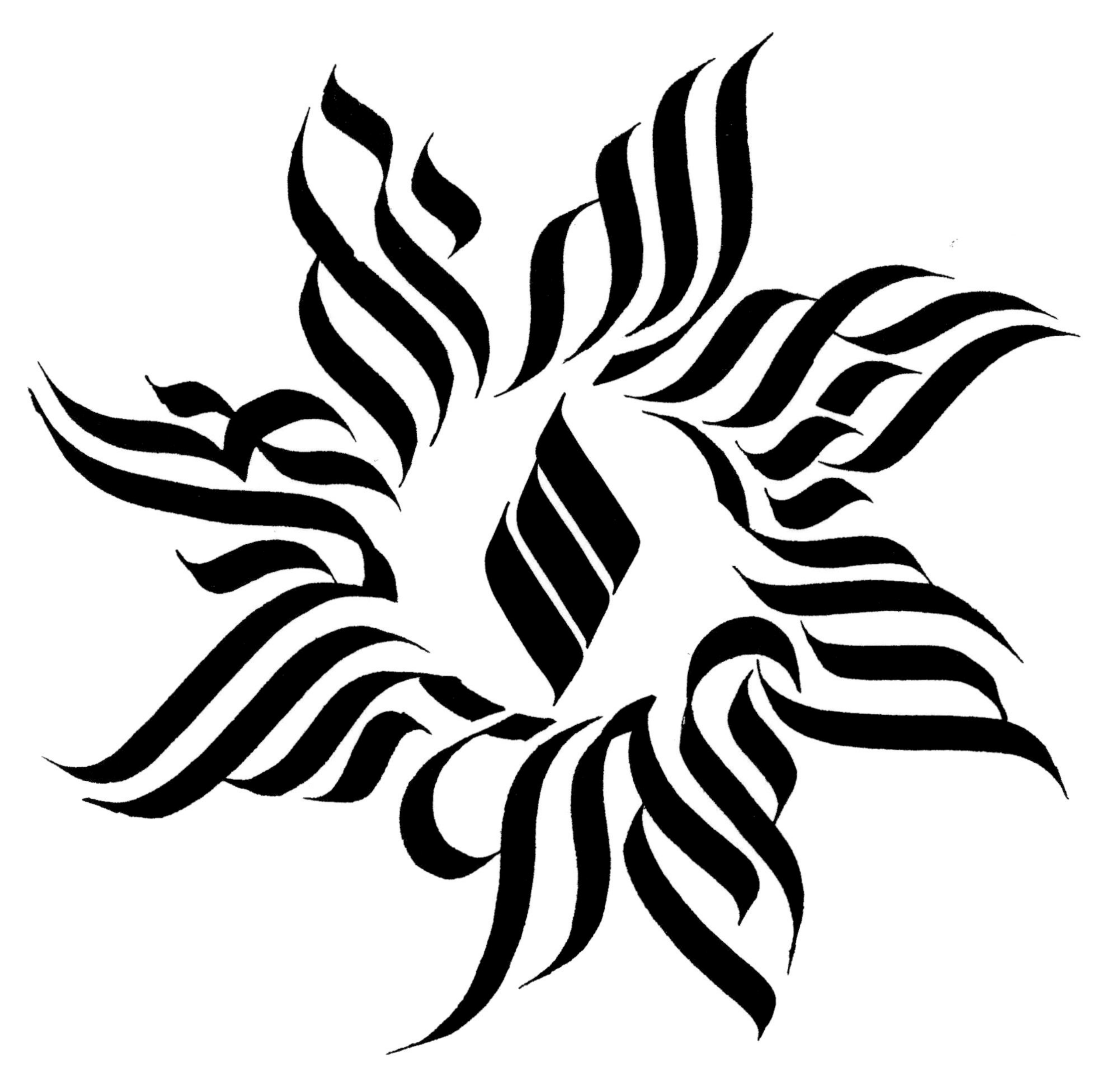

Gabriel Wolff
I Am My Beloved's, 2013

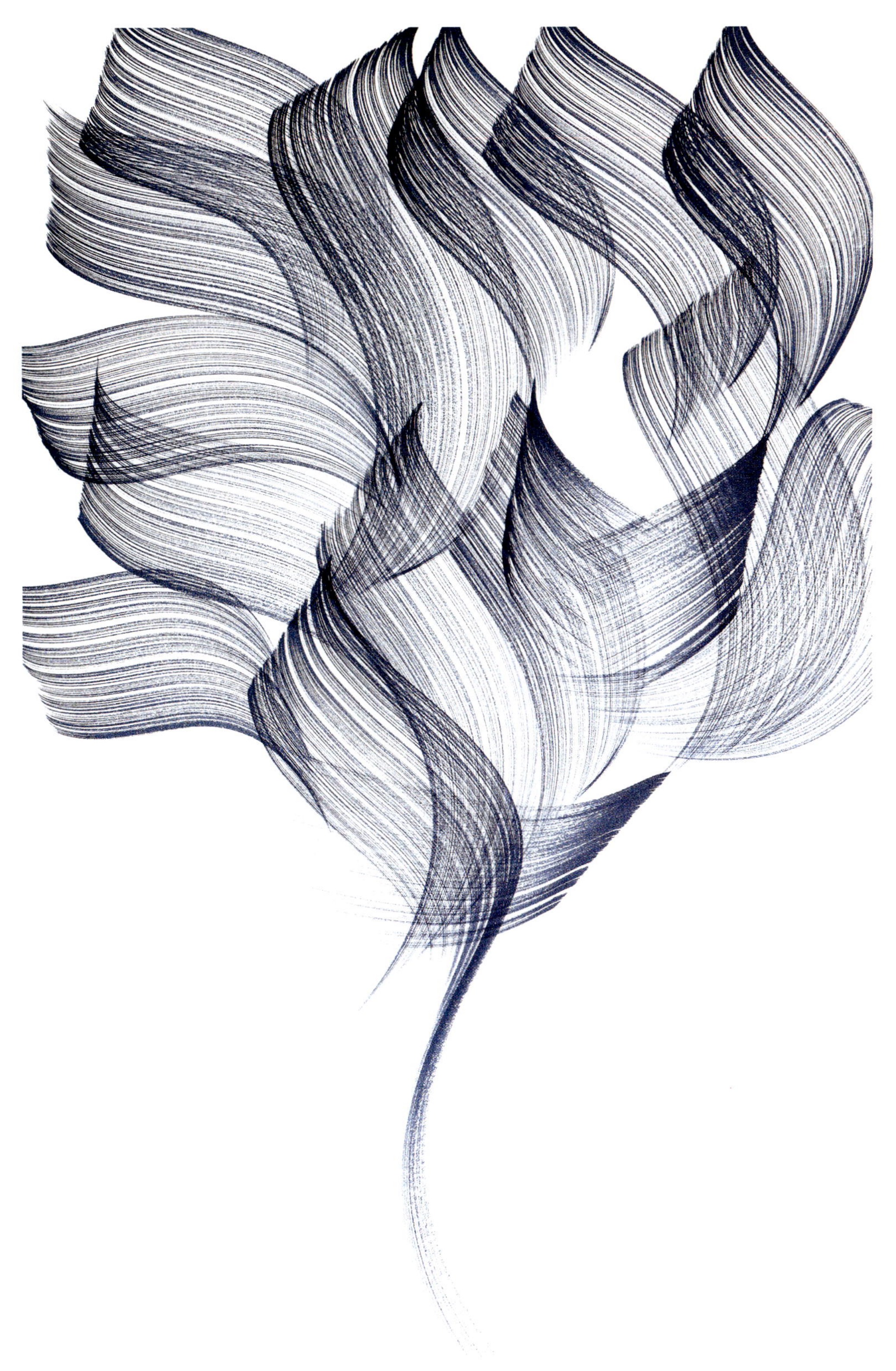

Michael D'Anastasio
Jerusalem, 2012

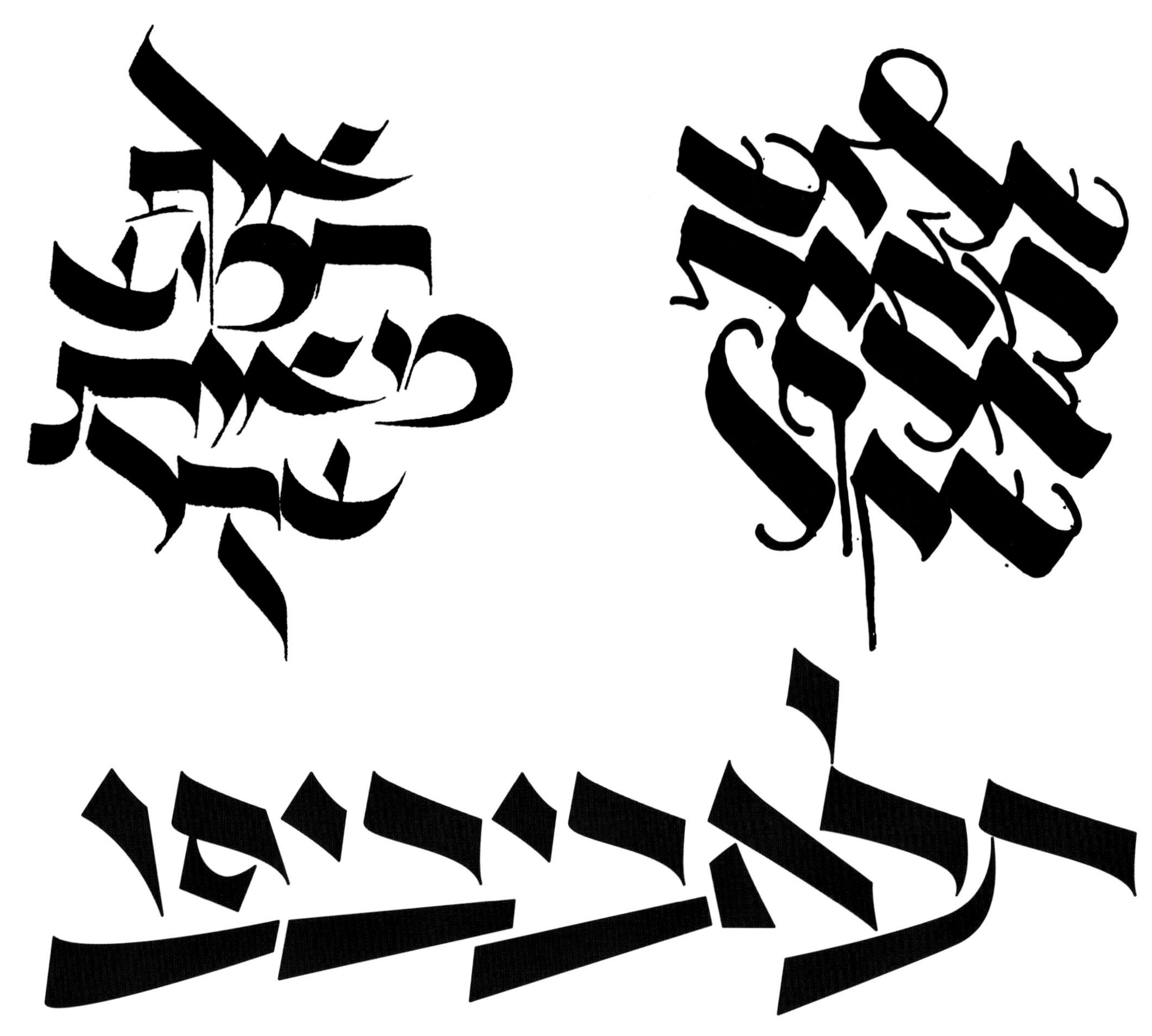

Guy Tamam
TOP LEFT: *Fifteen Hundred Shekel, 2015*
TOP RIGHT: *Three Hundred Thousand Shekel, 2015*
BOTTOM: *Tel Aviv Yaffo, 2018*

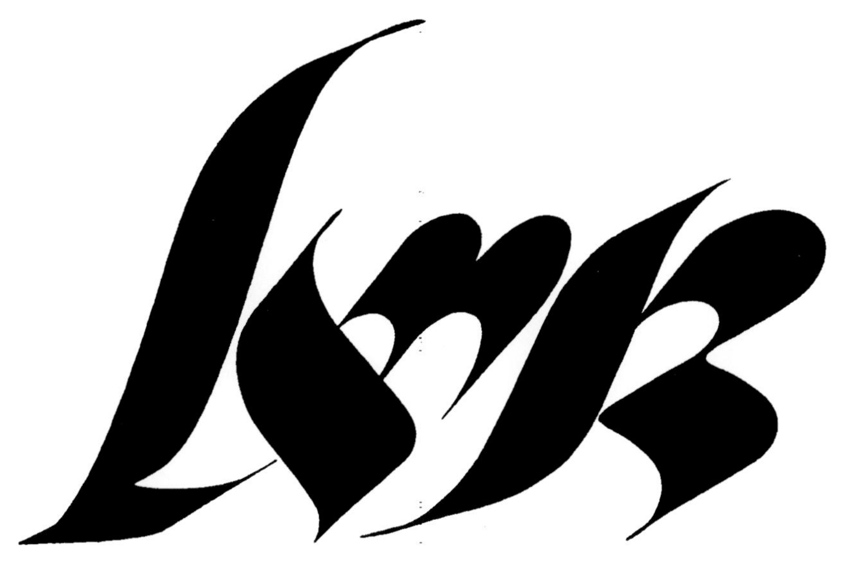

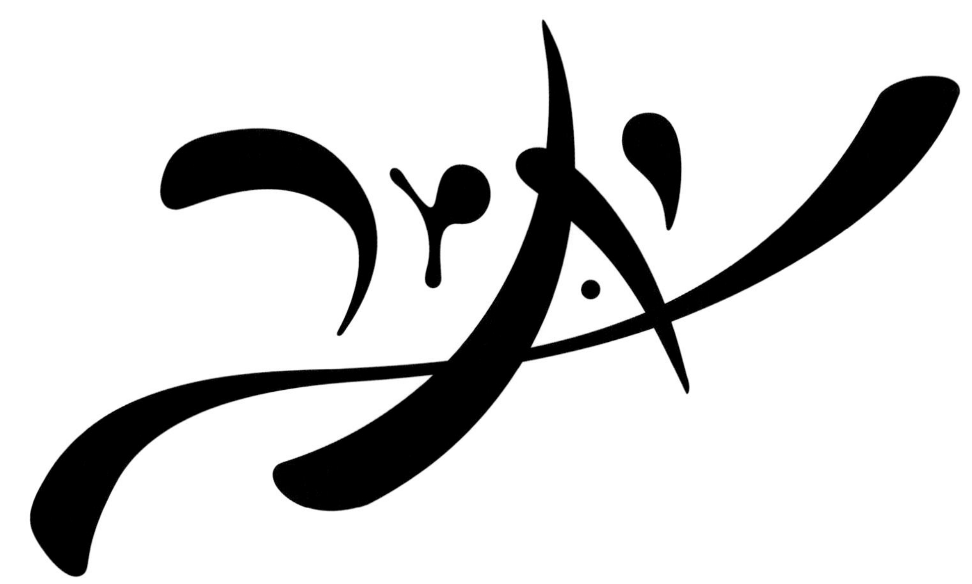

TOP: Lynn Broide
Daniel, 1991
BOTTOM: Baruch Naeh
Lettering from the logo of the Yatir Winery, 2003

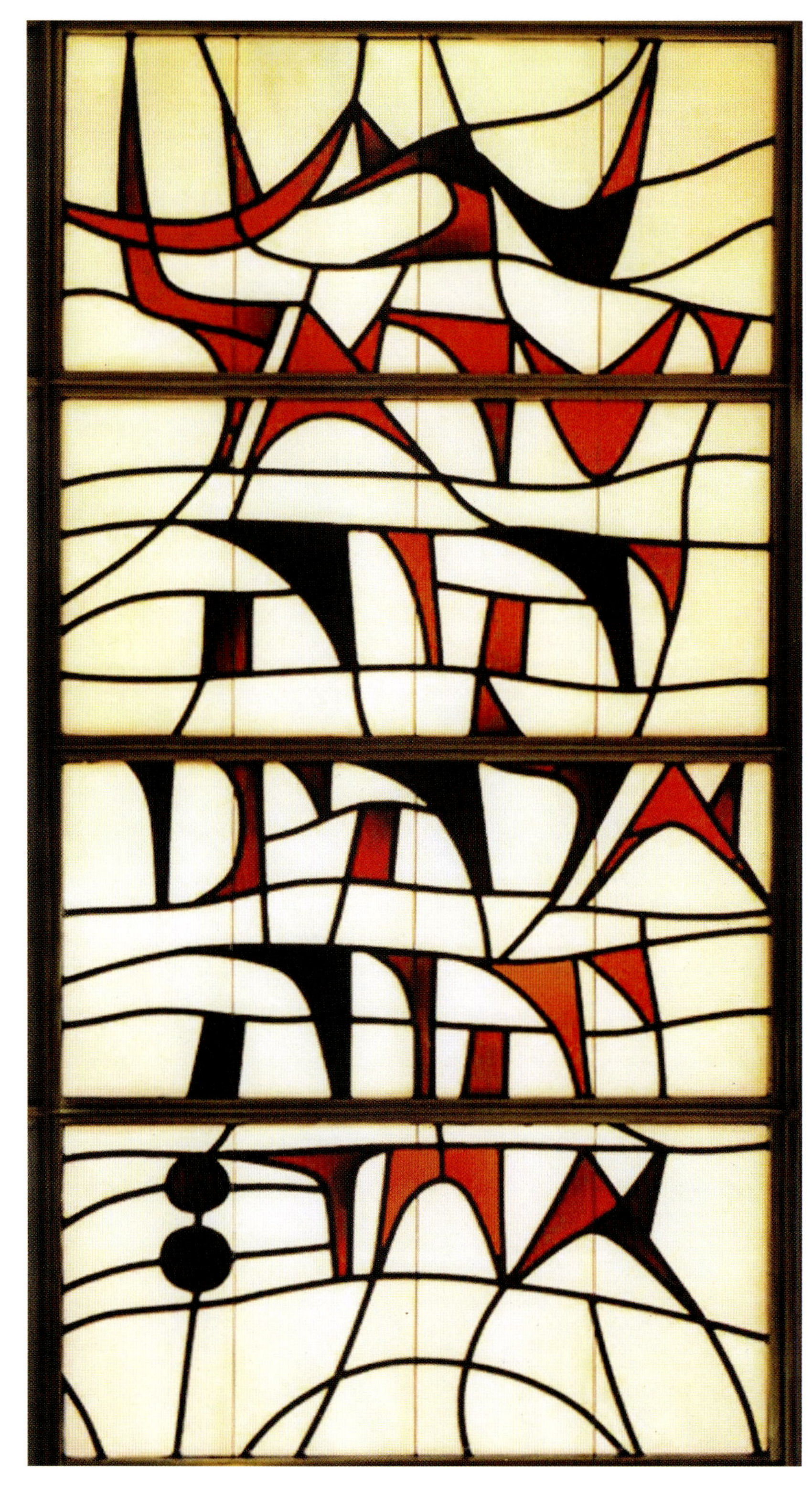

Designer: Nisan Engel
Shma Yisrael, 1974
Larchmont Temple, Larchmont, New York

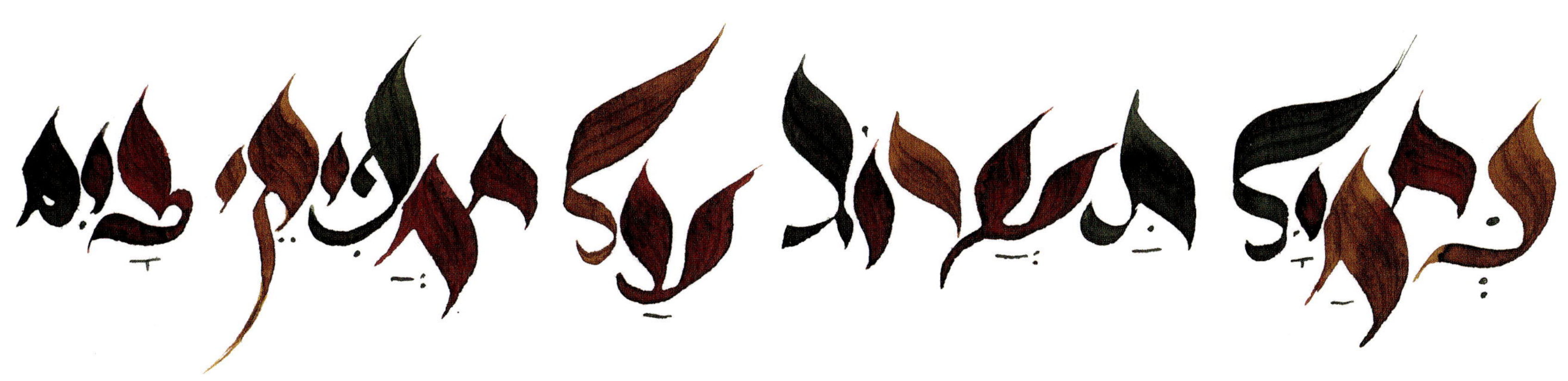

David Goldstein
As the Deer Pants for Streams of Water . . . (from Psalm 42), 2020

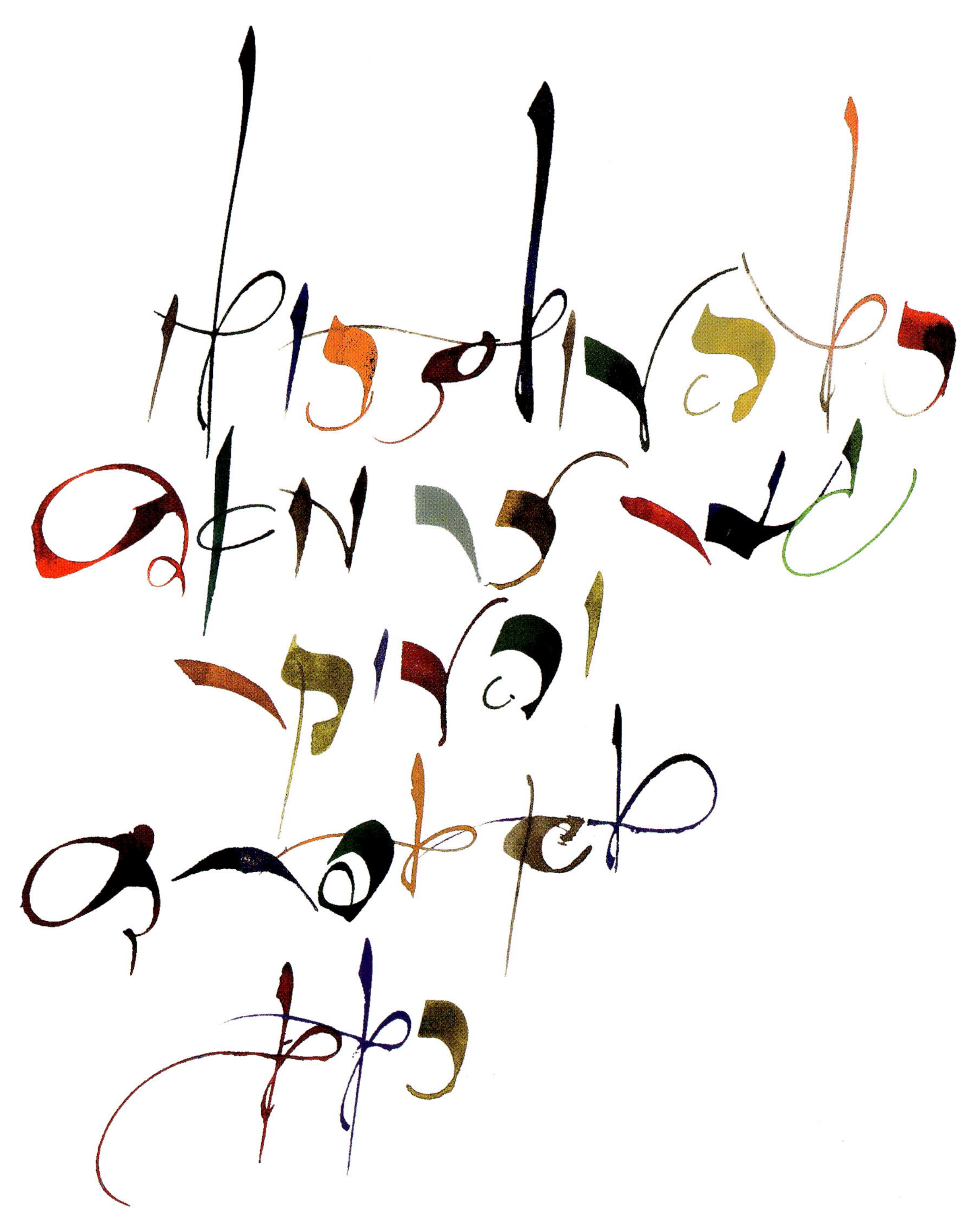

ר' נחמן

Izzy Pludwinski
The Whole World Is a Narrow Bridge, 2018

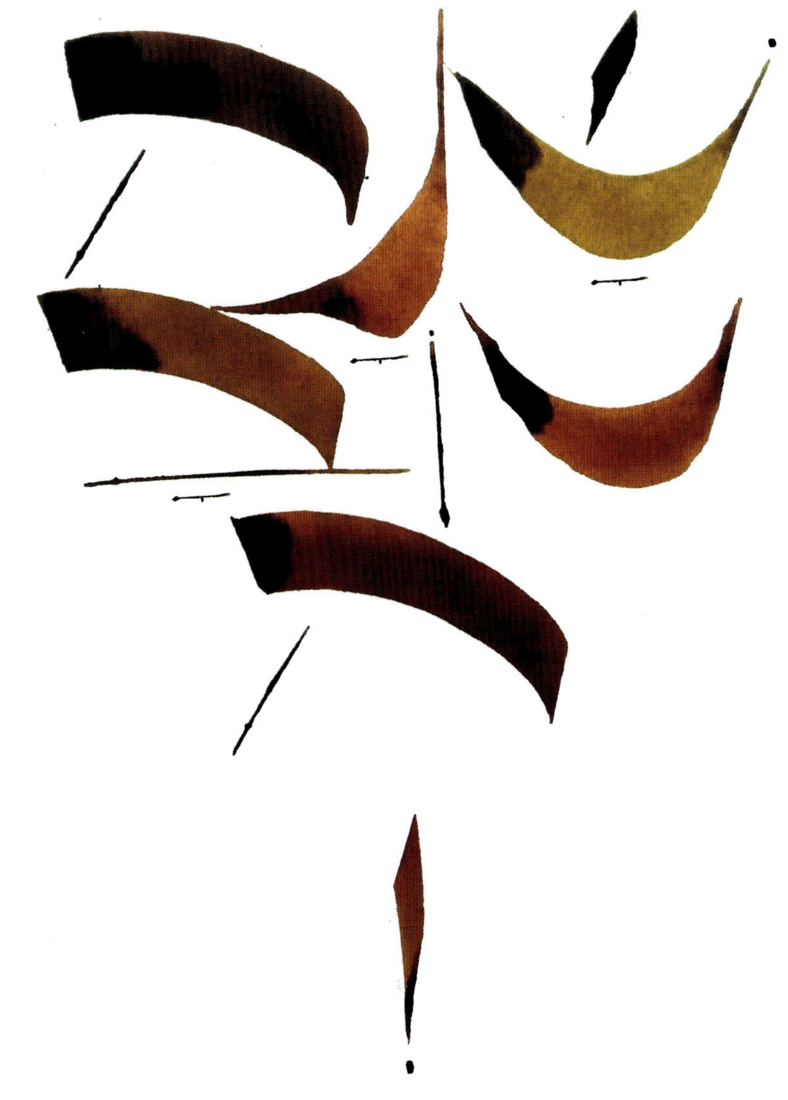

Izzy Pludwinski
Shanah Tovah! (A Good Year!), 2020

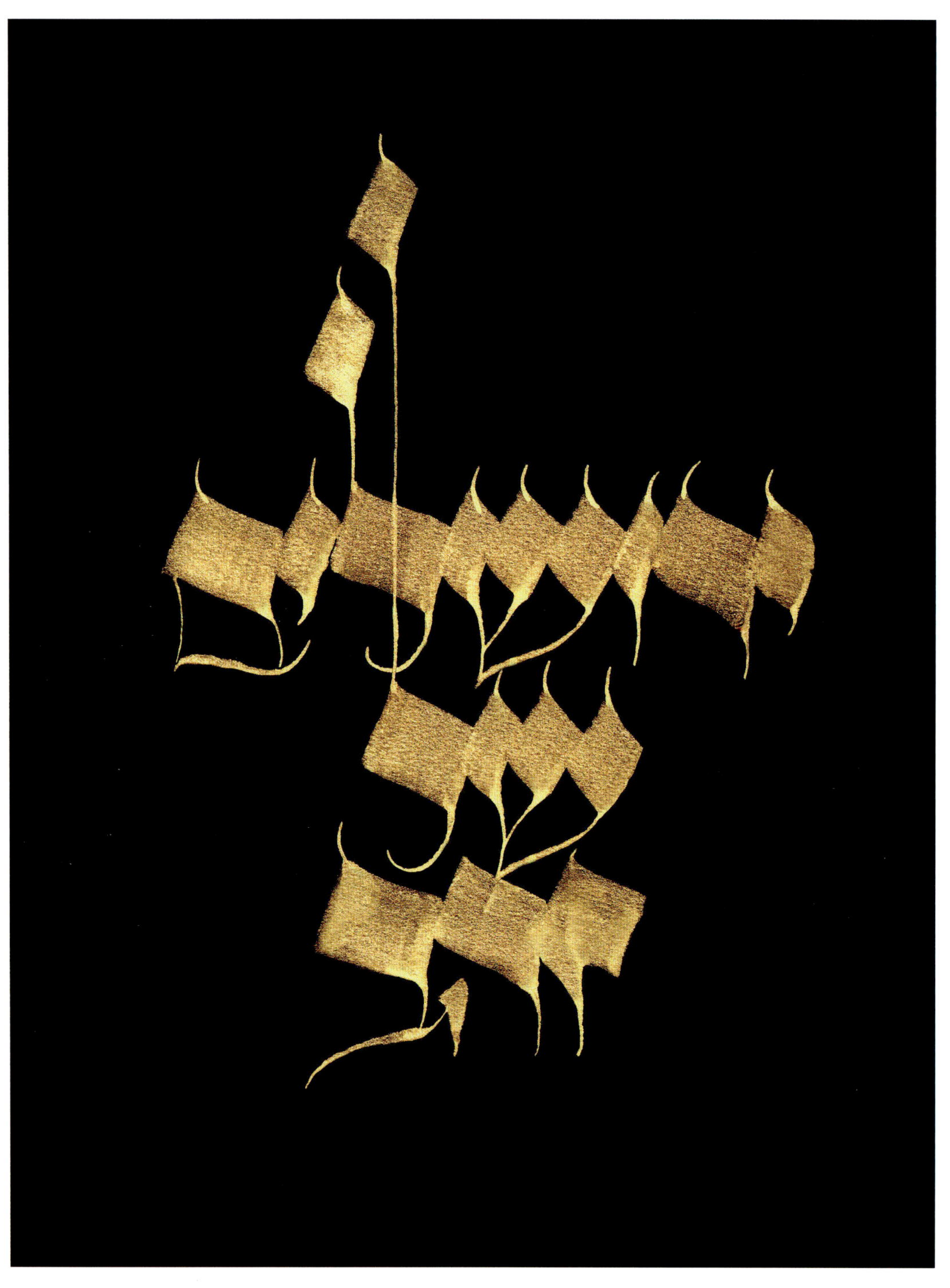

David Goldstein
Jerusalem of Gold, 2019

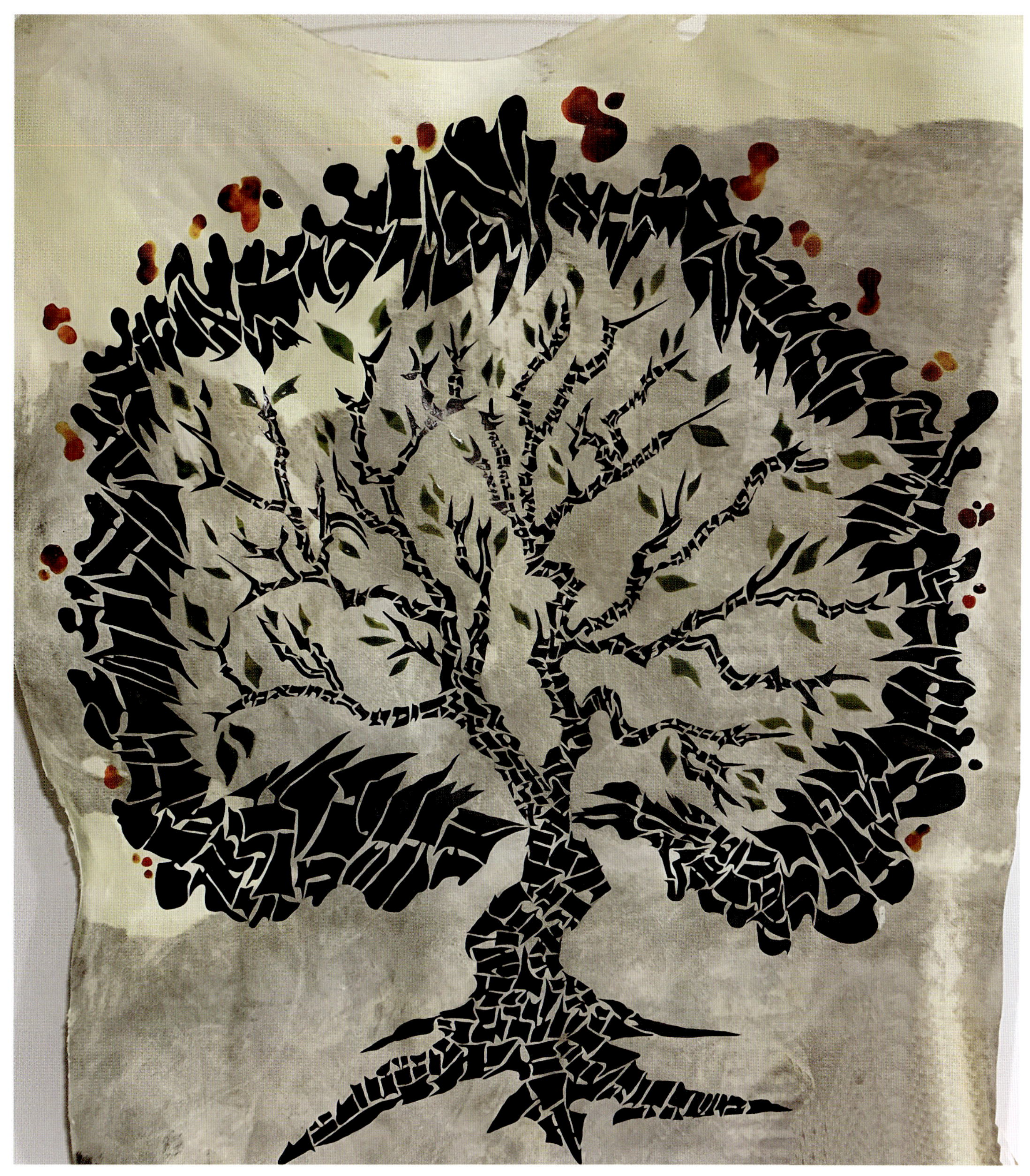

Nathaniel Smith
Burning Bush, 2020
Micrography from
Exodus 3 and 4

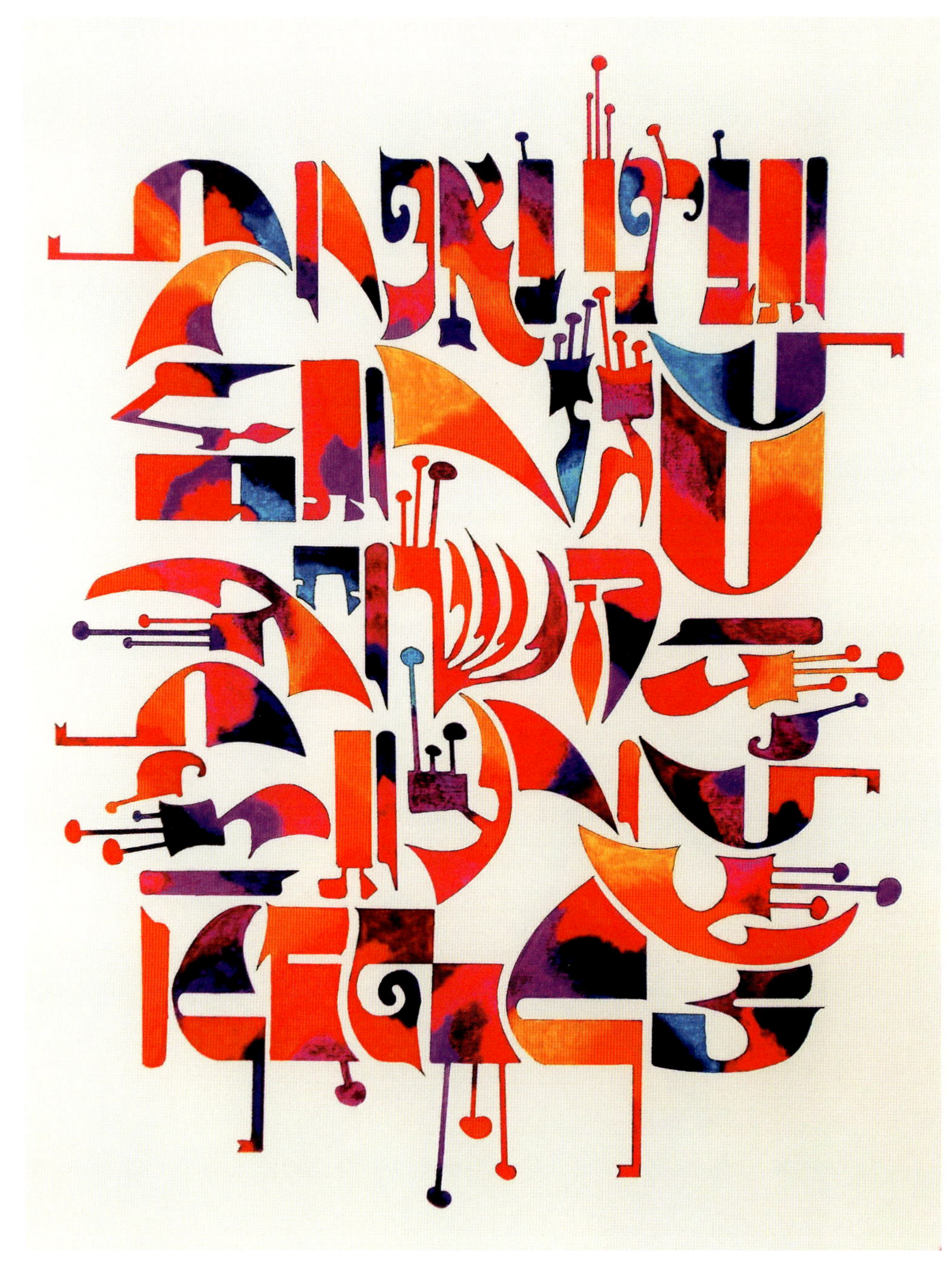

Moran Haynal
Calligraphy 10, 2018

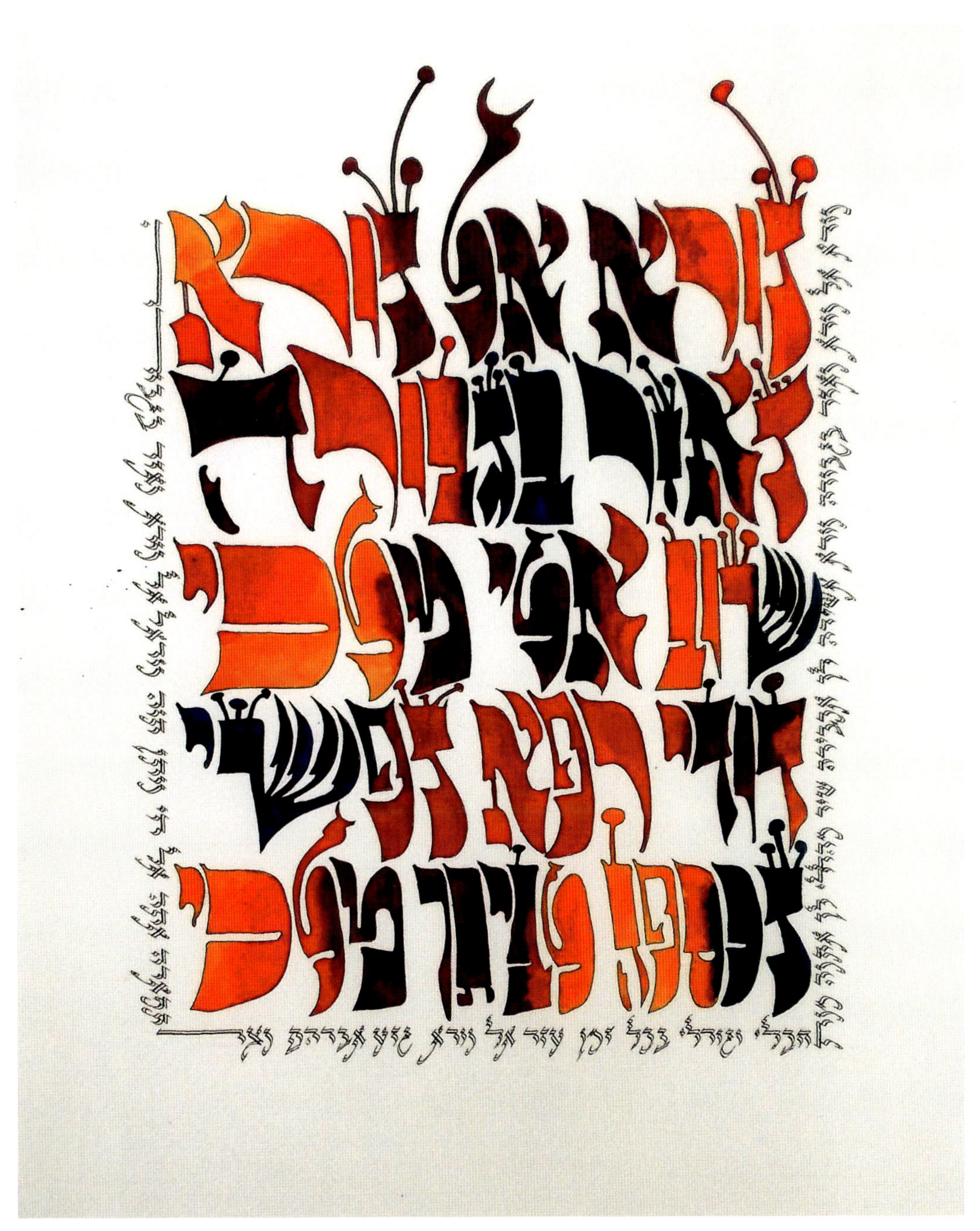

Moran Haynal
Calligraphy 5, 2016

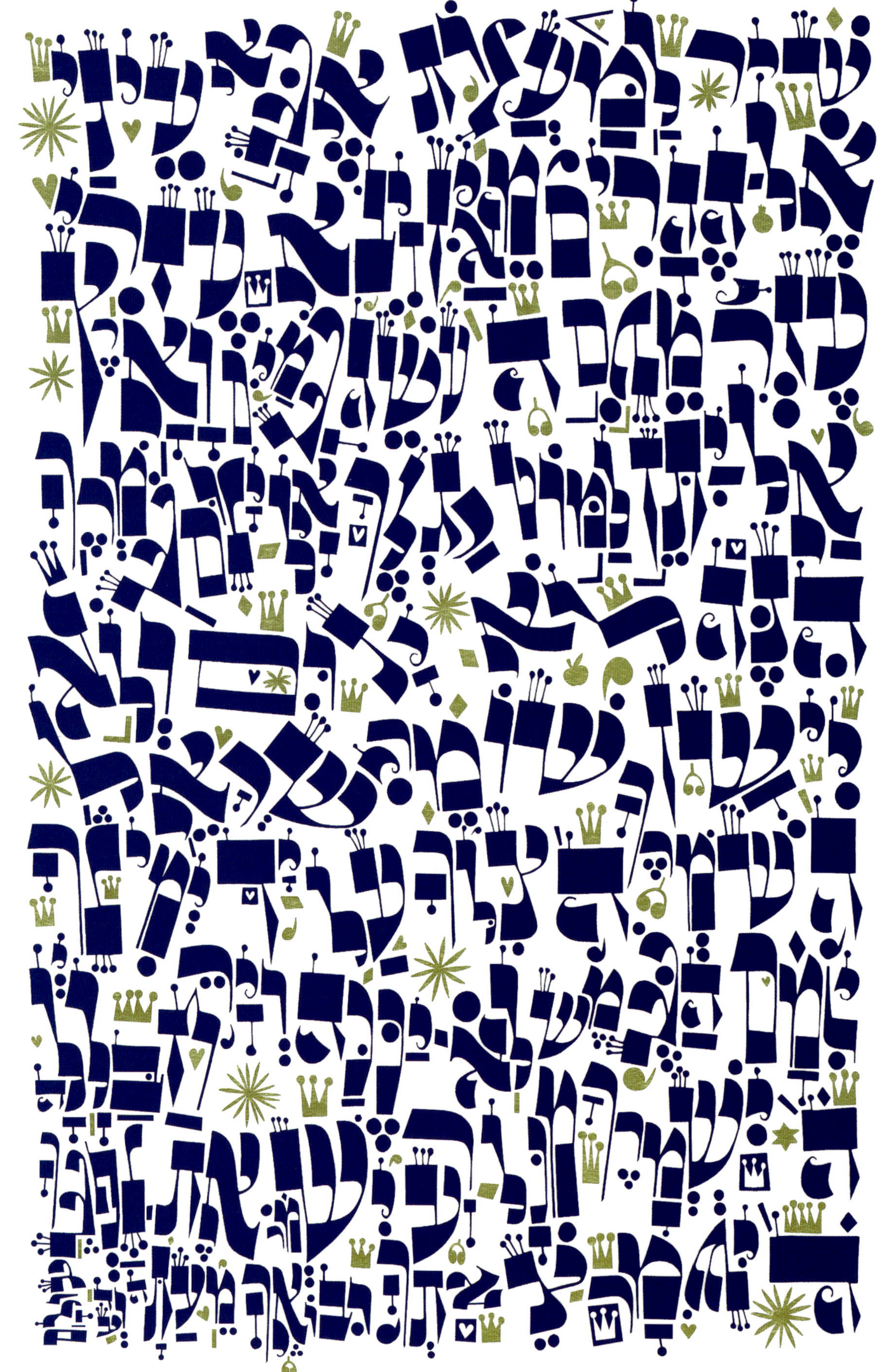

Josh Baum
Psalm 121, 1996

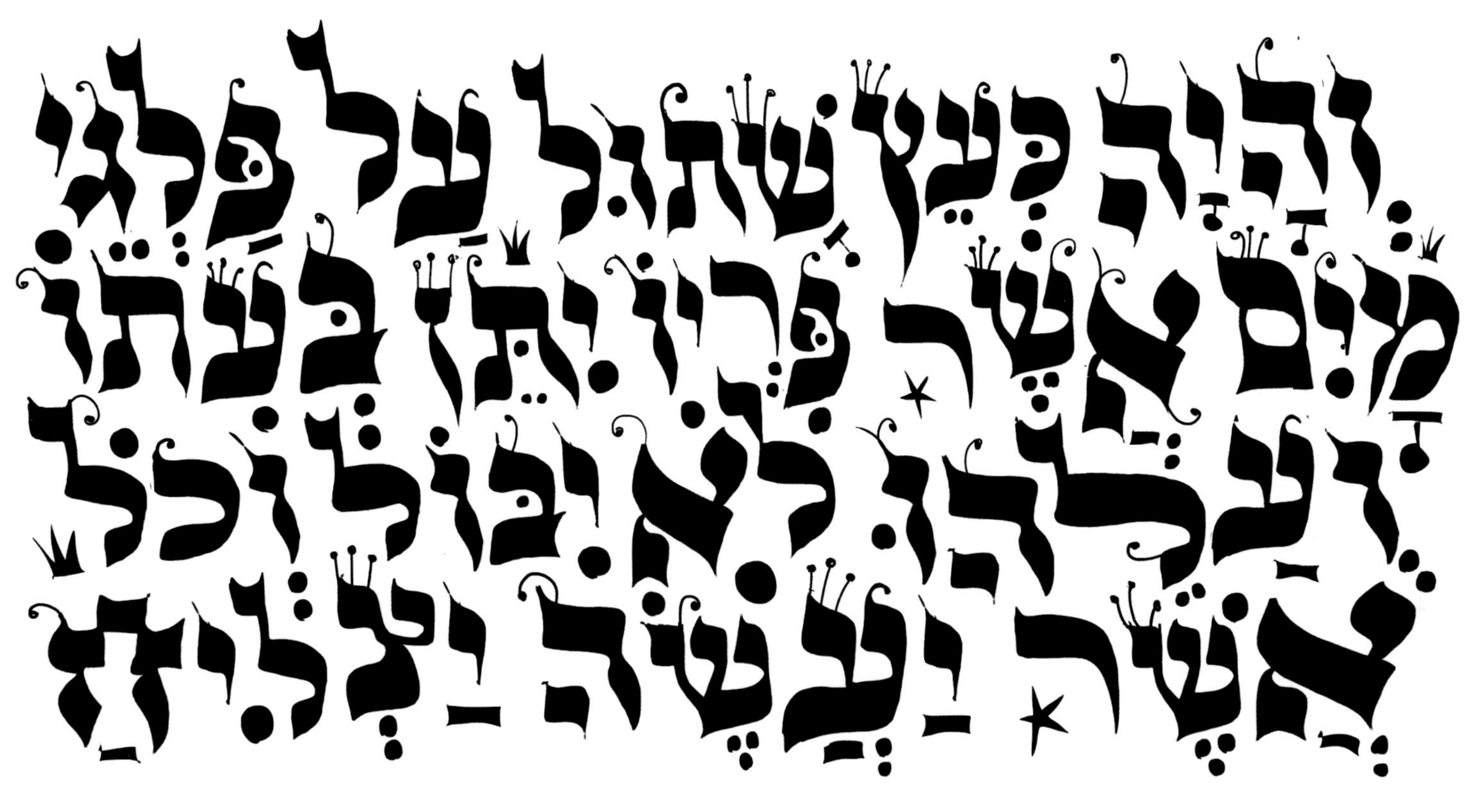

Josh Baum
Psalm 1:3, 2010

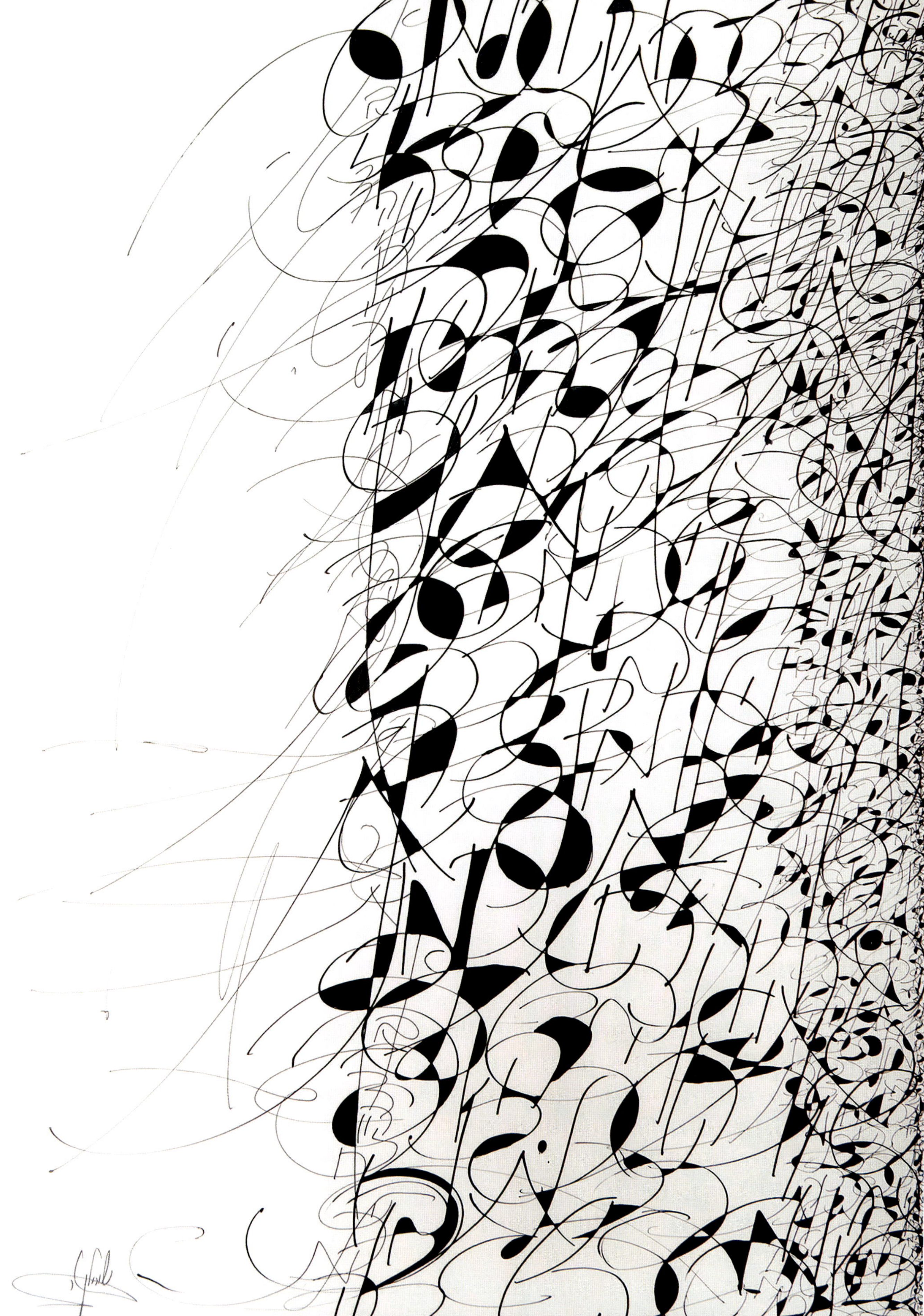

Shiri Lanzer
Improvisation, 2014

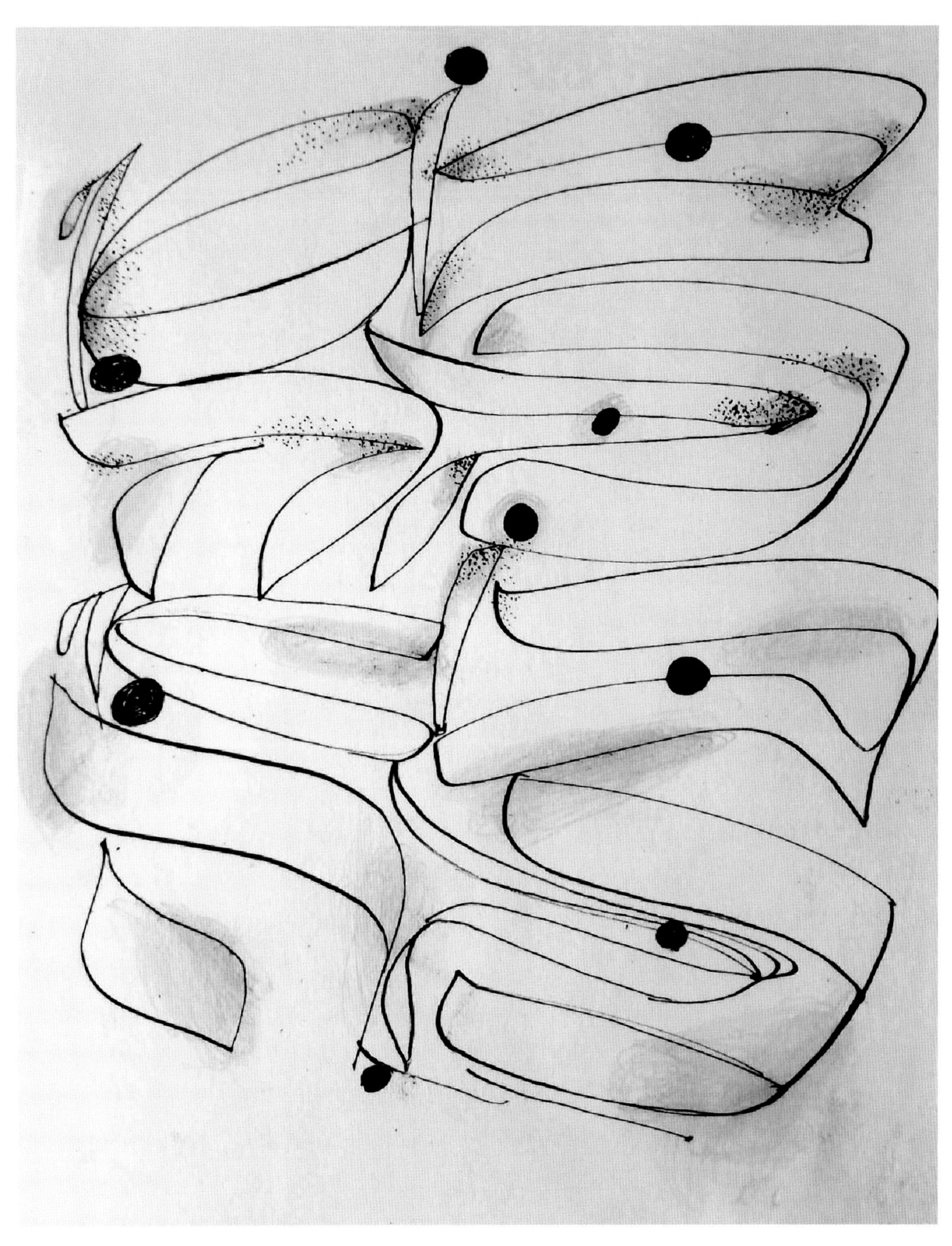

Lynn Broide
Come O Bride, late 1990s

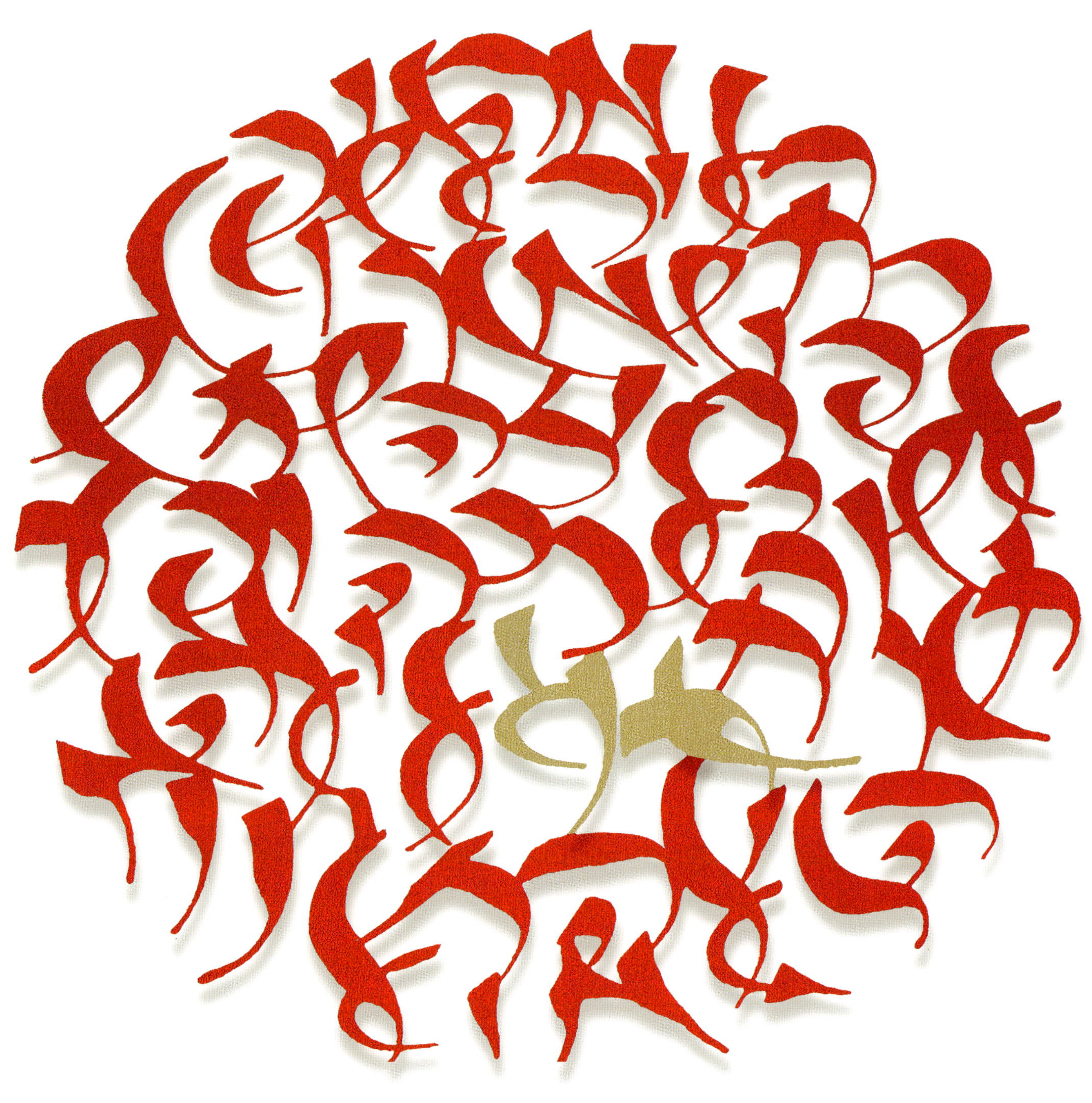

Ilanit Scharff Vigodsky
What Was Tonight, poem by the artist, 2020

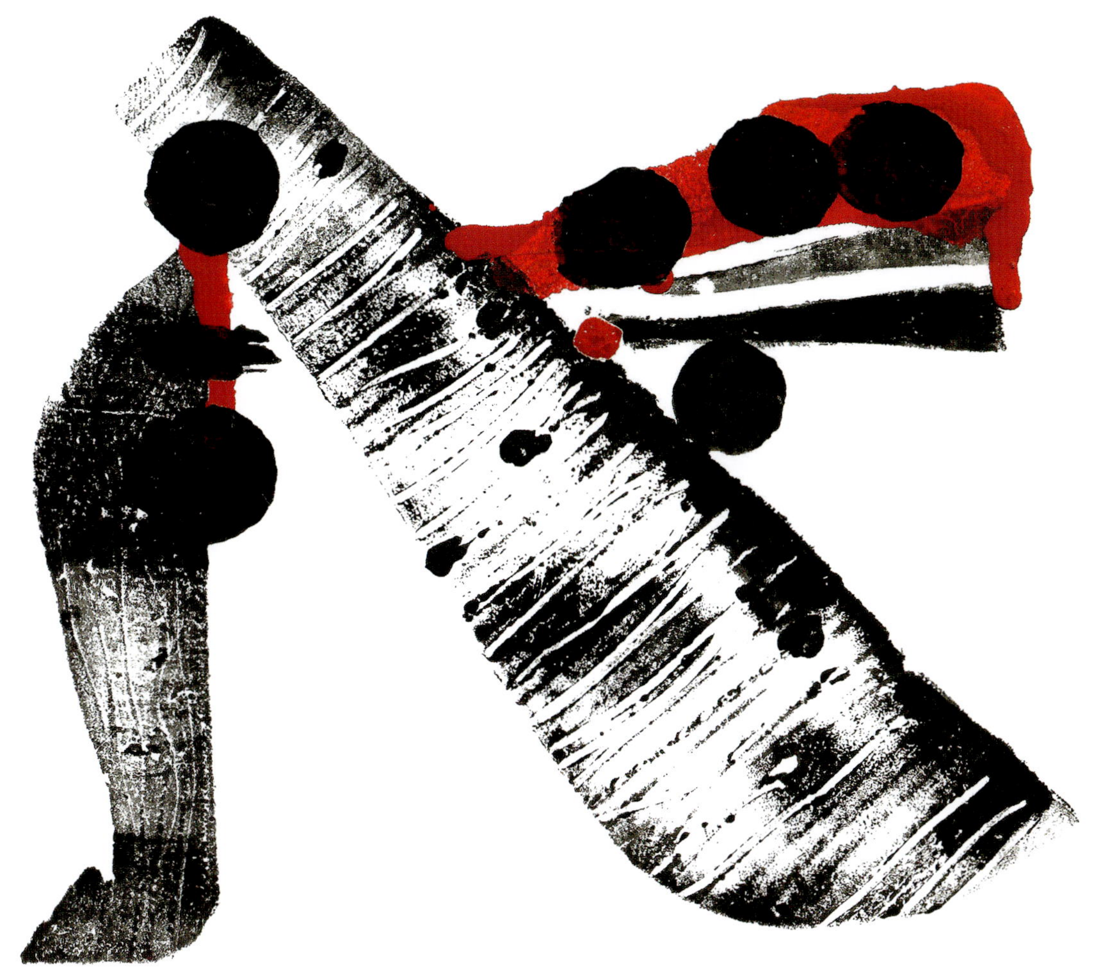

Itamar Heifetz
Aleph, 2021

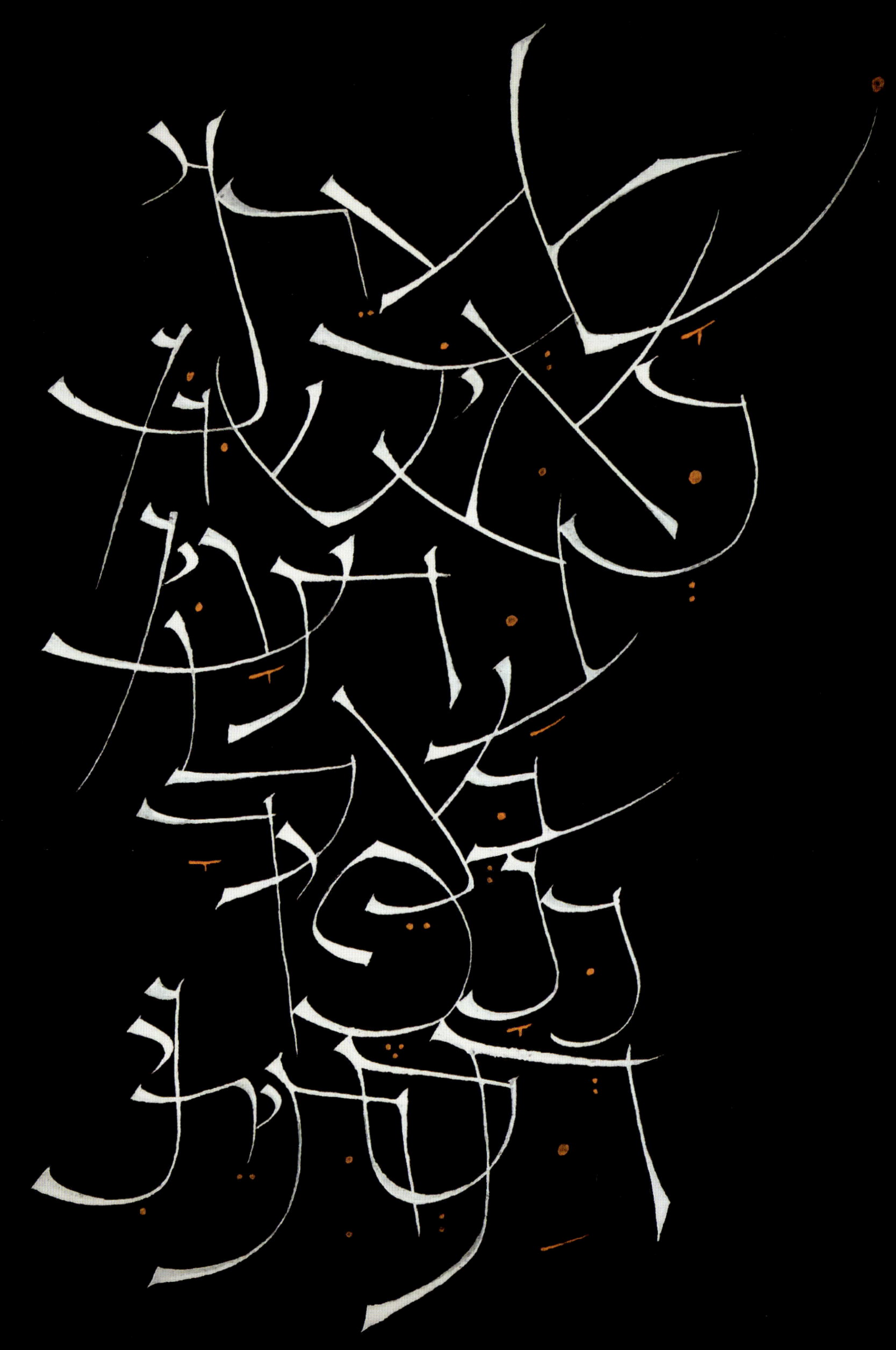

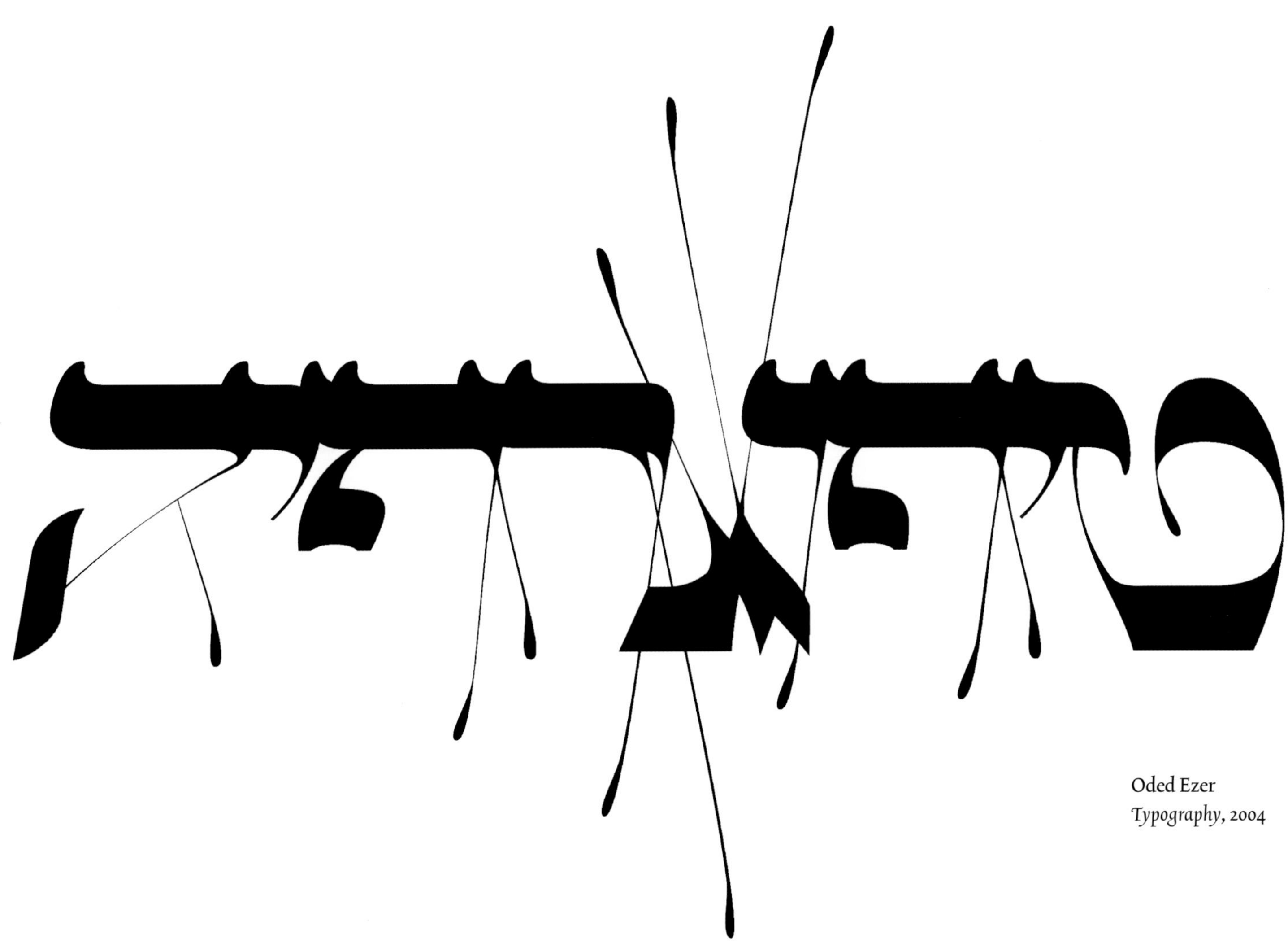

Oded Ezer
Typography, 2004

FACING PAGE: David Goldstein
Watch Over Me as the Apple of Your Eye, 2020
Based on Psalm 17:8

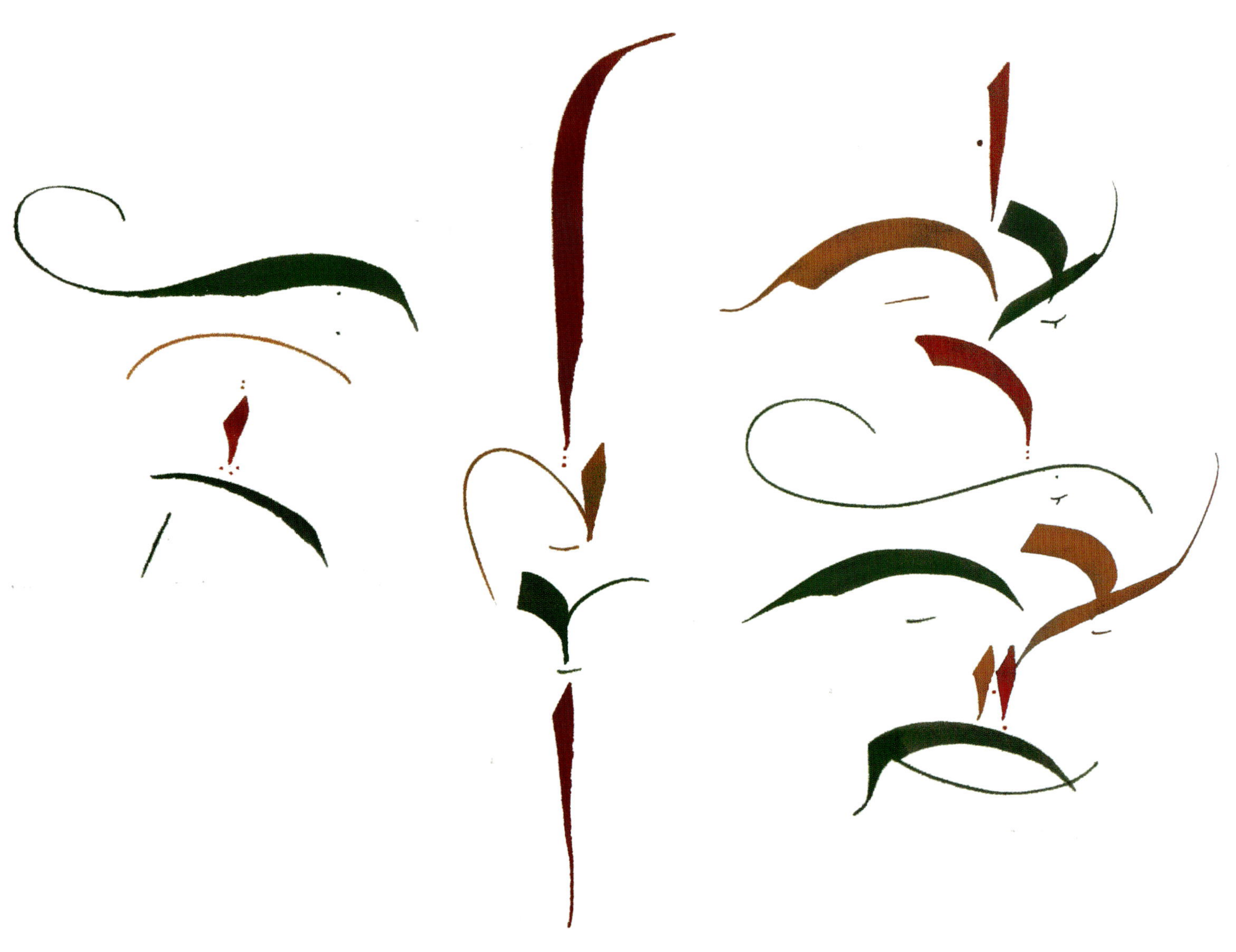

Izzy Pludwinski
And You Shall Choose Life, 2016
From Deuteronomy 30:19

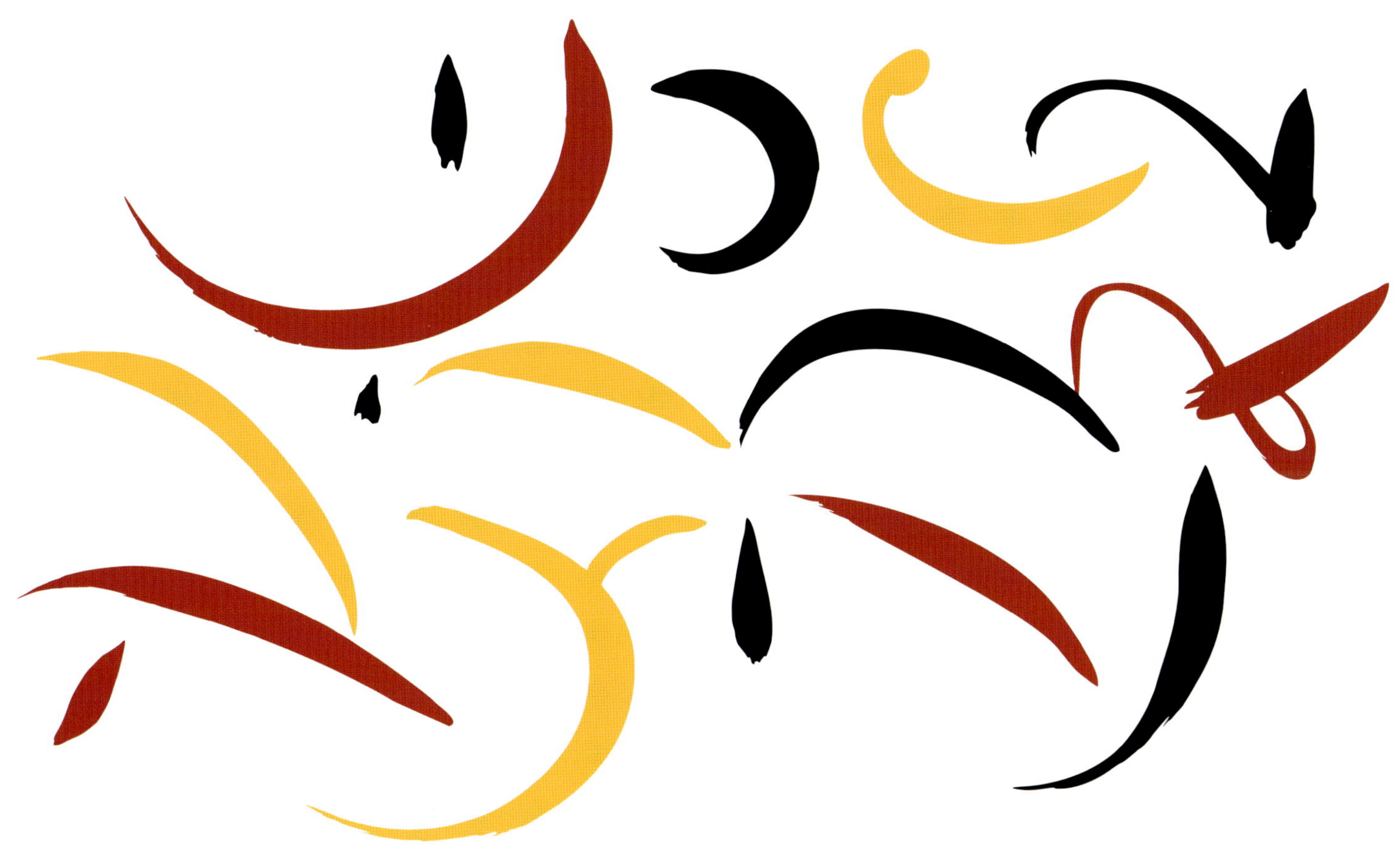

Izzy Pludwinski
Draw Me after You and We Will Run, 2006
From the *Song of Songs* 1:4

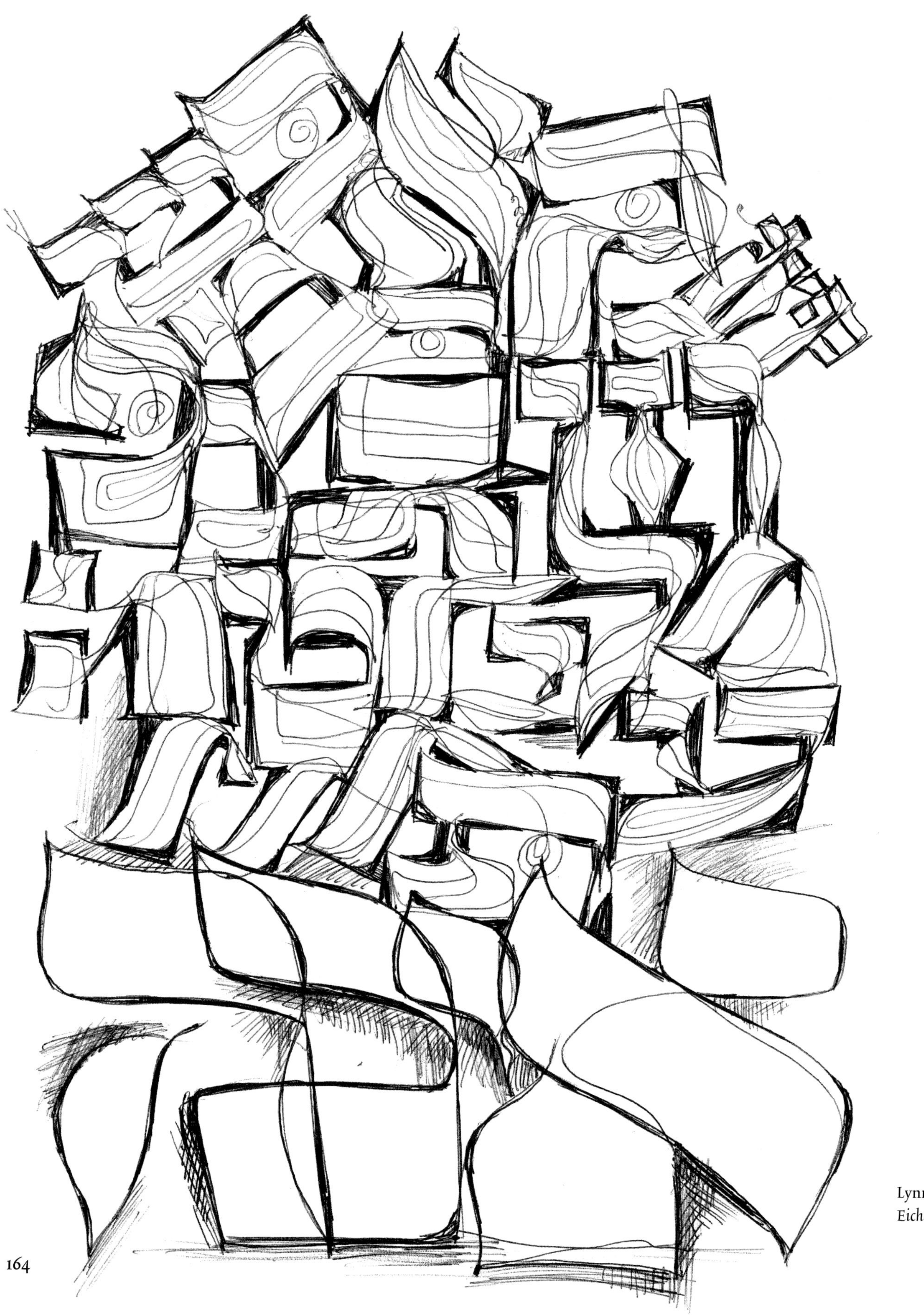

Lynn Broide
Eichah, c. 2018

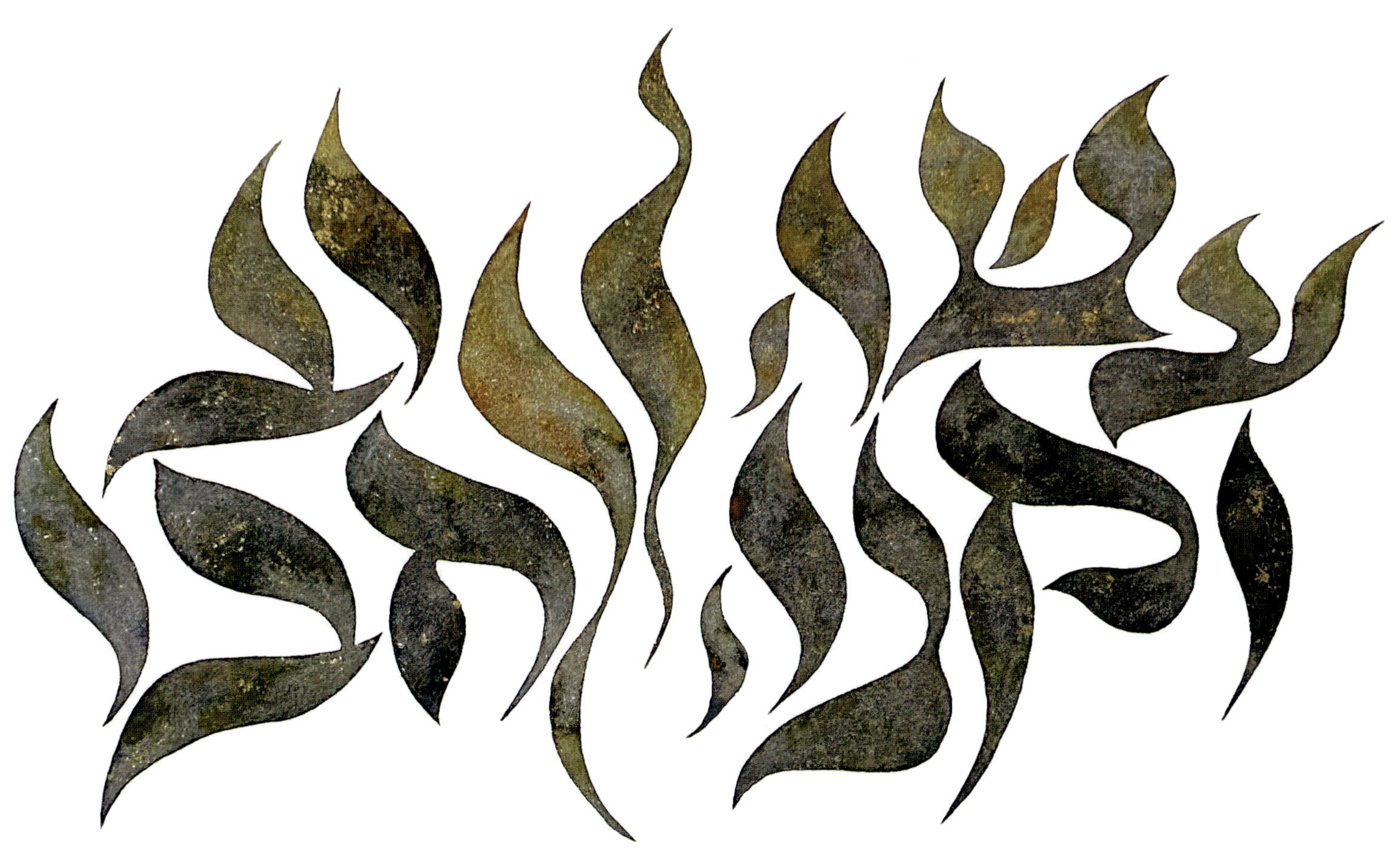

Karen Ness
Acquire a Teacher . . . , 2022

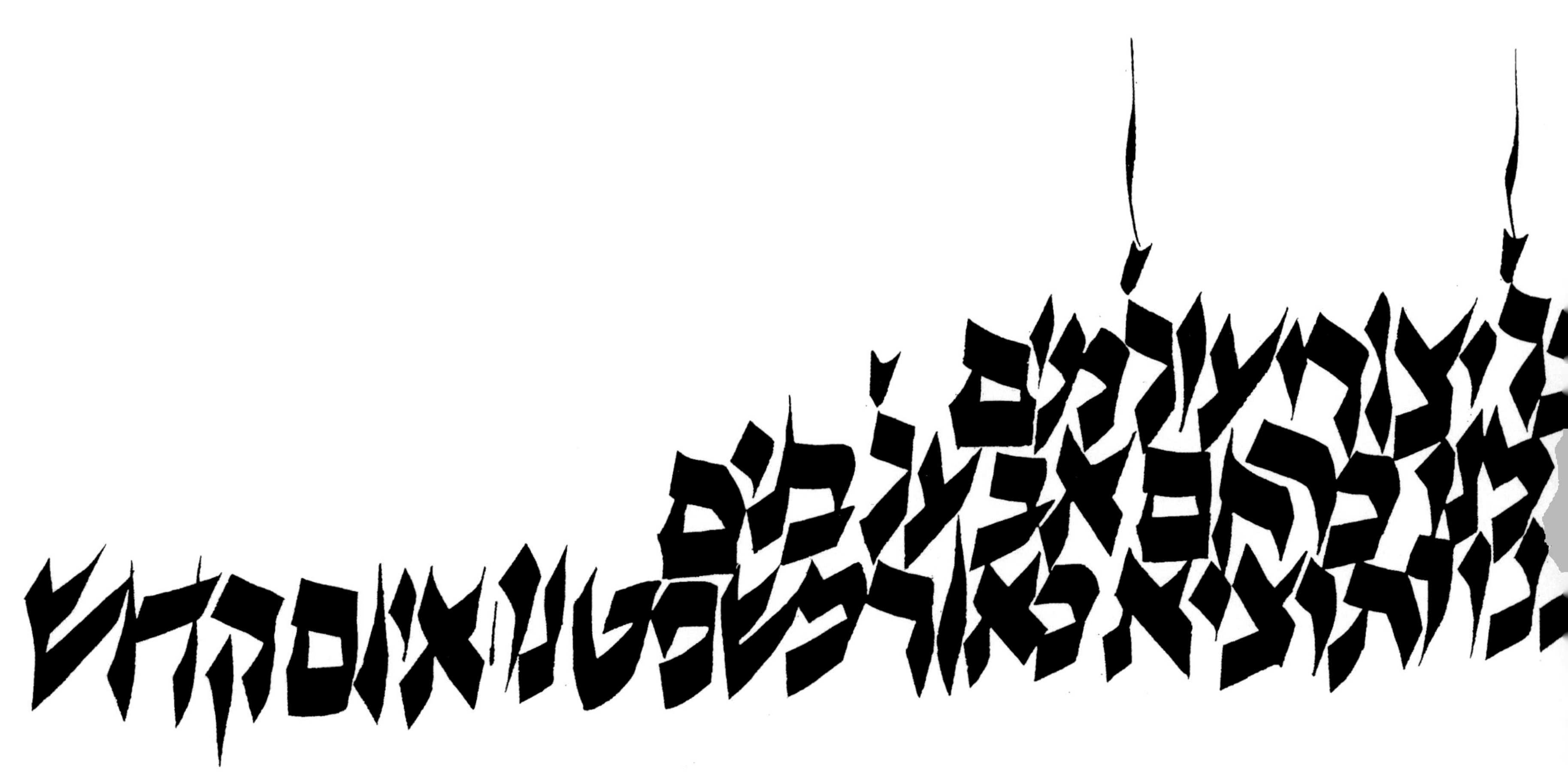

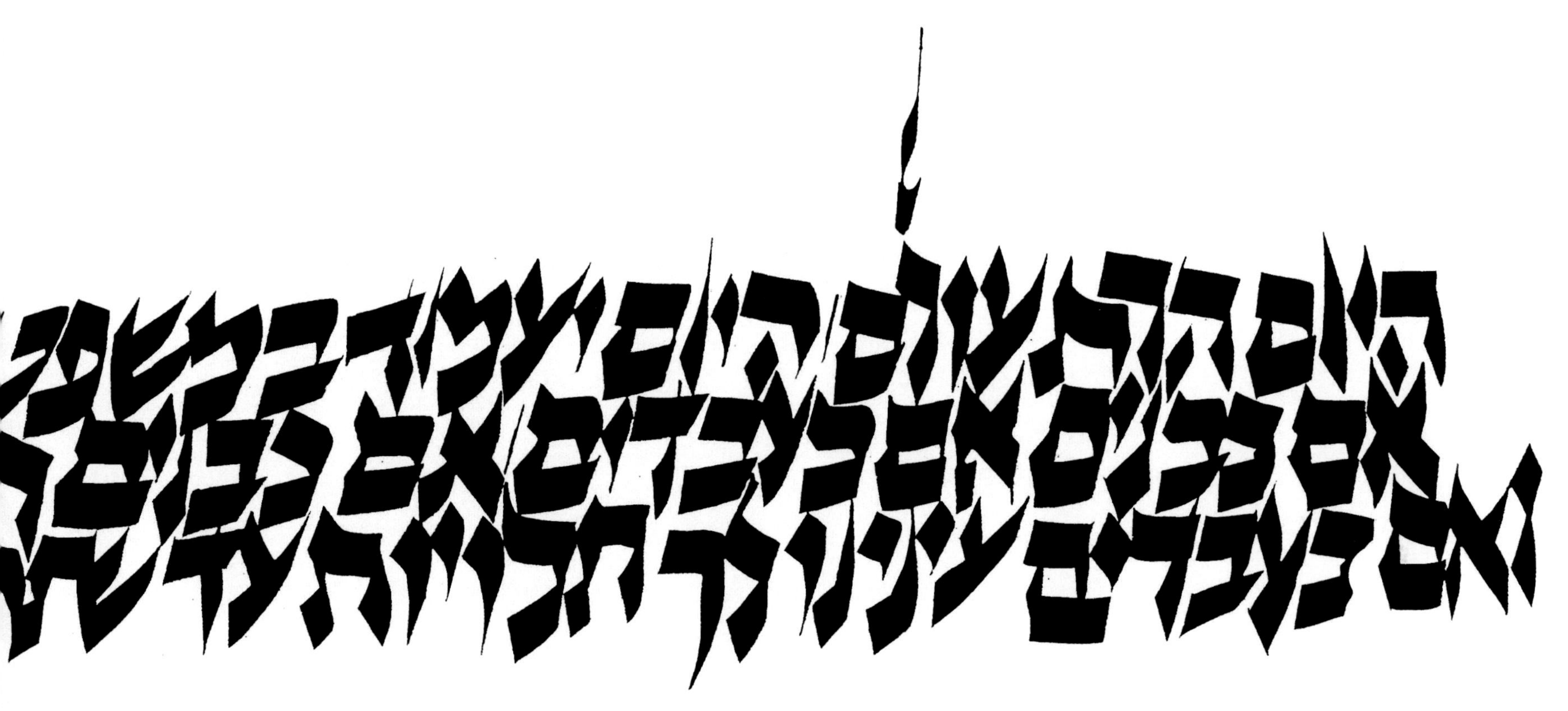

Lynn Broide
Today Is the Birth of the World, 1991

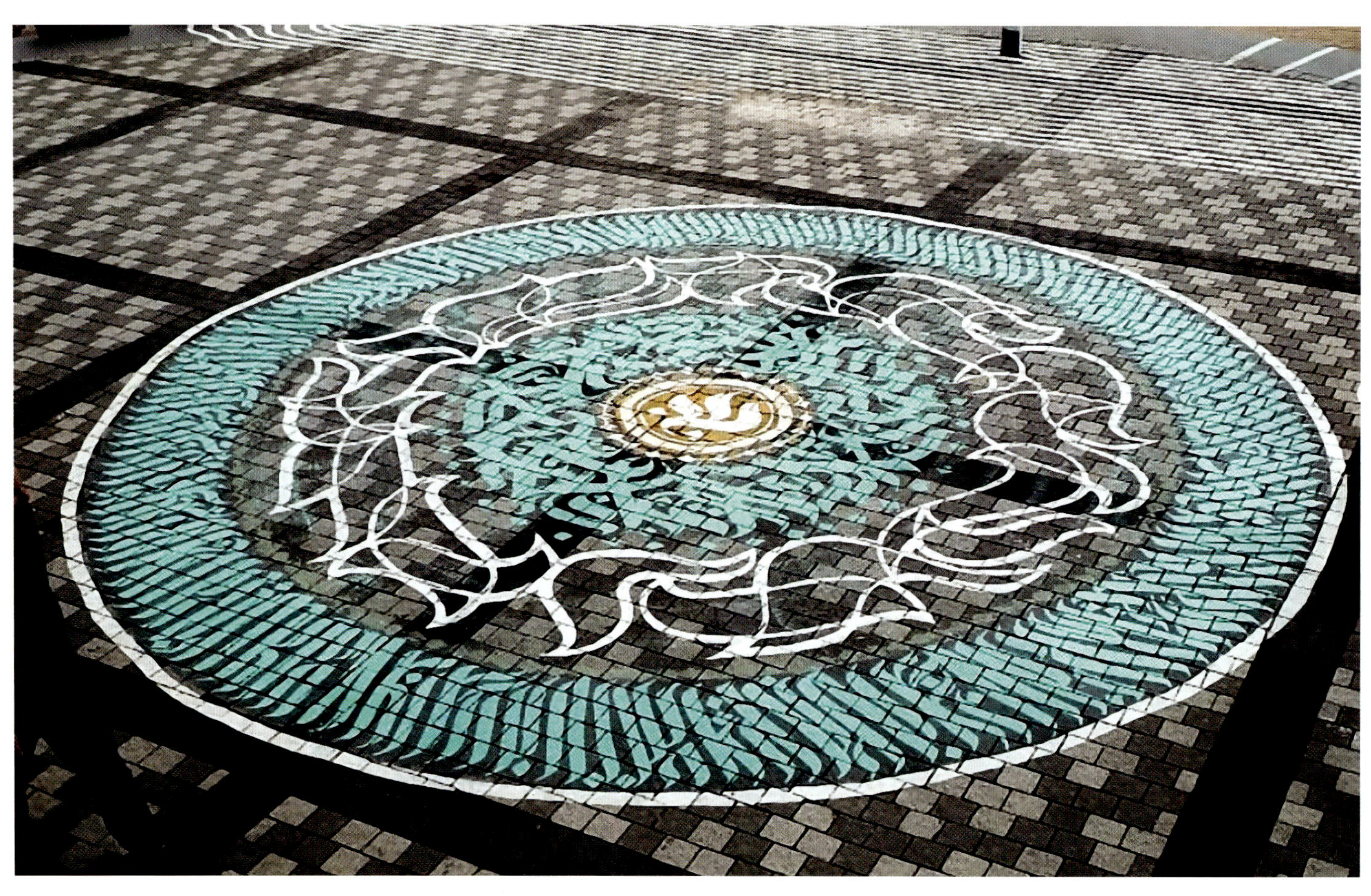

Ira Dayan
Circle of Blessing, c. 2018

5
Street Art & Fine Art

The twenty-first century has seen a global rise in street art and graffiti, and naturally this has attracted creative Hebrew letterers. These young artists have taken the art of lettering out of the studio to the walls and buildings of the city, thus exposing the public to new possibilities in creative Hebrew lettering.

On the other side of the coin, fine artists have incorporated Hebrew letters into their paintings, the focus on the mystique of these forms and symbols being intrinsic to the content of their art.

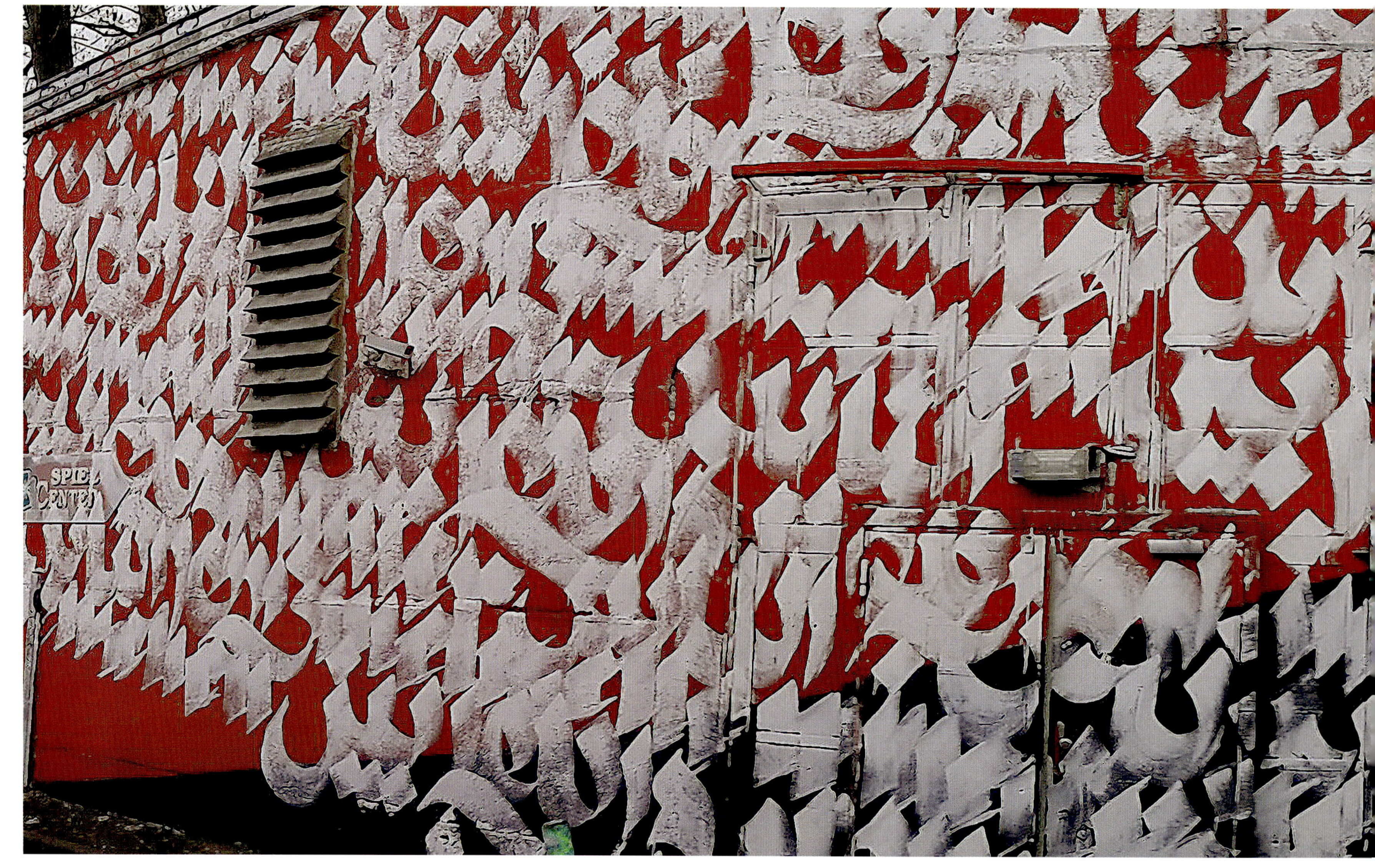

Part of the mural series Among Refugees Generation Y.

*In the words of the artist: "*Among Refugees Generation Y *is a series of temporary, site-specific, and multilingual (Yiddish, German, Arabic) calligraphy murals in the public space of Berlin, inspired by the story 'Among Refugees' (1923) by the Yiddish writer Dovid Bergelson (1884–1952), who lived and worked in Berlin in the 1920s."*

This series integrates languages to reach a harmonious visual manifestation of Berlin's cultural hybridity.

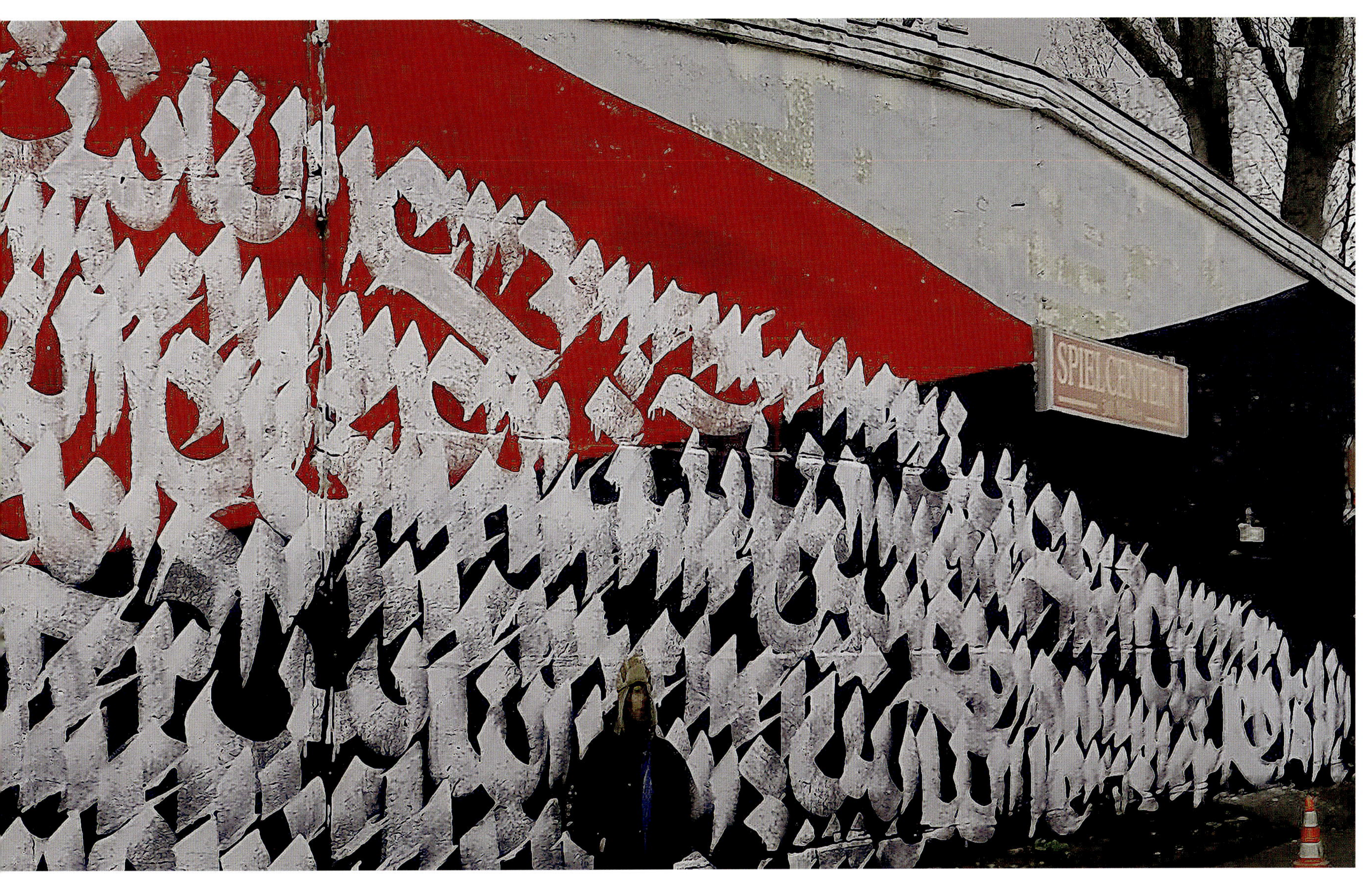

Ella Ponizovsky Bergelson
People Among People, 2019
Lime paint on plaster, 20 x 5.5 m
Mensch Meier, Berlin
Photo by Lea Fabrikant

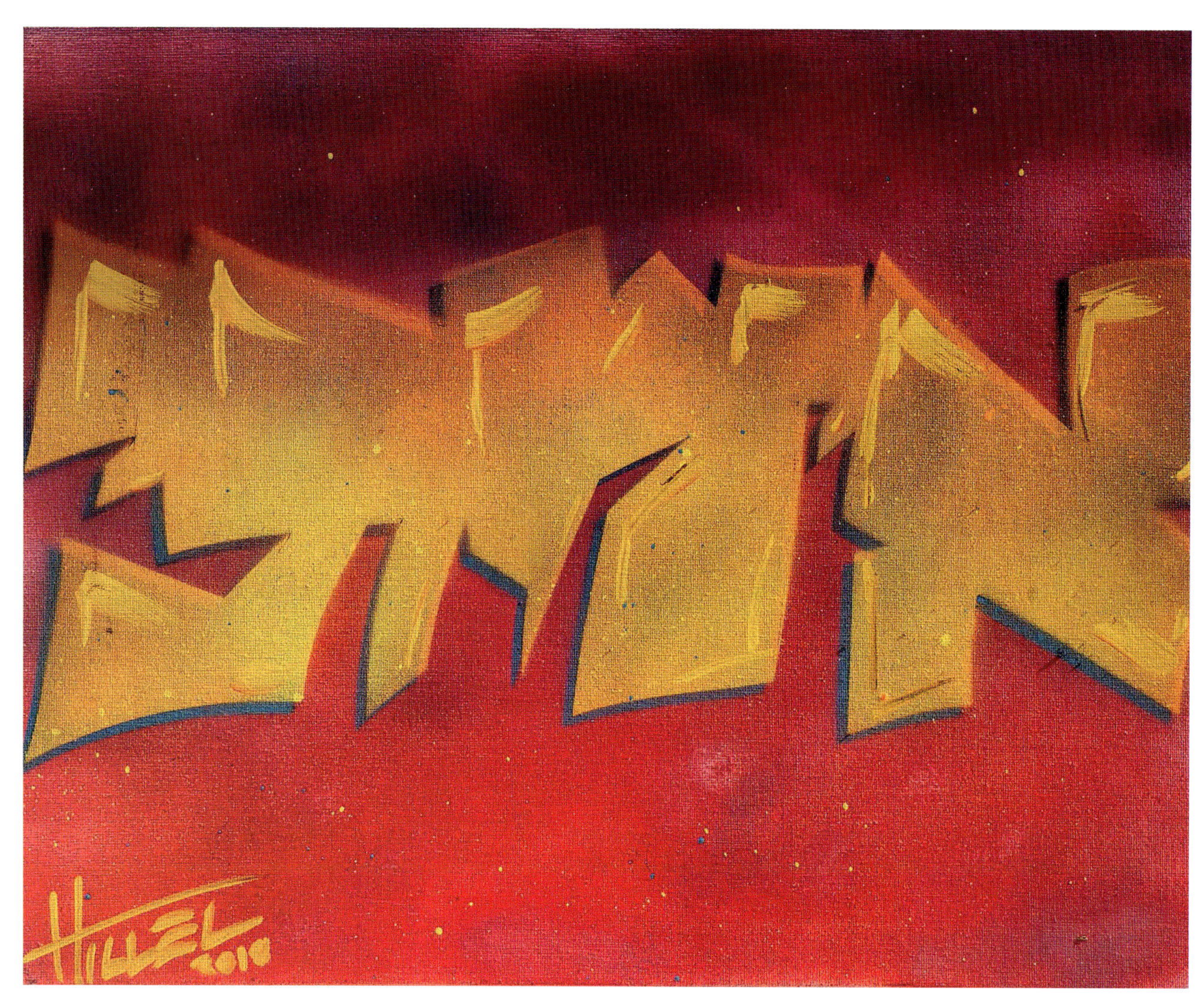

Hillel Smith
When? 2018

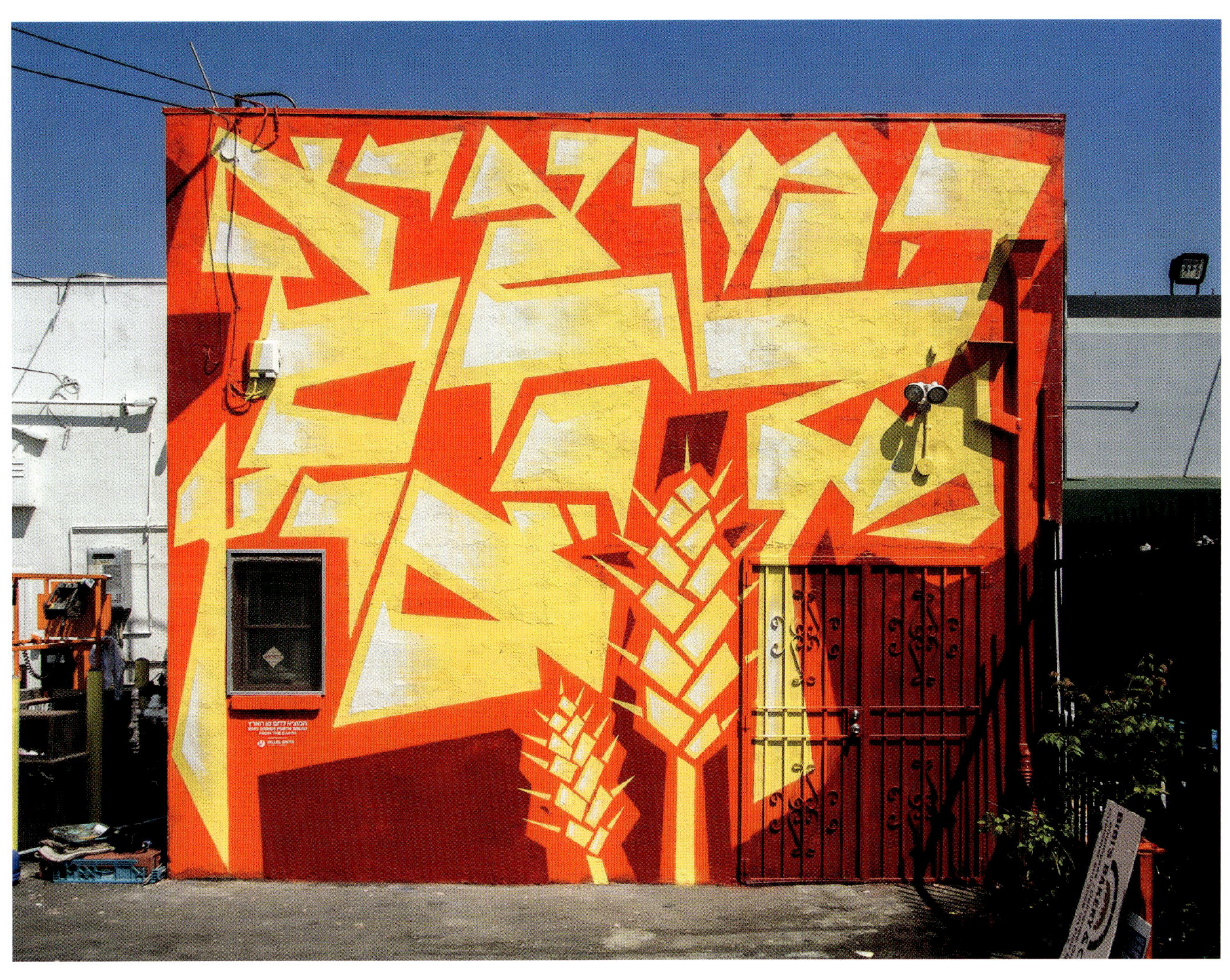

Hillel Smith
Who Brings Forth Bread from the Land
Sign on bakery, 2016

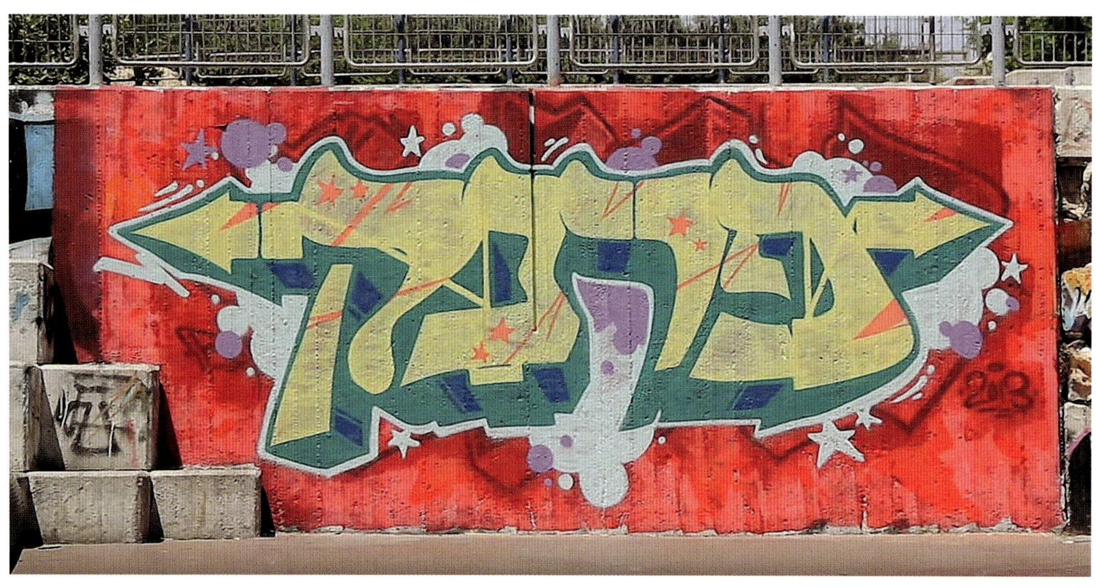

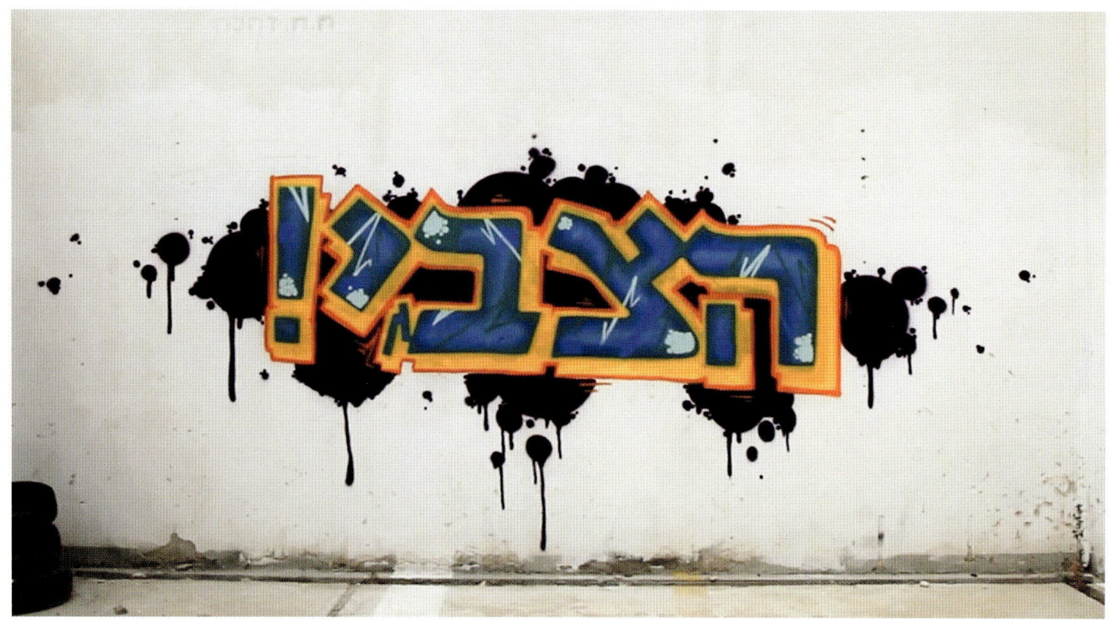

Asaf Mendelovitch
Graffiti series of interpretations of the names of popular Hebrew typefaces
TOP: *Frank-Reuhl*
BOTTOM: *Hatzvi, 2014*
FACING PAGE: *Hadassah, 2014*

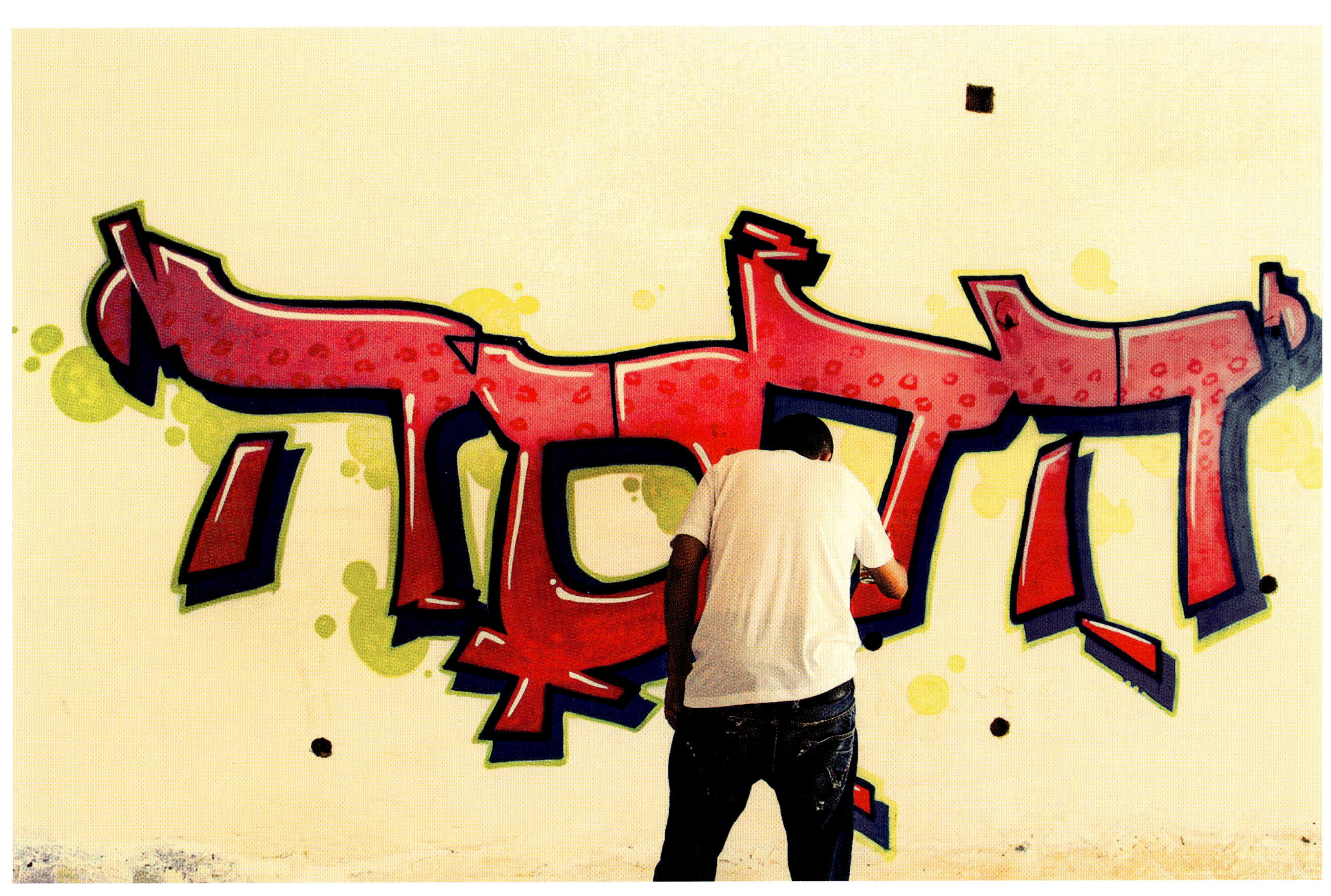

What I find interesting in graffiti is that the artists seem to completely deconstruct the letters, divide them into their individual strokes, then redesign the shapes of each of the strokes in a creative and often surprising manner, and then put it all back together. This is a far cry from how traditional lettering artists approach their forms. It is sometimes hard to read the word or words (often just their tag), but the result can be exciting from a purely graphic perspective.

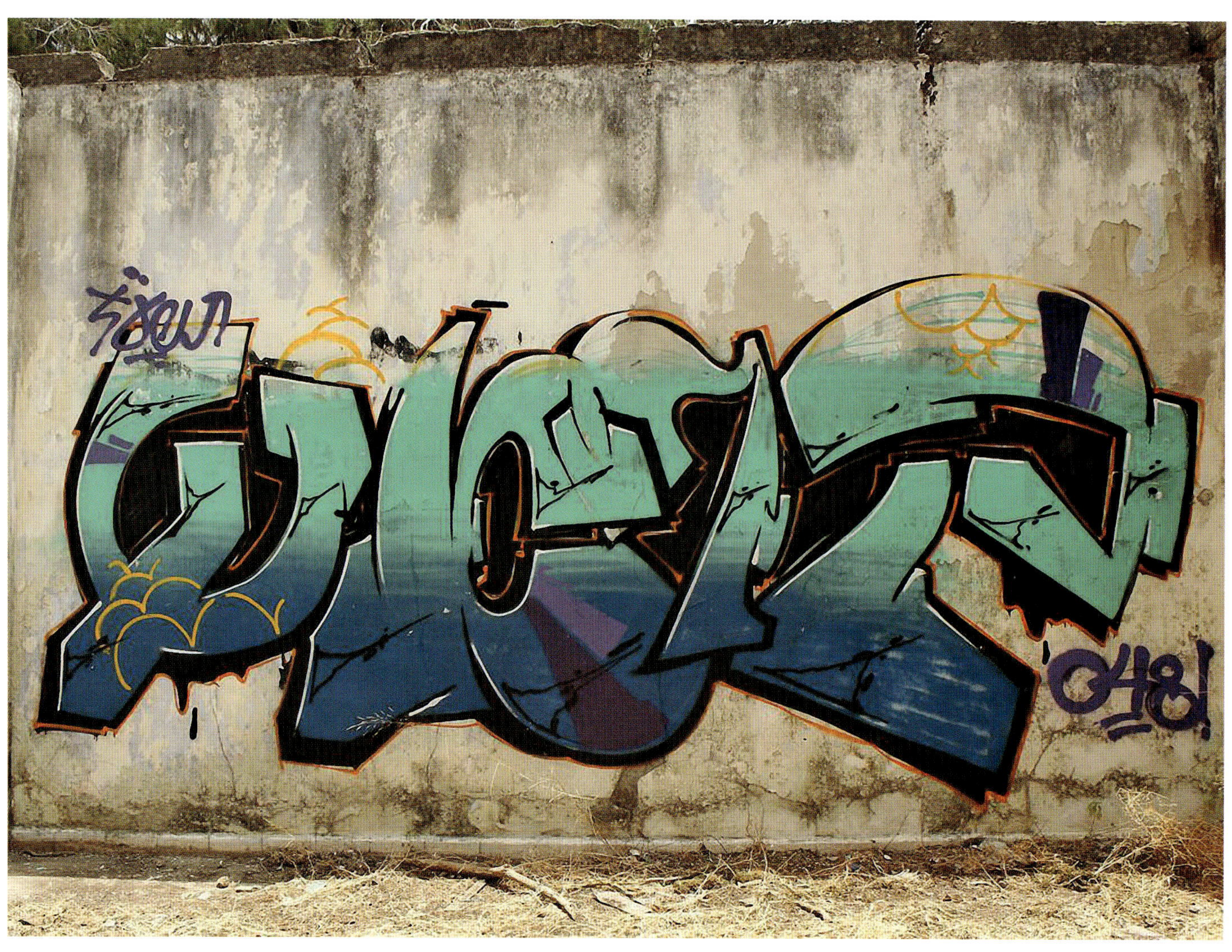

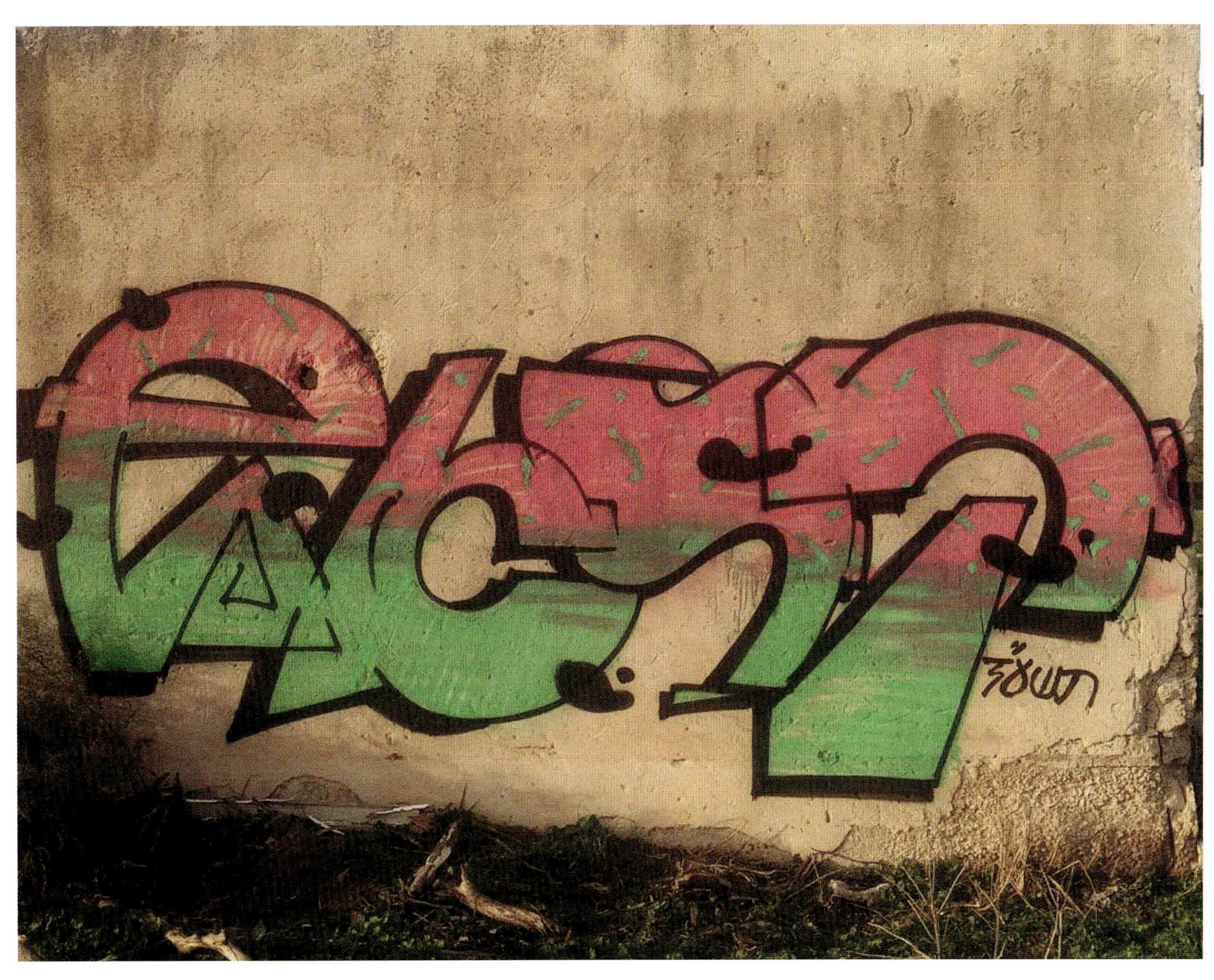

LEFT AND ABOVE:
Crash 048
Crash, 2017

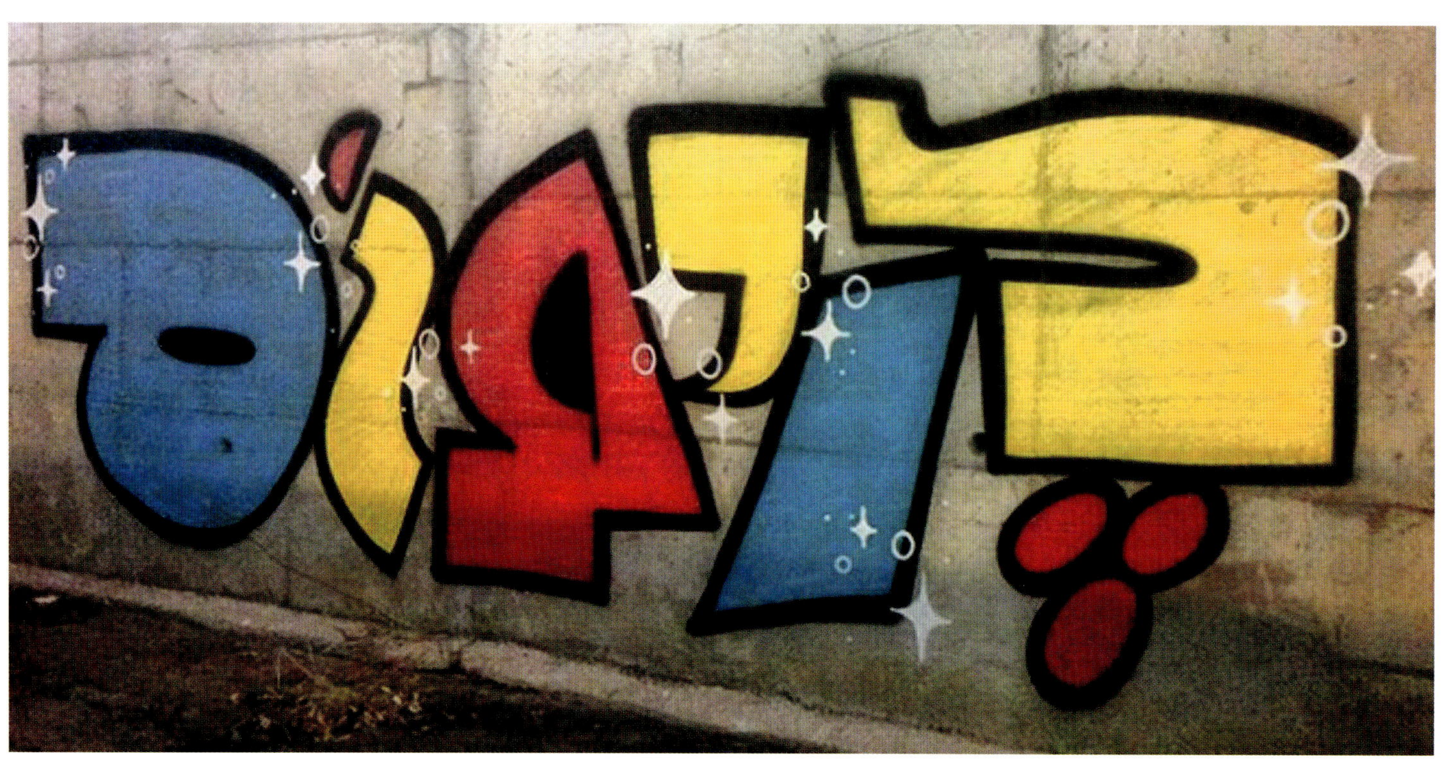

LEFT AND RIGHT:
Keos 048
Keos, 2015

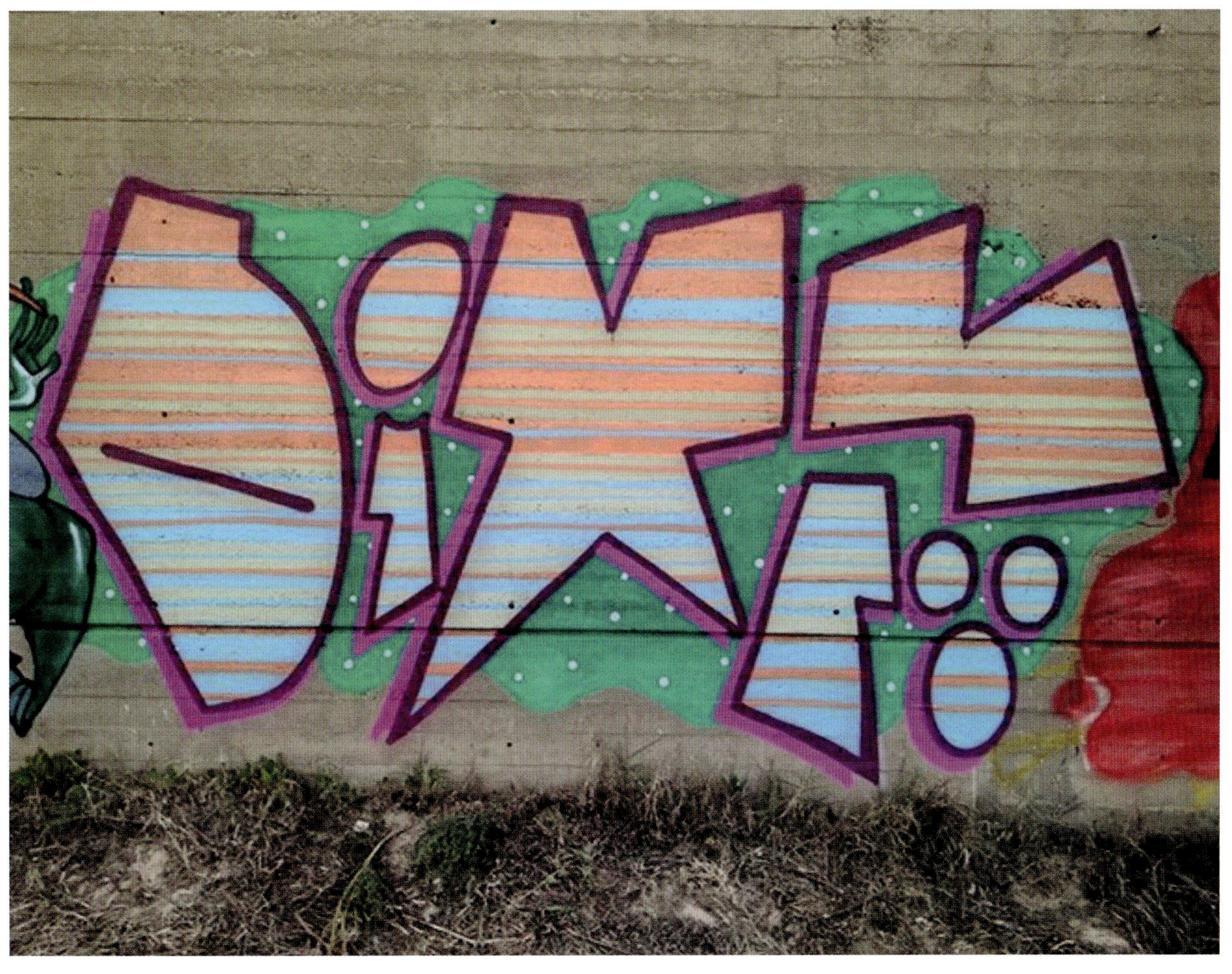

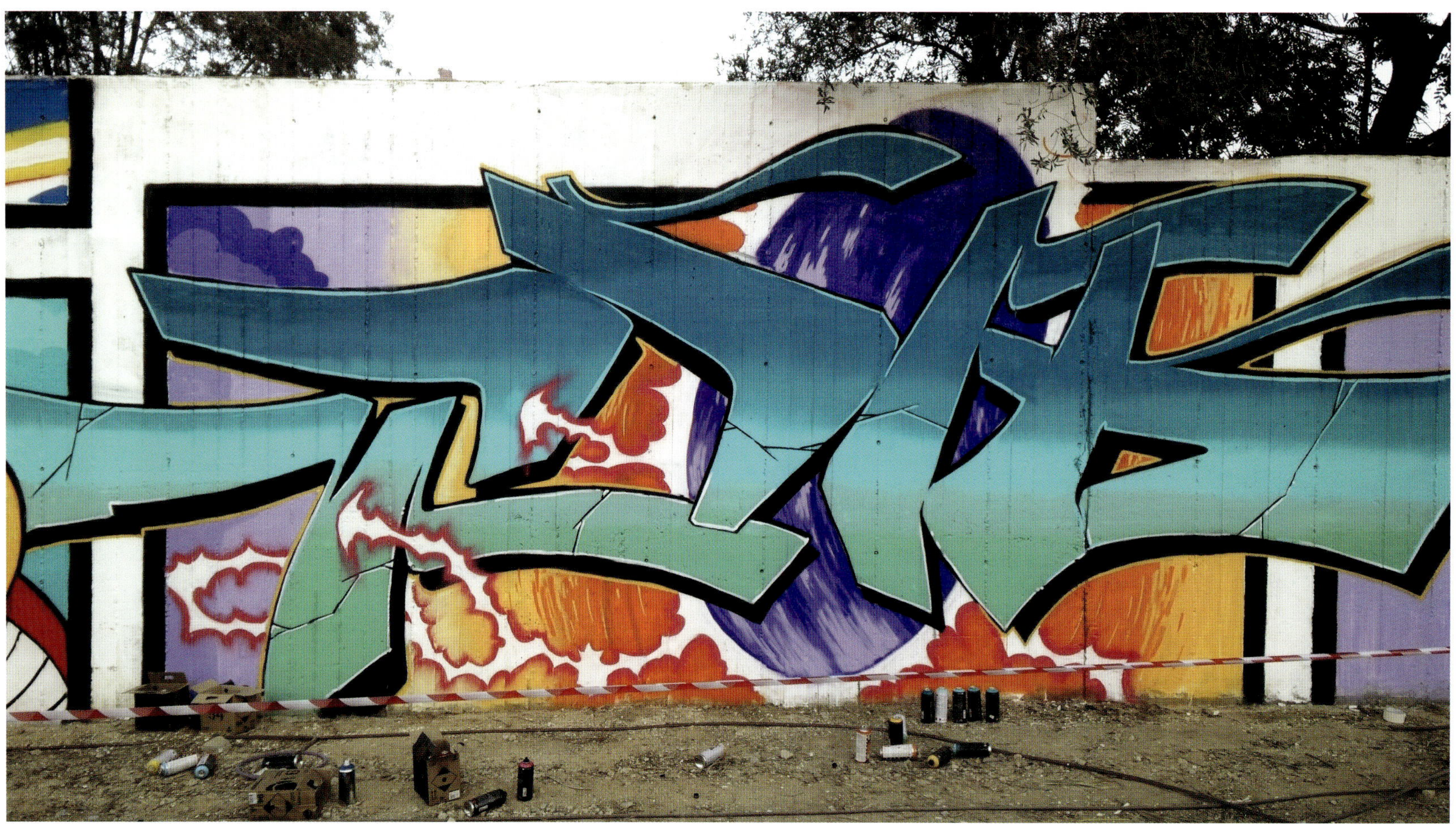

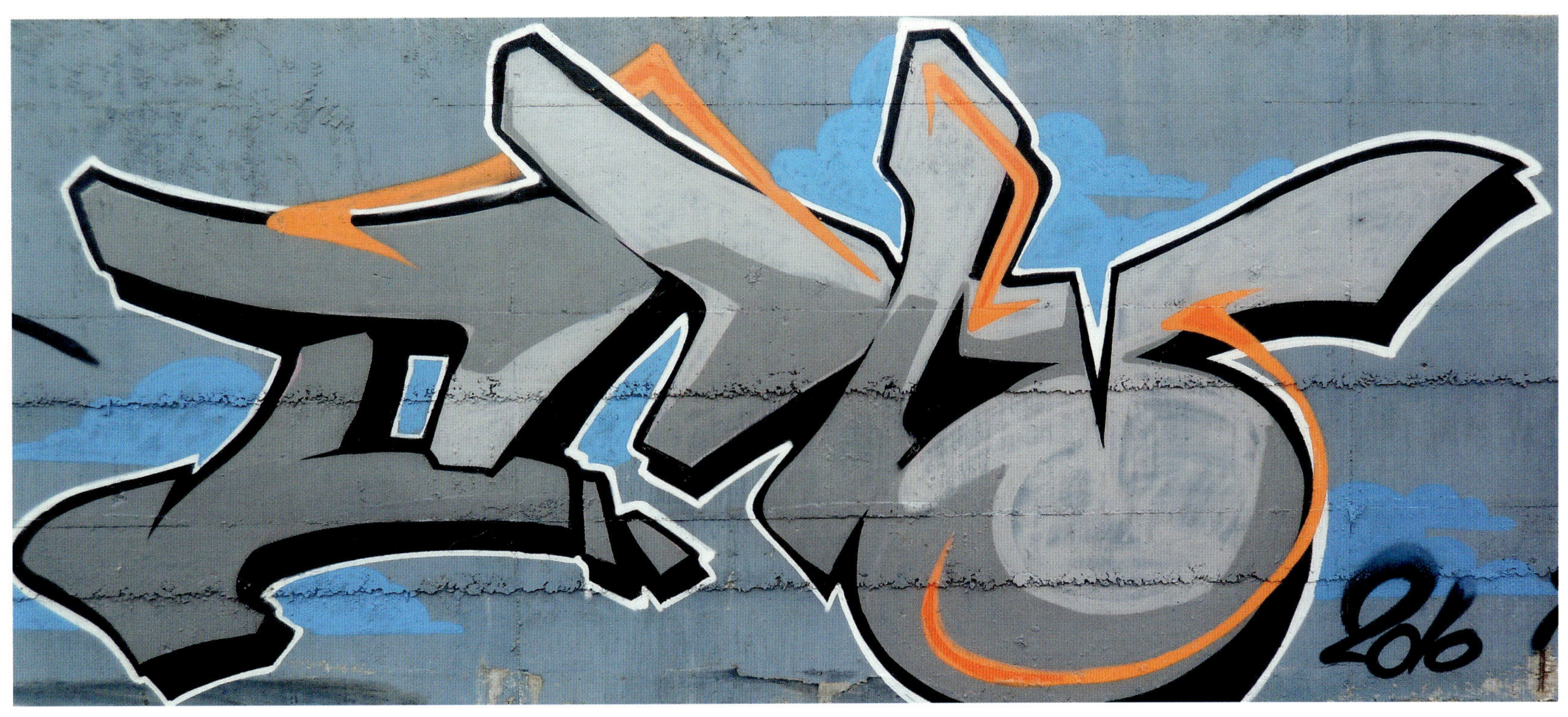

LEFT AND ABOVE:
Orek
Orek, 2010

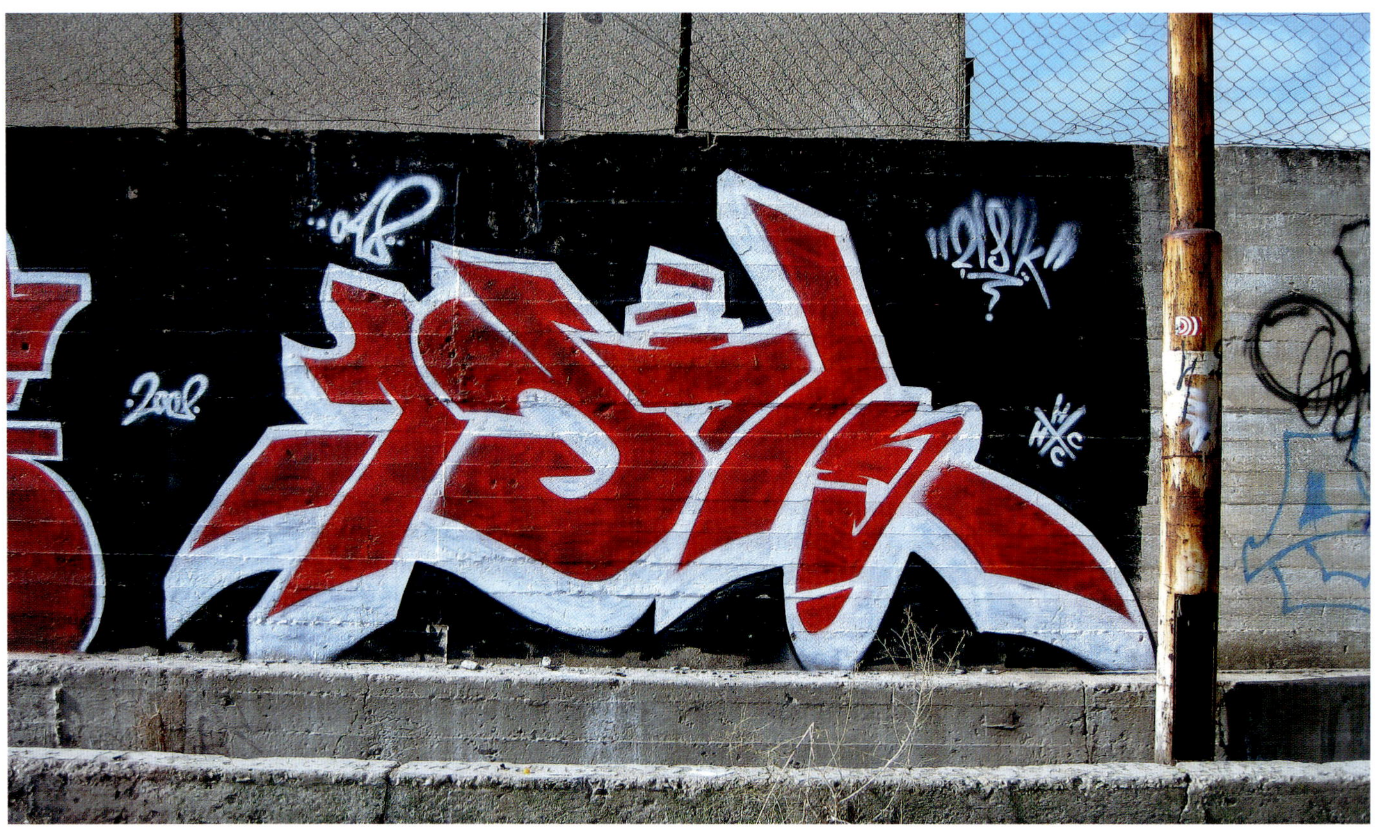

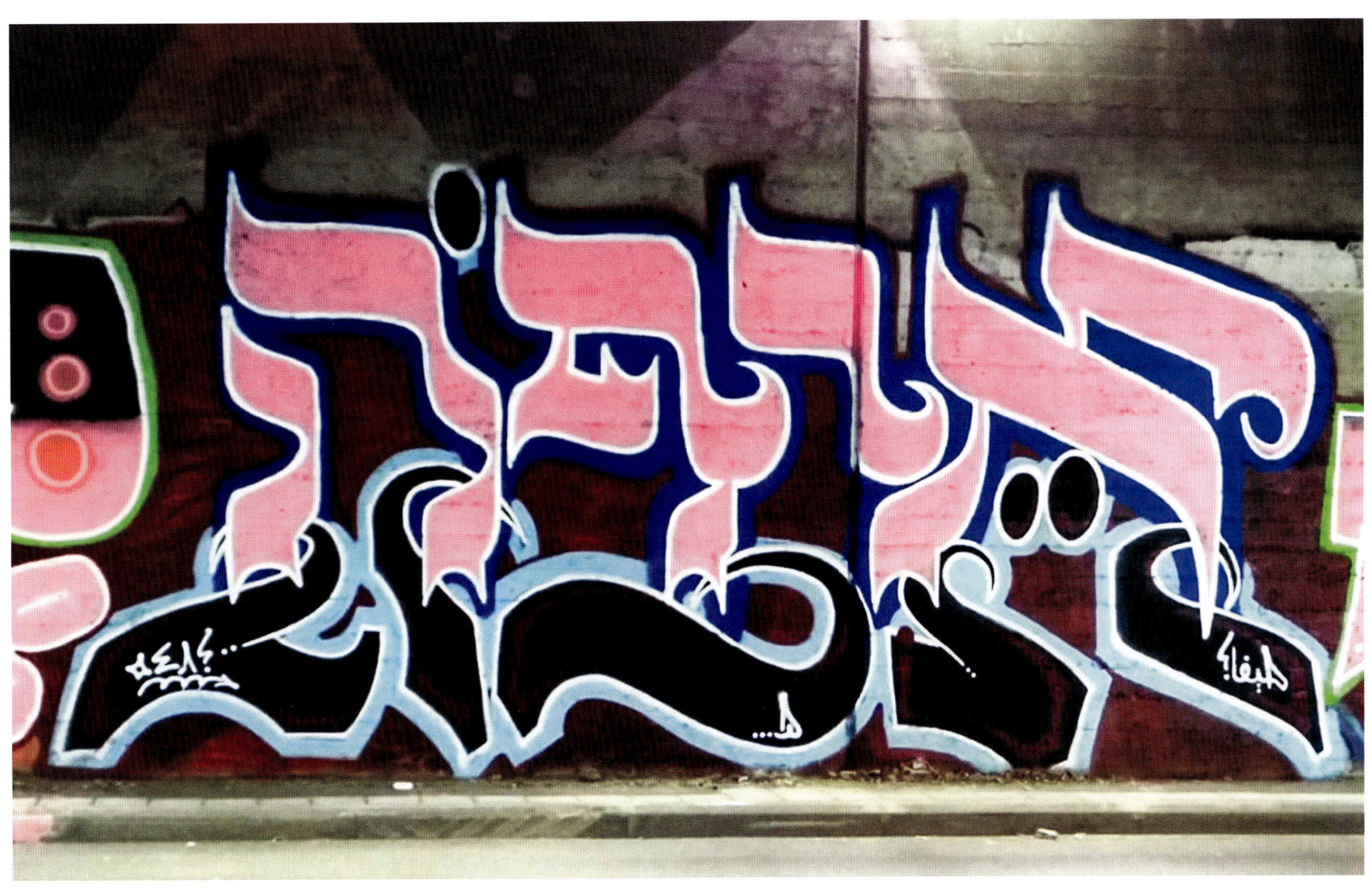

LEFT AND ABOVE:
AIFOE 048
Aifoe, 2010

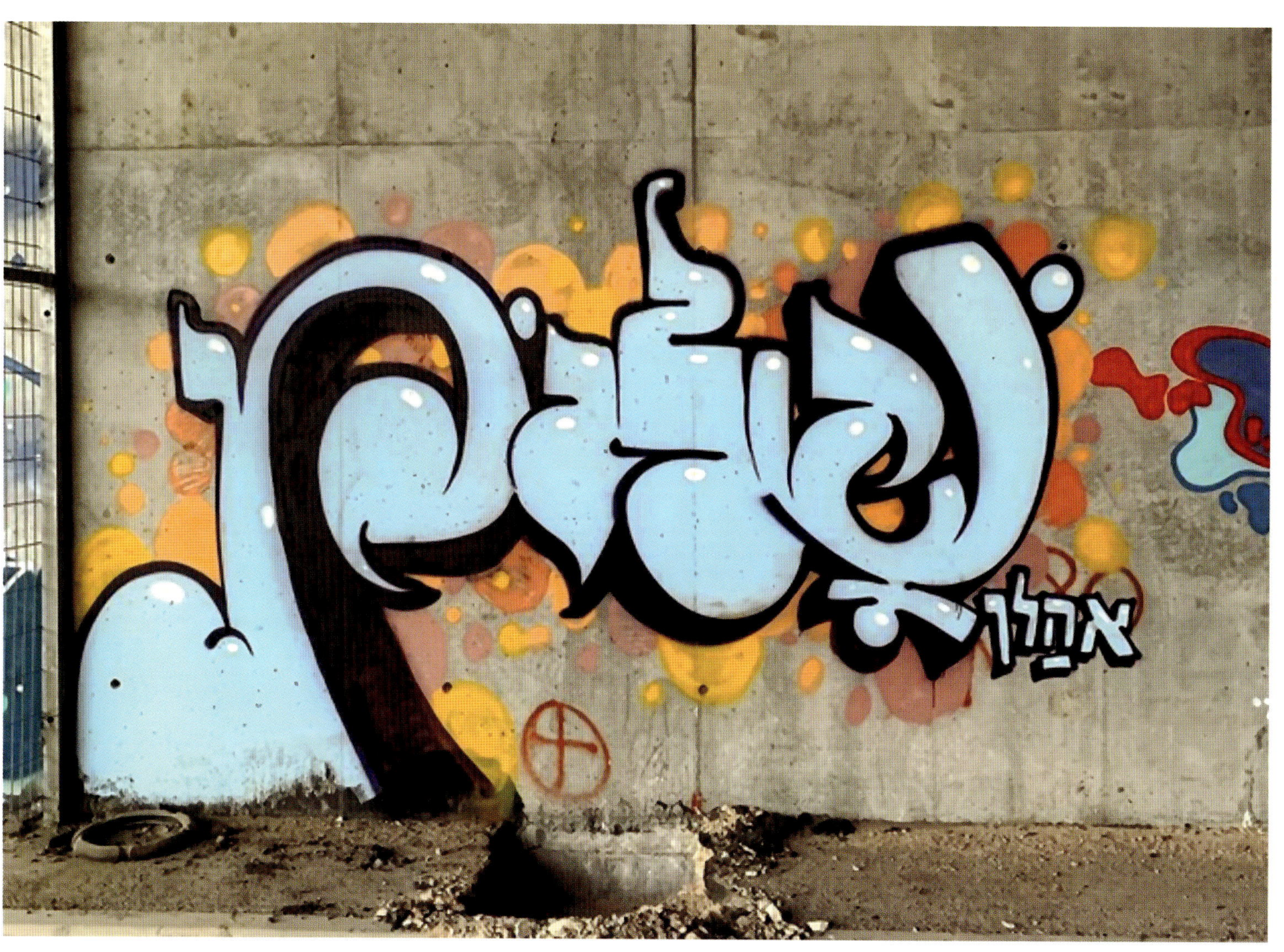
אהלן

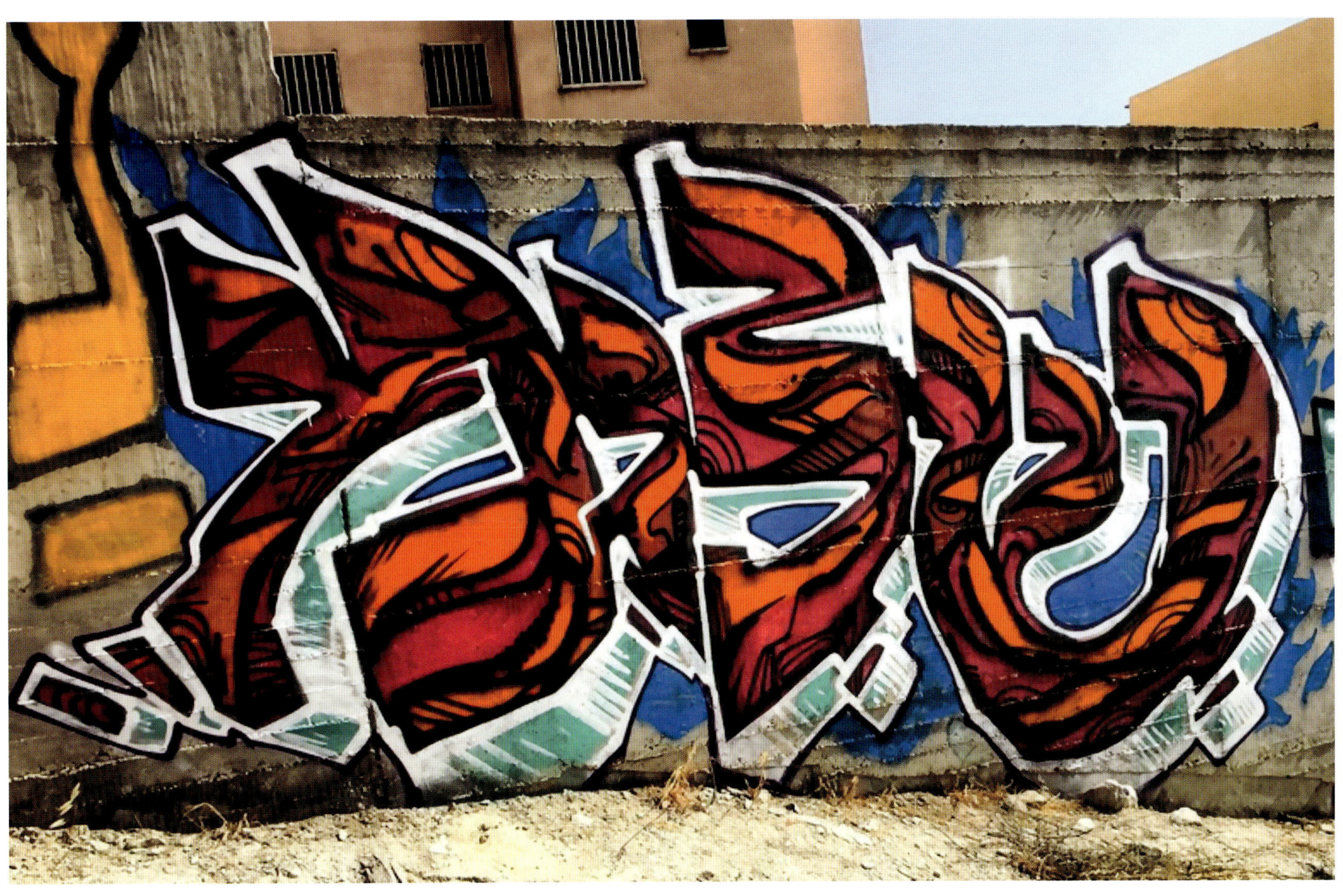

LEFT AND ABOVE:
Shalom
Shalom, 2018

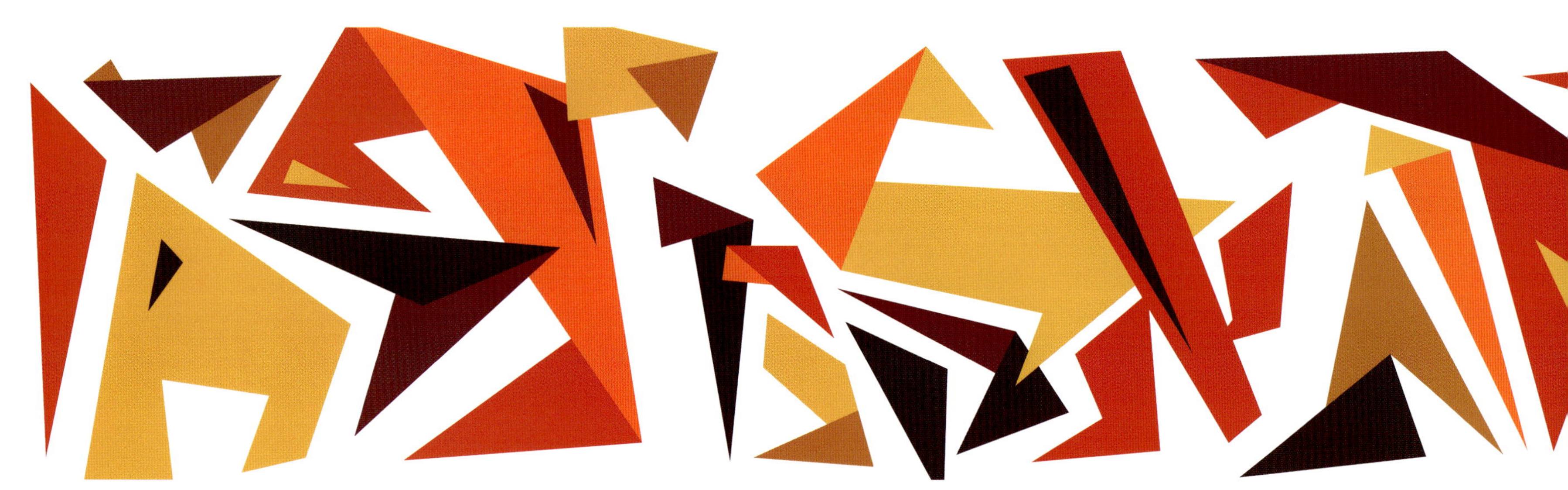

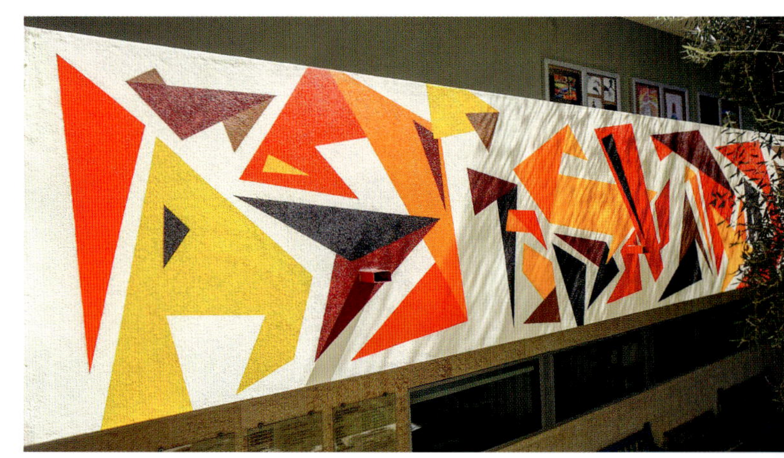

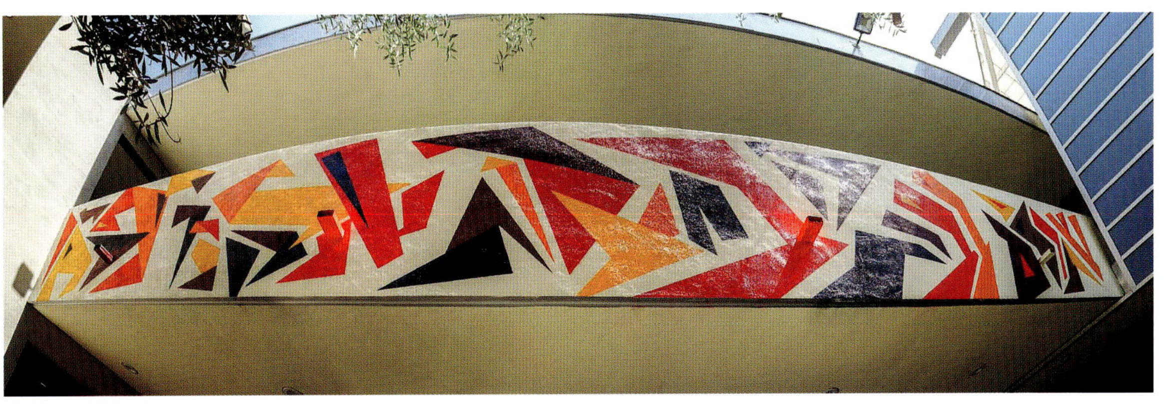

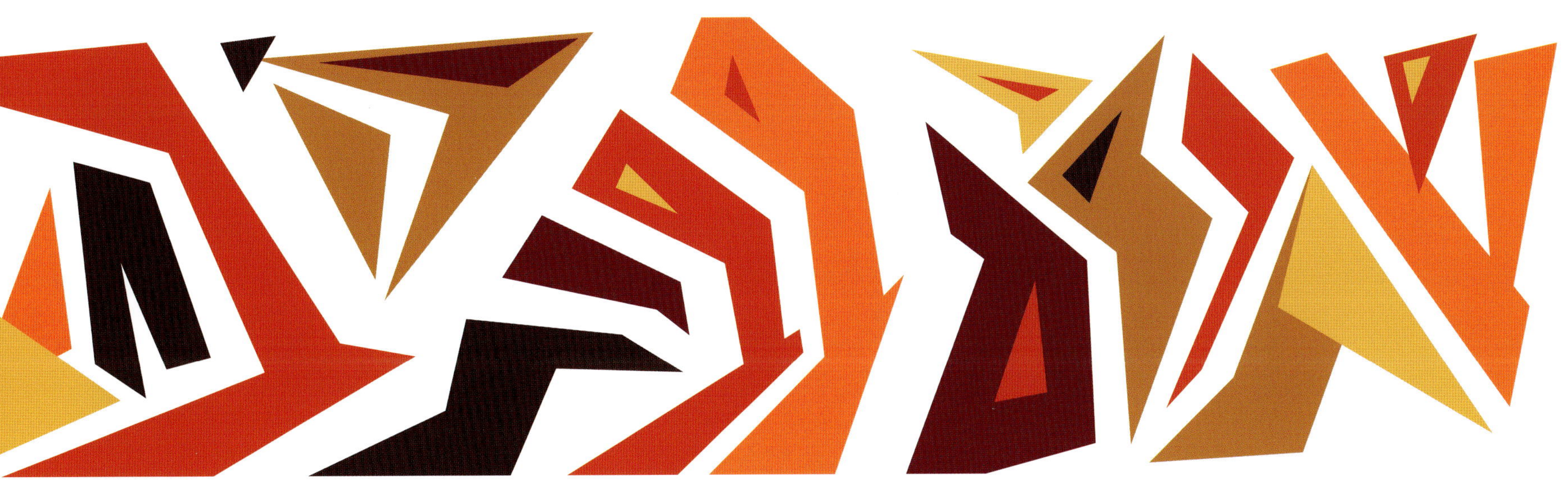

"Planted in the house of Hashem,
they will flourish in the courtyards of our God"

Hillel Smith
YULA Courtyard mural, 2017
From Psalms 92:14

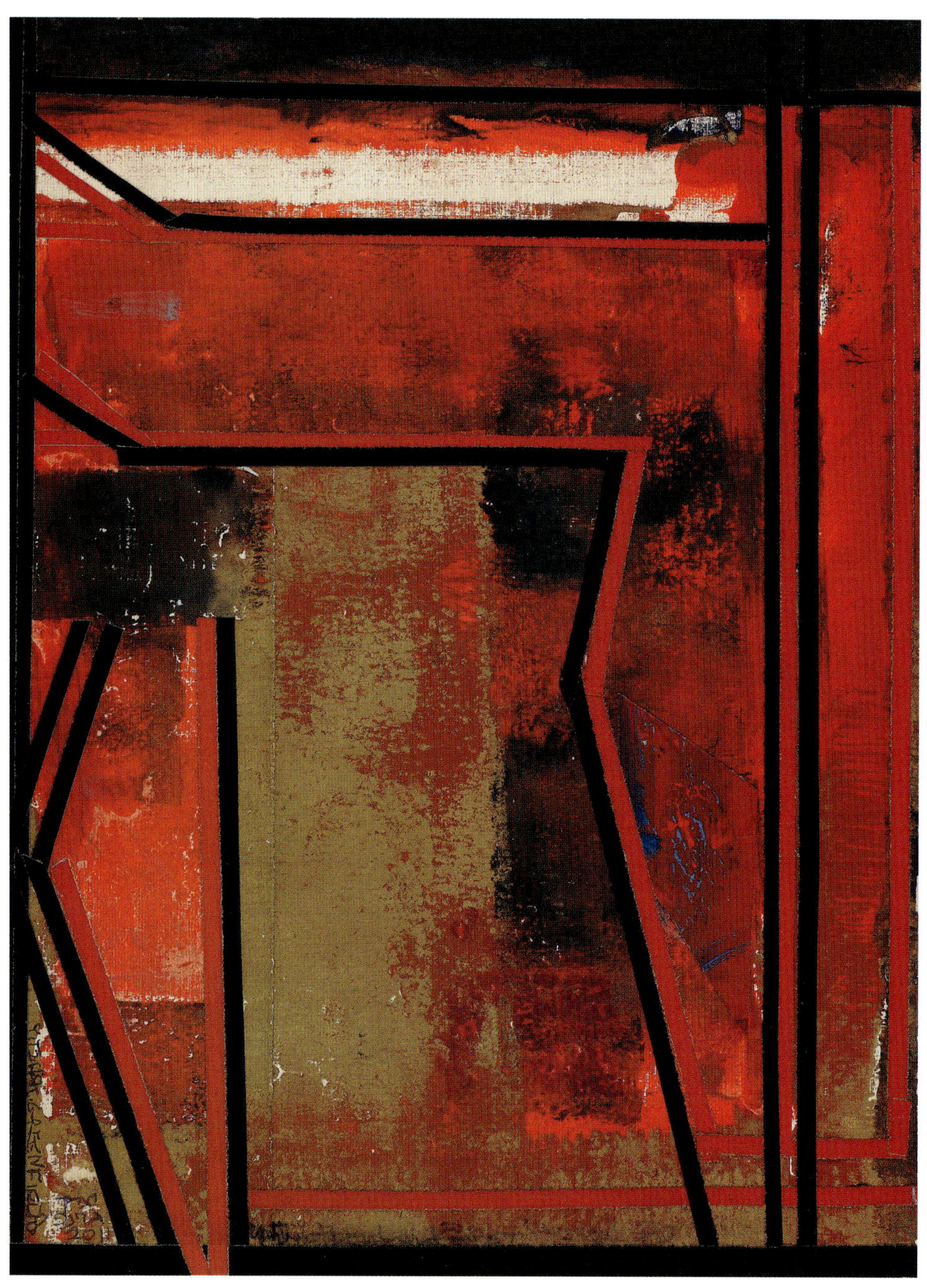

Yitzchak Greenfield
Hebrew Letter Heh, 2011

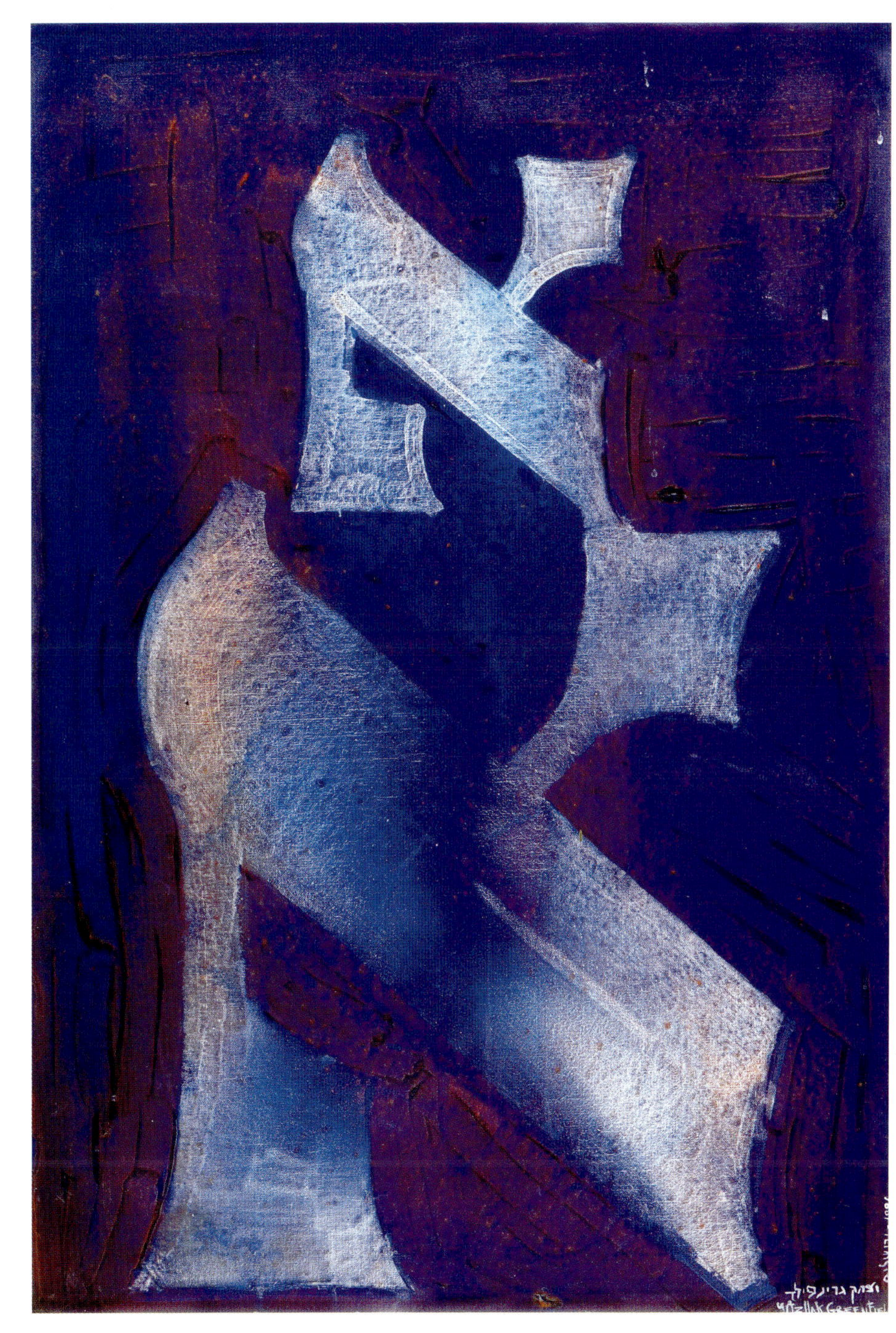

Yitzchak Greenfield
Hebrew Letter Alef, 1995

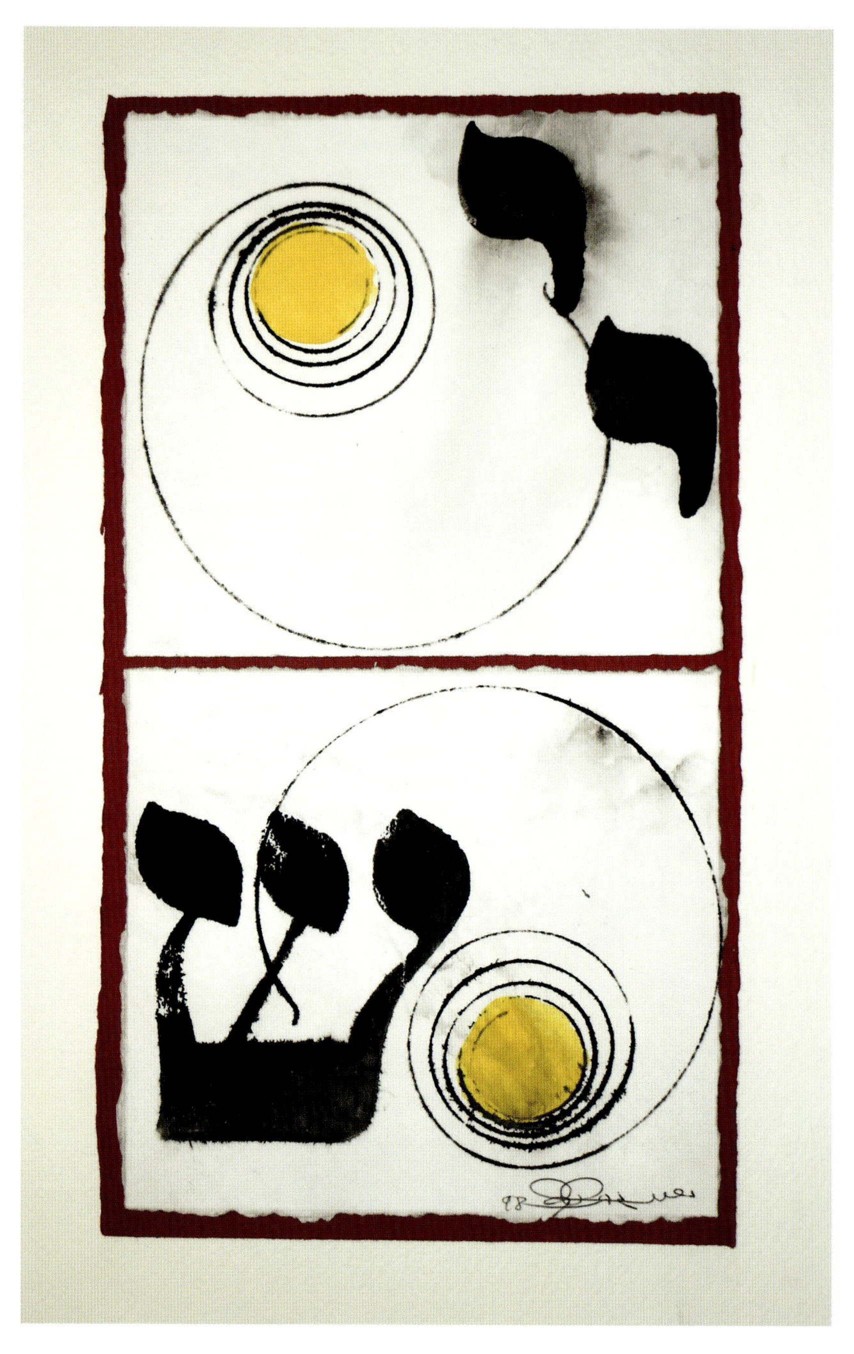

Yitzchak Greenfield
Meeting of God's Names, c. 2000

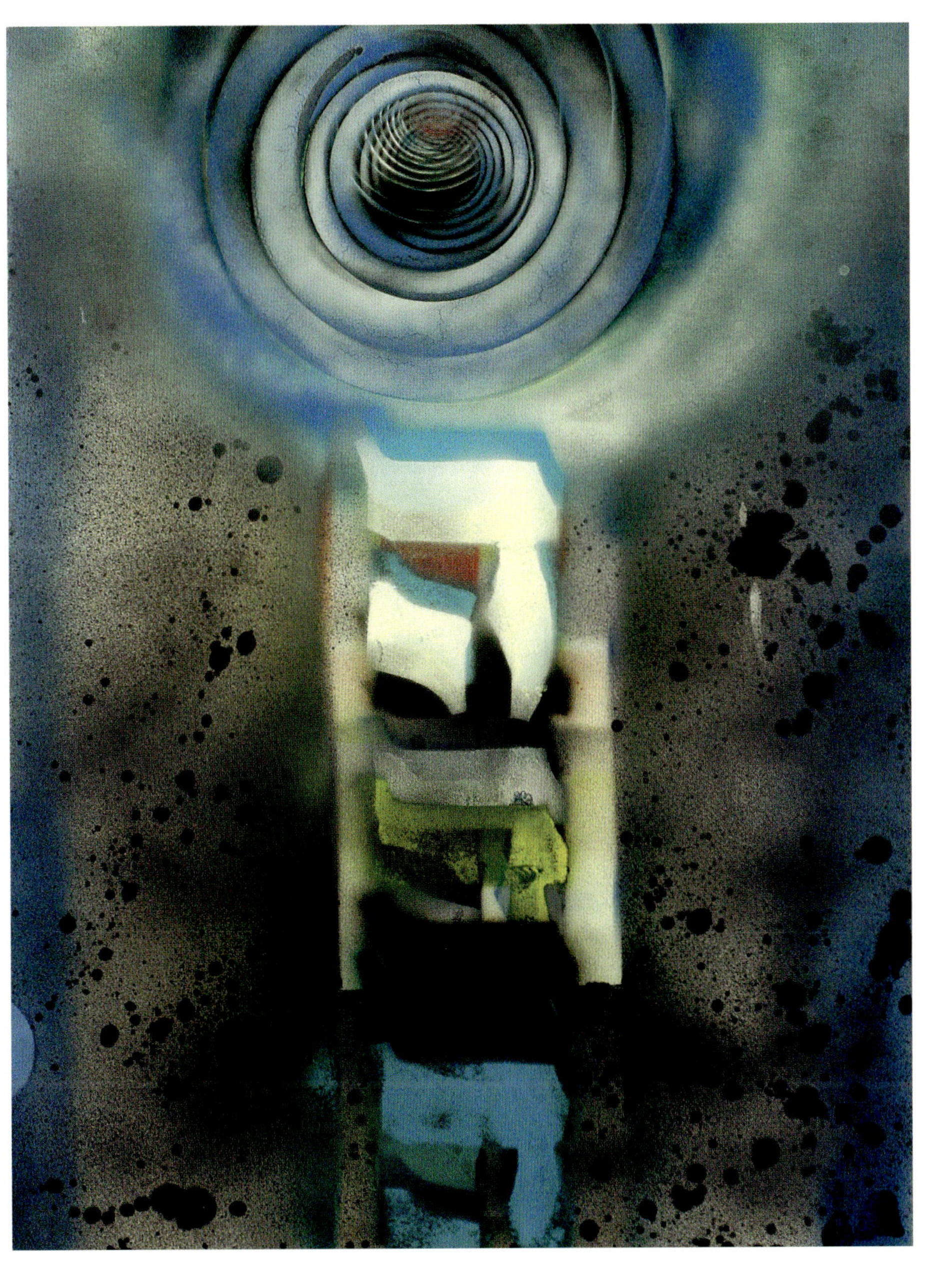

THIS PAGE: Yitzchak Greenfield
The Birth of the Heh, 2008
OVERLEAF: David Rakia
Detail from *Letters in Grey*, 2002

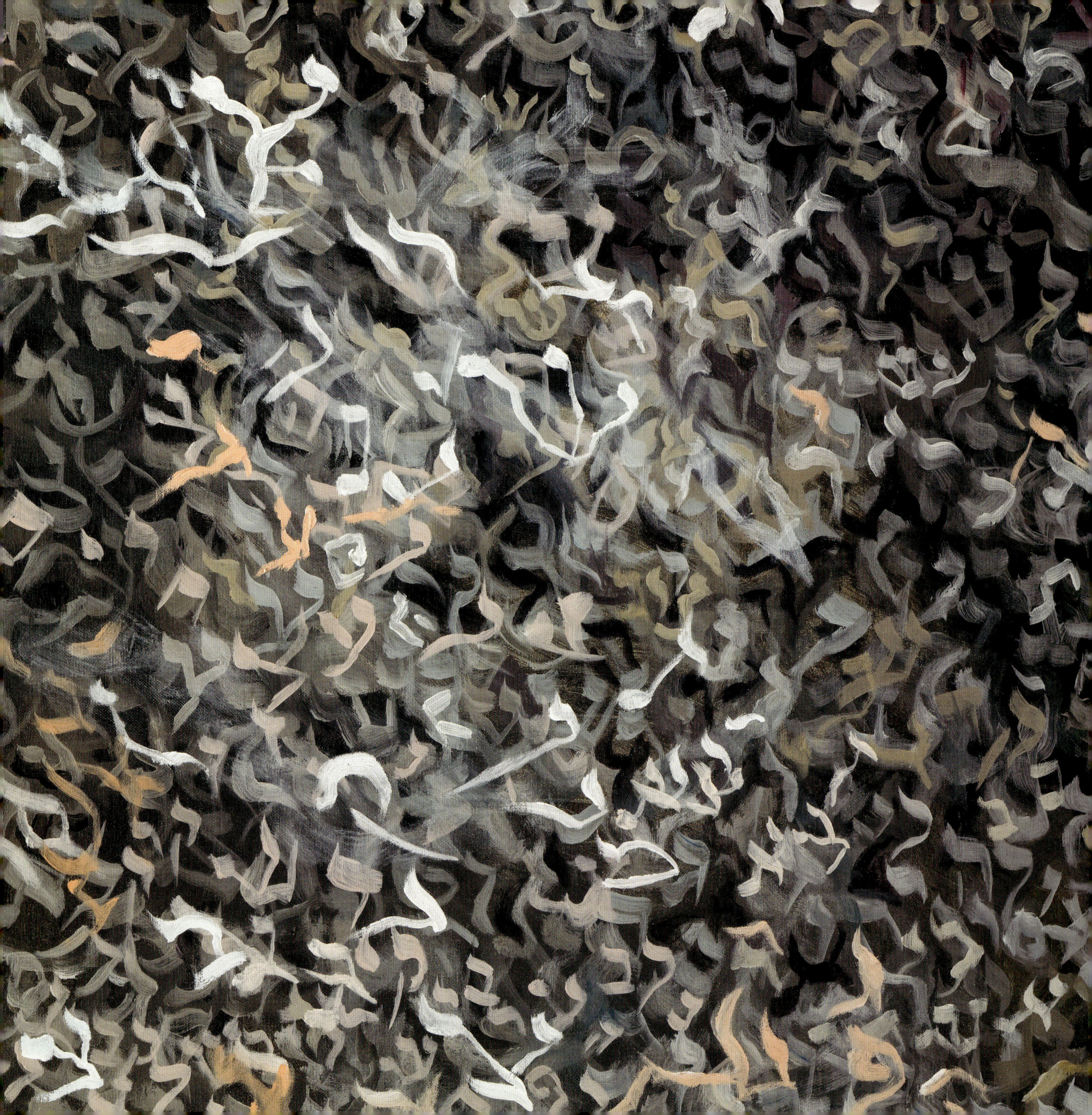

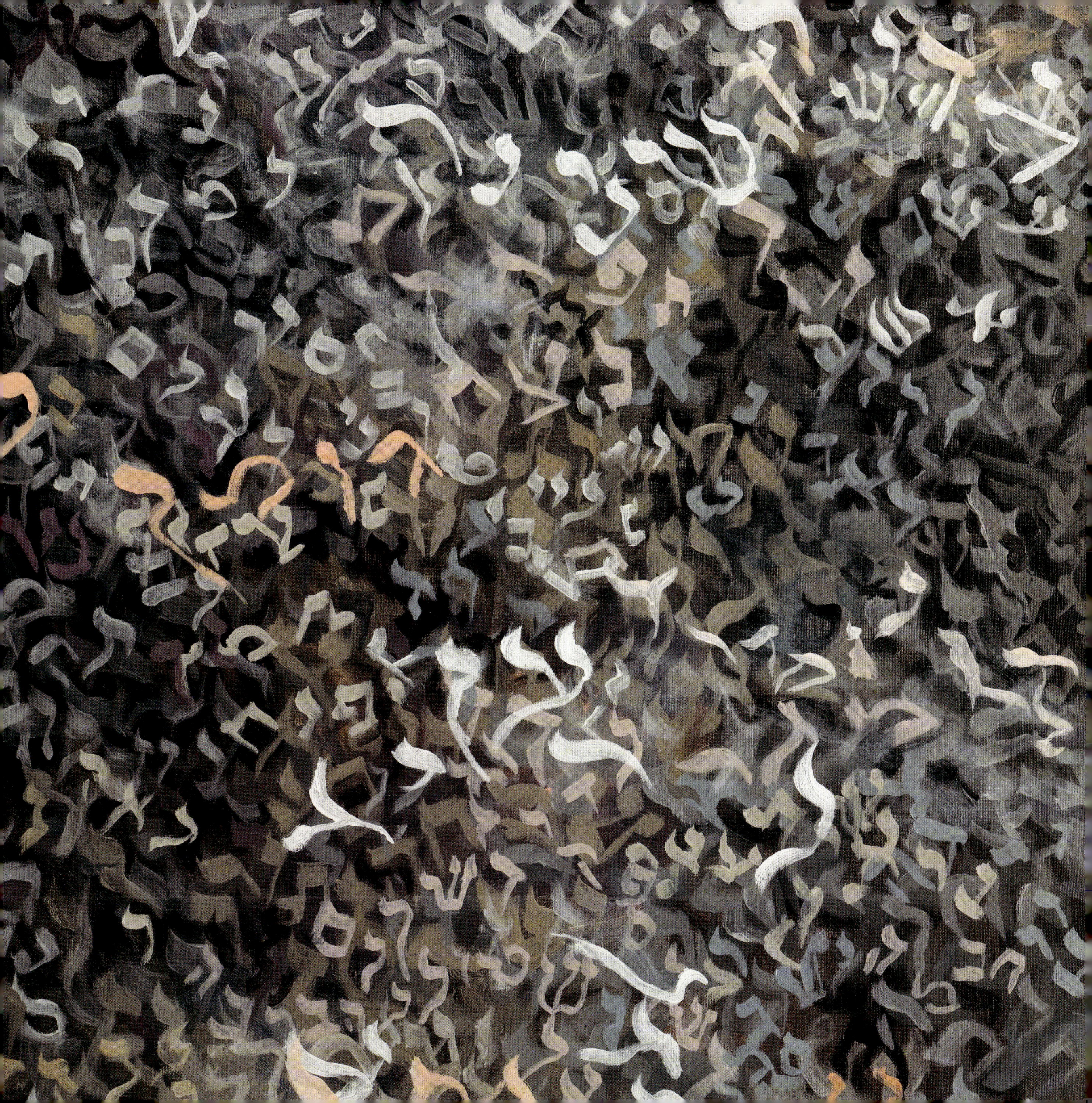

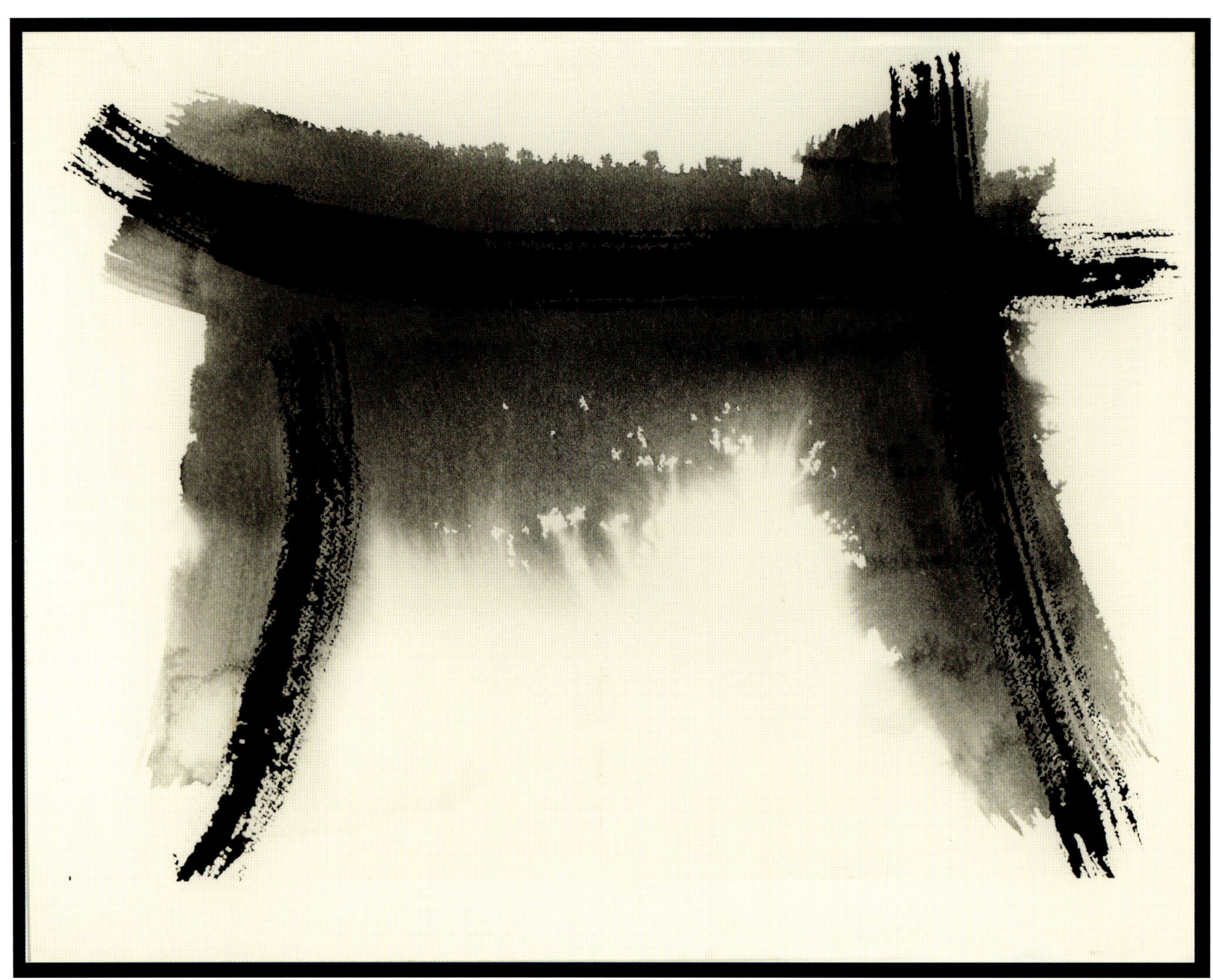

In the artist's words, Mystical Images *"is a transformative art experience. It synthesizes my background as a lettering artist, my pursuit of the Jewish mystical path, and my reverence for the beauty and simplicity of Japanese Zen Art. Exploring imagery, dreams, and meditation, I seek to integrate the concept of notan—the harmonious interaction between positive and negative space—with Hebrew letterforms that evolve into abstract symbols."*

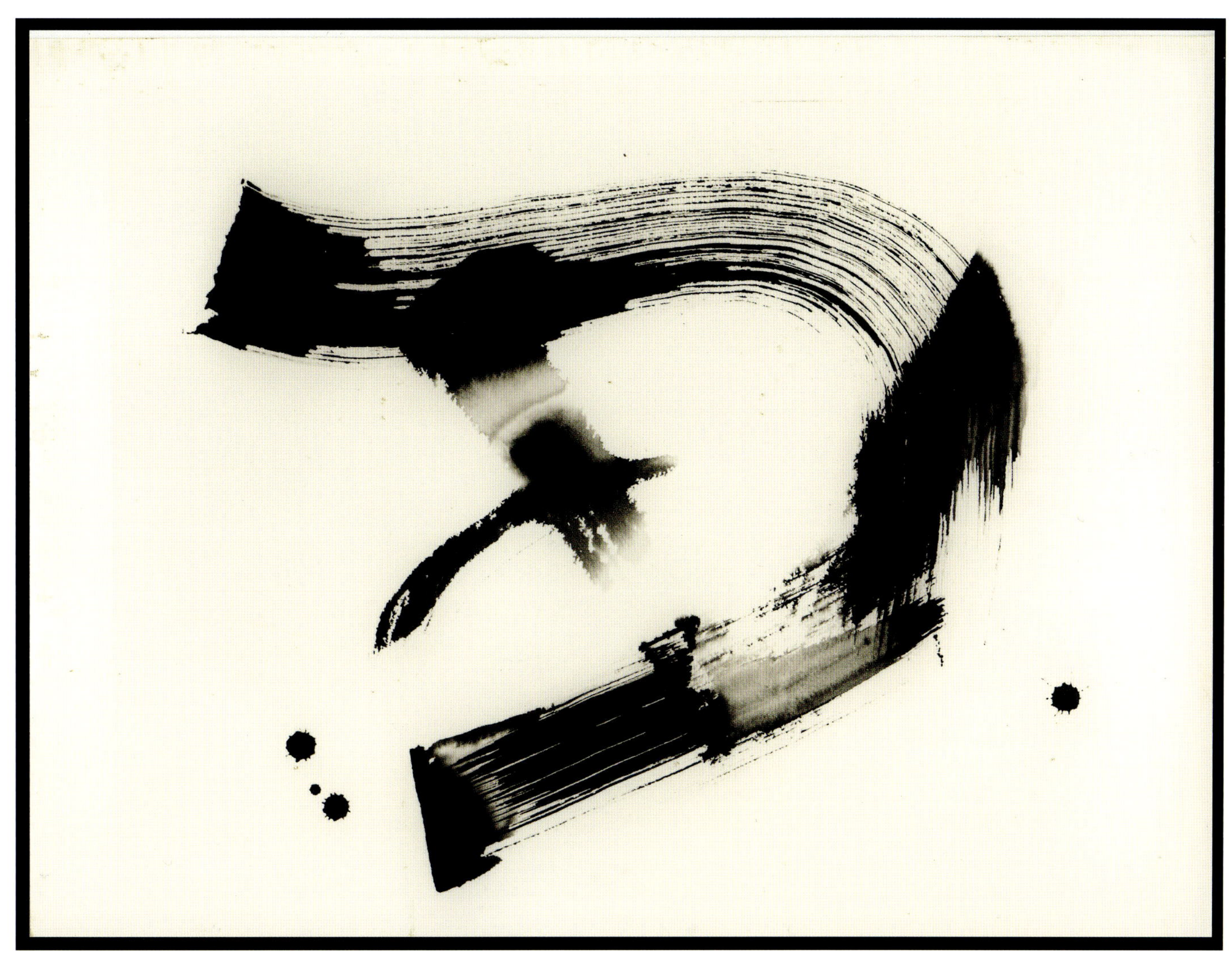

Edna Miron Wapner
FACING PAGE: *Heh*, from *Mystical Images* series, 1991
ABOVE: *Peh*, from *Mystical Images* series, 1991

Again in the artist's own words, "I made hand rubbings of original stone fragments onto a page and then added brushstrokes of paint. I sought to create a dialogue between past and present, and to express my sense of powerlessness at the unrelenting cycle of violence in our land."

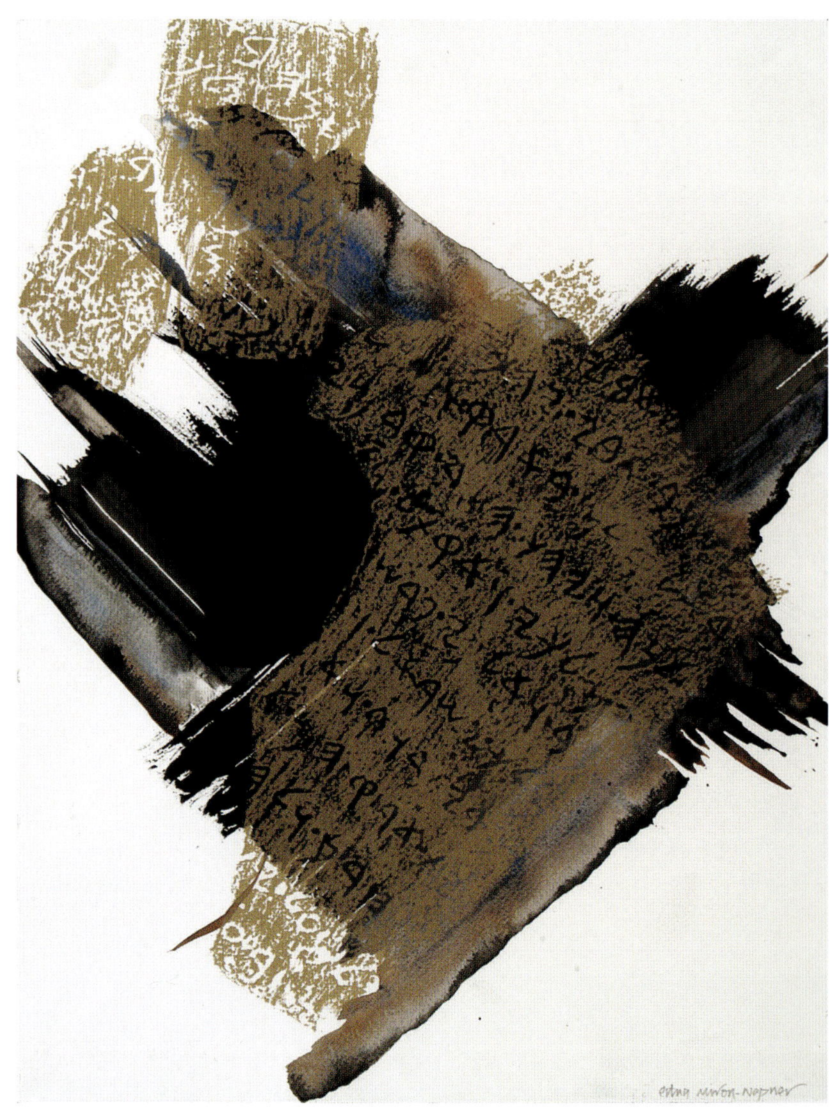

Edna Miron-Wapner
Dialogue 7, 1998–1989

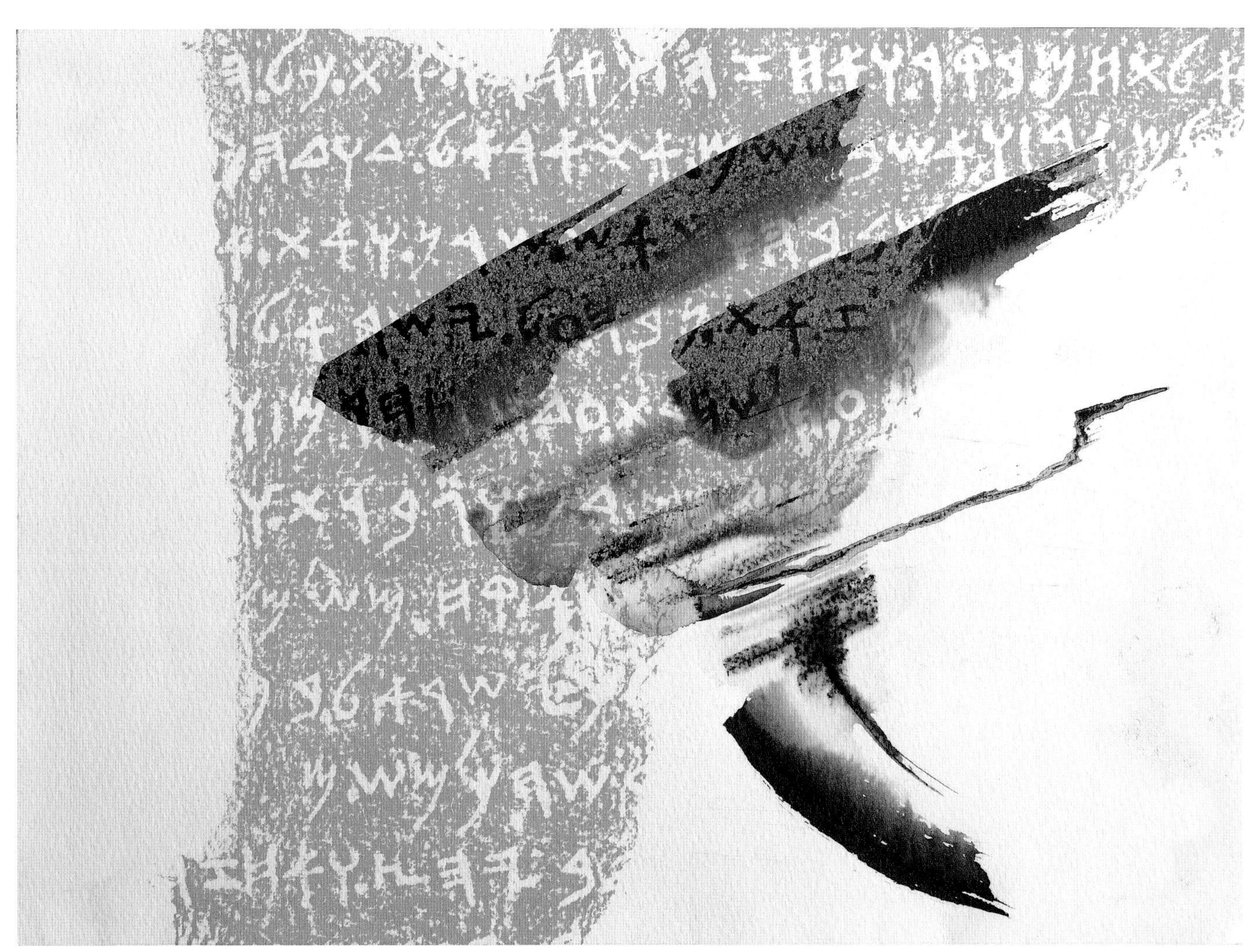

Edna Miron-Wapner
Dialogue 8, 1998–1999

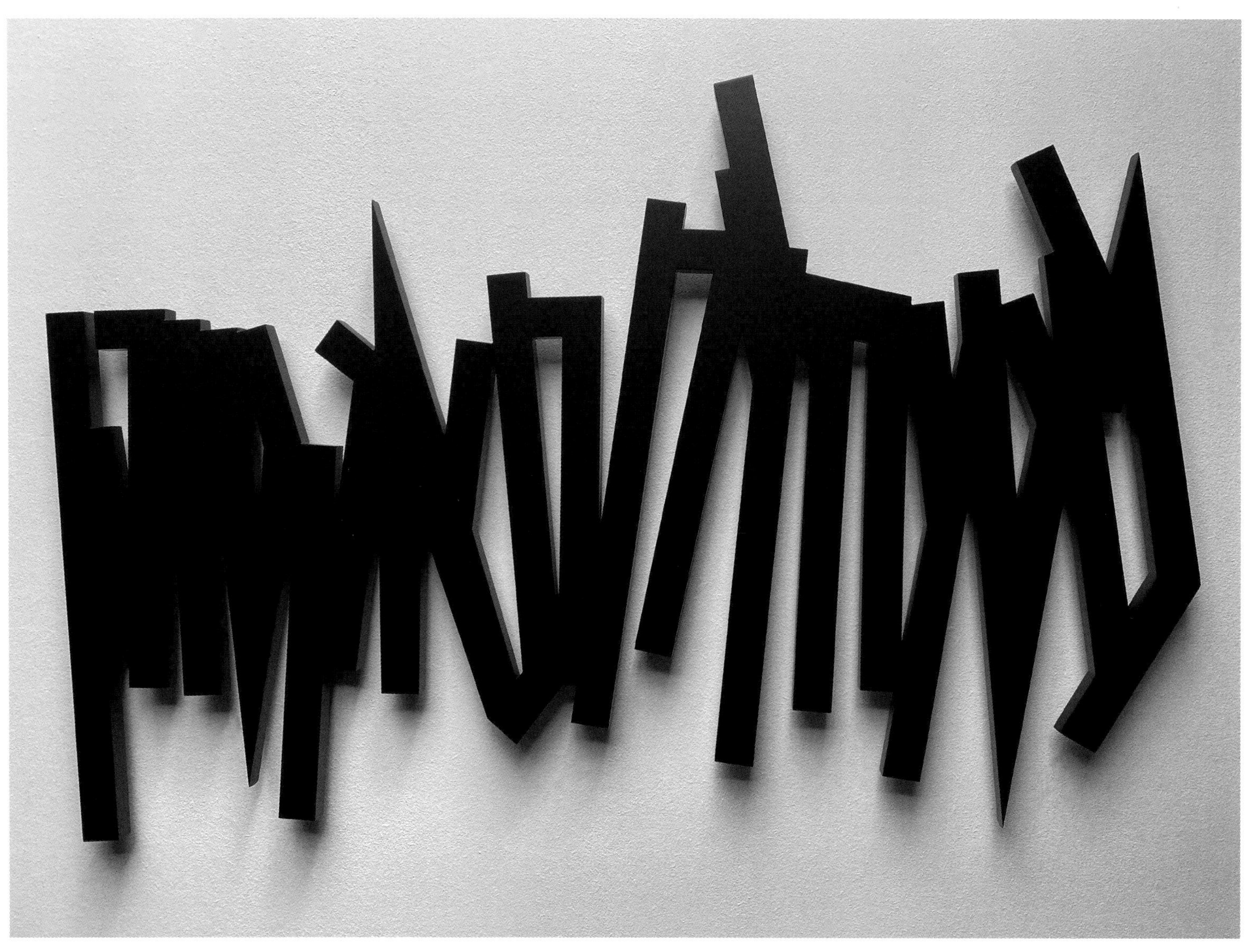

Above and following page: From Mouraud's Shmues *series, these painted aluminum bas-reliefs are conversations (*shmues *in Yiddish). They dialogue with each other, with whoever looks at them, with whoever tries to read them. Writings, grammars, and reading directions are intermingled. The words are signs while being indecipherable. They are extracted from poems of Yiddish literature (Avrom Sutzkever, A. Leyeles, Irena Klepfisz, et al.) that touched the artist. They are fragments, snippets of a language consumed by Nazi barbarism and assimilation, an almost invisible presence, similar to memories or ghosts. What has disappeared (re)appears, appears like a flash on the surface of the wall and stands out.*

Tania Mouraud
Muterlekher Nokturn (Nocturne maternelle), 2020
Bas-relief, painted aluminum, 52 x 81.5 x 1.5 cm

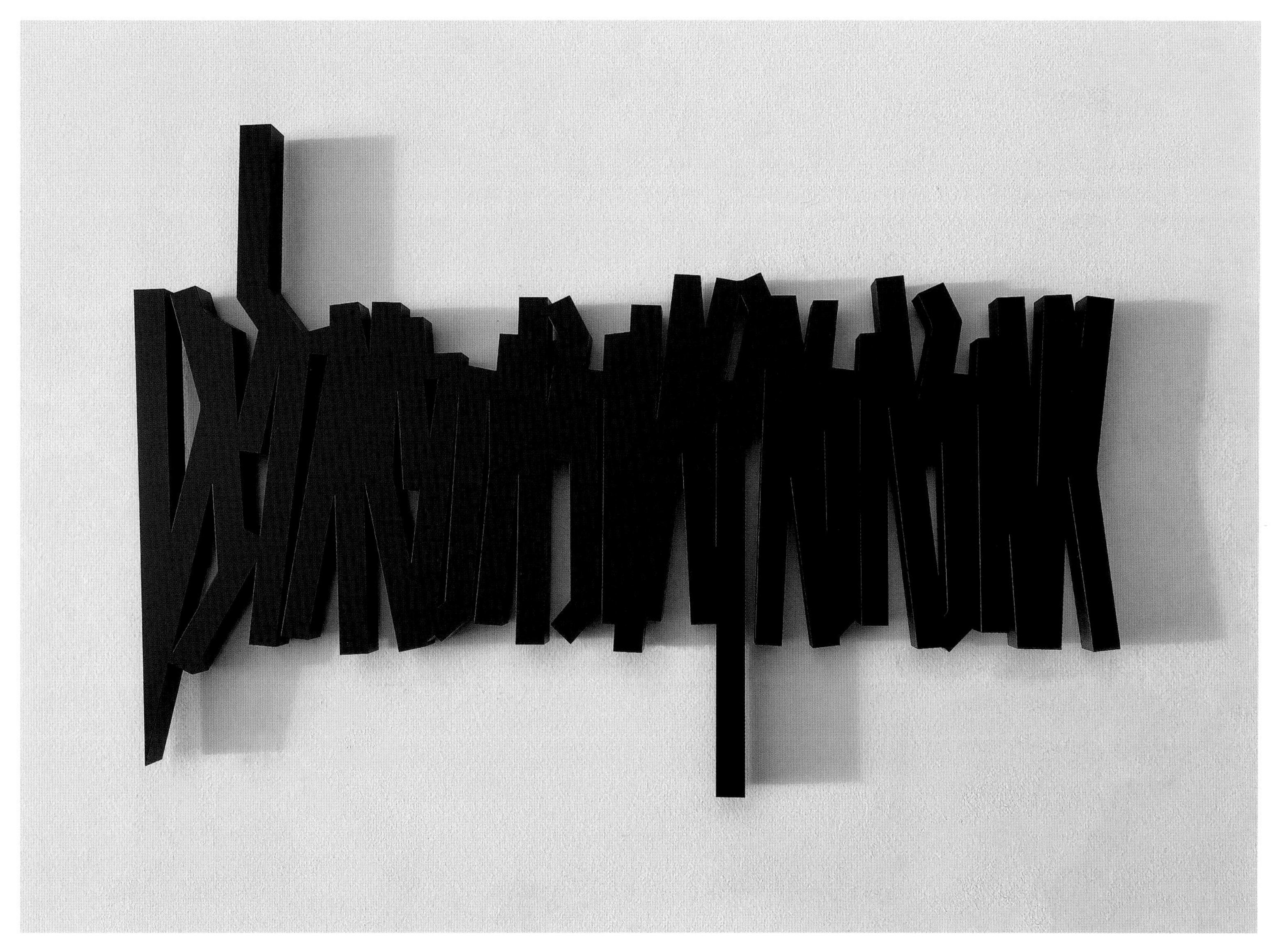

Tania Mouraud
Shmues—Oysyes in oysyes farlibt (Lettres amoureuses des lettres), 2020
Bas-relief, painted aluminum

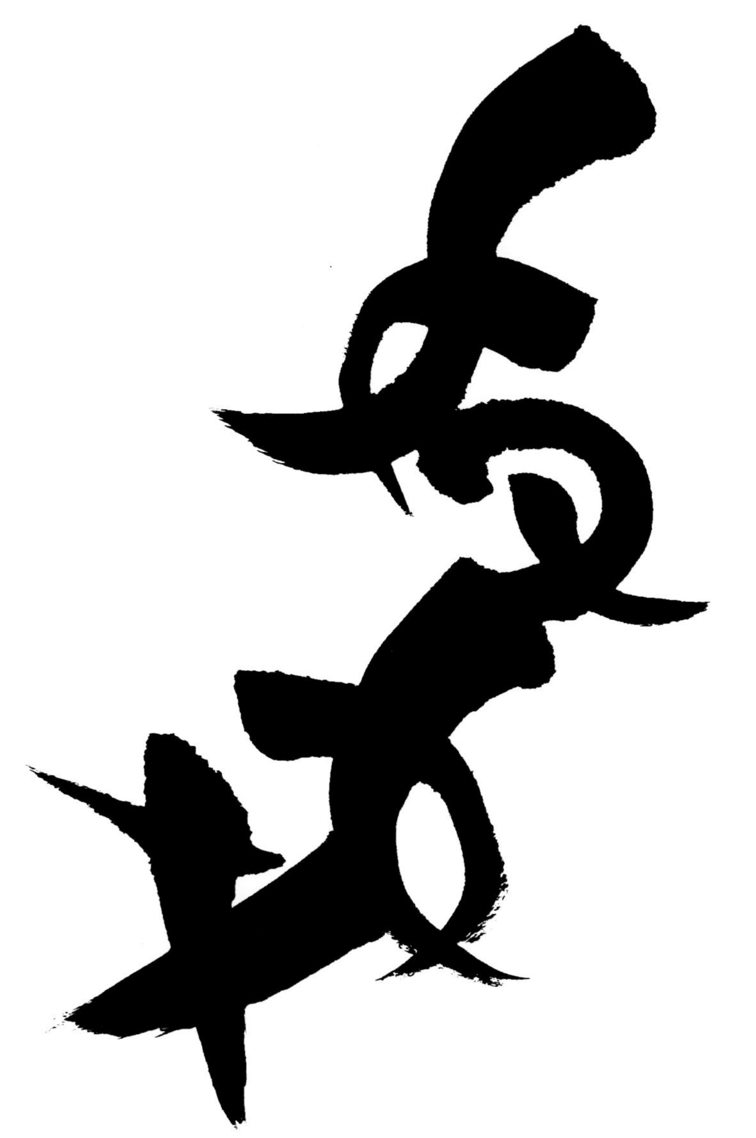

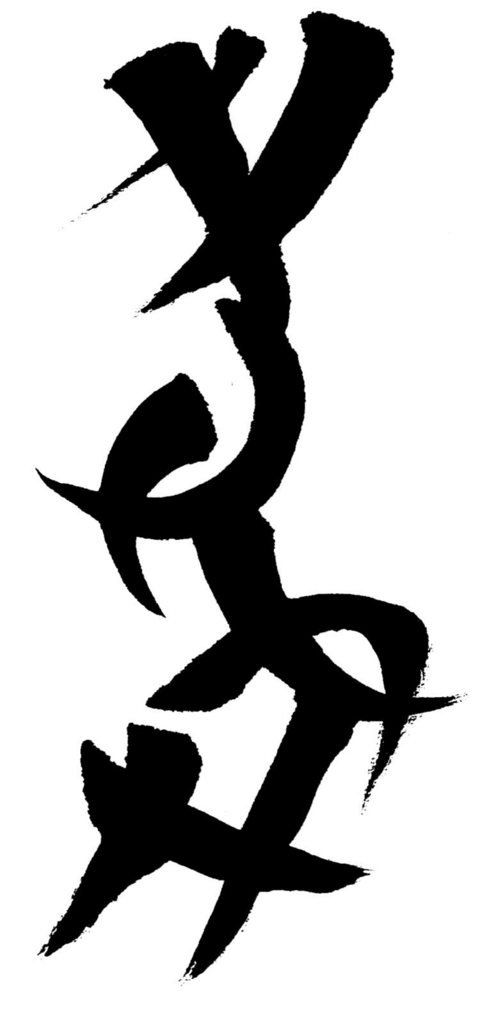

Ilanit Scharff Vigodsky
From Time to Time, poem by the artist, 2020

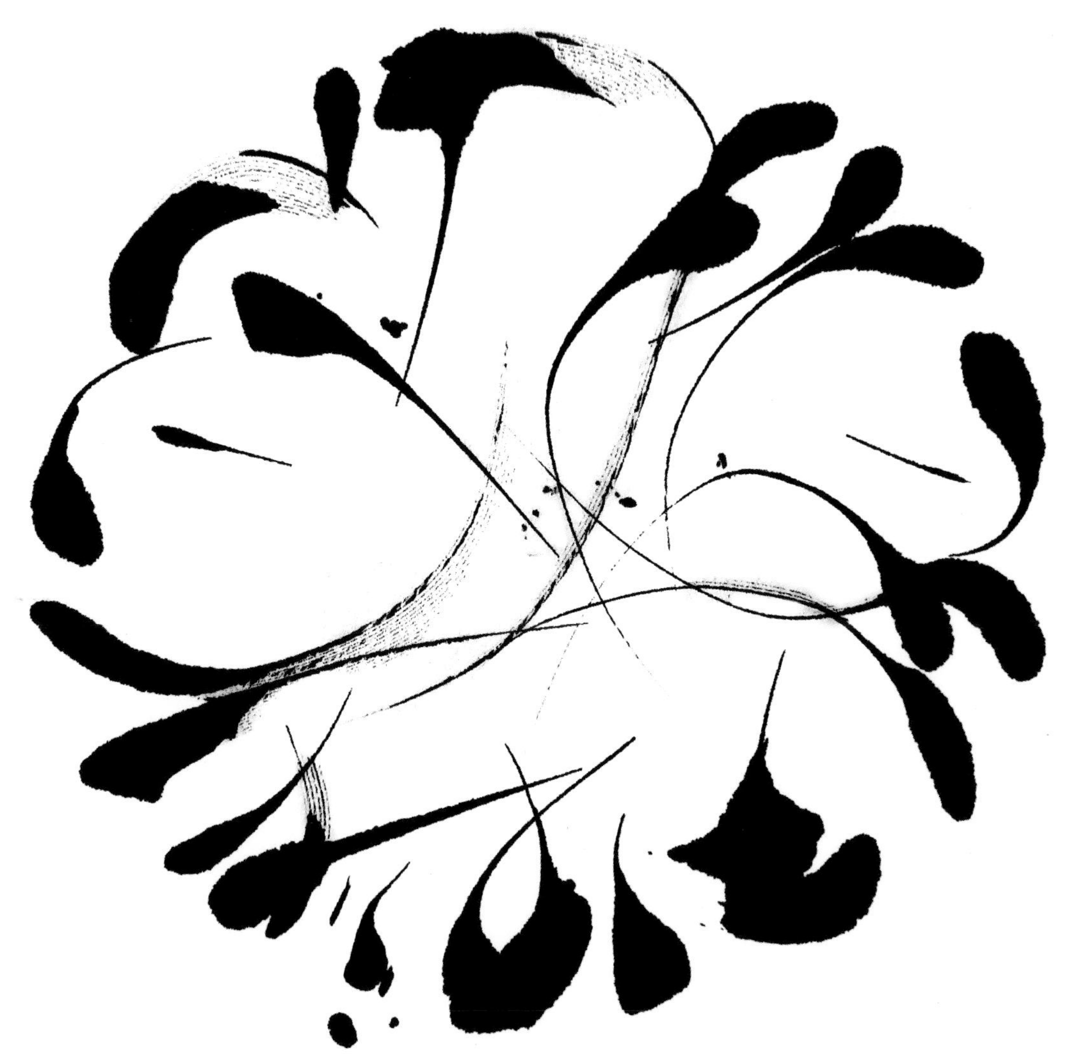

Ilanit Scharff Vigodsky
Untitled, 2020

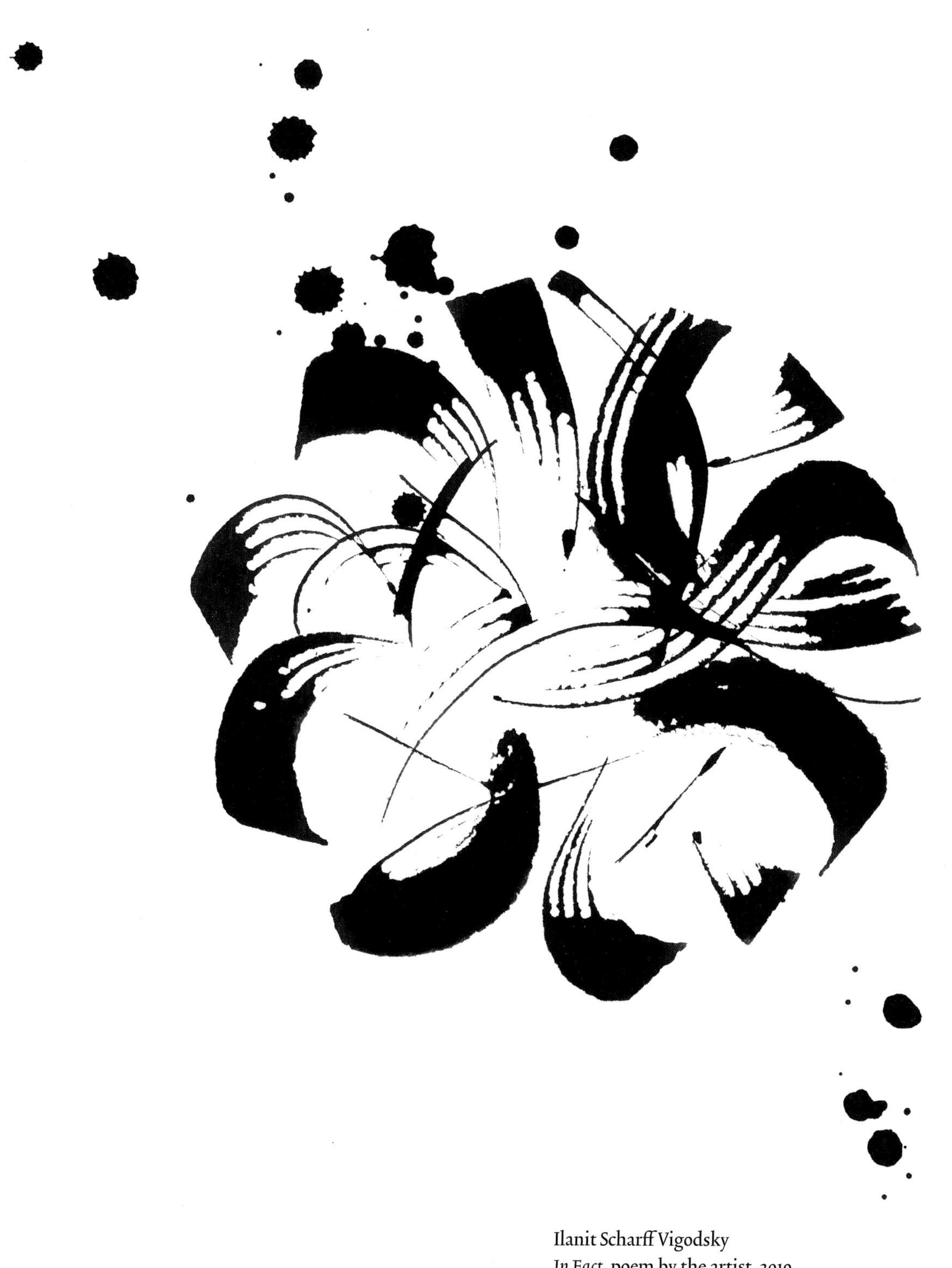

Ilanit Scharff Vigodsky
In Fact, poem by the artist, 2019

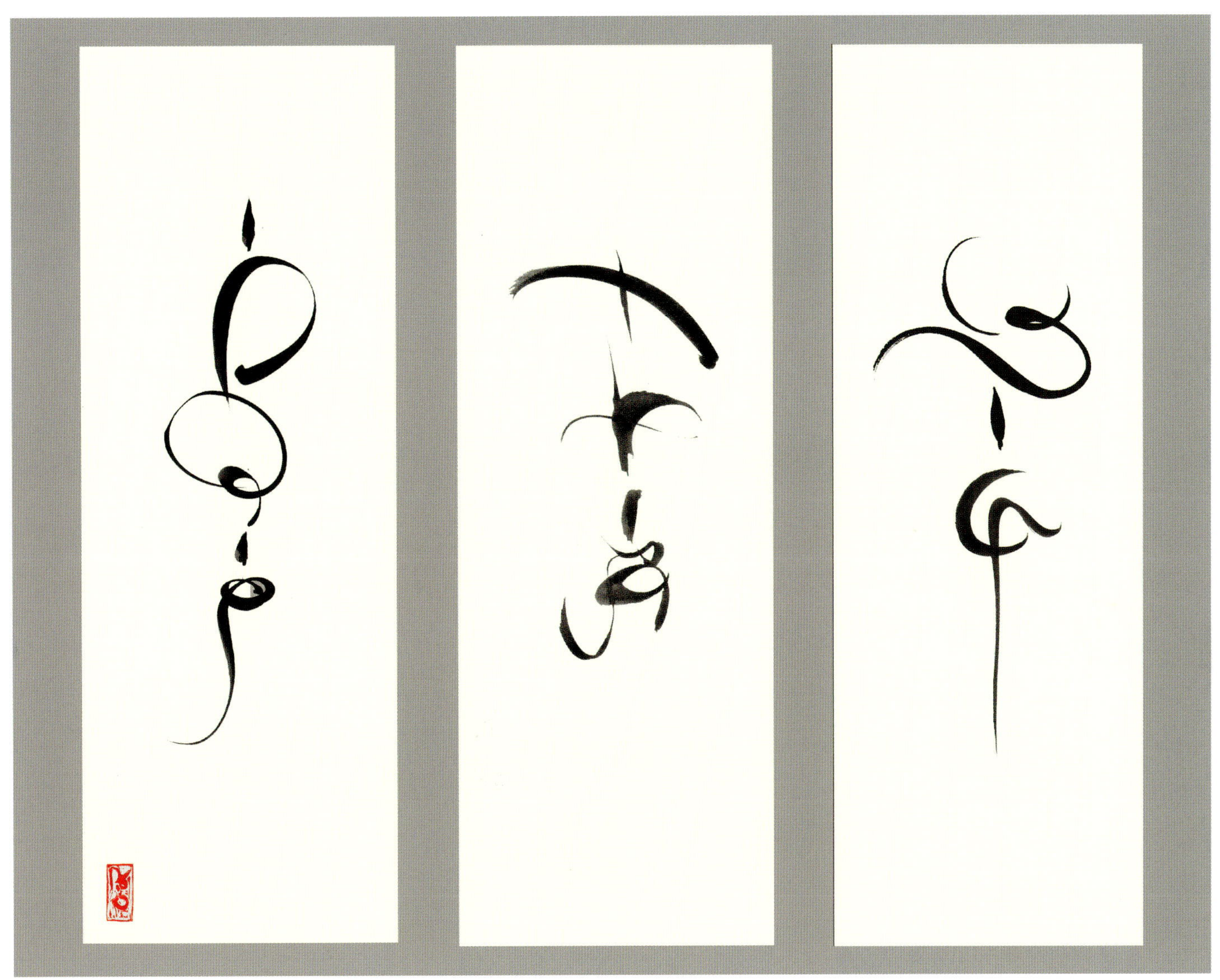

Izzy Pludwinski
Laughter, Dream, Children, 2013

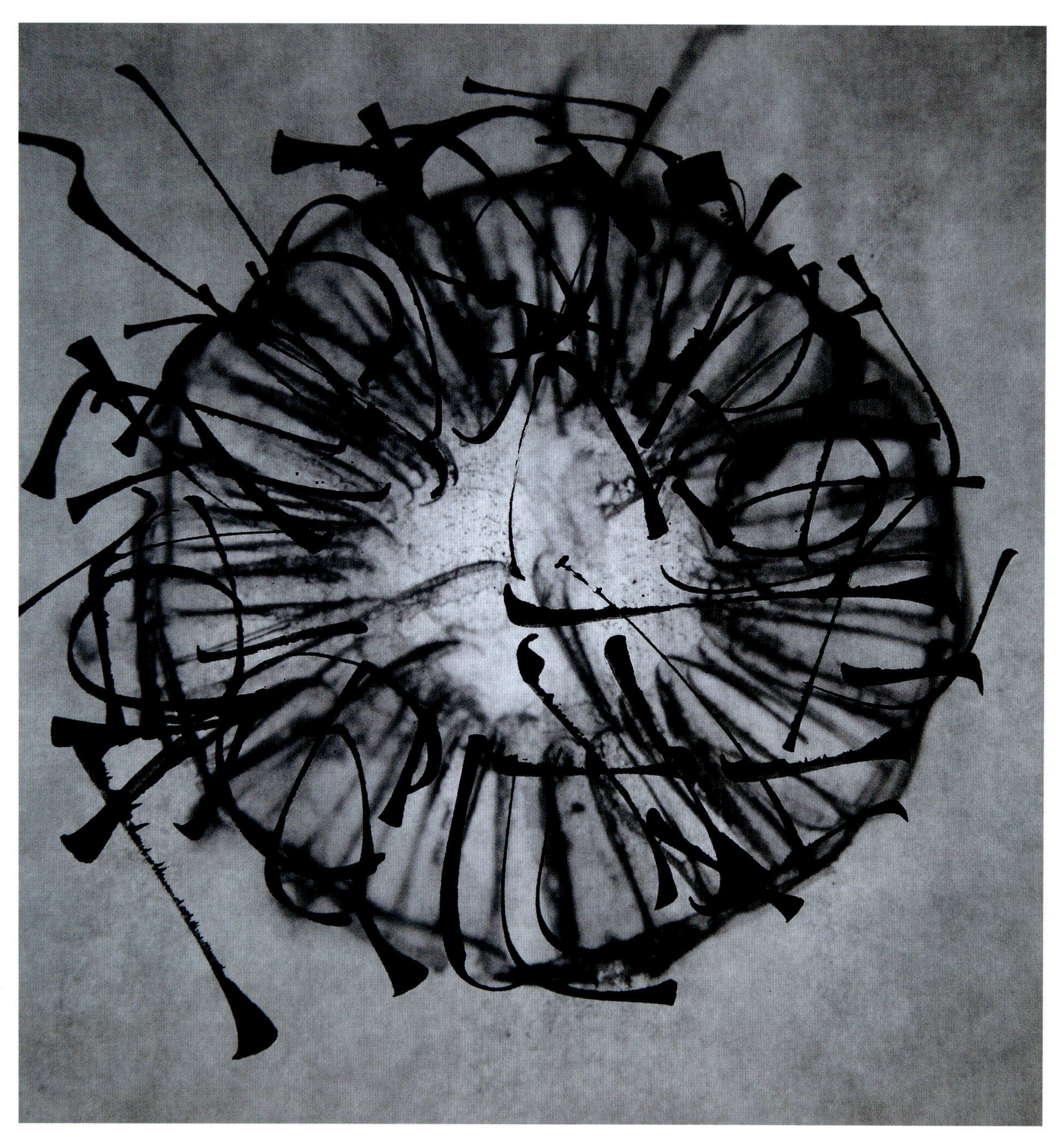

Michel D'Anastasio
Aleph-bet, 2009

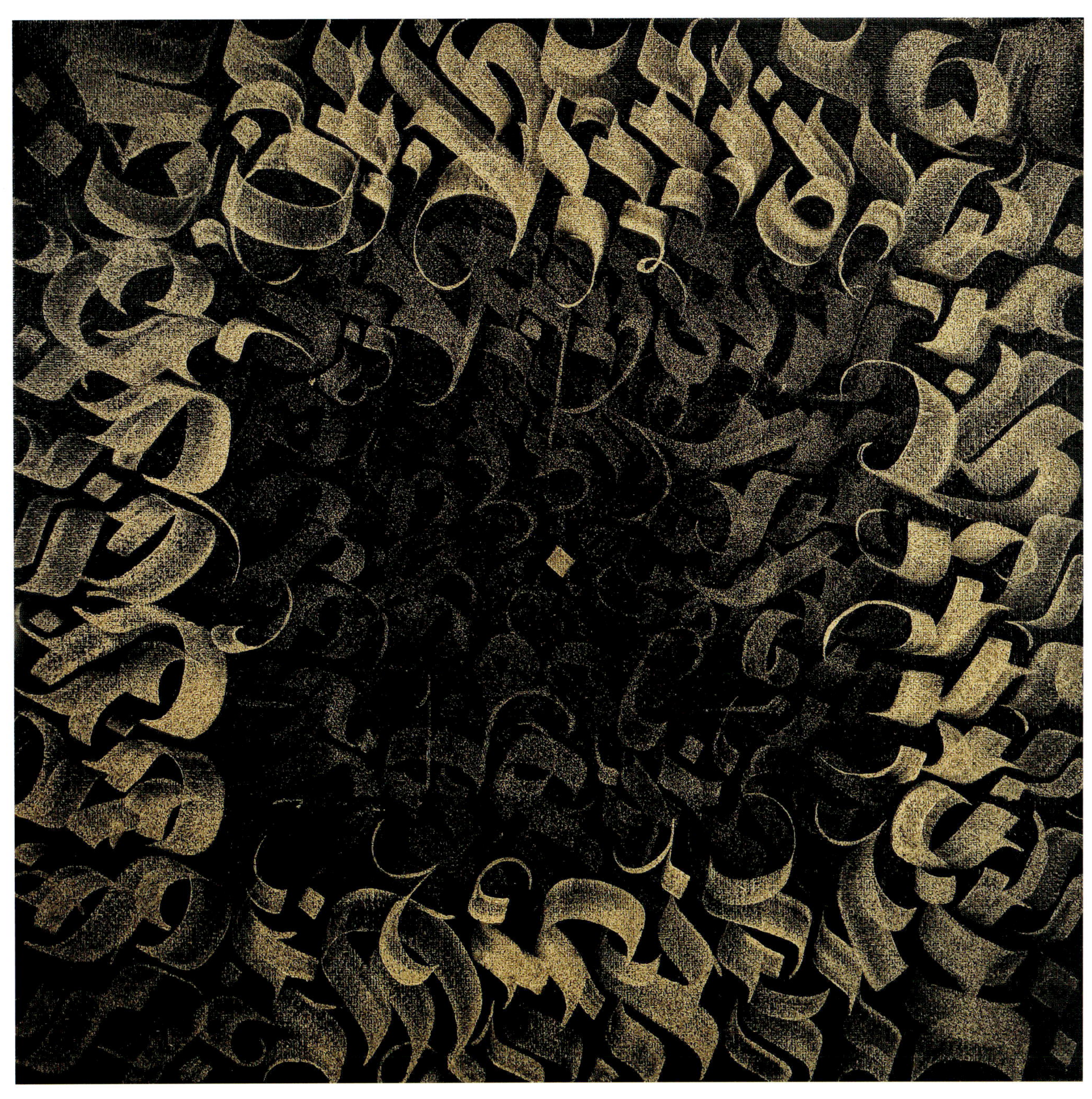

Ohad Naor
Untitled, 2021

In the words of the artist, "Every person has a planet that matches his attributes—all he has to do is to travel there and live his life in it."

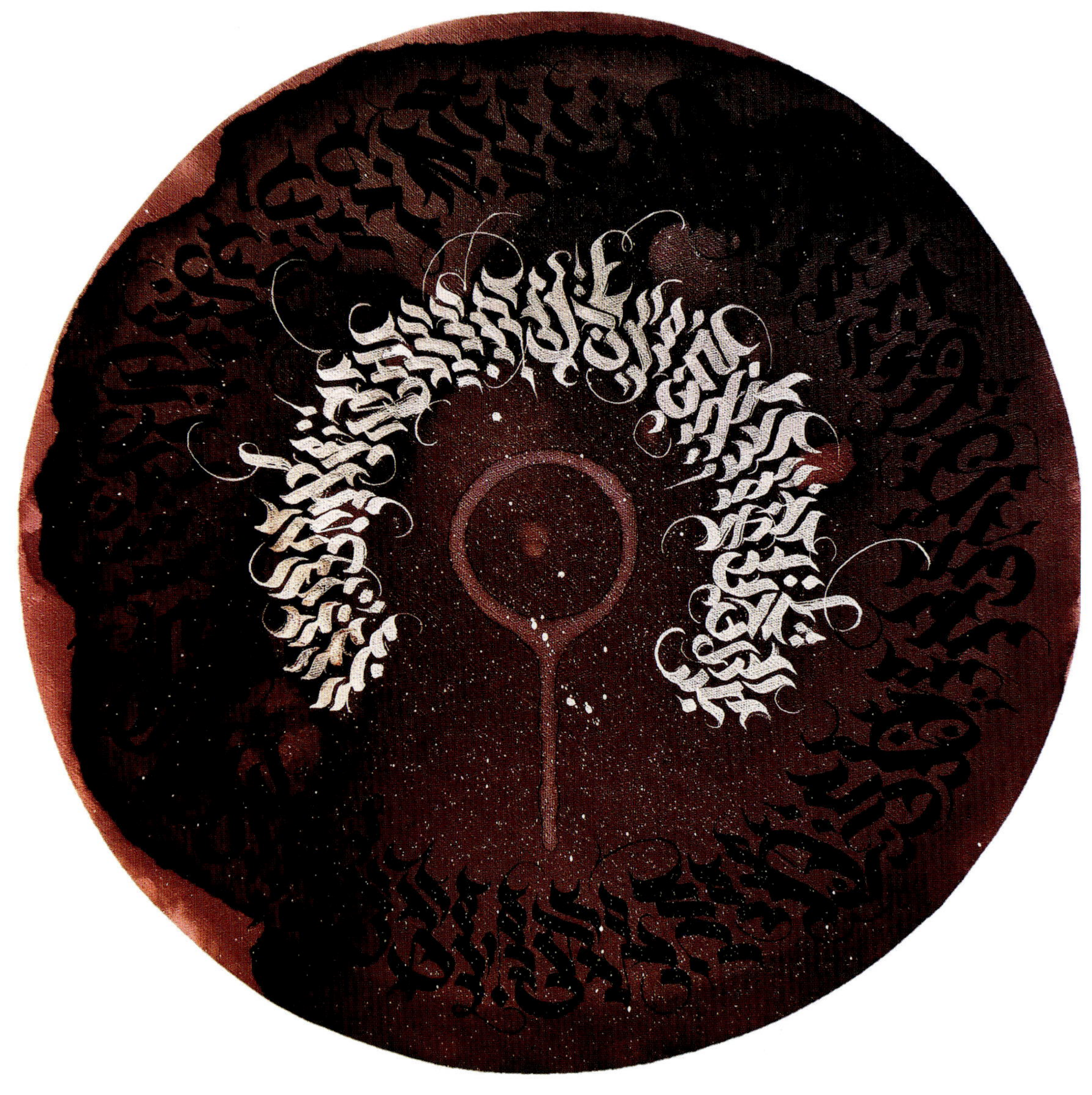

Ohad Naor
A Different Planet, 2021

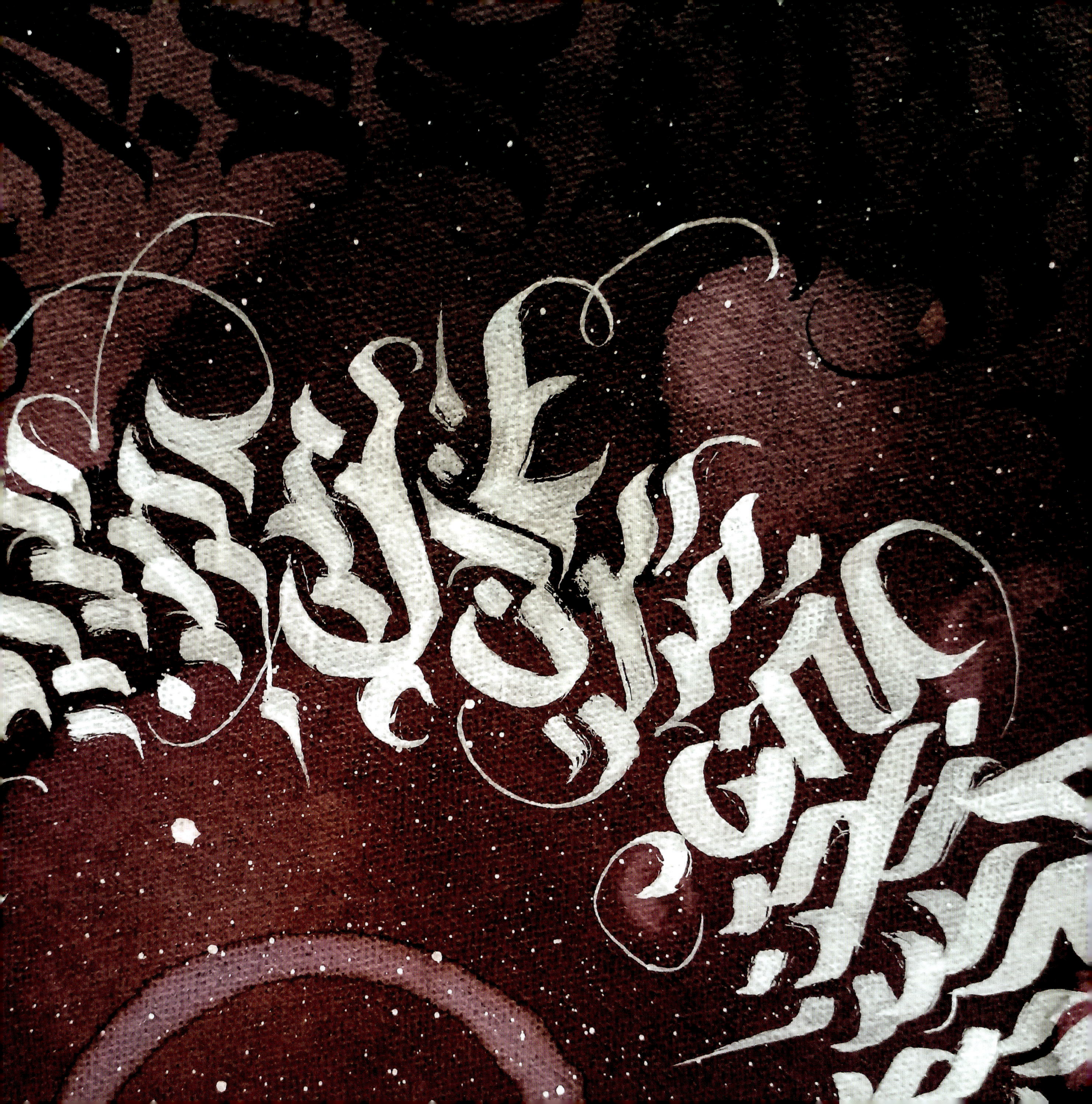

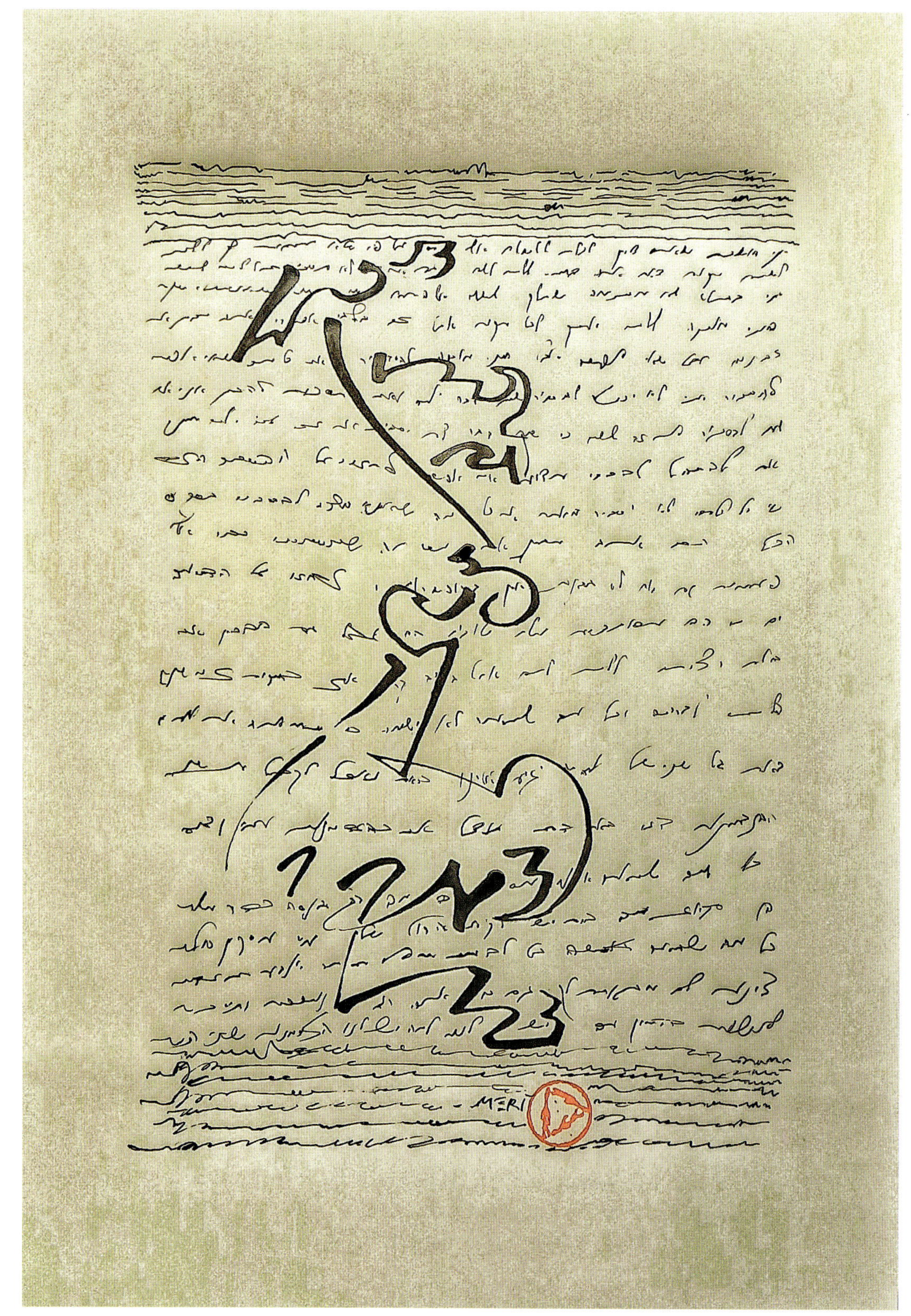

Meri Karako
The Lines between the Lines, 2021

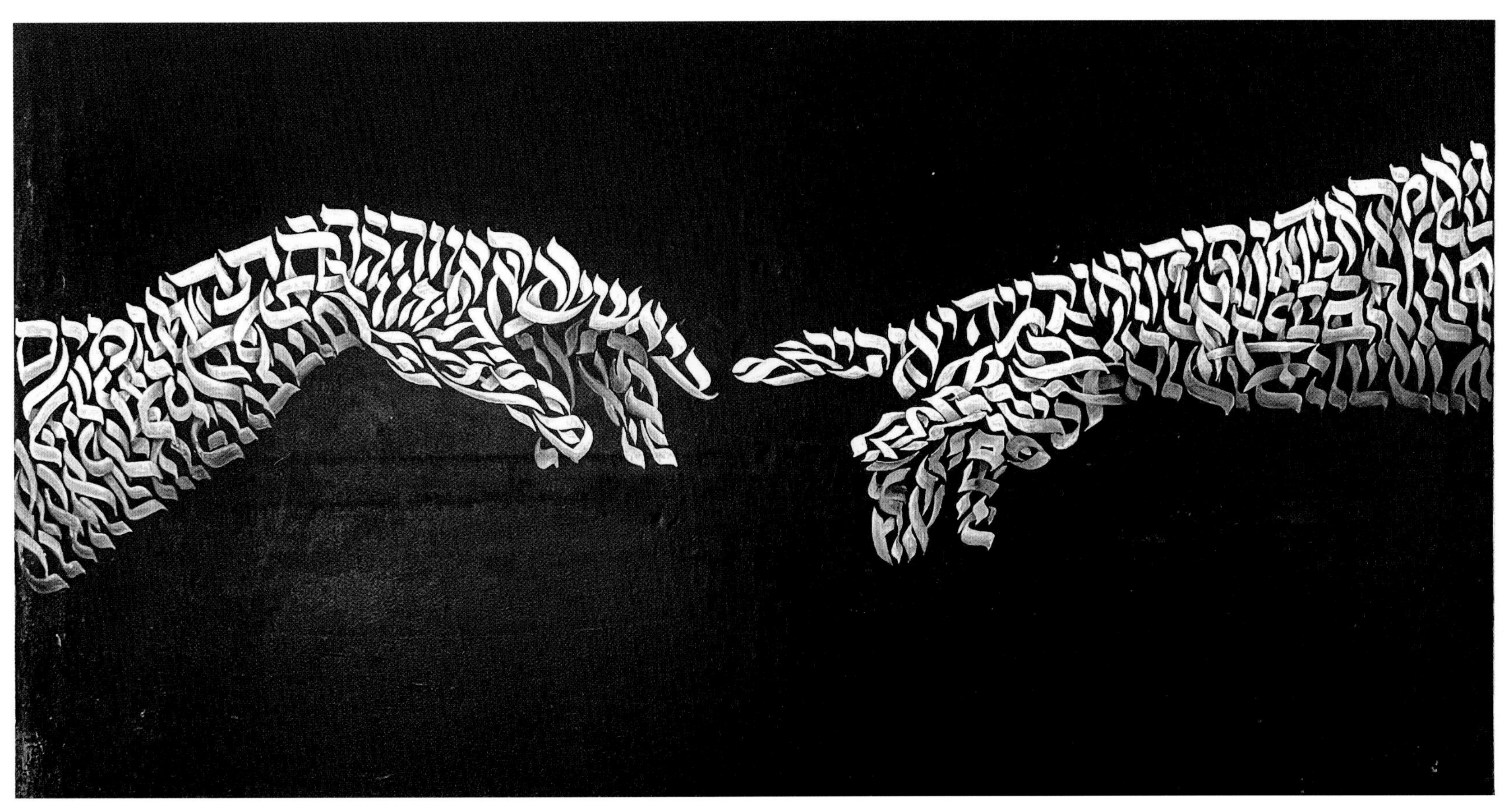

Gabriel Wolff
Genesis, 2017

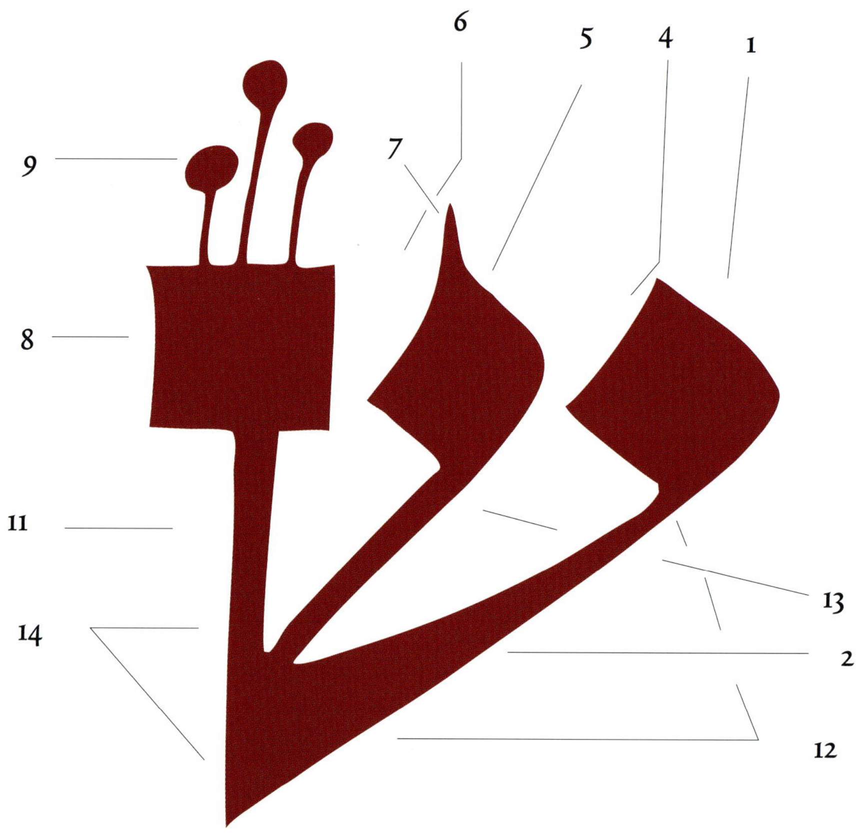

An example of the rules regarding the writing of the letters in the sacred script. Here is the letter shin *as is written in the* Beit Yosef *Ashkenazic tradition. The diagram is modeled after an illustration from a book on the laws of writing. The numbers refer to the notes accompanying the illustration, which explain all the fine points required to form this letter properly.*

6

Sacred Writing

A Jewish scribe of ritual objects is called a Sofer STaM—STaM being an acronym for Sefer Torah, Tefillin, and Mezuzot. These are three of the religious objects that must be handwritten as opposed to printed. Examples of each are presented here. There is a *hiddur mitzvah*, an enhancement of the commandment, for the objects to be written as beautifully as possible. To quote from one of the law books, "all those that write Torah scrolls, Tefillin and Mezzuzot that are good and kosher, their reward is doubled and multiplied."

And yet, ironically, the lettering on these objects is almost never seen. The mezuzah parchment is rolled and affixed to a doorpost. The tefillin parchment is rolled and sewed into black boxes. And the Torah scroll too is kept rolled and only opened during the synagogue readings. In other words, the beauty is kept mostly hidden, giving it a different purpose, as well as a mystique and mystery in line with the sacred.

וישכם אבימלך בבקר ויקרא לכל עבדיו
וידבר את כל הדברים האלה באזניהם
וייראו האנשים מאד ויקרא אבימלך
לאברהם ויאמר לו מה עשית לנו ומה
חטאתי לך כי הבאת עלי ועל ממלכתי
חטאה גדלה מעשים אשר לא יעשו עשית
עמדי ויאמר אבימלך אל אברהם מה ראית
כי עשית את הדבר הזה ויאמר אברהם כי
אמרתי רק אין יראת אלהים במקום הזה
והרגוני על דבר אשתי וגם אמנה אחתי בת
אבי הוא אך לא בת אמי ותהי לי לאשה
ויהי כאשר התעו אתי אלהים מבית אבי
ואמר לה זה חסדך אשר תעשי עמדי אל
כל המקום אשר נבוא שמה אמרי לי אחי
הוא ויקח אבימלך צאן ובקר ועבדים
ושפחת ויתן לאברהם וישב לו את שרה
אשתו ויאמר אבימלך הנה ארצי לפניך
בטוב בעיניך שב ולשרה אמר הנה נתתי
אלף כסף לאחיך הנה הוא לך כסות עינים
לכל אשר אתך ואת כל ונכחת ויתפלל
אברהם אל האלהים וירפא אלהים את
אבימלך ואת אשתו ואמהתיו וילדו כי עצר
עצר יהוה בעד כל רחם לבית אבימלך על
דבר שרה אשת אברהם   ויהוה
פקד את שרה כאשר אמר ויעש יהוה לשרה
כאשר דבר ותהר ותלד שרה לאברהם בן
לזקניו למועד אשר דבר אתו אלהים ויקרא
אברהם את שם בנו הנולד לו אשר ילדה
לו שרה יצחק וימל אברהם את יצחק בנו בן
שמנת ימים כאשר צוה אתו אלהים ואברהם
בן מאת שנה בהולד לו את יצחק בנו ותאמר

Detail from a fifteenth-century Torah scroll written on leather, as in Sephardic tradition

יהודה ער ואונן וימת ער ואונן בארץ כנען ויהיו
בני יהודה למשפחתם לשלה משפחת השלני
לפרץ משפחת הפרצי לזרח משפחת הזרחי ויהיו
בני פרץ לחצרן משפחת החצרני לחמול משפחת
החמולי אלה משפחת יהודה לפקדיהם ששה
ושבעים אלף וחמש מאות בני
יששכר למשפחתם תולע משפחת התולעי
לפוה משפחת הפוני לישוב משפחת הישבי
לשמרן משפחת השמרני אלה משפחת
יששכר לפקדיהם ארבעה וששים אלף ושלש
מאות בני
זבולן למשפחתם לסרד משפחת הסרדי לאלון
משפחת האלני ליחלאל משפחת היחלאלי אלה
משפחת הזבולני לפקדיהם ששים אלף וחמש
מאות בני יוסף למשפחתם
מנשה ואפרים בני מנשה למכיר משפחת המכירי
ומכיר הוליד את גלעד לגלעד משפחת הגלעדי
אלה בני גלעד איעזר משפחת האיעזרי לחלק
משפחת החלקי ואשריאל משפחת האשראלי
ושכם משפחת השכמי ושמידע משפחת
השמידעי וחפר משפחת החפרי וצלפחד בן
חפר לא היו לו בנים כי אם בנות ושם בנות
צלפחד מחלה ונעה חגלה מלכה ותרצה אלה
משפחת מנשה ופקדיהם שנים וחמשים אלף
ושבע מאות אלה בני אפרים
למשפחתם לשותלח משפחת השתלחי לבכר
משפחת הבכרי לתחן משפחת התחני ואלה בני
שותלח לערן משפחת הערני אלה משפחת בני

Scribe and date unknown
Detail from an Ashkenazic Sefer
Torah scroll

Some samples of writing from different Torah scrolls. The two different styles in the Ashkenazic tradition were written with a bird-feather quill. Compare especially the shapes of the shin *and the* heh*.*

Scribe and date unknown
Detail from Torah scroll, Ashkenazic writing

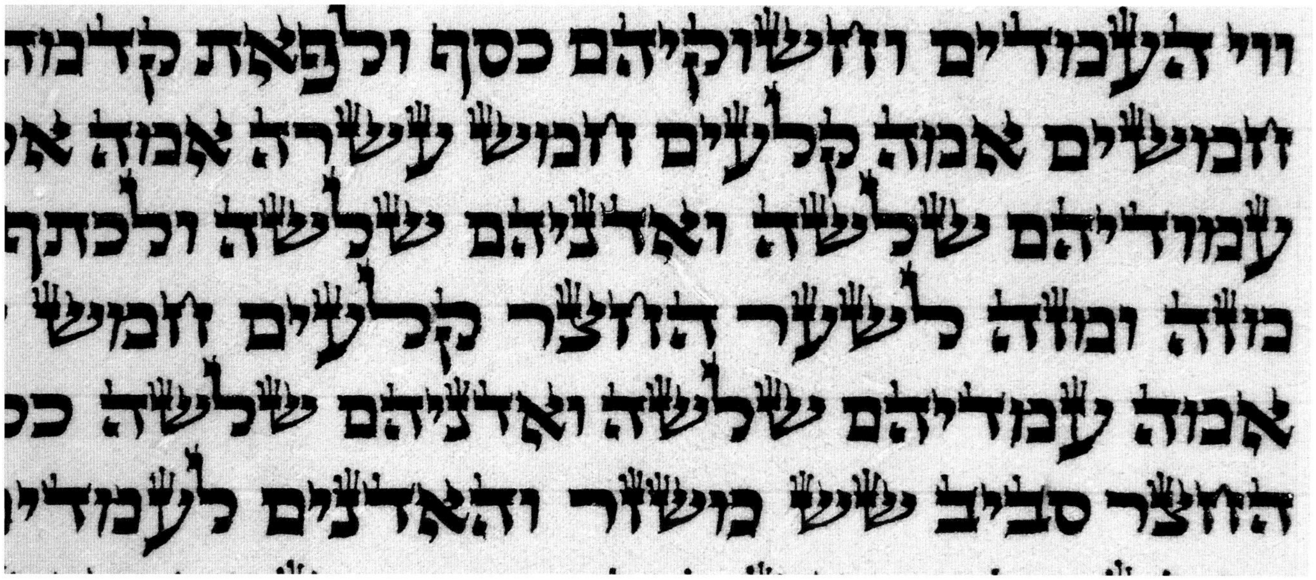

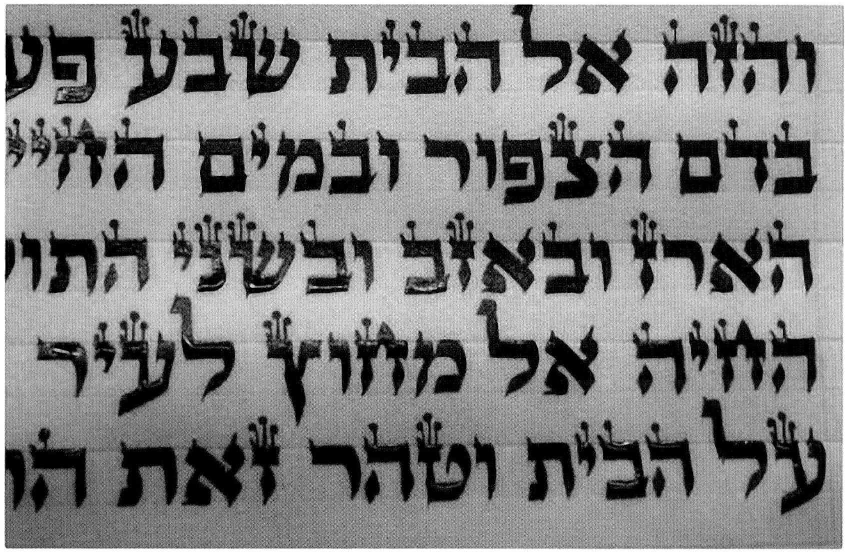

TOP: Yossi Gilad
Detail from Torah scroll
Ashkenazic Beit *Yosef* writing, 2018–2019
BOTTOM: Moshe Levi
Detail from Torah scroll
Sephardic writing

והיה כי יבאך יהוה אל ארץ הכנעני כאשר נשבע לך ולאבתיך ונתנה לך והעברת כל
פטר רחם ליהוה וכל פטר שגר בהמה אשר יהיה לך הזכרים ליהוה וכל פטר חמר
תפדה בשה ואם לא תפדה וערפתו וכל בכור אדם בבניך תפדה והיה כי ישאלך בנך
מחר לאמר מה זאת ואמרת אליו בחזק יד הוציאנו יהוה ממצרים מבית עבדים ויהי כי
הקשה פרעה לשלחנו ויהרג יהוה כל בכור בארץ מצרים מבכר אדם ועד בכור בהמה
על כן אני זבח ליהוה כל פטר רחם הזכרים וכל בכור בני אפדה והיה לאות על ידכה
ולטוטפת בין עיניך כי בחזק יד הוציאנו יהוה ממצרים

שמע ישראל יהוה אלהינו יהוה אחד ואהבת את יהוה אלהיך בכל לבבך ובכל
נפשך ובכל מאדך והיו הדברים האלה אשר אנכי מצוך היום על לבבך ושננתם
לבניך ודברת בם בשבתך בביתך ובלכתך בדרך ובשכבך ובקומך וקשרתם
לאות על ידך והיו לטטפת בין עיניך וכתבתם על מזזות ביתך ובשעריך

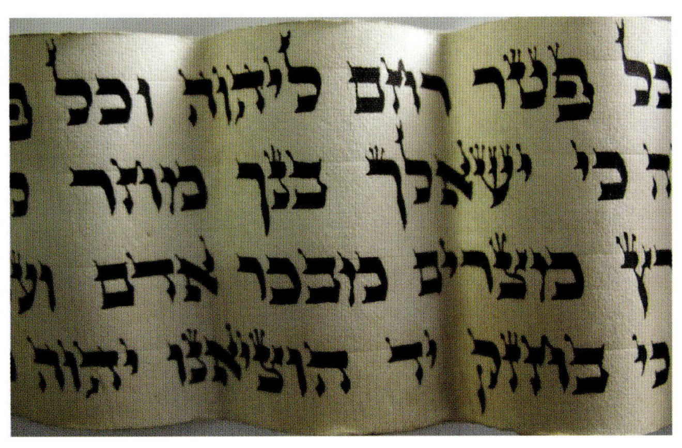

TOP: Jonathan Essebag
Tefillin, Ashkenazic script style, 2020
MIDDLE: Baruch Danon
Tefillin, Sephardic script style
BOTTOM: Scribe and date unknown
Tefillin, Chabad script style

שמע ישראל יהוה אלהינו יהוה אחד ואהבת את
יהוה אלהיך בכל לבבך ובכל נפשך ובכל מאדך והיו
הדברים האלה אשר אנכי מצוך היום על לבבך ושננתם
לבניך ודברת בם בשבתך בביתך ובלכתך בדרך
ובשכבך ובקומך וקשרתם לאות על ידך והיו לטטפת
בין עיניך וכתבתם על מזזות ביתך ובשעריך

והיה אם שמע תשמעו אל מצותי אשר אנכי
מצוה אתכם היום לאהבה את יהוה אלהיכם ולעבדו
בכל לבבכם ובכל נפשכם ונתתי מטר ארצכם בעתו
יורה ומלקוש ואספת דגנך ותירשך ויצהרך ונתתי
עשב בשדך לבהמתך ואכלת ושבעת השמרו לכם
פן יפתה לבבכם וסרתם ועבדתם אלהים אחרים
והשתחויתם להם וחרה אף יהוה בכם ועצר את
השמים ולא יהיה מטר והאדמה לא תתן את יבולה
ואבדתם מהרה מעל הארץ הטבה אשר יהוה נתן לכם
ושמתם את דברי אלה על לבבכם ועל נפשכם וקשרתם
אתם לאות על ידכם והיו לטוטפת בין עיניכם ולמדתם
אתם את בניכם לדבר בם בשבתך בביתך ובלכתך
בדרך ובשכבך ובקומך וכתבתם על מזוזות ביתך
ובשעריך למען ירבו ימיכם וימי בניכם על האדמה
אשר נשבע יהוה לאבתיכם לתת להם כימי השמים
על הארץ

Aaron Shaffier
Mezuzah, Chabad script style, 2021

המלך חור כרפס ותכלת אחוז בחבלי בוץ וארגמן
על גלילי כסף ועמודי שש מטות זהב וכסף על
רצפת בהט ושש ודר וסחרת והשקות בכלי זהב
וכלים מכלים שונים ויין מלכות רב כיד המלך
והשתיה כדת אין אנס כי כן יסד המלך על כל רב
ביתו לעשות כרצון איש ואיש גם ושתי
המלכה עשתה משתה נשים בית המלכות אשר
למלך אחשורוש ביום השביעי כטוב לב המלך
ביין אמר למהומן בזתא חרבונא בגתא ואבגתא
זתר וכרכס שבעת הסריסים המשרתים את פני
המלך אחשורוש להביא את ושתי המלכה לפני

Izzy Pludwinski
A column from a *Scroll of Esther*, 2019

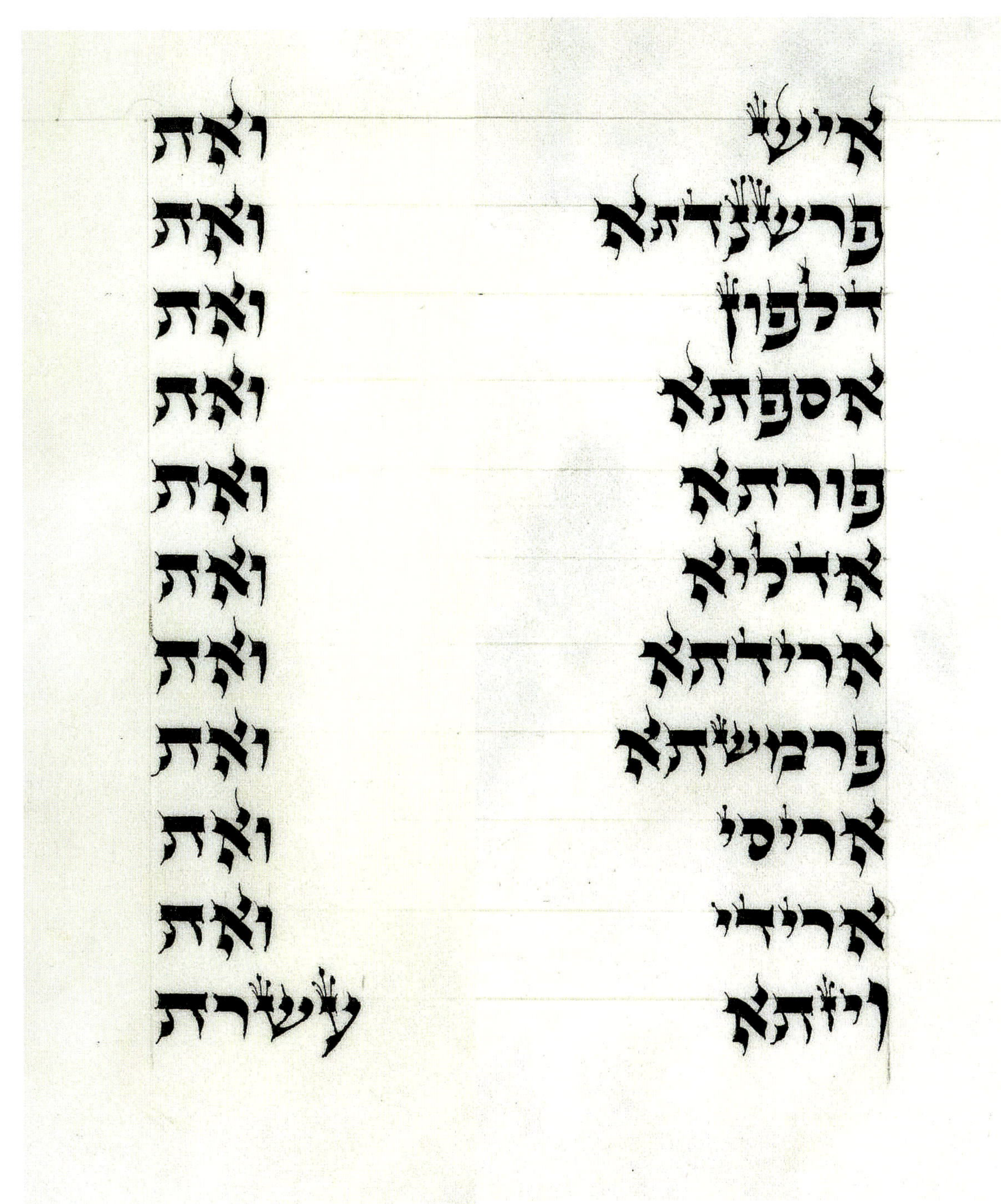

Izzy Pludwinski
A column from a *Scroll of Esther*, 2004

Perhaps a fitting way to end this book. The image shows the bottom of the final column of a Torah scroll that the scribe has just finished. The scribe has outlined the last three words. At this point, as part of a siyum hasefer *(completion of the Torah) ceremony, members of the congregation are often invited to fill in the letters in ink, thus participating in the writing of the Torah.*

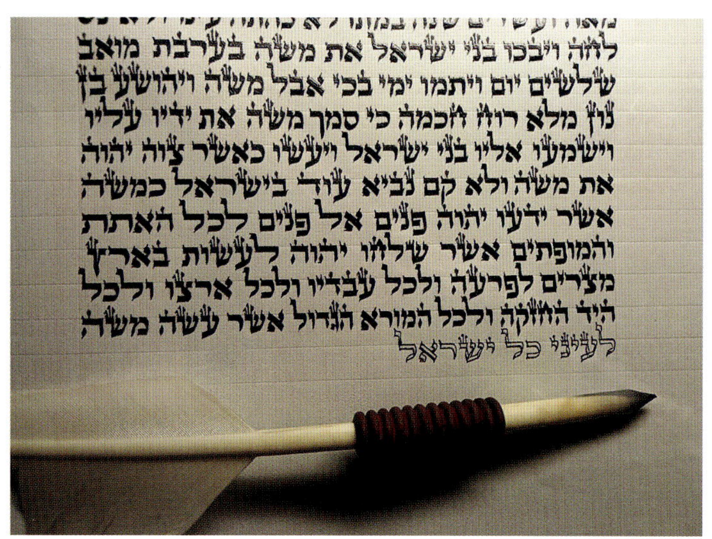

לחה ויבכו בני ישראל את משה בערבת מואב
שלשים יום ויתמו ימי בכי אבל משה ויהושע בן
נון מלא רוח חכמה כי סמך משה את ידיו עליו
וישמעו אליו בני ישראל ויעשו כאשר צוה יהוה
את משה ולא קם נביא עוד בישראל כמשה
אשר ידעו יהוה פנים אל פנים לכל האתת
והמופתים אשר שלחו יהוה לעשות בארץ
מצרים לפרעה ולכל עבדיו ולכל ארצו ולכל
היד החזקה ולכל המורא הגדול אשר עשה משה
לעיני כל ישראל

Moshe Levi
Detail of last column of a Torah scroll

Acknowledgments

WHERE TO BEGIN? I started out on this journey naively thinking this would be a relatively simple book to write. How wrong I was! It turned out to be a long and complicated endeavor that could not have been accomplished without the cooperation and generosity of many people.

First and most obviously, my thanks go to all the artists whose works constitute this book. It was a joy to search and research the wonderful creative work that is being done in Hebrew lettering, and I am grateful for all the artists' willingness to share their works here.

A very special thanks and gratitude to David Goldstein. It is good to have people to bounce ideas off of, to hear opinions from, and to argue with. David is a highly regarded calligrapher and graphic artist, and I turned to him, if not daily, then at least weekly, with ideas and questions. His enthusiasm and support for the book, as well as his input, were invaluable in keeping me going when I was feeling despair and frustration. And add to that his graphics wizardry in improving the images wherever possible.

Karen Ness too was a huge help and always made herself available to my endless conundrums. Her keen sense of design, which holds to the highest standards, and practical common sense helped simplify problems. My deeply felt thanks to her.

And much appreciation and thanks to Misha Beletsky for his practical and professional advice in the early stages of my work on the book and later on, for his professional contribution to its design.

Sharon Mintz, curator of Jewish art at the Jewish Theological Seminary, was extremely generous in allowing me to use images from the wonderful JTS Special Collections Library. Her advice and recommendations were invaluable, and I deeply thank her. Helen Brandshaft was extremely helpful in providing information as well as obtaining images of the works of Ismar David.

Other people and institutions deserving mention for generously allowing use of their images are Nanette Stahl, librarian at the Yale University Library Judaica Collection, Gabriel Goldstein, curator at the North Carolina Museum of Art, and the Royal Danish Library.

A big thanks to Professor Dov-Ber Kerler for his kind help in providing both information and actual images of certain Yiddish books and journals.

At the very last stages of writing this book, I was introduced to a magnificent Judaica collector: William Gross. His kindness and generosity in allowing the images from his collection to be used contributed greatly to this book.

Thanks to the artists' relatives who gave permission to use the works of the artists.

Matthew Miller at Koren Publishers, although not able in the end to publish the book, recommended me to Brandeis University Press, which proved to be a most fruitful connection. Thank you.

And lastly, to the staff at Brandeis University Press for enthusiastically believing in this book and for their high standards of professionalism.

—Izzy Pludwinski

Brandeis University Press acknowledges with gratitude the generous support of the Martin J. Gross Family Foundation.

Some Useful Terms

Lettering artists use certain terms to classify Hebrew scripts, which the average reader might not be familiar with. Here are short explanations of some of the terms mentioned throughout the book.

התהלך לפני והיה תמים

MIZRACHI (ORIENTAL, ERETZ YISRAEL) SQUARE SCRIPT
One of the earliest formal styles to develop from the scripts found on the Dead Sea Scrolls. Written in Israel, Syria and Egypt. Some salient features are the shape of the roofs of the letters, which seem to be written in two strokes—a sloped stroke followed by a horizontal stroke, and the shape of *mem*. Note too the very tall lameds which were incorporated when there was enough room - a feature also seen in the Dead Sea Scrolls.

ASHKENAZIC SQUARE SCRIPT
This term is used to describe the script that was developed in the Northern European countries, such as Germany and France, reaching its aesthetic heights in the beautiful illuminated manuscripts of the Middle Ages. These has had a strong influence on contemporary lettering artists. The script is characterized by high contrasts between the thick horizontal strokes and thin vertical strokes. In the Middle Ages these letters were written with a quill made from the feathers of a bird, such as goose. To achieve this contrast the pen's nib was held at an angle close to 90 degrees. Diamond shaped strokes were often added to the very thin vertical strokes to add weight to the legs.

SEPHARDIC SQUARE SCRIPT
This term is used to describe the script that was developed in the Southern European countries, such as Spain, Portugal, and Italy. They were written with a reed pen. Compared to the Ashkenazic script the contrasts between horizontal and vertical strokes are less pronounced, which makes for easier readability. The pen's nib was held at a less extreme angle, usually 65–75 degrees. Most Hebrew fonts today are based on Sephardic script forms.

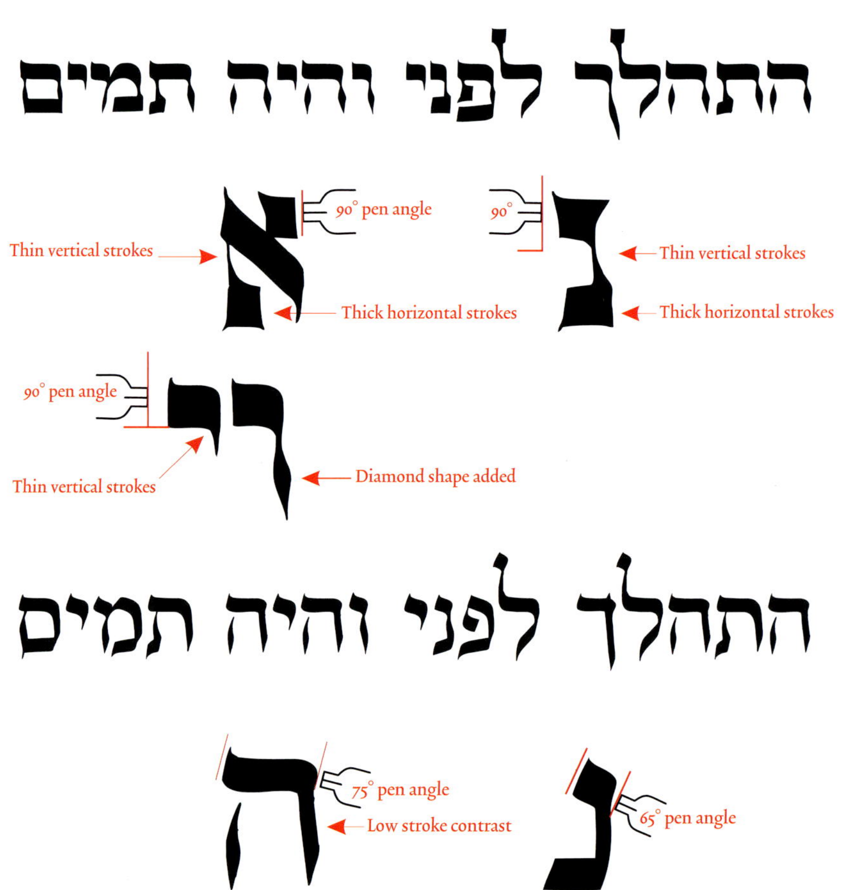

YERUSHALMI SCRIPT

A modernized script that developed from the forms used on the scrolls found at Qumran, near the Dead Sea. One of its unique characteristics is the triangular serif that is formed as a beginning stroke on many of the letters.

התהלך לפני והיה תמים

Triangular serif

SEMI-CURSIVE SCRIPT

A general term for less formal scripts, with simpler shapes that can be written quicker. They exist in many different forms, two of which are shown here: the medieval Italian (*above*) and the medieval Ashkenazic (*below*).

התהלך לפני והיה תמים

התהלך לפני והיה תמים

STAM SCRIPT (ASHURIT)

STaM in an acronym for Sefer Torah, Tefillin, and Mezuzah—the three religious articles in Judaism that must be handwritten. The script is considered holy and has many laws prescribing exactly how it must be written. Note the *tagim* (crowns) on certain letters. Above is an example of Ashkenazic STaM and below, Sephardic STaM.

ובכל נפשך ובכל מאדך

ובכל נפשך ובכל מאדך

CONTEMPORARY HANDWRITING

A semi-cursive script that sometimes exhibits cursive (interconnecting letters) qualities. These developed out of eighteenth-century German semi-cursives.

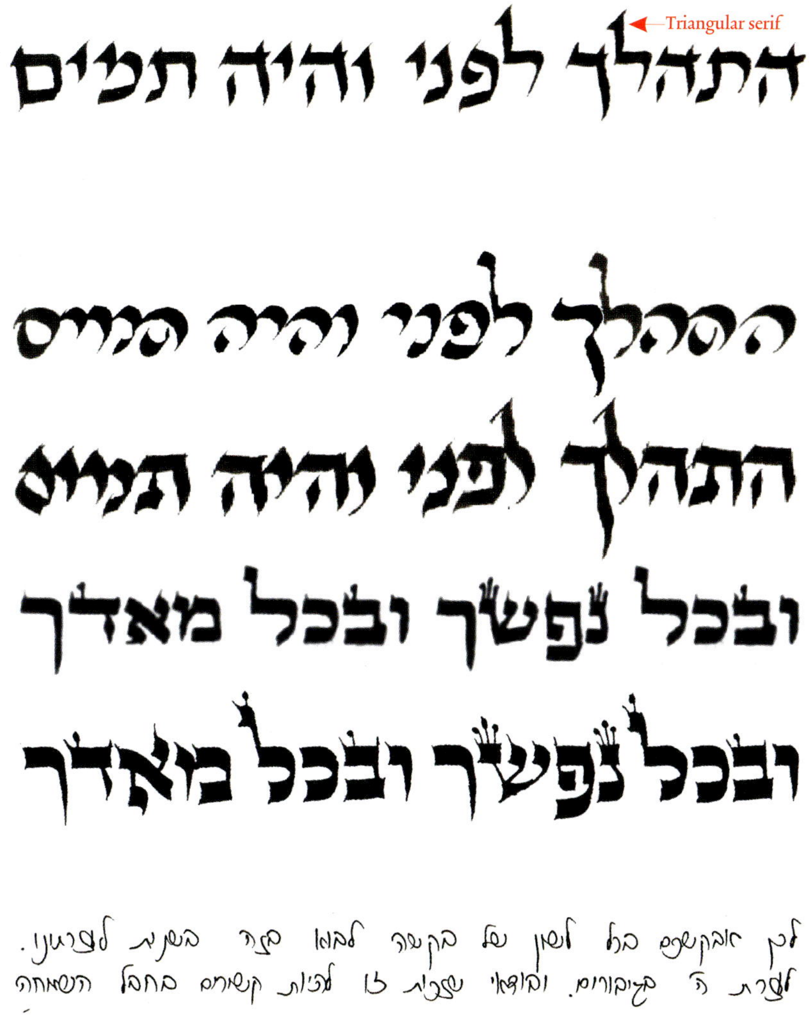

Index of Contributing Artists

Illustration Credits

Page xii: Mesad Hashavyahu Ostracon replica, seventh century BCE. Archaeological Museum Beit Miriam, Kibbutz Palmahim. Photo by Hanay: commons.wikimedia.org/wiki/File: Mesad_Hashavyahu_Ostracon_Replica_1.JPG. Licensed under the Creative Commons—Attribution-ShareAlike 3.0 Unported license.

Page 3: Edna Miron-Wapner. Silkscreen print from a rubbing of the Meshe Stele, 1998–1999. Courtesy of Edna Miron-Wapner.

Page 4: Izzy Pludwinski. *Chesed*, Paleo-Hebrew script, 2017.

Page 5: Ilya Yakubovich. *Yah* (Yud-Heh ligature), Paleo-Hebrew script, 2019. Courtesy of Ilya Yakubovich.

Page 6: *Commentary on Habakkuk*, Qumran, first century BCE. Shrine of The Book, The Israel Museum, Jerusalem. © The Israel Museum, Jerusalem, photo by Ardon Bar-Huma.

Page 7: Felix Greenberg. *Book of Ruth*, 1959. © Emunah Academic College of Arts and Design.

Page 8: *Shelach Lecha*, portion of the Torah, 1106–1107 CE. Jewish National and University Library. Public Domain.

Page 9: Zvi Narkiss, font designer. Details from the *Keter Yerushalayim*. N. Ben Zvi Printing Enterprises, 2002. Courtesy of Nahum Ben Zvi.

Page: 10: *Mahberet Hatigan*, Yemenite Bible L66: Pentateuch, Yemen, 1400. Courtesy of The Library of the Jewish Theological Seminary.

Page 11: Oded Ezer. *Kadim* font, 2020. © Oded Ezer, 2020.

Page 12: *Prato Haggadah*, MS 9478, page 10, Spain, 1300 CE. Courtesy of The Library of the Jewish Theological Seminary.

Page 13: Joel Ben Simeon. *Ashkenazi Haggadah*, Germany, fifteenth century. The British Library. © The British Library Board.

Page 14: *Shiviti*, Jerusalem, 1912. Courtesy of the Beinecke Rare Book & Manuscript Library, Yale University.

Page 15: Moshe Levi. *Psalm 142*, 2021. Courtesy of Moshe Levi.

Page 16: Moshe ben Mordechai. *Shiviti*, 1875. Gross Family Collection, Tel Aviv.

Page 17: Moshe Yosef Avraham. From an illuminated compendium of texts for Passover, Iraq, 1883. Gross Family Collection, Tel Aviv.

Page 18: Amulet, Iran, c. 1900. Gross Family Collection, Tel Aviv.

Page 19: Amulet, Iran, c. 1930. Gross Family Collection, Tel Aviv.

Page 20: Details from Bible, Poligny, France, 1300. Courtesy of Bibliothèque Nationale de France.

Page 21: Details from Bible, Poligny, France, 1300. Courtesy of Bibliothèque Nationale de France.

Page 22: M. Giovanbattista Palatino. *Tools of Handwriting*, 1540–1545. Courtesy of Getty Research Institute. Public domain.

Page 23: Giovanni Antonio Tagliente. *Lo presente libro insegna la vera arte de lo excellente scrivere de litere*. Bibliothèque Nationale de France. Public domain.

Page 24: Details from the *Ashkenazi Haggadah*, Germany, fifteenth century. © The British Library Board.

Page 25: Details from the *Herlingen Haggadah*, Vienna, 1730. BCB 388, Braginsky Collection, Zurich. Photography by Ardon Ben-Hama, Ra'anana, Israel.

Page 26: *The Rothschild Machzor*, MS 8892, page 149, Florence, 1492. Courtesy of Library of the Jewish Theological Seminary.

Page 27: *The Rothschild Machzor*, detail, MS 8892, page 149, Florence, 1492. Courtesy of The Library of the Jewish Theological Seminary.

Page 28–29: Book of Genesis, c.1250–1300. Reprinted with the kind permission of Les Enluminures.

Pages 30: *Sefer Mitzvot Katan*, 1201–1400. Courtesy of Bibliothèque Nationale de France.

Page 31: *Sefer Mitzvot Katan*, detail, 1201–1400. Courtesy of Bibliothèque Nationale de France.

Page 32: Detail from *Guide to the Perplexed*, Southern Spain, 1479. Courtesy of Bibliothèque Nationale de France.

Page 33: Rosh Av Bet Din be-Kopenhagen. From *Drashot ve-hidushim al parashat ha-shavu'a* (enlarged detail), eighteenth century. Courtesy of the Royal Danish Library, David Simonsen Collection.

Page 34: Malla Carl. From *If I Forget Thee O Jerusalem* (detail), late twentieth century. Courtesy of Nechama Carl.

Page 36: Franzisca Baruch. Top: *Title for Haggadah*, 1921. Bottom: Logo for Haaretz newspaper, 1936.

Page 37: Zev Lipman. *In Memory of Rudolph Koch*, mid–late twentieth century. Courtesy of Danny Lipman.

Page 38: Siegmund Forst. Lettering in cover illustration from *A Lifetime in Arts and Letters*, 1993. Courtesy of Benjamin Forst.

Page 39: Zev Lipman. Greeting card for the New Year, mid- to late twentieth century. Courtesy of Danny Lipman.

Page 40: Zev Lipman/Studio Roli. Left: Logo proposal for Israel's twentieth anniversary, c.1968. Top right: Logo proposal for Tel Aviv Museum, n.d. Bottom right: Logo proposal for the city of Beer Sheva, n.d. Courtesy of Danny Lipman.

Page 41: Zev Lipman. Sample calligraphy page in *The Art of Hebrew Lettering* by L. F. Toby, c. 1951. Courtesy of Danny Lipman.

Page 42: Zev Lipman. *I Will Raise Jerusalem above All My Joy*, mid- to late twentieth century. Courtesy of Danny Lipman.

Page 43: Ada Yardeni. Page from *The Passover Haggadah*. Carta Publishers, 1976.

Pages 44–45: Abram Games. Design for the *Encyclopedia Judaica*, 1969. © 1969 Estate of Abram Games.

Page 46: Arieh Allweil. Title page for a fully illustrated *Megillat Ruth*, 1939. Courtesy of the artist's family.

Page 47: Top: Designer unknown. Publisher: Avraham Yoseph Shteibel, Leipzig, 1923. Bottom: Designer unknown. Publisher: Yidbukh, Buenos Aires, 1957.

Page 48: Zvi Narkiss. Left: Design sketch for medal commemorating the 1979 peace accord with Egypt. Right: Design sketch for "Am Yisrael Chai" medal. Gift of Tamar Narkiss Gal, Harish, and Ruth Shoub, Kibbutz Nachshon, for The Israel Museum, Jerusalem. © The Israel Museum, Jerusalem, photo by Ofrit Rosenberg.

Page 49: Top left: Gideon Keich. "They Still Bring Forth Fruit . . . ," 1982. Top right: Zvi Narkiss. "Hear O Israel,"

1980. Bottom right: Nathan Karp. "Am Yisrael Chai," 1982. Bottom left: Ben Shahn. Commemorative medal celebrating the twentieth anniversary of El Al Israel Airlines, 1969. Images courtesy of the Israel Coins and Medals Corporation.

Page 50: Top: Yaakov Stark. Hebrew monogram designs (edited), 1915. © The Israel Museum, Jerusalem, original photo by Elie Posner. Bottom: Joy Rosenblum. Hebrew monogram designs, 1994. Courtesy of Joy Rosenblum.

Page 51: Top: Ismar David. Detail from invitation announcing the opening of the Kaiser-Fraiser Auto Company, 1951. Courtesy of Helen Brandshaft. Bottom: Shavit Yaakov. Satirical logo for tobacco company, 2020. Courtesy of the artist.

Page 52: Ludwig Yehudah Wolpert. Bronze gates of the synagogue at Kennedy International Airport, New York, 1968.

Page 53: Ludwig Yehudah Wolpert. *Mezuzah*, 1951. Gift of Dr. Ludwig Y. Wolpert in honor of the fiftieth wedding anniversary of Drs. Abram and Frances Pascher Kanof. Courtesy of North Carolina Museum of Art, Raleigh.

Page 54: Left: Chava Wolpert Richard. *Memorial Lamp*, c. 1980. Gift of Drs. Abram and Frances Pascher Kanof. Image courtesy of North Carolina Museum of Art, Raleigh. Right: Ludwig Yehudah Wolpert. Shecheyanu pin, c. 1970s (?).

Page 55: Fred Pauker. Cornerstone certificate for High-Tech Park in Beer Sheva, Israel, 1984. Courtesy of Evelyn Pauker.

Page 56: Moshe Chatumi. *Book of Lamentations*, 1960. © Emunah Academic College of Arts and Design.

Page 57: Top: Arnona Rozin. Selected pages from *Greek Mythologies*, c. 1960(?). © Emunah Academic College of Arts and Design. Bottom: *Chaham, Rasha*, by student of Yerachmiel Shechter, c. 1960. © Emunah Academic College of Arts and Design.

Page 58: Yerachmiel Shechter. *Chad Gadya*, c. 1930s. © Emunah Academic College of Arts and Design.

Page 59: Top: Yerachmiel Shechter. *Chad Gadya*, c. 1930s. © Emunah Academic College of Arts and Design. Bottom: Elly Gross. Design for the Israel Medical Association, 1965–70. The Elly Gross Archive, The National Library of Israel. © The National Library of Israel.

Page 60: Zvi Narkiss. *Traveler's Blessing*, c. 1970s. Courtesy of Sharon Binder.

Page 61: Design for cover of the *Koren Siddur*, 1971. © Koren Publishers Jerusalem, Ltd.

Page 62: Ismar David. *Priestly Blessing*, 1976. Courtesy of Helen Brandshaft.

Page 63: Ismar David. Sketch for *Priestly Blessing*, c. 1980. Courtesy of Helen Brandshaft.

Page 64: Ismar David. *Ten Commandments*, design above the ark at Temple Aaron, St. Paul, Minnesota, 1957. Courtesy of Helen Brandshaft.

Page 65: Ismar David. *Peace to Israel* pendant, n.d. Courtesy of Helen Brandshaft.

Page 66: Ada Yardeni. From the *Gates of Jerusalem Haggadah*. Carta Jerusalem, 1978.

Page 67: Ismar David. *Let the Heavens Rejoice*, from Psalm 96, n.d. Courtesy of Helen Brandshaft.

Page 68: Lili Wronker. *For Love Is Stronger than Death*, mid-late twentieth century. Courtesy of Rona Wronker.

Page 69: Fred Pauker. From *Memorial Book for Ben-Gurion University*, 1984. Courtesy of Evelyn Pauker.

Page 70: Fred Pauker. *Traveler's Prayer*, 1975. Courtesy of Evelyn Pauker.

Page 71: Malla Carl. *A Woman of Valor*, late twentieth century. Courtesy of Nechama Carl.

Page 72–73: Zvi Narkiss. From *Great Is Peace*, Masada Press, 1979. Photograph by Ruth Yehoshua.

Page 74: Barbara Wolff. *Psalm 104*, 2006–07. Courtesy of Barbara Wolff.

Page 75: Arthur Szyk. *The Four Questions from The Haggadah*. Łódz, Poland, 1935. Courtesy of Irvin Ungar, Historicana.

Page 76: Ruth Lubin, calligrapher, and Irina Oblovsky, artist. From *Passover Haggadah*, 2006. Courtesy of Ruth Lubin.

Page 77: Ruth Lubin. Detail from a *Shir Hashirim* book, 2007. Courtesy of Ruth Lubin.

Page 78: Sharon Binder. *The Four Species*, 2002. Courtesy of Sharon Binder.

Page 79: Malla Carl. *Prayer for Blessing for the New Month*, late twentieth century. Courtesy of Nechama Carl.

Page 80: Avraham Borshevsky. Right: *Psalm 33:1*, 2007. Left: *Philip*, 2017. Courtesy of Avraham Borshevsky.

Page 81: Malla Carl. *Prayer after Lighting the Shabbat Candles*, late twentieth century. Courtesy of Nechama Carl.

Page 82: Sharon Binder. Design for a chuppah, 2016. Courtesy of Sharon Binder.

Page 83: Zina Dorman. *The Old Man and the Sea*, 2014. Courtesy of Zina Dorman.

Page 84: Lynn Broide. *Eliyahu*, design for Bar-Mitzvah invitation cover, 1993. Courtesy of Lynn Broide.

Page 85: Fred Pauker. *Logo for Israel Bibliophiles*, 1980–81. Courtesy of Evelyn Pauker.

Page 86: Top: Fred Pauker. Detail from cover of *Midrash Yerushalayim*, c. 1982. Courtesy of Evelyn Pauker. Bottom: David Goldstein. *Bereshit*, 2016. Courtesy of David Goldstein.

Page 87: David Goldstein. *Through Two Points Only One Straight Line Can Pass*, text by Yehuda Amichai. © Schocken Publishing House Ltd., Tel Aviv, Israel. Image courtesy of David Goldstein.

Page 88: Akiva Roszkowski. *Home Blessing*, 2019. Courtesy of Akiva Roszkowski.

Page 89: Melanie Dankowicz. *Hebrew Clock*, 2012. Courtesy of Melanie Dankowicz.

Page 90: Lettering on the building of the Officer's Training School. Lettering designer unknown, as per Zvi Hecker, architect of Bahad 1. Building constructed in the 1960s.

Page 91: Joseph Hirsch. Top: Lettering detail from part of a ketubah design, n.d. Bottom: Lettering for street sign in the Jewish Quarter, Jerusalem, designed in 1968. Courtesy of the Hirsch Family.

Page 92-93: Carved lettering on the building of the Ponevezh Yeshivah, Bnei Brak, early twentieth century. Image source: https://creativecommons.org/licenses/by-sa/3.0, via Wikimedia Commons.

Page 94: Karen Ness. *Ketubah*, 2011. Courtesy of Karen Ness.

Page 95: Ted Scott Kadin. *Ketubah*, 2011. Courtesy of Ted Scott Kadin.

Page 96-97: Gina Jonas. *Ketubah*, 2003, Courtesy of Gina Jonas.

Page 98-99: Josh Baum. *Ketubah*, 2011. Courtesy of Josh Baum

Page 100: Izzy Pludwinski. Page from *The Song of Songs (Shir Hashirim)*, 2020.

Page 101: Izzy Pludwinski. "I Am Dark and Beautiful," from *Shir Hashirim*, 2018.

Page 102: Izzy Pludwinski. *Shir*, digital font used for a limited edition of *The Song of Songs*, 1999.

Page 103: Izzy Pludwinski. *Ashkanizzy*, digital font designed for a Pentateuch, 2014.

Page 104: Izzy Pludwinski. *Floating Letters*, 2021.

Page 106: Ilene Winn-Lederer. *Acanthus Hebrew Aleph-Bet*, 2012. Courtesy of Ilene Winn-Lederer.

Page 107: Lawrence Kushner. *Hebrew Aleph-Bet*, c. 1975.

Page 108: Josh Baum. *Hebrew Aleph-Bet*, 2002. Courtesy of Josh Baum.
Page 109: Izzy Pludwinski. *Hebrew Aleph-Bets*, 2016.
Page 110: Izzy Pludwinski. *Hebrew Aleph-bet*, 2022.
Page 111: David Goldstein. *Hebrew Aleph-Bet*, 2021. Courtesy of David Goldstein.
Page 112: David Goldstein. *Hebrew Aleph-Bet*, 2020. Courtesy of David Goldstein.
Page 113: Kalman Gavriel. *Alef-Bet Circle*, 2018. Courtesy of Kalman Gavriel.
Page 114: Elhanan Ben Uri. *Alef-Bet*, 2019. Courtesy of Elhanan Ben Uri.
Page 115: David Goldstein. *Hebrew Aleph-Bet*, 2021. Courtesy of David Goldstein.
Page 116: Michel D'Anastasio. *Aleph-Bet*, 2012. Courtesy of Michel D'Anastasio.
Page 117: Shiri Lanzer. *Aleph-Bet*, 2014. Courtesy of Shiri Lanzer.
Page 118: Lynn Broide. *Aleph-Bet*, c. 2019. Courtesy of Lynn Broide.
Page 119: Michel D'Anastasio. *Hebrew Aleph-Bet*, 2016. Courtesy of Michel D'Anastasio.
Page 120: Izzy Pludwinski. *Cursive Hebrew Aleph-Bet*, 1995.
Page 121: Izzy Pludwinski. *Brush Aleph-Bet*, 2002.
Page 122: Ben Shahn. *Aleph-Bet*, 1954. © 2022 Estate of Ben Shahn/ Licensed by VAGA at Arts Rights Society (ARS), NY.
Page 123: Josh Baum. *Aleph-Bet*, 2002. Courtesy of Josh Baum.
Page 124: Josh Baum. *Squashed Aleph-Bet*, 2003. Courtesy of Josh Baum.
Page 125: Alan Rafael Najman. *Aleph-Bet*, 2010. Courtesy of Alan Rafael Najman.
Page 126: Tal Becker. *Hebrew Letters*, 2020. Courtesy of Tal Becker.
Page 127: *Alephs*. Left to Right: Top: Guy Tamam, Izzy Pludwinski, Ben Natan. Middle: Fred Pauker, Sagi Carmi. Aleph-lamed ligature, from the Amsterdam Mahzor, 1670; Bottom: Ben Natan, Izzy Pludwinski, Moshik Nadav. Courtesy of the artists.
Page 128-129: Anna Zakai. *Illustrated Letters from Shir Hashirim* (colored letters), 2015–16. Courtesy of Anna Zakai.
Page 128-129: Zina Dorman. *Hebrew Initial Letters* (in black and white), 2015. Courtesy of Zina Dorman.
Page 130: Lynn Broide. *Aleph*, c. 2010. Courtesy of Lynn Broide.
Page 132: Cover of Tealit, Yiddish journal focusing on theater and literature, 1923. Cover designer unknown.
Page 132: Below: *Pompadour*, lettering from book cover. Designer unknown. Publisher: Literarishe Farlag, 1918.
Page 133: Top: Henryk Berlewi. Lettering on cover for *Albatross*, a journal for new writing and graphic arts, Berlin, 1923. Bottom: Cover for *Oksn*, book by Y. Kipnis, 1923. Designer unknown.
Page 134: David Moss. "Psalm 105:4" from *A Pueblo Portfolio*, 2004. © 2021 David Moss. Courtesy of Bet Alpha Editions.
Page 135: David Moss. "Mizrach Plaque" from *A Pueblo Portfolio*, 2004. © 2021 David Moss. Courtesy of Bet Alpha Editions.
Page 136: Michel D'Anastasio. *I Am My Beloved's*, 2020. Courtesy of Michel D'Anastasio.
Page 137: Michel D'Anastasio. *Adam, Adamah, Adom*, 2011. Courtesy of Michel D'Anastasio.
Page 138: Izzy Pludwinski. *Two Are Better Than One*, 2002.
Page 139: David Goldstein. *Lech lecha*, 2017. Courtesy of David Goldstein.
Page 140: David Goldstein. *Abstract Texture*, 2020. Courtesy of David Goldstein.
Page 141: Michel D'Anastasio. *Shabbat Shalom*, 2012. Courtesy of Michel D'Anastasio.
Page 142: Gabriel Wolff. *I Am My Beloved's*, 2013. Courtesy of Gabriel Wolf.
Page 143: Michael D'Anastasio. *Jerusalem*, 2012. Courtesy of Michel D'Anastasio.
Page 144: Guy Tamam. Top left: *Fifteen Hundred Shekel*, 2015. Top right: *Three Hundred Thousand Shekel*, 2015. Bottom: *Tel Aviv Yaffo*, 2018. Courtesy of Guy Tamam.
Page 145: Top: Lynn Broide. *Daniel*, 1991. Courtesy of Lynn Broide. Bottom: Baruch Naeh, lettering from the logo of the Yatir Winery, 2003. Courtesy of Yatir Winery.
Page 146: Nisan Engel. *Shma Yisrael*, 1974. Larchmont Temple, Larchmont, New York. Courtesy of Larchmont Temple.
Page 147: David Goldstein. *As the Deer Pants for Streams of Water . . .* (from Psalm 42), 2020. Courtesy of David Goldstein.
Page 148: Izzy Pludwinski. *The Whole World Is a Narrow Bridge*, 2018.
Page 149: Izzy Pludwinski. *Shanah Tovah! (A Good Year!)*, 2020.
Page 150: David Goldstein. *Jerusalem of Gold*, 2019. Courtesy of David Goldstein.
Page 151: Nathaniel Smith. *Burning Bush*, 2020. Micrography from Exodus chapters 2 and 3. Courtesy of Nathaniel Smith.@nathanjulius.
Page 152: Moran Haynal. *Calligraphy 10*, 2018. Courtesy of Moran Haynal.
Page 153: Moran Haynal. *Calligraphy 5*, 2016. Courtesy of Moran Haynal.
Page 154: Josh Baum. *Psalm 121*, 1996. Courtesy of Josh Baum.
Page 155: Josh Baum. *Psalm 1:3*, 2010. Courtesy of Josh Baum.
Page 156: Shiri Lanzer. *Improvisation*, 2014. Courtesy of Shiri Lanzer.
Page 157: Lynn Broide. *Come O Bride*, late 1990s. Courtesy of Lynn Broide.
Page 158: Ilanit Scharff Vigodsky. *What Was Tonight*, poem by the artist, 2020. Courtesy of Ilanit Scharff Vigodsky.
Page 159: Itamar Heifetz. *Aleph*, 2021. Courtesy of Itamar Heifetz.
Page 160: David Goldstein. *Watch Over Me as the Apple of Your Eye*, Psalm 17:8, 2020. Courtesy of David Goldstein.
Page 161: Oded Ezer. *Typography*, 2004. © 2004 Oded Ezer.
Page 162: Izzy Pludwinski. *And You Shall Choose Life*, 2016. From Deuteronomy 30:19.
Page 163: Izzy Pludwinski. *Draw Me after You and We Will Run*, 2006. From *The Song of Songs* 1:4.
Page 164: Lynn Broide. *Eichah*, c. 2018. Courtesy of Lynn Broide.
Page 165: Karen Ness. *Acquire a Teacher . . .*, 2022. Courtesy of Karen Ness.
Page 166-167: Lynn Broide. *Today is the Birth of the World*, 1991. Courtesy of Lynn Broide.
Page 168: Ira Dayan. *Circle of Blessing*, c. 2018. Courtesy of Ira Dayan.
Page 170-171: Ella Ponizovsky Bergelson. *People Among People*, part of the mural series "Among Refugees Generation Y," Mensch Meier, Berlin, 2019. Courtesy of Ella Ponizovsky Bergelson. Photo by Lea Fabrikant.
Page 172 Hillel Smith. *When?* 2018. Courtesy of Hillel Smith.
Page 173: Hillel Smith. *Who Brings Forth Bread from the Land*, sign on bakery, 2016. Courtesy of Hillel Smith.
Page 174: Asaf Mendelovich. Graffiti interpretations of classical Hebrew fonts: *Frank-Reuhl, Hatzvi*, 2014. Courtesy of Asaf Mendelovich.
Page 175: Asaf Mendelovich. Graffiti interpretations of classical Hebrew fonts: *Hadassah*, 2014. Courtesy of Asaf Mendelovich.
Page 176: Crash 048. *Crash*, 2017.
Page 177: Crash 048. *Crash*, 2017.
Page 178: Keos 048. *Keos*, 2015.
Page 179: Keos 048. *Keos*, 2015.
Page 180: Orek. *Orek*, 2010.
Page 181: Orek. *Orek*, 2010.
Page 182: AIFOE 048. *Aifoe*, 2010.
Page 183: AIFOE 048, *Aifoe*, 2010.
Page 184: Shalom. *Shalom*, 2021.
Page 185: Shalom. *Shalom*, 2018.
Page 186-187: Hillel Smith. *"Planted in the house of Hashem, they will flourish in the*

courtyards of our God," YULA Courtyard Mural, 2017. Courtesy of Hillel Smith.
Page 188: Yitzhak Greenfield. *Hebrew Letter Heh*, 2011. Courtesy of Yitzhak Greenfield.
Page 189: Yitzhak Greenfield. *Hebrew Letter Alef*, 1995. Courtesy of Yitzhak Greenfield.
Page 190: Yitzhak Greenfield. *Meeting of God's Names*, c. 2002. Courtesy of Yitzhak Greenfield.
Page 191: Yitzhak Greenfield. *The Birth of the Heh*, 2008. Courtesy of Yitzhak Greenfield.
Page 192-193: Overleaf: David Rakia, detail from *Letters in Grey*, 2002. Courtesy of David Rakia, Rakia Gallery.
Page 194: Edna Miron-Wapner. *Heh*, from *Mystical Images* series, 1991. Courtesy of Edna Miron-Wapner.
Page 195: Edna Miron-Wapner. *Peh*, from *Mystical Images* series, 1991. Courtesy of Edna Miron Wapner.
Page 196: Edna Miron-Wapner. *Dialogue 7*, 1998–99. Courtesy of Edna Miron-Wapner.
Page 197: Edna Miron-Wapner. *Dialogue 8*, 1998–99. Courtesy of Edna Miron-Wapner.
Page 198: Tania Mouraud. *Muterlekher Nokturn* (nocturne maternelle), 2020. ©Tania Mourand, ADAGP.
Page 199: Tania Mouraud. *Shmues – Oyses in oyses farlibt* (lettres amoureuses des lettres), 2020 ©Tania Mourand, ADAGP.
Page 200: Ilanit Scharff Vigodsky. *From Time to Time*, poem by the artist, 2020. Courtesy of Ilanit Scharff Vigodsky.
Page 201: Ilanit Scharff Vigodsky. *Untitled*, 2020. Courtesy of Ilanit Scharff Vigodsky.
Page 202: Ilanit Scharff Vigodsky. *In Fact*, poem by the artist, 2019. Courtesy of Ilanit Scharff Vigodsky.
Page 203: Izzy Pludwinski. *Laughter, Dream, Children*, 2013.
Page 204: Michel D'Anastasio. *Aleph-bet*, 2009. Courtesy of Michel D'Anastasio.
Page 205: Ohad Naor. *Untitled*, 2021. Courtesy of Ohad Naor.
Page 206-207: Ohad Naor. *A Different Planet*, 2021. Courtesy of Ohad Naor.
Page 208: Meri Karako. *The Lines between the Lines*, 2021. Courtesy of Meri Karako.
Page 209: Gabriel Wolff. *Genesis*, 2017, from the collection of Edward and Judith Vays, Roslyn, New York. Courtesy of Gabriel Wolff.
Page 212: Detail from a fifteenth-century Torah scroll written on leather, Sephardic tradition. The National Library of Israel. Public domain.
Page 213: Detail from an Ashkenazic Sefer Torah scroll. Scribe and date unknown.
Page 214: Detail from an Ashkenazic Sefer Torah scroll. Scribe and date unknown.
Page 215: Top: Yossi Gilad. Detail from Torah scroll, Ashkenazi Beit Yosef writing, 2018–19. Photo courtesy of Neta Naor. Bottom: Moshe Levi. Detail from Torah Scroll, Sephardi writing. Courtesy of Moshe Levi.
Page 216: Top: Jonathan Essebag. Tefillin, Ashkenazic script style, 2020. Photo courtesy of Jonathan Essebag. Middle: Baruch Danon. Tefillin, Sephardic script style. Photo courtesy of Baruch Danon. Bottom: Tefillin, Chabad script style, Sofer and date unknown. Image source: http://hebrewstam.blogspot.com/2016/01/blog-post_21.html/.
Page 217: Aaron Shaffier. *Mezuzah*, Chabad script style, 2021. Courtesy of Aaron Shafier.
Page 218: Izzy Pludwinski. A column from a *Scroll of* Esther, 2019.
Page 219: Izzy Pludwinski. A column from a *Scroll of* Esther, 2004.
Page 220: Moshe Levi. Detail of last column of Torah Scroll. Courtesy of Moshe Levi.

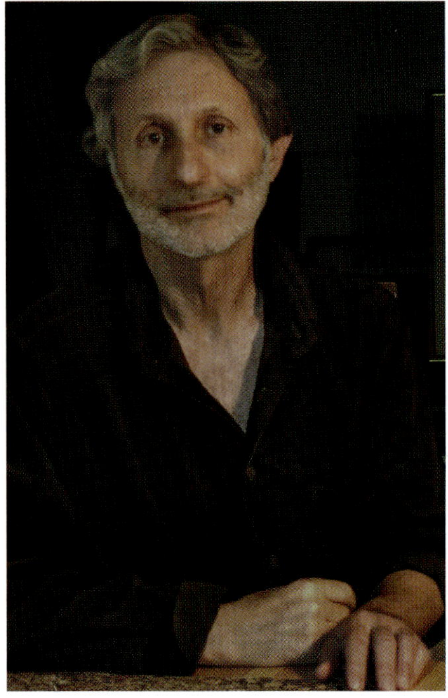

About the Author

IZZY PLUDWINSKI is a Jerusalem-based professional calligrapher and Sofer STaM. He is the author of *Mastering Hebrew Calligraphy*, which was chosen as a finalist for the National Jewish Book Awards in 2014.

His works have been included in international exhibitions in England, the US, and Russia, and he has had several solo exhibitions in Israel. His works have been featured many times in the prestigious *Letter Arts Review* journal.

Though firmly entrenched in the world of traditional Judaica, Izzy's calligraphic passion lies in finding ever-new expressive forms for the Hebrew *aleph-bet*—a path that has led him anywhere from font development to Zen-influenced abstract Hebrew calligraphy.

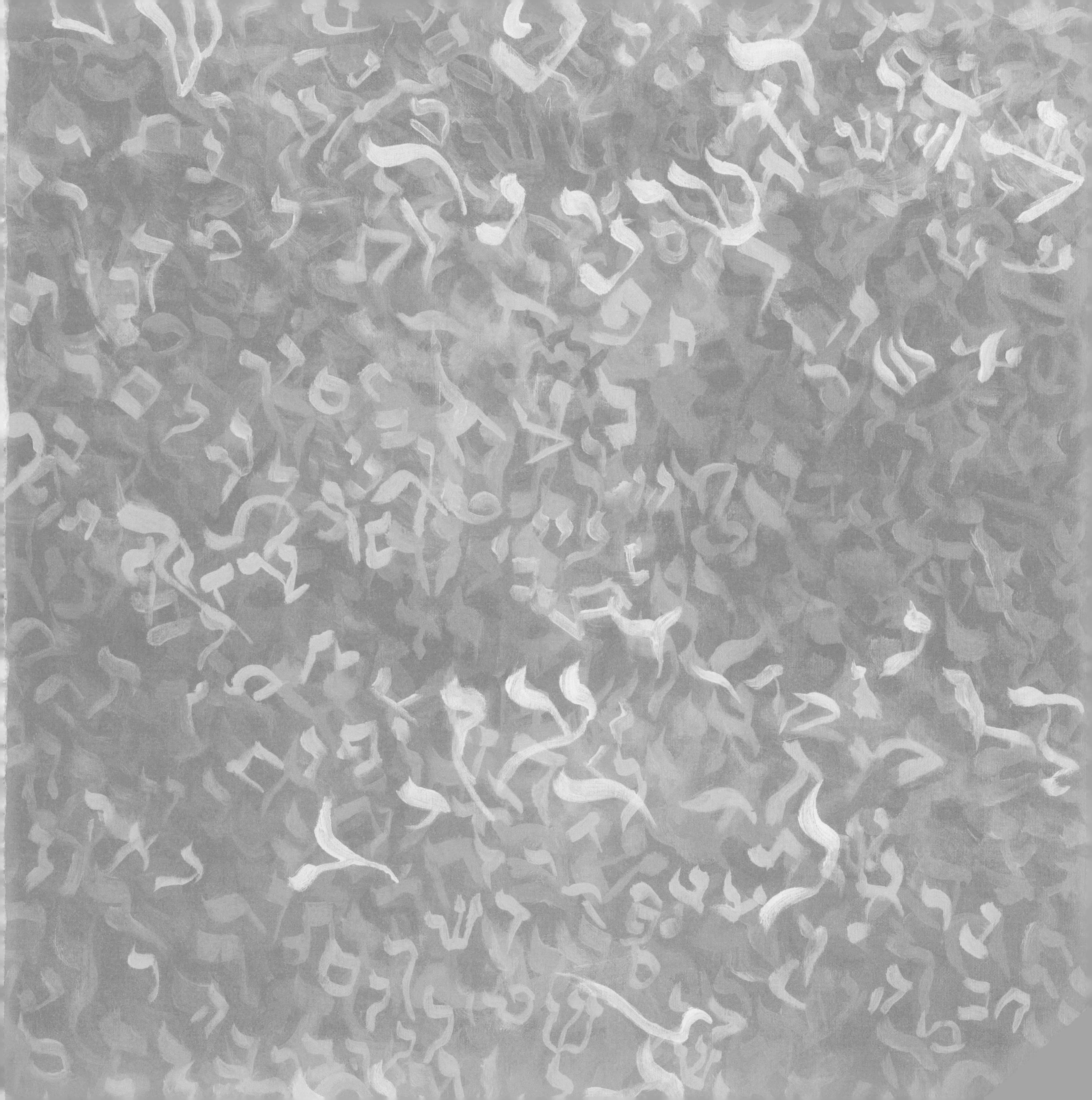

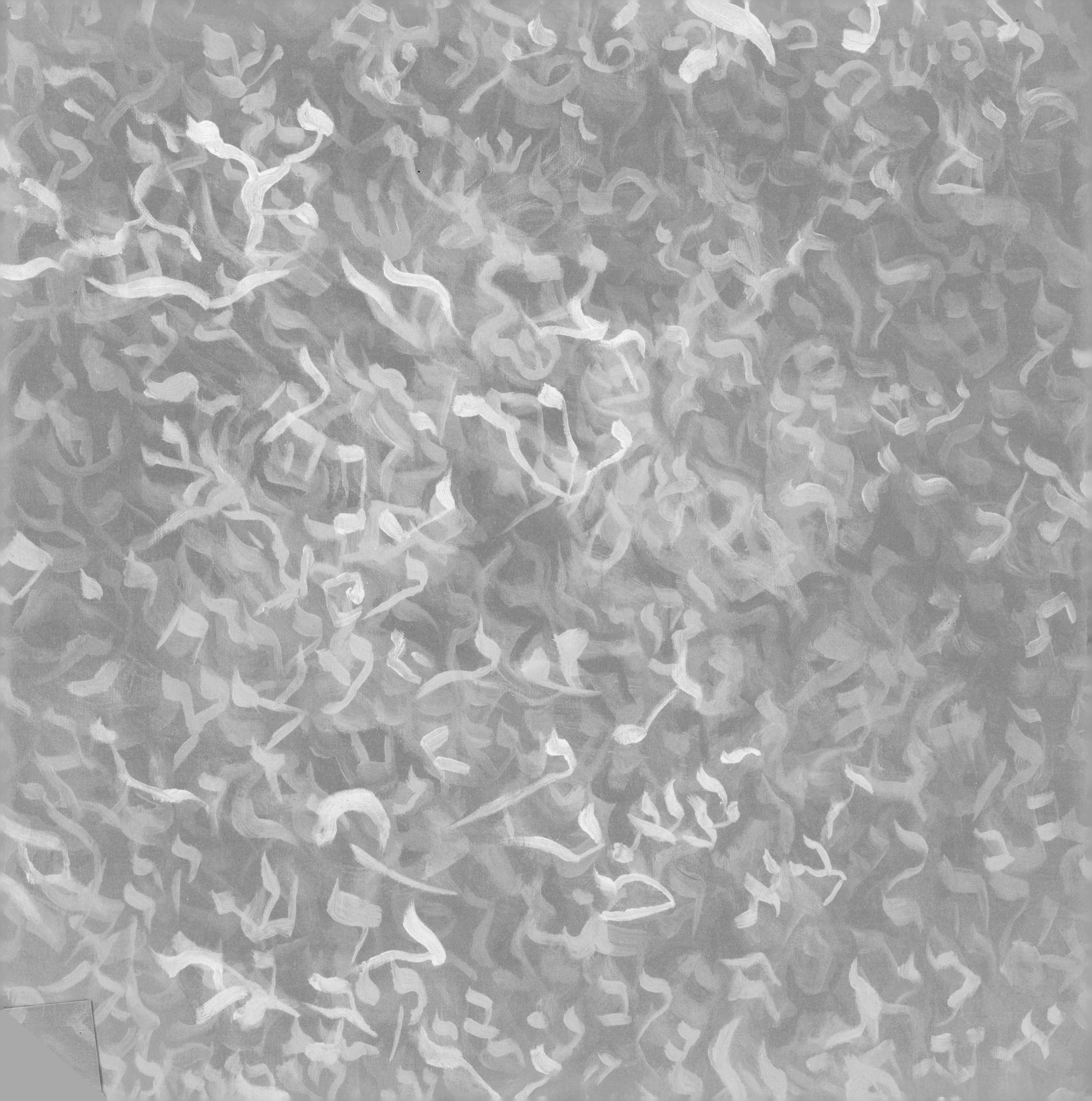